THE GOSPEL *of* MARK

THE GOSPEL *of* MARK

A Liturgical Reading

CHARLES A. BOBERTZ

Ⱦ
BakerAcademic
a division of Baker Publishing Group
Grand Rapids, Michigan

© 2016 by Charles A. Bobertz

Published by Baker Academic
a division of Baker Publishing Group
P.O. Box 6287, Grand Rapids, MI 49516-6287
www.bakeracademic.com

Printed in the United States of America

Library of Congress Cataloging-in-Publication Data
Names: Bobertz, Charles A., 1957- author.
Title: The gospel of Mark : a liturgical reading / Charles A. Bobertz.
Description: Grand Rapids : Baker Academic, 2016. | Includes bibliographical references and index.
Identifiers: LCCN 2016017289 | ISBN 9780801035692 (pbk.)
Subjects: LCSH: Bible. Mark—Criticism, Narrative. | Rites and ceremonies—Biblical teaching. |
    Rites and ceremonies in the Bible. | Worship in the Bible. | Worship—Biblical teaching.
Classification: LCC BS2585.52 .B63 2016 | DDC 226.3/06—dc23
LC record available at https://lccn.loc.gov/2016017289

16   17   18   19   20   21   22   7   6   5   4   3   2   1

This book is dedicated to the memory of my parents,
Sarah (Hall) and William Bobertz.
Their love of learning was infectious.
May they now enjoy the eternal banquet with Christ.

Contents

Acknowledgments

After working on a book for many years there is in one's heart more gratitude than can possibly be expressed. I would like to thank my family: my wife of thirty-four years, Mary, and my now-grown children, Sarah and Thomas. Their constant love and support brightened every day in which I was working on this project. I would like to thank my faculty and staff colleagues in the department and School of Theology at St. John's University in Minnesota. It is a privilege to teach New Testament in a place that gives witness to fifteen hundred years of Benedictine liturgy and prayer. The dean of the School of Theology, Bill Cahoy, deserves a special note of gratitude for his constant encouragement of my writing. My students throughout the years, graduate and undergraduate, have pushed me in ways that made the final version of this book better. Several of these graduate students, including Mark Nussberger, Shawn Powers, and Ben De Bono, provided valuable research assistance. In addition I would like to thank all those colleagues who have read all or parts of this book. Their comments and reactions helped me to think through so much of what is presented here. Of these Stephen J. Patterson of Willamette University, my closest friend since we grew up together on the plains of South Dakota, deserves special thanks. Finally, I am so very grateful for the financial support given to me in these years of writing by the faculty development committee at St. John's University.

Abbreviations

Old Testament

Gen.	Genesis	Song of Sol.	Song of Solomon
Exod.	Exodus	Isa.	Isaiah
Lev.	Leviticus	Jer.	Jeremiah
Num.	Numbers	Lam.	Lamentation
Deut.	Deuteronomy	Ezek.	Ezekiel
Josh.	Joshua	Dan.	Daniel
Judg.	Judges	Hosea	Hosea
Ruth	Ruth	Joel	Joel
1–2 Sam.	1–2 Samuel	Amos	Amos
1–2 Kings	1–2 Kings	Obad.	Obadiah
1–2 Chron.	1–2 Chronicles	Jon.	Jonah
Ezra	Ezra	Mic.	Micah
Neh.	Nehemiah	Nah.	Nahum
Esther	Esther	Hab.	Habakkuk
Job	Job	Zeph.	Zephaniah
Ps. (Pss.)	Psalm (Psalms)	Hag.	Haggai
Prov.	Proverbs	Zech.	Zechariah
Eccles.	Ecclesiastes	Mal.	Malachi

New Testament

Matt.	Matthew	1–2 Cor.	1–2 Corinthians
Mark	Mark	Gal.	Galatians
Luke	Luke	Eph.	Ephesians
John	John	Phil.	Philippians
Acts	Acts	Col.	Colossians
Rom.	Romans	1–2 Thess.	1–2 Thessalonians

1–2 Tim.	1–2 Timothy	1–2 Pet.	1–2 Peter
Titus	Titus	1–3 John	1–3 John
Philem.	Philemon	Jude	Jude
Heb.	Hebrews	Rev.	Revelation
James	James		

Ancient Texts

Did.	Didache	Irenaeus, *Haer.*	*Adversus haereses*
Ignatius, *Eph.*	*To the Ephesians*	LXX	Septuagint
Ignatius, *Smyr.*	*To the Smyrnaeans*	Pliny, *Ep.*	*Letter to Trajan*
Ignatius, *Trall.*	*To the Trallians*		

General and Bibliographic

AASF	Annales Academiae scientiarum fennicae
AER	*American Ecclesiastical Review*
ALBO	Analecta lovaniensia biblica et orientalia
ANRW	*Aufsteig und Niedergang der römischen Welt: Geschichte und Kultur Roms im Spiegel der neueren Forschung.* Part 2, *Principat.* Edited by Hildegard Temporini and Wolfgang Haase. Berlin: de Gruyter, 1972–
ASBT	Acadia Studies in Bible and Theology
AsSeign	*Assemblées du Seigneur*
AThR	*Anglican Theological Review*
BBB	Bonner biblische Beiträge
BBR	*Bulletin for Biblical Research*
BETL	Bibliotheca ephemeridum theologicarum lovaniensium
Bib	*Biblica*
BibInt	Biblical Interpretation Series
BibLeb	*Bibel und Leben*
BiBR	Bibliographies for Biblical Research
BJRL	*Bulletin of the John Rylands University Library of Manchester*
BJS	Brown Judaic Studies
BR	*Biblical Research*
BRBS	Brill's Readers in Biblical Studies
BRev	*Bible Review*
BTB	*Biblical Theology Bulletin*
BZ	*Biblische Zeitschrift*
BZNW	Beihefte zur Zeitschrift für die neutestamentliche Wissenschaft und die Kunde der älteren Kirche
CBQ	*Catholic Biblical Quarterly*
CBQMS	Catholic Biblical Quarterly Monograph Series
CC	*Cross Currents*
CNT	Commentaire du Nouveau Testament

ConBNT	Coniectanea biblica: New Testament Series
CS	*Chicago Studies*
CSP	Cambridge Studies in Philosophy
CurBR	*Currents in Biblical Research*
CurTM	*Currents in Theology and Mission*
EBib	*Etudes bibliques*
Enc	*Encounter*
EPR	Études d'Histoire et de Philosophie Religieuses
EstBib	*Estudios biblicos*
ETL	*Ephemerides theologicae lovanienses*
EvT	*Evangelische Theologie*
ExpTim	*Expository Times*
FB	Forschung zur Bibel
FCNTECW	Feminist Companion to the New Testament and Early Christian Writings
FF	Foundations and Facets
FRLANT	Forschungen zur Religion und Literatur des alten und neuen Testaments
FT	*First Things*
HR	*History of Religions*
HTKNT	Herders theologischer Kommentar zum Neuen Testament
HTR	*Harvard Theological Review*
HvTSt	*Hervormde teologiese studies*
ICC	International Critical Commentary
IEJ	*Israel Exploration Journal*
Int	*Interpretation*
IRGLS	*International Rennert Guest Lecture Series (Israel)*
JAAR	*Journal of the American Academy of Religion*
JBL	*Journal of Biblical Literature*
JBR	*Journal of Bible and Religion*
JBT	*Jahrbuch für Biblische Theologie*
JECS	*Journal of Early Christian Studies*
JHI	*Journal of the History of Ideas*
JHR	*Journal of the History of Religions*
JHS	*Journal of Hellenic Studies*
JR	*Journal of Religion*
JSJ	*Journal for the Study of Judaism in the Persian, Hellenistic, and Roman Periods*
JSNT	*Journal for the Study of the New Testament*
JSNTSup	Journal for the Study of the New Testament: Supplement Series
JSOT Press	Journal for the Study of the Old Testament Press, an imprint of Sheffield Academic
JSP	*Journal for the Study of the Pseudepigrapha*
JSQ	*Jewish Studies Quarterly*
JTS	*Journal of Theological Studies*
JTSA	*Journal of Theology for Southern Africa*
KBANT	Kommentare und Beiträge zum Alten und Neuen Testament
LB	*Linguistica Biblica*
List	*Listening: Journal of Religion and Culture*
LNTS	Library of New Testament Studies

LQ	*Lutheran Quarterly*
LTQ	*Lexington Theological Quarterly*
MT	*Modern Theology*
NedTT	*Nederlands theologisch tijdschrift*
Neot	*Neotestamentica*
NGS	New Gospel Studies
NovT	*Novum Testamentum*
NTL	New Testament Library
NTS	*New Testament Studies*
Per	*Perspectives*
PMLA	*Proceedings of the Modern Language Association*
ProEccl	*Pro ecclesia*
PRSt	*Perspectives in Religious Studies*
PSB	*Princeton Seminary Bulletin [Supplement]*
RB	*Revue biblique*
RelSRev	*Religious Studies Review*
RevExp	*Review and Expositor*
SBLSP	*Society of Biblical Literature Seminar Papers*
SBT	Studies in Biblical Theology
SE	*Studia Evangelica*
Semeia	*Semeia*
SemeiaSt	Semeia Studies
SJT	*Scottish Journal of Theology*
SL	*Studia Liturgica*
SR	*Studies in Religion*
ST	*Studia Theologica*
StPatr	Studia patristica
SwJT	*Southwestern Journal of Theology*
TC	Traditio Christiana
Them	*Themelios*
ThTo	*Theology Today*
TJT	*Toronto Journal of Theology*
TLZ	*Theologische Literaturzeitung*
TST	Toronto Studies in Theology
TTCSG	T&T Clark Study Guides
TTZ	*Trierer theologische Zeitschrift*
TW	*This World*
TynBul	*Tyndale Bulletin*
USQR	*Union Seminary Quarterly Review*
VC	*Vigiliae christianae*
WUNT	Wissenschaftliche Untersuchungen zum Neuen Testament
ZAW	*Zeitschrift für die alttestamentliche Wissenschaft*
ZDPV	*Zeitschrift des deutschen Palästina-Vereins*
ZKT	*Zeitschrift für katholische Theologie*
ZNW	*Zeitschrift für die neutestamentliche Wissenschaft und die Kunde der älteren Kirche*
ZTK	*Zeitschrift für Theologie und Kirche*

Prologue

In Mark 8:2–4, a curious dialogue occurs between Jesus and his disciples. A large crowd has gathered:

> Jesus: "I have compassion for the crowd, for they have remained with me for three days and do not have anything to eat. If I send them away hungry to their house they will grow weary on the way, for some of them have come from a great distance."
>
> Disciples: "How is it possible for someone to feed these people with loaves here in the wilderness?"

An initial reading of the setting and the dialogue of this scene is straightforward enough. There are a great many people in an uninhabited area, and there is no food to feed them. There is concern that some may not have the energy to make it back to their own homes for lack of food. The stage is set for a miracle performed by Jesus that will result in the crowd being fed.

So far, so good. This might be all there is to the dialogue. But now consider how one might read this same dialogue differently from a different context, a context that takes seriously the fact that the earliest Christians engaged in a ritual meal they called the "Lord's Supper" (described by Paul in 1 Cor. 11:17–34), an early form of the ritual Eucharist practiced by many Christians in churches today.

Who is the crowd here, and where do they come from? Why does the dialogue specifically refer to *three days* (*hēmerai treis*)?[1] Where else does the

---

1. This book is intended for a general audience as well as for scholars and students of the Gospel of Mark. Often Greek words and short phrases will be important. For readers who do not control the Greek, I will include a translation and transliteration of the Greek words, sometimes in their root form and sometimes in the inflection in which they appear in the Greek text. I presume readers who do control the Greek can easily consult

Gospel of Mark refer specifically to three days? Why does the narrative specifically state that they are in the *wilderness* (*erēmos*), a place laden with meaning as part of the story of Israel's exodus from Egypt? Is the reference here to not having anything to eat simply about eating or about not eating the Lord's Supper? If the latter, then what does it mean that *these people*, who have come from a long way away, are not to be fed *loaves* (*artos*) at the ritual of the Lord's Supper? Are the disciples here worried about finding enough food or about feeding *these people* in the wilderness? Are the *loaves* that would feed them ordinary bread, or is this the ritual food of the Lord's Supper? In sum, does the disciples' question imply that *these people* ought not to be fed *these loaves* here in *this place* of wilderness?

Later in this book I will delve deeply into an interpretation of this dialogue, but for now I only want to highlight the obvious: assumptions held by the reader of a story have a great impact on how a story is interpreted.[2] The narrative story of Mark *reads* differently if one presumes that the ritual practices of the early Christians (what I will refer to as Christian liturgy) inform the creation of the story, that is, why Mark was written in the first place, and why it was disseminated to its earliest readers. After all, a loaf (*artos*) can be just food, and a wilderness (*erēmos*) can be just a lonely place.

In this book I read the Gospel of Mark with the assumption that its creator and earliest readers were often gathered within the experience of emotionally and spiritually powerful rituals, primarily an initiation immersion ritual called baptism and a house-based ritual communal meal called the Lord's Supper.[3] I claim that the narrative of Mark was first and foremost a story about Jesus created to convince the original readers and hearers of the story that there was a correct way to understand and practice these rituals in the context of violent persecution and an expectation of the imminent return of Jesus as Lord and judge of history.[4]

---

the standard Greek text, now online: *Novum Testamentum Graece*, 28th ed., http://www .nestle-aland.com/en/read-na28-online/.

2. Robert Fowler's commentary on Mark, *Let the Reader Understand*, discusses the experience of the reader of the text, an experience that, along with the meaning of the text, changes with the location of the reader (26–40). In the present study I propose what might be termed an "ideal reader," an ancient reader located within the emotional and cognitive experience of the ritual gatherings of the Christian community in Mark's time. This is the ancient liturgical reader of Mark.

3. For background on the turn in modern scholarship to reading Mark as a created narrative, see Iverson and Skinner, eds., *Mark as Story*, 1–16. For a description of early Christian ritual meal practice, see McGowan, *Ancient Christian Worship*, 26–36; for ritual immersion (baptism), see 135–67.

4. Mark Allan Powell's description of narrative criticism is germane to what I hope to accomplish here: "Whereas historical critics are expected to suspend faith commitments temporarily

Yet I would like to accomplish something more in the pages that follow. When I refer to the narrative and the reader of Mark I am, as I say above, primarily interested in an interpretation of Mark that locates the creation and reception of the narrative within the experience of a reality largely created by early Christian ritual practice. And to be honest such a reading, as all attempted readings of Mark, must perforce rely on a good bit of hypothetical reconstruction. But I also want to include in my description of the "reader"—often implicitly—a modern reader of Mark who would benefit from understanding the possibilities of interpreting Mark on the basis of his or her own liturgical location and practice. Despite the best efforts of historical scholars in the past two hundred years, there will never be *the* reading of Mark,[5] but *readings* will continue to enter into the scholarly conversation as we keep trying to understand better the origins of Christianity. I intend this book to be just one of those readings, an entry into the conversation with other plausible readings of Mark, but one that appeals to contemporary Christians who are themselves gathered to baptize and eat the Lord's Supper (Eucharist).

Baptism, as contemporary historians of liturgy would understand it, would have been a precise ritual of immersion, probably full immersion. It would have included disrobing (probably naked), ritual bathing, and a formal "rising" from the water to be reclothed.[6] The ritual would have quite physically enacted a separation from the previous social, political, and religious world of the one washed and his or her incorporation into the new social, political, and religious community of the Christian house church. Baptism would have been followed by the eating of a communal meal in an ancient house, the Supper of the Lord, a meal that would have, in the establishment of sacred space, *physically* marked both participation in, and the external boundary of, that particular Christian community.[7]

I will argue that the ancient story we call the Gospel of Mark was created to convey a particular understanding of these two rituals to the community,

---

in order to interpret texts from the perspective of objective, disinterested historians, narrative critics may be expected to adopt faith commitments temporarily in order to determine how texts are expected to affect their implied readers" ("Narrative Criticism," 244). My commitment is to read Mark from within the liturgically gathered community, past and present.

5. Modern attempts to provide the *definitive* reading of Mark are legion (Mark 5:9). For descriptions, see, e.g., A. Y. Collins, *Mark*, 19–42; Marcus, *Mark 1–8*, 64–69; Iverson and Skinner, *Mark as Story*, 11–16; Telford, *Interpretation of Mark*, 1–61; Kealy, *History of the Interpretation of the Gospel of Mark*, 90–237.

6. Gal. 3:27; Col. 3:9–11, discussed in Meeks, *First Urban Christians*, 150–57. I am reminded here of an ancient mural at the monastery of Subiaco, perhaps sixth century, that features the naked Jesus being baptized by John.

7. Meeks, *First Urban Christians*, 157–63.

an interpretation which of course implies that there was an understanding of these rituals that Mark opposed. Thus I come to the heart of the argument of the book you are about to read: one reading of the Gospel of Mark is that it is fundamentally a presentation in narrative form of a theological rationale, in a time of communal crisis evoked by persecution,[8] for Gentile and female inclusion in the defined ritual space of the Lord's Supper of the house churches. Thus the narrative presents a theological argument similar to that posed by Paul in Galatians: Jews ought not to back away from eating the Lord's Supper with the Gentiles, for Gentiles too have been baptized into the death of Christ and so belong to Christ (Gal. 2:11–13; 3:27–29; Rom. 6:3–11). Moreover it is this ritually gathered community of Jews and Gentiles, men and women, at the meal, the body of Christ (Rom. 12:4–5; Mark 14:22), which now—precisely because it is this *body* of Jews and Gentiles, men and women—suffers horrific persecution amid the expectation of the imminent return of the resurrected Christ (13:9–27; 16:7–8).

The particular importance of Augustine's and, later, Luther's understanding of Paul as centered in justification by grace through faith (Eph. 2:5, 8) rather than by works often makes it difficult for us to reimagine what was physically going on in the context of those early Christian house churches. Justification or salvation (the Greek word *sōzō* in Mark) was not some personal existential reality or spiritual awareness, as it is so often thought to be today, but quite literally a place at the sacred ritual meal. The concrete physical reality that lurks behind the complex theological argument that Paul presents, especially in Galatians and Romans, is who belongs within the actual ritual space of the Lord's Supper in the house churches. And it would have been *the* question because it would have been—especially at times of persecution for simply being a Christian—at the center of early Christian communal definition. Only those at the meal, the *body* of Christ, would be saved at the moment of judgment when Christ returned (Mark 13:13).

That the issues surrounding Gentile and female inclusion at the Lord's Supper were at the center of early Christian experience is hardly surprising to anyone familiar with the writings left to us by the ancient churches.[9] The lengthy and carefully developed argument in Paul's Letter to the Romans

---

8. Mark 13 (esp. 13:2), the so-called apocalyptic discourse, makes it clear that the narrative is being written in the context of the social and political chaos generated by the Jewish revolt against Rome (AD 66–73). This chaos was keenly felt in the area of Galilee and southern Syria, where I believe Mark was written. For discussion see Marcus, *Mark 1–8*, 33–37; contra A. Y. Collins, *Mark*, 7–10, who argues for a Roman provenance.

9. Stendahl, *Paul among Jews and Gentiles*, 1–67. In the title essay, Stendahl argues that the discussion of law versus grace in Paul's letters functions primarily as an apology for full status, a place at the one table, for Gentile converts within the Christian community.

justifying the mission to the Gentiles and their inclusion in the church, judged by many ever since to be the most important theological text in the Christian canon, must have been written to convince actual readers of the letter in Rome who would have hesitated to agree with Paul. And judging by the care and precision of the letter, it does not seem likely that Paul himself was assured of their agreement with his position. Indeed the Letter to the Galatians reveals an utterly exasperated writer willing to resort to ad hominem attack in the face of challenging opposition (Gal. 5:12). And even a quick read of the second-century, and largely apologetic, book of Acts indicates that the story of controversy over the inclusion of Gentiles was at the center of the church's collective memory.[10] The story of Peter's dream and the conversion of the Gentile Cornelius with his (Gentile) household (Acts 10:1–35; cf. 10:45; 11:2–3) and the accounts of the resistance Paul encounters in his mission beginning at Acts 13 (13:46) both indicate that this controversy, along with the subsequent and successful inclusion of Gentiles in the Pauline mission, was at the heart of Luke-Acts's understanding of the churches' history.

My reading of Mark suggests that what was primarily at issue in the church of Mark, wherever in the Mediterranean world it was located[11]—and most likely it was written in the midst of the chaos created by the Jewish revolt against Rome (AD 66–73)—was the relationship between the ritual of baptism and the full participation of Gentiles with Jews in the Lord's Supper within the house churches. This is not the usual way Mark has been understood within the tradition or by the vast majority of modern scholars.[12] Early tradition would posit that Mark was created to write down Peter's preaching and so preserve the words of Jesus at a time when the original disciples were beginning to die.[13]

10. On the dating of Acts to the second century, see the extensive discussion in Richard Pervo, *Dating Acts: Between the Evangelists and the Apologists* (Santa Rosa, CA: Polebridge, 2006), 1–28.

11. Donahue, "Quest for the Community of Mark's Gospel," 819–34.

12. Even a cursory reading of several major modern commentaries and monographs reveals how seldom the issue of ritual participation, the inclusion of Gentiles in the Lord's Supper of the house churches, is understood as central to the narrative purpose of Mark. Representative examples would include A. Y. Collins, *Mark*, 1–125; Marcus, *Mark 1–8*, 25–39; Donahue and Harrington, *Mark*, 1–47; Black, *Mark*, 27–40; Focant, *Mark*, 1–21; Moloney, *Mark*, 16–20; Malbon, *Narrative Space and Mythic Meaning*, 6–14; Tolbert, *Sowing the Gospel*, 90–126; France, *Mark*, 20–22; van Iersel, *Mark*, 51–53. In this regard, I should take special note of Standaert, *L'Évangile selon Marc*, 32–41. Standaert argues that the occasion for writing the Gospel of Mark was recitation in the ritual gathering on the Easter vigil. Though Standaert shares my interest in the ritual setting of the Markan Christians, my argument centers not on a specific celebration (e.g., an Easter vigil) but on the common ritual practices of baptism and—especially—the eating of the Lord's Supper within the house churches.

13. This is based on an interpretation of what the ancient church historian Papias reported about the writing of Mark. See Kürzinger, *Papias von Hierapolis*, discussed in Juel,

Some modern scholars, reading especially chapter 13, would argue that Mark was written to encourage the community to remain faithful to Christianity at a time of war and horrific persecution.[14] For these scholars Mark tells the story of Jesus the faithful martyr who sets the example for would-be martyrs to follow.[15] Some see Mark as an apology, an ancient explanation, for why the Messiah of Israel had to suffer and die an ignoble death on a cross only to be glorified by God.[16] Indeed in reading a cross-section of the major studies of the Gospel in the last fifty years or so, the heyday of modern historical criticism, one can conclude without too much difficulty that there is little or no agreement as to why one of the most important texts in the history of the world was in fact written.[17]

Even beyond the fact that we are not sure *why* Mark was written, we are not even sure what sort of text Mark actually is. I suspect most Christians familiar with the Gospel of Mark think of it as a sort of life of Jesus. But scholars have long noticed that Mark does not tell us very much about the life of Jesus. Unlike the Gospels of Matthew and Luke, there is no story of Jesus's birth—and unlike Luke, there is no story of Jesus's boyhood. Mark simply begins with the story of Jesus's baptism by John in the wilderness and then quickly tells us how Jesus, in a very short time, gathered disciples in and beyond Galilee, rode with an entourage into Jerusalem at the Passover, and was crucified by the Romans. This is hardly a biography by modern standards. And even by ancient standards of biography Mark is missing key elements.[18] So what sort of literature is Mark?

The fact is that if we accept Mark as the first written Gospel—and most scholars do agree on this at least—then there is really nothing quite like it in the ancient literature that has survived to our day.[19] Scholars discuss how Mark draws on various forms of ancient literature, yet there appears to be no one type of ancient literature, no one genre, that completely explains the

---

Master of Surprise, 13. See also Culpepper, *Mark*, 3–18; Marcus, *Mark 1–8*, 21–24; van Iersel, *Mark*, 51.

14. A. Y. Collins, *Mark*, 11–14.

15. Marcus, *Mark 1–8*, 28–29.

16. Gundry, *Mark*, 1–3.

17. Major modern commentaries provide a ready review of this scholarship. See, e.g., Focant, *Mark*, 14–19; Marcus, *Mark 1–8*, 25–39; A. Y. Collins, *Mark*, 1–93; Moloney, *Mark*, 11–15; Donahue and Harrington, *Mark*, 3–16. A list of attempts is provided by Watts, *New Exodus in Mark*, 1–2; Black, *Disciples according to Mark*, 318–33, provides a strikingly negative evaluation of these efforts.

18. See the thorough discussion by Aune, "Problem of the Genre," 9–60. See also the critique of the work of Burridge, *What Are the Gospels?*, in Marcus, *Mark 1–8*, 62–64; A. Y. Collins, *Mark*, 22–33.

19. This is in fact Aune's conclusion: "Problem of the Genre," 44.

Gospel that has come down to us.[20] Almost like a new recipe, familiar foods have been recombined into a new dish.[21]

I do not intend to address the question of the ancient genre of Mark here. But I am convinced, and I hope I can convince my readers, that modern readers can make sense of the narrative and come closer to understanding why we have this Gospel. And this has to do with what I pointed out above: what was most pressing in the Christian experience of the first century was the controversy over whether baptized Gentiles (including female Gentiles) would have a place at the Lord's Supper with Jews in the same house church, this at a time when the very definition of what it meant to be a Christian was the difference between persecution and freedom (8:34–35; 13:9). I am convinced the Gospel of Mark was an attempt to provide a definitive answer to that question by telling the story of how Jesus himself began the Gentile mission, inviting Gentiles to be a part of the community, and how Jesus himself in the story understands his own death to be the ritual means by which the Gentiles ought to be included in the Lord's Supper. In effect Mark pulls out, in fact creates, the trump card of Jesus himself to settle once and for all the issue of the Gentile mission at the time of the writing of the Gospel, the issue of who is included at the table of the house church.[22]

Mark is a deeply symbolic narrative created to help its readers understand the necessary death of Jesus Messiah as the foundation of the Gentile mission and thus the inauguration of the reign of God. This kingdom, according to Mark, came into ritual reality in the physical gathering of the Christians in

20. Discussions of the genre of Mark are legion. Almost every major commentary on Mark considers the issue. See especially A. Y. Collins, *Mark*, 15–84, for an extended discussion of the relationship of Mark to contemporary historical and literary genres (both non-Jewish and Jewish). Her conclusion is that Mark may be understood as an ancient historical monograph that focuses on the deeds of Jesus but which is also influenced by additional literary influences (42). Also important to the question of genre is the study by Robbins, *Jesus the Teacher*. Boring, *Mark*, 6–9, provides a good discussion of Mark's unique narrative qualities with respect to the genre of ancient Hellenistic biography.

21. See especially the discussion in Marcus, *Mark 1–8*, 64–69.

22. Marxsen, *Mark*, firmly established that the narrative of Mark often directly reflects the experiences of a specific Christian community in the first century. It is obvious from what I propose here that I agree with those who have since that time understood Mark as such a transparent narrative. Yet I know of no current studies that argue for the ritual setting of the Christian house churches as the primary setting and inspiration for the experiences that have found their way into the narrative of Mark. I do agree with Marxsen that Mark, writing from and to the Christian community in Galilee, expected the imminent parousia (the return of Christ to gather the elect) to take place on behalf of the persecuted community in Galilee for whom Mark writes (Mark 13:26–27). See Marxsen, *Mark*, 166–89; Roskam, *Gospel of Mark*, 73–74, also places the writing and audience in Galilee during the Jewish revolt (AD 66–73). For pertinent references see A. Y. Collins, *Mark*, 96–97.

communal meal in an inclusive house church, and that ritual reality was about to become the final ordering of time and history itself (13:26–27; 14:25). But there is more. It is not just the death of Jesus Messiah, but all faithful death— ritual death (baptism) and actual death (martyr)—that creates the ritual space that is in fact the physical in-breaking of God's reign. Jesus in the narrative of Mark does set the example of the faithful martyr and so encourages the would-be martyrs of Mark's day, but the purpose for faithful death is pro- vided in the first ten chapters of Mark. The death of Jesus and the death of martyrs *create* the church of Jews and Gentiles, the gathered community of the one loaf, the in-breaking of a new Genesis garden, the anticipated goal of history and time itself.[23]

I will argue throughout this book that the Gospel of Mark was created as just this sort of symbolic narrative.[24] One might agree that all narratives are symbolic (words point to realities other than the words themselves) but not in the same way. As the first Gospel chronologically, Mark is unique because it was created to answer a question that was at the heart of early Christian self-definition: What gives legitimacy, in the face of Jewish reluctance and opposition, to the presence of Gentiles in the Lord's Supper of the house churches? The answer is carefully developed in Mark's symbolic narrative, which weaves in and out of the time of Jesus and the much later time of the church of Mark.[25] Through baptism, ritual entry into the death of Jesus, Gentiles are given a place at the Lord's Supper (7:28–29), where they share in the one loaf of bread with the Jews (8:14–21; 14:22–26). The Gospel of Mark does tell the story of Jesus's ministry and his death, but it is a story crafted with purpose: Jesus must die in order to be a ransom for the many (*polys*; 10:45) and a covenant for the many (*polys*) in his blood (14:24).[26] His death is the means by which, enacted in the ritual death of baptism, Gentiles (including Gentile women) have come to have a place at the Lord's Supper of Mark's house church. In other words, Mark presents an understanding of these

23. The emphasis on the one loaf (*artos*) as ritually enacting the unity of the community is paralleled in Ignatius, *Eph.* 20.

24. For the history and impact of reading Mark primarily as a narrative, see Powell, "Nar- rative Criticism," 19–43.

25. Hedrick, "What Is a Gospel?," 255–68; Malbon, *Narrative Space and Mythic Meaning.*

26. I understand the specific use of the term *many* (*polys* in Greek) to include Gentiles. The language here in Mark has remarkable affinities to the language used by Paul at Rom. 5:15 to characterize how Jesus's death is salvific for the Gentiles, that is, for the many (*polys*): "For if in the transgression of the one [Adam] many [*polys*] died, how much more did the grace of God and the gracious gift of the one person Jesus Christ overflow for the *many* [*polys*]." See also Rom. 5:19: "For just as through the disobedience of one person [Adam] the many [*polys*] were established as sinners, so through the obedience of one person [Christ] the many [*polys*] will be established as righteous."

rituals which closely follows Paul's understanding, but which he presents not by an occasional letter (e.g., Galatians) or even lengthy theological argument (Romans) but through a symbolic presentation of the story of Jesus which we call the Gospel of Mark.

The characters within the Gospel play symbolic roles that have a distinct relationship to the lived reality of the church of Mark in a time immediately following the fall of the second Jewish temple to the Romans (AD 70).[27] Jewish leaders in the narrative, for example, oppose Jesus because they represent distinct Jewish opposition to the very existence of early Christian churches in Mark's time. As Paul tells us, some Jewish leaders rejected the nascent Christian communities and even became a source of persecution (1 Cor. 15:9; 2 Cor. 11:24; cf. Mark 13:9). Ironically, in the narrative created by Mark these leaders are responsible for the death of Christ, which, enacted in ritual baptism, becomes the means by which the Christian community of Jews and Gentiles comes into being. In other words, in Mark the Jewish leaders are responsible for the *necessary* death of Jesus (3:6; 8:31; 11:18) at the hands of the Romans, thereby bringing into existence the community opposed by some Jews of Mark's own time.

I will also argue that in Mark the narrative portrayal of the Jewish disciples of Jesus (Peter, James, John, and the other nine),[28] as well as the portrayal of the (obviously) Jewish extended family of Jesus in Mark 3:20–35 and 6:1–6, is often transparent to the known resistance among some early Jewish Christians to the idea of eating the Lord's Supper in the same house with baptized Gentile Christians. For a description of this reality in the early churches we need look no further than Paul's description in Galatians 1–3 of certain events in Antioch that took place early in Paul's ministry of establishing house churches in which Jews and Gentiles did eat the Lord's Supper together. What we can garner from Paul's description is that (1) Paul and other Jews of his Christian community in Antioch ate the Lord's Supper with Gentiles; (2) certain "men from James" visited the community (presumably from the Jerusalem church) and caused Peter and other Jewish members of the community to withdraw from table fellowship with Gentile members of the community; and (3) Paul argues his case for Gentile inclusion at the meal on the basis of the ritual of

---

27. For a discussion of recent scholarship on the role of characters in Mark, see Malbon, "Characters in Mark's Story," 45–69; see also Black, *Disciples according to Mark*, 319–40. Discussions of the date of Mark are to be found in almost every major commentary on that Gospel. Central to this discussion is whether the reference in Mark 13:2, "not one stone upon a stone," is a reference to the Roman destruction of the Jerusalem temple in AD 70. I accept that it is.

28. There is a long history of studies of the portrayal of the disciples in Mark. For references see Henderson, "Concerning the Loaves," 3–26, esp. 3n3.

baptism: "For as many of you as were *baptized* into Christ have been clothed in Christ. You are neither *Jew nor Greek*, slave nor free, *not male and female*, for you are all one in Christ Jesus" (Gal. 2:11–3:29).[29]

Finally, in Mark there are the famous minor characters.[30] For the most part these characters are transparent to the positive case Mark wants to make about Gentile inclusion on the basis of baptism. Whereas the Jewish disciples and Jewish family of Jesus often appear to either oppose or show consternation concerning the Gentile mission, the Gentile characters are often welcomed and accepted by Jesus (2:1–12; 7:25–30; 10:45–52).

This brings us finally to the symbolic character of Jesus in Mark's narrative. He is in this narrative the *resurrected* Christ known from the heart of early Christian liturgy, the Lord's Supper. He represents right practice (e.g., Jesus presides over the feeding of Gentiles at the ritual meal, 6:41; 8:6–7) based on a proper theological understanding of the role and purpose of Jesus in his earthly ministry. Mark understands the purpose of Jesus's ministry and life, and especially his death, to have been the creation of the inclusive church, enacted now in the rituals through which the Gentiles come into full participation in the life of the church. Jesus himself is the seed which must fall into the earth (*eis tēn gēn*) in order to resurrect (*anabainō*) and become the abundant yield, Jews and Gentiles, men and women, gathered as the body of Christ in the early Christian church (4:8; cf. 1:10; 6:51). Jesus must die as a ransom for the *many* (10:45); his blood is the blood of the new covenant poured out for the *many* (14:24). The inclusive ritual meal, in turn, is the place in which the resurrection is enacted: it is the Gentile paralytic who is resurrected (*egeirō*; 2:12), and the twelve-year-old Jewish girl who also rises (*egeirō*; 5:41); it is the "body of Christ" (14:22) that dies and rises and so accomplishes the moment of in-breaking of God's reign on earth (1:10–11; 15:39). Throughout the Gospel there are glimpses of this reality: the retreat of the demons (1:26; 7:30), the eradication of disease (1:34), healing of bodies (3:5; 5:29), and resurrection from death itself (4:38–39). The readers (or hearers[31]) of Mark could experience this story and simultaneously realize that it was their own story, that it was written from, and spoke back to, the experience of their ritual gathering of Jews and Gentiles rooted in the death, resurrection, and now imminent return of Christ (16:7). This story of Jesus, located and enacted within the ritual setting of baptism and meal,

---

29. When italics appear in my Scripture translations, they have been added for emphasis.

30. Joel Williams, *Other Followers of Jesus*; Malbon, "Major Importance of Minor Characters," 58–86. Shiner, *Follow Me*, provides a useful study of ancient methods of characterization.

31. That Mark was written for oral performance is a distinct possibility: see Shiner, *Proclaiming the Gospel*.

would become the foundational story of this particular ritually inscribed community and eventually all of Christianity.

Stories, once written, take on a life of their own. And in some ways it hardly mattered to subsequent centuries that Mark indeed may have had an original purpose in creating and telling the story in the way that he did. In later centuries, and especially following the Protestant Reformation, the Gospel of Mark became a story about the individual Jesus rather than the crucified and resurrected body of Christ, the ritually enacted *body of Christ* who is the character Jesus in the narrative. It also became a story about existential faith in Jesus rather than the inclusive ritual place enacted by Jesus, a story of atonement for sin rather than a story of atonement for *Gentile* sin. Even more egregious, in the centuries following the seventeenth-century Enlightenment, Mark came to be read quite literally as a sort of history of Jesus, a positivistic description of what actually happened. The new standard of truth for the narrative was, and continues to be, some sort of literal history, and Mark (and the rest of the Bible) has often been forced to meet that standard.[32]

Yet the attempt to read Mark as literal historical truth results in neither history nor truth. And that is tragic because such a reading fails to capture both the literary and theological genius of Mark and fails to bring that genius into conversation with the contemporary church and world. As a narrative created from the experience of powerful rituals, Mark invites readers of every generation to enter into that experience and re-create both the experience and story of Jesus in our own time. A narrative world of symbols and symbolic action invites not closure, not definitive answers, but exploration: as it has been since the time of Mark, the search for meaning and identity is at the heart of being Christian in the world.

Finally, I should say a word about what prompted me to write this book after teaching New Testament and early Christian history to graduate and undergraduate students for twenty-five years. And here I might take my cue from Mark and tell a story. I recently directed a study-abroad program in London, and while there I took a group of students to visit two churches in one afternoon in the area of Knightsbridge. The first church was Brompton Oratory, perhaps the most "Catholic" of the Catholic churches in all of London: paintings, stained glass, hundreds of candles, crucifixes and statues of saints, the Eucharist, marked by a burning candle, obviously reserved in the tabernacle. The second church was only a short walk from the first. The

---

32. Conservative Protestant Christian scholarship still accepts this standard for reading Mark. See, e.g., Gundry, *Mark*, 1. Alarmingly for me as a Roman Catholic, and despite the acceptance of critical method by the Second Vatican Council (*Dei Verbum*), some recent Catholic scholarship on Mark is also based on such a literal reading: see, e.g., Healy, *Mark*, 17–26.

Church of Scotland is a large Presbyterian church, simple and dignified, with low dais and preaching pulpit, plain walls and clear glass, without any of the Catholic "stuff" that filled the Brompton Oratory.

In the world of biblical scholarship Mark has most often been read from the point of view of the Church of Scotland: simple and highly rational, a text of existential faith in which the climax is the isolated verbal confession of the individual Peter that Jesus is the Messiah (8:29). But then I began to ask whether Mark could not also be read from inside the Brompton Oratory, a story of deep symbolism and ritual complexity, a story not so much about individual existential faith but communal sacrament and mystery; a story not about Jesus so much as the *body of Christ*. And from that point on my reading of Mark began to change and formed the book that (I hope) you are about to read.

This book is not a commentary. But it will present a careful reading of selected portions, based on my own translations, of all sixteen chapters of the Gospel from the perspective of understanding the entire Gospel as a symbolic narrative inspired by Mark's understanding of the sacred reality—what we now call sacrament—of baptism and the Lord's Supper. I will take up issues in interpretation as they arise, some in the body of the text and some in the footnotes, but will make every effort to provide a straight-through reading to show how Mark can be understood as a symbolic narrative created for a particular purpose in the midst of the most pressing controversy of the earliest Christian church: In a time of persecution and martyrdom simply for being Christian, on what basis should Gentiles (including Gentile women) be allowed to enter the house churches and participate fully in the early Christian community? Finally, I should say here again that while I hope this book is read by other scholars, it is not written primarily for them. Rather, I hope I can convince anyone interested in the Second Gospel that there is a way to read the Gospel that speaks from and to the heart of Christian liturgical experience.

Introduction

In the Beginning: Creation versus Chaos and the Liturgical Reading of Mark

At his baptism in Mark, Jesus resurrects (*anabainō*) from the waters (1:10). In ancient apocalyptic thought, a part of the religious and literary context for reading Mark,[1] the waters of chaos/death actively resist the Spirit of God in creation.[2] And it is therefore sometimes difficult for the modern reader to understand the liturgical symbolism, based in an apocalyptic worldview, which undergirds Mark's narrative presentation.[3]

From the standpoint of a liturgical practice which must have emerged prior to the writing of Mark and even Paul's earliest letters,[4] it may well be that Christians connected the ritual power of baptism in water to the apocalyptic defeat of demonic forces, the immersion ritual itself being the place of battle

---

1. The apocalyptic context for Mark is best described in A. Y. Collins, *Mark*, 42–84.

2. For a survey of apocalyptic thought and the so-called combat myth, see DiTomasso, "Apocalypses and Apocalypticism," 235–86; for the ancient Near Eastern setting of the myth and its extension into the early Christian period, see A. Y. Collins, *Combat Myth*, and Garrett, *Temptations of Jesus*, 36–40.

3. Levenson, *Creation*, defines *apocalyptic* in this way: "The central affirmation of apocalyptic is that the evil that occurs within history is symptomatic of a larger suprahistorical disequilibrium that requires, indeed invites, a suprahistorical correction. As evil did not originate with history, neither will it disappear altogether *in* history, but rather *beyond* it, at the inauguration of the coming world" (50).

4. Paul writes during the decade of the 50s in the first century. He makes numerous references to both baptism (e.g., Rom. 6:3; Gal. 3:27–28) and the Lord's Supper (e.g., 1 Cor. 10:16–17; 11:17–34) and expects his audience to be familiar with these rituals.

between the powers of chaos (water) and divine power.[5] In Mark, Jesus rises (*anabainō*) from the river Jordan, the waters of baptism, and is declared by the divine voice to be the beloved Son (1:10–11).[6] He then immediately engages the forces of Satan (chaos) in the wilderness (1:13). Only after this confrontation does Jesus begin his ministry in the Gospel, often confronting demons, water, darkness, and death (chaos) and defeating them all (1:23; 4:35–41; 5:41; 7:30; 9:17). So from the beginning of the Gospel to its end the cosmic struggle between the divine power that orders creation—the Spirit now within Jesus (1:10)—and chaos has been joined.

The important work of Jon Levenson in interpreting the Genesis creation narrative, utilizing comparative material from ancient Jewish and Near Eastern mythology, places this mythology of the struggle of God against chaos into its proper liturgical and ritual context.[7] Ultimately, Levenson argues, within ancient Judaism it was the defining of ritual order within the temple cult that marked out the order of creation amid the constant assault of chaos.[8] *Ritual action in the cult, especially ritual sacrifice, literally sustained in the face of chaos the order of the entire cosmos.*[9] Further, Levenson argues that what is depicted in descriptions of the ancient Jewish temple cult is the constant possibility, a cosmic threat, of a return to chaos from the order of the seven-day creation established by ritual action. Most important for my argument in this book, however, is Levenson's convincing argument that God's sovereignty over chaos in ancient Judaism—which will come into the early Christian understanding of its own ritual activity—was a *liturgical reality*, realized and then enacted in the cultic system of the Jerusalem temple on Mount Zion. With the performance of the ritual cult the temple mount (Zion) becomes the phenomenological cosmic mountain. The order of creation itself, achieved by God's ordering of chaos in the first six days of creation, is established on the seventh day (Sabbath) and proceeds from Zion (temple), and so Zion becomes the junction and conduit between heaven, earth, and hell. Moreover, in the

5. See my extended discussion of this reality in "That by His Passion," 91–98.

6. The echo here is Ps. 2:7 and Isa. 42:1–2. Both texts point to the adoption of the Davidic king as God's representative who possesses the divine Spirit. That the Davidic king is given the power to contest chaos is indicated in Ps. 88:26 (LXX): "I will place his hand upon the sea [*thalassa*] and his right arm upon the rivers."

7. I base what follows on a general reading of two books by Levenson: *Creation* and *Death and Resurrection*.

8. Levenson, *Creation*, xxv–xxvii.

9. Ibid., 85–86. See p. 127: "It is through the cult that we are enabled to cope with evil, for it is the cult that builds and maintains order, transforms chaos into creation, ennobles humanity, and realizes the kingship of God who has ordained the cult and commanded that it be guarded and practiced."

cult, primordial mythical time is present as opposed to what we might describe or experience as time or temporality. The cosmic mountain is therefore also always the sacred wilderness as well as the primordial garden of Eden. It is the cultic enactment of sacred space which manifests the achieved order of the seven-day creation. Here in the ritual space is the first creation, untarnished by time, *surrounded yet unaffected* by threats of chaos.[10]

The major liturgical festival of Passover (Mark 14:1) is obviously important in Mark as the time in which Jesus is betrayed, brought to trial, and crucified, yet leaves the tomb empty. Passover is celebrated within Judaism as the divine victory over the waters of chaos: the Red Sea is pushed back by divine wind (*anemos*; Exod. 10:13 LXX; Mark 4:37; 6:51), just as in the opening verse of Genesis the divine Spirit pushes back the waters of chaos. This victory is followed by the salvific appearance of dry land, upon which the carefully ordered sanctuary is built. This sanctuary, with its intended cultic practice, seals and enacts in ritual practice the victory of God in establishing the ordered creation (dry land) over chaos (water).[11] Sometime after the fall of the first temple in 587 BC, Isaiah described a new exodus, a new path (*hodos*), straight and level, which will bring the Lord again to be with his people (Isa. 40:3–5 LXX) and again establish the ordered creation (Genesis).[12] This is the path or way (*hodos*) which the Gospel of Mark describes as the death of Jesus (10:52), the way (*hodos*) through the baptismal death of Christ in the waters of chaos, the way by which Jesus rises (*anabainō*; 1:10; 4:8; 6:51), orders chaos (4:39; 6:51), and comes to be with the Gentiles in a new sanctuary, the new sacred space of the ordered creation, the wilderness (1:2–3, 12; 6:31; 8:4).[13] For Mark this new sacred space, the restoration of the Genesis creation, is the inclusive ritual space of the Lord's Supper. It is the resurrected body of Christ (14:22).

Jesus was a Jew, and the earliest Christian churches emerged from ancient Judaism prior to the fall of the second temple. As a result, this basic understanding of the function of ritual practice and the role it played in the struggle between chaos and creation would have deeply influenced their emerging understanding of their own unique ritual practices (baptism and meal). In baptism the power of chaos, death in the waters, was defeated by divine power

10. Ibid., 90–99.
11. Exod. 39–40; the parallelism between the establishment of the ordered creation in Genesis and the creation of the tabernacle in Exodus is, according to Levenson, too striking for coincidence. See Levenson, *Creation*, 85.
12. The depiction of a new Genesis in Isa. 11:1–12 clearly informs the narrative of Mark: the Spirit of the Lord rests upon the messianic figure (11:2) who will gather the outcasts from the four corners of the earth (11:12).
13. For extensive discussion, see Watts, *New Exodus*, 96–121.

in the resurrection. In Mark, for example, Jesus rises (*anabainō*) from the waters to confront Satan in the wilderness (1:10–13), and amid opposition, he creates the sacred space of the Lord's Supper (6:30–44; 8:1–9; 14:17–26). This is the ritual meal that enacted the resurrection, a ritual space of ordered creation which, as the enactment of the wilderness and the Genesis garden, celebrated God's cosmic victory over chaos and evil.[14]

It is this basic understanding of resurrection, sacred space, chaos, and new creation enacted in ritual that I am, at every turn, attempting to read back into the narrative of Mark. As we shall see in the pages that follow, there are many ways in which the narrative character of Jesus in Mark can and should be understood as depicting a liturgical reality, the one who literally enacts the order of creation against chaos.[15] Overall, Jesus's ministry in Mark is the establishment of a new creation and a new temple realized in the Lord's Supper gatherings as the inclusive (Jew and Gentile, men and women) body of Christ in the early Christian house churches. When Jesus heals, he restores bodies to the perfect state of Genesis (1:42; 3:5; 5:29) and so invites these characters to this new reality, that is, to be part of the meal. He resurrects (*diegeirō*) to calm the waters of chaos (4:39) and walks upon the sea (chaos) and, in a demonstration of resurrection power, rises (*anabainō*) into the boat with his disciples (6:47–52). Most important, Jesus will become in his death and resurrection the new temple itself, the ritually enacted body of Christ (14:22–25), the house of prayer for all the Gentiles (11:17).

For the liturgically located reader, both ancient and modern, it would be difficult without this understanding to fully engage the Gospel of Mark. For

14. For the seven-day creation as the celebration of God's triumph over chaos, see Levenson, *Creation*, 66–77. In Mark this is the importance both of the implied number seven in the first ritual meal narrative (five loaves plus two fish) and of the explicit *seven* loaves of the second ritual meal in the wilderness (8:1–9): the Gentiles (represented by the universal number of four thousand) have been gathered into the new creation (*seven loaves*).

15. I am more or less opting out of the recent scholarly debate over whether Jesus is depicted as human (Davidic king) or divine (Yahweh) in Mark, especially with respect to his mastery of water (chaos) in 4:35–41; 6:47–52. For details and references, see Kirk and Young, "I Will Set His Hand," 333–40. This debate depends on the prior assumption that the narrative character in Mark is only or primarily an individual, divine or human, while my sense is that Jesus in Mark is the *resurrected* Jesus and so also possesses a liturgical and corporate identity. Jesus in Mark is the "one loaf" (8:14–21) and the "body of Christ" (14:22), transparent to the ritual practice and identity of Mark's house churches. When Jesus dominates the water (chaos) in 4:35–41 and 6:47–52, it is the new creation, the liturgical gathering, which emerges from the chaos of Jesus's (baptismal) death. In many ways this debate clarifies why I wrote this book. Almost all modern scholarship, in tune with modern and Protestant sensibilities, focuses on Jesus and other characters in Mark, whether narrative or historical, as individuals. I focus on the ways in which every aspect of Mark—characters, time, and places—reflects the realities of the ritual setting of the early house churches.

such a reader, the character of Jesus and the other characters, as well as all of their words and actions, is deeply symbolic and reflect most of all the *reality* experienced within these rituals. Jesus as a character will both proclaim and bring into reality the reign of God, which he in his character, through ritual death and resurrection, already manifests (5:30; 9:2–3). He is both an individual figure in the story and a symbolic corporate figure. Put differently, Jesus in the narrative is a sacramental reality,[16] a literary character wherein the church that Mark experiences and envisions in ritual practice, Jews and Gentiles, men and women, is revealed. In Mark Jesus is Jesus from Nazareth, a real person inside of time, *and* Jesus the risen Christ, a real person who has transcended time. The church of Mark's day in the ritual gathering of the Lord's Supper is both inside of time (experiencing the reality of persecution and human needs of all sorts) and outside of time (within their rituals experiencing the reality of the new creation, the reign of God). It is the sheer genius of Mark to create a narrative character Jesus as well as other characters who reflect exactly this dual reality of the Lord's Supper among the Christians of Mark's time. For Mark the body of Christ is both inside and outside of time.[17]

Finally, readers of Mark, both ancient and modern, have puzzled over why Mark would have Jesus Christ, Son of God (1:1), baptized for repentance and the forgiveness of sins (1:4). Yet if the ritual of baptism in Mark is part of this larger struggle between creation and chaos, then Jesus in the act of baptism is both beginning the struggle against death and chaos and completing that same struggle (rising out of death and chaos). This is in fact the struggle which the gathered community of Mark's day has both begun and completed in their own rituals of baptism and the Lord's Supper. And here is the tricky part that is central to Mark's purpose: *in Mark the resurrected Christ must die on the cross in order to be the resurrected Christ.* On one level of the narrative the character Jesus of Nazareth has to move through ordinary time and be

16. This understanding is crucial to my reading of Mark. The idea of sacrament here is that it is two things at once. For example, eucharistic bread is bread and more than bread. Baptismal water is water and more than water. Jesus as a sacramental character is an individual man in the narrative and more than an individual man. Sacraments as such convey a particular sacred reality beyond what we might term ordinary reality.

17. The argument can and should be made that this unique narrative quality of time in the Gospels (i.e., the story of Jesus of Nazareth is transparent to the story of the later Christian communities) emerges from liturgy itself. For liturgy reflects actual time (the experience of the participants) and time before (e.g., the words and actions of a past Jesus made present) and time after (the consummation of time itself). I will argue that all of the characters in Mark act primarily as this sort of liturgical symbol. Peter, James, and John, for example, are ciphers for elements in the Christian community who will not or do not understand that the reality of the resurrection is based on the cross and so includes the Gentiles who enter the community through ritual baptism into Jesus's death (8:32–33; 10:38–40).

crucified by the Romans in about AD 30. On another level the character Jesus in Mark has already been crucified and resurrected. He has been baptized into his own death and rises into the story as the divine voice of God, proclaimed as beloved Son (1:11). Yet the status of the latter, the resurrected Son of God, is completely dependent on the actions of the former, Jesus of Nazareth, in choosing to follow through with his martyrdom on the cross.[18] There is both victory (resurrection) and continued struggle (the way, *hodos*, of the cross). So also at the time Mark was written, members of the house churches were moving through ordinary time to their own martyrdoms while being gathered in the Lord's Supper outside of time as the body of Christ (13:9–13). Already crucified in baptism and risen in meal, they are now called on by Mark to be willing to suffer and die in order to become, as Jesus is in the narrative, what they already are (8:33).

The opening baptismal scene in Mark tells us that the death of Jesus in Mark, the passion narrative (14:1–16:8), is ritually enacted martyrdom. It is the ritual death that literally enacts the ordered creation already present in Jesus as he rises from the water chaos of baptism.[19] And this too is the link to the rituals of baptism and cultic meal within the Christian community, both within the narrative and in the later time of Mark's church. When Jesus in Mark moves to his death, he does so as the temple sacrifice itself (11:17–25), as the epitome of a new cultic ritual that both defeats chaos (death) and manifests the new creation (resurrection; 14:58). For Mark the proper understanding of the rituals of baptism and the Lord's Supper begins and moves forward this story of Christ. Indeed the proper understanding of these rituals is embedded within the narrative, as we shall have occasion to explore throughout this book. This understanding, the baptism of the Gentiles into the death of Christ and their presence, both men and women, at the ritual meal, is the foundation of how Mark tells the story of Jesus and how he wants the story of Jesus to be told within the ritual gatherings of the church in his own time. Thus within the narrative when Jesus faces strong opponents—including disease and water and demons and death, and even his own will—yet overcomes them to accept death as the will of the Father (14:36), it is the death (sacrifice) that unleashes the creative Spirit of God to defeat chaos and bring new creation (1:10; 4:35–41; 15:37). The church of Mark, gathered to enact the rituals of baptism and Supper, must also overcome these opponents (especially their own doubts about martyrdom) to enact in ritual the final gathering of

18. This is the point of the temptation scene at Gethsemane in Mark 14:32–42.
19. As in John 1:1–18, one could argue that the Markan prologue is the entire story: Jesus is "Christ and Son of God" (1:1) who must die (baptismal death, 1:9) in order to be declared "beloved Son" (1:11).

a unified humanity, Jews and Gentiles, men and women (13:27; 14:22–24). This is liturgical ritual centered on martyrdom, a martyrdom that is in turn given its meaning from liturgical ritual.

From the very beginning of Mark's narrative, therefore, it is not possible to understand what Mark is attempting to convey without realizing that the story itself emerges from Mark's experience of the cultic reality of his own church. Yet the story Mark has created attempts to convey a particular understanding of that reality in the way he has constructed the overall progression of the narrative from baptism (1:10) to the inclusion of the Gentiles and women in the ritual meals of the wilderness (6:30–41; 8:1–9) to the final ritual meal of the one loaf (8:14–21; 14:17–26) announcing the meaning of Jesus's death (14:22–25). It is just this dynamic that I hope this book conveys.

1

The Early Gentile Mission
and Explanation

1:1–4:34

Mark 1

Baptismal Death and Resurrection

The beginning of the gospel of Jesus Christ, the Son of God. As it is written
in Isaiah the prophet: "Behold I send my *messenger* in front of you, who will
prepare your *way* [*hodos*]"; a voice of one crying in the *wilderness* [*erēmos*],
"Prepare the *way* [*hodos*] of the Lord, immediately make straight his path."

And John the Baptizer came into the wilderness [*erēmos*] preaching a baptism
of repentance for the forgiveness of sins. And there came out to him everyone
from the region of Judea and all of Jerusalem, and they were baptized by him
in the river Jordan confessing their sins. John was clothed in camel's hair, and
had a leather belt around his waist, and he ate locusts and wild honey. And he
preached, saying, "One who is stronger than I is coming behind me. I am not
fit to bend down and loosen the straps of his sandals. I have baptized you with
water, but he will baptize you with the Holy Spirit."

And it happened in those days that Jesus came from Nazareth in Galilee
and was baptized in the Jordan River by John. And immediately resurrecting
[*anabainō*] from the water, he saw the heavens split [*schizō*] and the Spirit

descending as a dove enter into him. And a voice came from the heavens: "You are my beloved Son. I am well pleased with you." And immediately the Spirit cast him into the wilderness [*erēmos*]. (1:1–12)

Jesus dies and rises from the dead in the first chapter of Mark. He does so through the ritual of baptism, that is, the *way* (*hodos*). As Paul tells us in Romans 6:3–4, some early Christians of Mark's time considered the ritual of immersion in water to be the enactment of a ritual death in Christ out of which the new Christian rises to a new reality, to be, as Paul states it, in newness of life (*kainotēti zōēs*). There is no guarantee, of course, that this is the basis on which Mark is presenting the story of Jesus's baptism, but there are plenty of clues in the opening verses that would bring the liturgical reader of Mark[1] to realize the connection here between Jesus's ritual baptism, his death on the cross, and his resurrection into "newness of life."

Mark begins his narrative with an announcement taken from the prophets Malachi and Isaiah:

"Behold I send my *messenger* in front of you, who will prepare your *way* [*hodos*]"; a voice of one crying in the *wilderness* [*erēmos*], "Prepare the *way* [*hodos*] of the Lord."[2]

The prophet Malachi identifies this messenger with Elijah (Mal. 4:5), and so the reader of Mark understands that Elijah has now returned in the person of John the Baptist.[3] His voice crying out in the wilderness echoes the prophet Isaiah and in doing so sets the stage for the entire narrative structure of Mark to be the fulfillment of the ancient prophecy of Isaiah:

1. I begin to describe this reader in the prologue (note 2). I presume that Mark and his ancient readers (and also hearers, for there is good reason to presume the Gospel was also proclaimed orally) shared the formative experience of early Christian ritual performance and that Mark's original text is written from within that shared perspective. In addition the liturgical reader of Mark is also a modern reader who reads the story from the present formative experience and reality of Christian liturgy, especially baptism and Eucharist. Unless otherwise specified, when I refer to "the reader," it is this liturgical reader. For a discussion of this sort of reading from *within* a tradition, see Levenson, "Unexamined Commitments," 24–33.

2. The Scripture here is a conflation of Mal. 3:1 and Isa. 40:3.

3. The identification of John as Elijah is made explicit at Mark 9:13. The description of John's clothing and diet (hair shirt, leather belt, and bees' honey) also makes the identification of John with Elijah transparent: see 2 Kings 1:8. The link here between the clothing and diet of John (camel hair, leather belt, and wild honey) and the garden of Eden is important: the hair garment and leather belt recall the Septuagint version of Gen. 3:21 (God clothes Adam and Eve with leather tunics); the Jewish story *Joseph and Aseneth* (probably written around the time of Mark) has Aseneth (the heroine) eating honey made by the bees of the garden of Eden (*Joseph and Aseneth* 16:14). Mark's later narrative focus on the Sabbath (1:21; 2:23; 3:2; 6:2) and the number seven (6:38, implicit; 8:5–6, 20) also has the connotation of the edenic garden.

A voice crying in the *wilderness* [*erēmos*], prepare the *way* [*hodos*] of the Lord, make the paths of our God straight. All valleys will be filled, and all mountains and hills made low. Crooked paths will be straightened, and rough patches made smooth. And the glory of the Lord will be *seen* [*horaō*], and *all flesh* [*pasa sarx*] will *see* [*horaō*] the salvation of God because the Lord has spoken. (Isa. 40:3–5 LXX)[4]

Four key aspects to this prophecy set out the structure of Mark's narrative: (1) *wilderness*, (2) *the way*, (3) *all flesh*, and (4) *to see the salvation of God*.

As I will discuss in detail later in this book, the first eight chapters of Mark build toward two successive ritual meal gatherings which take place in the wilderness (*erēmos*; 6:32; 8:4). In the first meal narrative Mark describes, per Isaiah here, an exodus on dry land: the Gentiles arrive in the wilderness by land prior to Jesus and the Jewish disciples, who come by water (6:33–34). In the second ritual meal narrative in the wilderness, now in a Gentile place, Jesus tells his disciples to feed the Gentiles so that they do not falter *on the way* (*hodos*), namely, the way of Jesus toward passion and death (8:3).[5] Following the second meal narrative, and again on two separate occasions, Jesus cures a blind man. The first blind man comes to *see* clearly that the Gentiles have indeed come to eat the one loaf with the Jews (8:22–26), and the second blind man, the Gentile "son of Timaeus," comes to recognize (see) Jesus as the *Son of David* and then asks to follow Jesus *on the way* (*hodos*) to Jerusalem and his passion and death (10:52). Toward the end of the narrative, at the Last Supper immediately before his death, Jesus declares that the body of Christ, Jews and Gentiles (*all flesh*), has been gathered and that he will pour out his blood as the new covenant for the many (14:22–23). And so at his trial before the Sanhedrin Jesus declares that everyone will *see* (*horaō*) him coming on the clouds of heaven, that is, all will *see* the salvation of God (14:62).

Thus for the liturgical reader of Mark a great deal of the basic structure of the entire narrative is established in the opening announcement of the Isaiah-Malachi prophecy. The church of Jews and Gentiles (all flesh) will be

4. Watts, *New Exodus*, 370–74, sees the narrative structure of Mark as built on the framework of this new exodus event in Isaiah (Yahweh delivers his people from the power of the nations; Yahweh leads the people along the way of the Lord; Yahweh and his people arrive in Jerusalem in triumph). And while I share substantive agreement with Watts, I would add that the rituals of baptism and Eucharist would create this new Israel (all flesh, Jews and Gentiles) and so be the place in which such a new exodus would be experienced and communicated in the form of the Gospel.

5. Throughout Mark's Gospel, the "way [*hodos*]" refers to the death of Christ (4:4, 15; 10:52; 11:8). Here one notes especially the later story of the Gentile Bartimaeus, who is brought from blindness to sight and who then follows Jesus "on the way [*hodos*]" (10:52), precisely at the point in the narrative where Jesus undertakes his final journey to Jerusalem to be crucified.

gathered in the wilderness for the Lord's Supper in order to follow Jesus on the way to his passion and death in Jerusalem, followed by his resurrection and imminent return on the clouds of heaven for all to see. Yet in the meantime there will be misunderstanding, betrayal, and abandonment. And all of this, the story of Jesus and the story of the church, will be enacted in the narrated and performed rituals of baptism and meal.

Baptism and Cross

And John the Baptizer came into the wilderness preaching a baptism of repentance for the forgiveness of sins. And there came out to him everyone from the region of Judea and all of Jerusalem, and they were baptized by him in the river Jordan confessing their sins. John was clothed in camel's hair, and had a leather belt around his waist, and he ate locusts and wild honey. And he preached, saying, "One who is stronger than I is coming behind me. I am not fit to bend down and loosen the straps of his sandals. I have baptized you with water, but he will baptize you with the Holy Spirit." (1:4–8)

From the time even before Mark's Gospel to the present day there has been the expectation with the Jewish tradition that the prophet Elijah, who in the biblical story had been taken up in the fiery chariot to heaven (2 Kings 2:11), would someday return to usher in the messianic age.[6] Mark now continues to link the opening of the Gospel, the appearance of John (Elijah) baptizing people in the Jordan River in the *wilderness*, with the future death of Jesus on the cross, that is, the death which inaugurates the messianic age.

So it is that at the end of the narrative the utterance of the bystander at the cross, "Let us see whether Elijah comes to pull him down" (15:36), is filled with specific irony tied to the beginning of the Gospel: if Elijah *would* pull Jesus from the cross, there would be no death and no ushering in of God's reign through his death. So also if Jesus had not been baptized by John (Elijah) into his own death to begin the Gospel, there would be no ministry, no ushering in of God's reign, in the narrative that follows.

So it is at the cross in the very next moment that Jesus dies and *gives out the Spirit (ekpneō;* 15:37).[7] Jesus thereby fulfills with his death at the end of

---

6. Collins, *Mark*, 49, 138–40; Marcus, *Mark 1–8*, 157. In modern Jewish settings the return is especially associated with the Passover Seder: Greenberg, *Jewish Way*, 156. In ancient apocalyptic writing contemporary to the writing of Mark the messianic age will usher in a new experience of the Genesis garden (Marcus, *Mark 1–8*, 139).

7. This is the more literal translation of *ekpneō* in the text of Mark 15:37; other translations such as the New American Bible simply have Jesus "breathing his last." I believe such translations miss the clear connection to the promise of the Spirit given at Mark 1:8.

the narrative what John predicts at the opening of the Gospel: "He will baptize you with the Holy Spirit" (1:8). This Spirit which comes from the death of Jesus is in fact the same Spirit that Jesus *receives* at his baptism, the ritual being distinctly narrated by Mark:

> And it happened in those days that Jesus came from Nazareth in Galilee and was baptized in the Jordan River by John. And immediately resurrecting [*anabainō*] from the water, he saw the heavens split [*schizō*] and the Spirit descending as a dove enter into him. And a voice came from the heavens: "You are my beloved Son. I am well pleased with you." And immediately the Spirit cast him into the wilderness [*erēmos*]. (1:9–12)

Reaching out to his readers who have also experienced the ritual of baptism, Mark would have these readers understand that Jesus enters into his own ritual death and resurrection in the baptism by John. Jesus resurrects (*anabainō*) from the waters of death. And at this moment the heavens are torn (*schizō*) and the Spirit descends upon Jesus. Again at the death of Jesus on the cross, and at the very moment the Spirit is released, the temple curtain is torn (*schizō*; 15:38).

For the reader of Mark it is as if the Spirit smashes through the curtain all the way back to the beginning of Mark's Gospel. The end and the beginning of the narrative have come together, and the events in the narrative will tell the story of Jesus, who must die because he has already died in baptism.[8] It is only by passing through death that Jesus becomes the resurrected beloved Son (1:11), who establishes the church, the body of Christ, in the narrative of Mark (14:22). It is only by their own endurance in persecution (13:9), including martyrdom as the fulfillment of their own baptismal death (8:34–35; 10:38–39), that the Christians in Mark's church, the body of Christ, Jews and Gentiles of the one loaf a generation later, can soon be gathered with Christ in the resurrection (8:35; 13:27). In short, a generation after Jesus's death on the cross, Mark will write the story of a faithful martyr Jesus as the unfinished story of the church of Mark.

8. In the earliest centuries of the Christian church, some churches celebrated the death, resurrection, and conception of Christ on the same day (Easter), and that day was apparently our March 25. Nine months following March 25 was December 25 (Christmas). Thus Christ was conceived—that is, became incarnate—at the moment of his death. Liturgically there would be no space between life and death, only the eternal life of Christ. As a narrative the Gospel of Mark reads exactly in this way. Mark's Jesus has already died and risen in baptism and now, though resurrected and outside of time, acts within time. In the same way those who have been baptized into his death in the church of Mark now constitute the ritual meal of the Lord's Supper, the ritual of the resurrected body of Christ within time. This also appears to be Paul's understanding of the Lord's Supper in 1 Cor. 11:29–30. See the discussion in McGowan, *Ancient Christian Worship*, 252–56.

When Jesus rises out of the chaotic waters of baptism, the Spirit as a dove enters into him, and a voice from the heavens proclaims that Jesus is the Son of God (1:11).[9] Jesus is then driven by this same Spirit into the wilderness. Liturgical readers find themselves drawn into both the story of Noah (the dove),[10] a story of new creation from the chaotic waters of the flood, and the story of Israel in the book of Exodus, a story of the creation of Israel in the wilderness out of the chaotic waters of the Red Sea (Exod. 15:1–22). As did Israel in the exodus event, Jesus here sojourns with God in the wilderness.

The Wilderness

And he was in the wilderness [erēmos] for forty days being tested by Satan. And he was with the wild beasts, and the angels ministered to him. (1:12–13)

The encounter with Satan in this wilderness sets yet another stage for the unfolding narrative drama.[11] For forty days—an obvious allusion to the forty years Israel spent in the wilderness—Jesus is put on trial by Satan. In an extension of the cosmic struggle between Jesus and Satan that is present throughout the narrative, Satan and the demons are introduced to the reader as the enemy of Christ, the resurrected one who, through his death (just ritually enacted), establishes the new people amid a new creation. Here as in Eden the wild beasts are apparently friendly (Gen. 1:30; Isa. 11:6–7). The liturgical reader knows why Satan and the demons know Jesus: chaos is the sworn enemy of creation. Hence the entire narrative will now unfold as a cosmic struggle between the forces of chaos (cosmic and human opponents of Jesus) and creation. The earthly opponents' desire to "destroy" Jesus (3:6; 11:18), and even the fear and opacity of the Jewish disciples (4:40; 6:50; 8:4), are part of the larger opposition of chaos to creation manifest in the crucified (baptized) and resurrected Christ and his gathering of Jews and Gentiles in the ritual meal (6:30–44; 8:1–9; 14:18–31). The central irony of the narrative is that the destruction of Jesus can result only in the resurrection of Jesus: as in the creation story of Genesis, the flood story, and the story of the exodus, creation overcomes chaos. This truth is manifest in the narrative already in the opening ritual of Jesus's baptism: Jesus must die in order to be the resurrected Christ (creation) in the narrative that follows.

---

9. This proclamation should be heard in light of the Gentile centurion's similar affirmation when Jesus dies on the cross and releases the Spirit: "Truly this man was the Son of God" (15:39).
10. Gen. 8:8–12.
11. For discussion, see Garrett, Temptations of Jesus, 55–60.

And after John was betrayed, Jesus came into Galilee preaching the gospel of God. He said, "The time is fulfilled and the kingdom of God draws near. Repent and believe in the gospel." And passing by the Sea [*thalassa*] of Galilee, he saw Simon and Andrew, the brother of Simon, casting [nets] into the sea. For they were fishermen. And Jesus said to them, "Come behind me and I will make you become fishermen of humans." And immediately they left the nets and followed him. And going along a bit further, he saw James, son of Zebedee, and his brother John. And they were mending nets in the boat. And immediately he called them, and they left their father Zebedee in the boat with the hired hands, and they went and followed him. (1:14–20)

After Jesus confronts Satan in the wilderness, he selects four disciples by the *Sea* (*thalassa*) of Galilee, an initial indication of the centrality of the Gentile mission in the narrative. A quite ordinary lake in Galilee has been designated as the *sea*, intimating to the liturgical reader the primeval waters of chaos out of which creation emerges.[12] It is this same sea/chaos which Jesus, his disciples, and "other boats" (Gentiles?) will cross on the way to the Gentiles and over which Jesus will triumph in an act of baptism and resurrection (4:35–41). It is also the sea/chaos upon which he will walk after the first feeding narrative (6:47–53) and upon which he will have a discussion in a boat about the one loaf of the ritual meal (8:10–21). As will become apparent later in our discussion, each of these events brings together the sea, primeval chaos, and the mission to bring Gentiles into the community. That is, the sea here has to be crossed to reach the Gentiles (4:35; 6:45). It is the cosmic opposition that must be defeated in order to bring together Jews and Gentiles into the ritual meal of the one loaf, the resurrected body of Christ, the new creation. For the liturgical reader of Mark, the sea is not just the sea.

The selection of "four" disciples here is deliberate. It is marked by the overall pattern of the narrative. Andrew, one of the disciples selected here, disappears altogether at key points in the narrative and returns to an active role only at Mark 13:3. It would have made more sense for only the three disciples who play a principal role throughout the narrative of Mark to be selected here.[13] Mark, however, wants to couple this first call of disciples with the Gentile mission, and calling *four* disciples here accomplishes just that.

12. Marcus, *Mark 1–8*, 432; Levenson, *Creation*, 14–25, notes that in Ps. 89 God's primeval victory over the waters of chaos is maintained by the Davidic throne, a theme not irrelevant to Mark's portrayal of Jesus as the Son of David (10:47).

13. The three disciples, Peter, James, and John, are the disciples present at the raising of the twelve-year-old girl (5:37), the Transfiguration (9:2), the apocalyptic discourse (13:3), and the Gethsemane garden (14:33). In addition, the narrative features Peter and then James and John in dialogue with Jesus in Mark 8–10.

Following Isaiah 11:12, and more generally in the ancient world, the number four was considered a type of universal number: there were four winds and four corners of the earth and four primal elements (air, fire, earth, and water).[14] So to select four disciples from the *sea* sets the stage for Mark's main narrative purpose: to establish the Jewish disciples' role in the Gentile mission despite their own reservations.[15]

This initial call narrative also links the disciples' eventual mission to the Gentiles with fishing. Jesus announces to Peter and Andrew that they will become "fishermen of humans" (1:17). Here Mark picks up on a more general tradition in the early church that links fishing with the early Christian mission.[16] Undoubtedly for Mark this is a reference to the Gentile mission: fish will be found and then served at the two wilderness meals of the Lord's Supper (6:38; 8:7). In addition, the second meal gathering will specifically state that "four" thousand were fed the fish.[17]

In the recruitment of the second pair of disciples the narrative emphasis is on a break with family in order to become a follower of Jesus. James and John leave their father in the boat to follow Jesus (1:20). As I will discuss in some detail below, in Mark the family and kinsmen of Jesus are transparent to Jews at the time of Mark's writing who resisted the Christian mission and actively sought to draw Christian Jews back to the synagogue. The narrative reflects this family tension not only at 3:31–35[18] and 6:1–6 but also in Mark 13, where family divisions and betrayal are a clear marker of the chaos that signifies the imminence of the return of the resurrected Christ (13:12, 27).

14. See Mark 2:3; 8:9; 13:27 (all with Gentile connotations); for the number four in its ancient context, see Pesch, *Das Markusevangelium*, 404. Irenaeus, a Christian bishop in the second century, uses the universal nature of the number four to argue for the four-Gospel canon (*Haer.* 3.11.8); see Gundry, *Mark*, 396.

15. At 6:41 the disciples serve the ritual meal with Gentiles apparently present; they are then forced (*anankazō*) into the boat to cross toward the Gentiles (6:45); at 8:4 the disciples resist providing the ritual meal to the Gentiles: "How is it possible for someone to feed these people with loaves here in the wilderness?"

16. John 21:1–14; Luke 5:1–11.

17. Peter and Andrew's apparent willingness to come behind (*opisō*) Jesus (1:17) is later matched by Peter's reluctance to accept Jesus's saying about the necessity of his death. There Jesus also commands Peter, as Satan, to come behind (*opisō*; 8:33).

18. The break with family is well illustrated in Mark 3:31–35. There Jesus is in his house with a crowd (3:20). His mother and his brothers are *outside* and want Jesus to come outside to them. Jesus responds by first looking at those around him in the house and then asking a rhetorical question about family: "Who are my mother and brothers?" Jesus then answers his own question with reference to the crowd (*ochlos*) *inside* the house: "Here are my mother and my brothers; whoever does the will of God is my brother, sister, and mother." It is not difficult to conclude that those who do the will of God have become the new family of Jesus. The Jewish family is left behind, and a new, more inclusive family, including Gentiles, is now based in the house church.

Here James and John leave not just their father but also the other Jews who work with the family fishing business. The narrative of Mark here seems to reflect the fact that Christian Jews often had to break family and village ties with other Jews in order to become Christians (10:29–30).

Jesus Begins His Ministry

And they came into Capernaum. And immediately on the Sabbath he entered the synagogue and taught. And they were astonished at his teaching. For he was teaching them as one with authority and not as the scribes taught. And immediately in their synagogue there was a man with an unclean spirit, and he cried out, saying, "What are you to us, Jesus the Nazarene? Have you come to destroy [apollymi] us? I know who you are, the Holy One of God." And Jesus rebuked him, saying, "Be silent and come out of him." And the unclean spirit convulsed him and cried out with a loud voice and came out of him. And they were all amazed and conversed amongst themselves, saying, "What is this? A new teaching with authority? He commands the unclean spirits and they obey him." (1:21–27)

After gathering the four disciples, Jesus begins his ministry in the synagogue in Capernaum, apparently his home village (2:1), with an exorcism (1:23–28).[19] This initial exorcism in the synagogue is marked by the incongruence of the actual event (an exorcism) and the response of the synagogue audience: "What is this? A new teaching [didachē]?" (1:27). Some scholars would argue that two different stories have been combined here (an exorcism story and a teaching story),[20] but it is more likely that this is a deliberate juxtaposition. The identification of the "unclean spirit" (1:23) indicates the confrontation is between the Spirit of creation that descended into Jesus at his baptism and the spirit of chaos (Satan) that opposed Jesus in the wilderness. The story also shows that this battle will not be easily won. Jesus commands the unclean spirit to be silent and come out of the man, but the spirit is hardly silent: it groans with a loud voice as it comes out (1:26). The Jewish people in the synagogue then hint at the connection between the authority of Jesus's teaching and the defeat of demonic chaos: "He commands the unclean spirits and they obey him" (1:27). Within the narrative the seed is therefore planted for some Jews in the synagogue to be converted.[21]

19. This marks the beginning of a small mission cycle in the narrative, for from Capernaum Jesus will follow his expanding fame (1:28) to the villages of Galilee (1:38) and then return to Capernaum (2:1).
20. Focant, *Mark*, 67–68.
21. That the house church or churches for which Mark writes started as a movement within the synagogue is quite obvious. Paul hints that he persecuted Christians within the synagogues (Gal. 1:13), and Acts records the pattern of mission to the synagogue followed by the formation

From Synagogue to House

Immediately he went out from the synagogue and came to the house [*oikia*] of Simon and Andrew, with James and John. Simon's mother-in-law lay there with a fever, and immediately they told him about her. And coming to her and grasping her hand, he resurrected her [*egeirō*]. And the fever left her, and she provided table service to them [*diakoneō*]. (1:29–31)

The narrative now shifts location from the synagogue to the "house of Simon and Andrew," in which the liturgical reader might see more than a hint that Mark is here transparent to a movement of some early Jewish Christians from synagogue to house church in which the experience of the resurrection and a ritual meal take place. Regardless, for any reader the boldness of the claim made within the house stands out in the story: Jesus *resurrects* (*egeirō*) Peter's mother-in-law by grasping her by the hand (physical touch), and she serves a meal for the group (*diakoneō*; 1:31). The liturgical reader immediately sees the connection between the resurrection and the physical restoration of creation: Peter's mother-in-law is resurrected amid the context of the ritual meal inside of the house. This is in fact a connection Mark will make again in chapter 6 when Jesus walks upon the water, rises into the boat, and then challenges his disciples to understand the meaning of the ritual meal (loaves; 6:52).[22]

Sundown

When it was evening and after the sun was down [*dynō*], they brought to him all those who were ill and possessed with demons. And the entire city was gathered at his door. And he healed many [*polys*] with illnesses of various kinds, and he cast out many demons, and he would not let the demons speak because they knew him. (1:32–34)

For the liturgical reader, the specific time reference at Mark 1:32, "it was evening and *after the sun was down* [*dynō*]," implies that the narrative has now moved to extend the time of the Jewish Sabbath into Christian Sunday, the day of resurrection.[23] The location of both space and time has now changed.

---

of house churches (Acts 6:9; 13–14). This is also the subject of Jesus's dialogue with the blind man in John, whose parents fear being ejected from the synagogue (John 9:22).

22. For a discussion of this feature of Mark's narrative, see Bobertz, "Our Opinion Is in Accordance," 79–90.

23. For a general discussion of the move from Jewish Sabbath to Christian Sunday in the early church, see Rordorf, *Sunday*; the more recent discussion in McGowan, *Ancient Christian Worship*, 219–22, appears to miss the evidence in Mark here.

Jesus's resurrection of Peter's mother-in-law in Peter's house has now brought the whole city from the synagogue to the door of the house (1:33). And now on Sunday in the house gathering Jesus does more of what he began in the exorcism in the synagogue and the resurrection of Peter's mother-in-law. He heals many who are sick with various illnesses and casts out many demons. What seems to have concerned theologians both in the early church and later centuries—that Jesus, apparently with limited power, healed only "many" who were diseased and cast out only "many demons"—is for the liturgical reader of Mark's narrative a quite deliberate description of a great manifestation of the reign of God as the ordered creation of the Sabbath is now extended into Sunday and beyond.

Resurrection and Wilderness

And very early in the morning, he resurrected [*anistēmi*] and came out and went into the wilderness place [*erēmos*], and there he prayed. And Simon and those with him pursued him. And they found him and told him that everyone was seeking him. And he said to them, "Let us go out into the market towns so that I might preach there, for this is why I came out [*exēlthon*] [to the wilderness]." (1:35–38)

"And very early in the morning, he *resurrected* and came out and went into the wilderness place, and there he prayed" (1:35). The dawn of Sunday now begins with the resurrection of Jesus.[24] Jesus comes out (*exēlthon*, of the tomb?) and is again in the wilderness, the place of both creation and temptation (1:13). Simon and *those with him* (who are these people?) seek him out there and, with more than a hint that Jesus's mission will include the Gentiles, claim that *everyone* (*pantes*) is seeking him. Jesus's response, "Let us go out into the market towns so that I might preach there, for this is why I came out [*exēlthon*]," signals to the liturgical reader that Jesus, as the crucified and resurrected Christ, has come to the wilderness to bring the Gentiles (everyone) into that ritual space. And indeed, following his mission and the mission of his disciples, the Gentiles will in fact gather with the Jews in the wilderness in the first and second ritual meal narratives (6:30–44; 8:1–9).

The Cure of a Leper

And he went out preaching in their synagogues in the whole of Galilee and cast out demons. And there came a leper beseeching him and kneeling down

---

24. The mark of time at Mark 1:35 is unmistakable: "exceedingly early [*lian prōi*] in the morning" refers to the time of the resurrection at Mark 16:2, "exceedingly early [*lian prōi*]."

[*gonypeteō*][25] before him. And he said to him, "If you will, you are able to make me clean." And with compassion he extended his hand and touched him. And he said to him, "I do wish this. Be made clean." And immediately the leprosy left him, and he was made clean. And he sternly charged him and sent him out, saying to him, "Show this to no one and say nothing to anyone, but go, show yourself to the priest and offer for the cleansing what is commanded by Moses as a witness to them." But he came out to preach in all sorts of places and spread the word, so that he [Jesus] was no longer able to enter a city in the open. So he was outside in the wilderness places, and they came to him from everywhere. (1:40–45)

The resurrected Christ now "comes out" to preach to the whole of Galilee. And it fits the emerging narrative pattern of Mark that Jesus is met by a leper (1:40–45). Second Kings 5 tells the story of Naaman, the Syrian general who was cured of leprosy by Elisha the prophet by *baptizing* (*baptizō*) himself seven times in the river Jordan (2 Kings 5:14 LXX). In the biblical story most likely serving as Mark's inspiration here, a Gentile who shows extraordinary faith is made clean by the command of the man of God and the power of baptism. So Mark begins the wider Galilean mission with the story of Jesus healing an unnamed leper, perhaps a Gentile on the model of Naaman, a leper who possesses extraordinary faith in Jesus. The leper both prostrates himself (*gonypeteō*) to Jesus and declares that if Jesus so desires he can make the leper clean.[26] If Mark's story of the leper is meant to recall the story of Naaman, who in the Old Testament narrative at first refused to humble himself out of pride, then the narrative seems transparent to Mark's purpose to show that Gentiles demonstrate remarkable faith, eagerness, and humility in joining the Christian church.

Hence the plea of the leper in Mark, "if you will," holds the audience of the narrative in some suspense: does Jesus will this? In other words, does Jesus will to include Gentiles in the reign of God? And if some of the ancient readers of Mark would have some doubt about this, that is, if they were Jews who resisted the inclusion of Gentiles at the Lord's Supper, then this story is meant to begin to erase the doubt. Jesus not only has compassion on the leper; he actually touches him (as he does Peter's mother-in-law) and thereby restores the leper's body to its intended state: the resurrected Christ again defeats chaos.

25. At least a strong variant reading. See 1:40 in *Novum Testamentum Graece*.
26. Extraordinary expressions of faith are also part of the following stories of the paralytic (2:1–11) and the Syrophoenician woman (7:26–30), stories that feature Gentiles who will not take no for an answer. Each of these stories demonstrates the unique determination of Gentiles within the narrative to become part of the reign of God.

And this brings us to the second part of the leper's plea: "you are able to make me clean." Mark here gets at the basis of any doubt his readers might hold: Jesus does have the capacity and the desire to use this capacity as the baptized and resurrected Son of God both to approve of and to authorize the inclusion of Gentiles in the Christian community. Through baptism the Gentiles of Mark's church can be made clean and fully eligible to participate in the Lord's Supper.

Jesus sternly commands the leper and sends him out, saying to him, "Show this to no one and say nothing to anyone, but go, show yourself to the priest and offer for the cleansing what is commanded by Moses as a witness to them" (1:44). Within the narrative this is a witness to both the Jewish temple priesthood and those Jews who would respect their authority: it would prove that Jesus really does have the capacity to cleanse the Gentile leper. Yet in Mark this might also be read as transparent to the Jewish readers in Mark's community still hesitant about the Gentile mission. Jesus in fact does have the capacity to include Gentiles in the reign of God.

Still the leper does not abide by Jesus's command. For Mark there is no need for the Christian mission to be authorized by the ritual authority of the temple. As Mark makes clear in 11:11–14, temple ritual sacrifices that would be offered for this sort of cleansing have been replaced with the ritual of the house church, the Christian Lord's Supper, the sacrifice of the body of Christ (13:2; 14:58). As well, here early in the narrative, there is already an intimation of how Mark understands the meaning of the passion narrative itself: Jesus, himself the temple, is destroyed in order to be resurrected as the restored creation (the body of Christ), manifest in the ritual meal gathering of Gentiles with the Jews.

In fact the leper did here exactly what Jesus did as he entered the greater area of Galilee: he *"came out* [his own baptism and resurrection?] to preach in all sorts of places" (1:45). And as a result of this Gentile's preaching, the word spreads, presumably to other Gentiles, "so that he [Jesus] was no longer able to enter a city in the open. So he was outside *in the wilderness places*, and they came to him from everywhere [*pantothen*]" (1:45). For the liturgical reader, the narrative here anticipates again the ritual meal gatherings of Jews and Gentiles in the wilderness meal narratives (6:30–44; 8:1–9). Jesus's mission will be to bring all of them, Jews and Gentiles, to the wilderness for the Lord's Supper. From there they will follow him on *the way* of his passion in Jerusalem and anticipate his imminent resurrection appearance.

So it is that Gentiles eagerly and in great numbers come to Jesus in the wilderness (and by analogy to the Christian community of Mark's time).

And just as in the first ritual meal narrative (6:30–44) when they arrive from "all the cities" to be fed with Jesus and the disciples in the wilderness (6:33), so here also they have arrived, narratively foreshadowing their inclusion with the Jews in the ritual meals to follow.

Mark 2

Mark 2:1–3:6 begins a series of five controversy stories in the Gospel.[27] These five stories culminate in the first overt notice in the Gospel that the opponents of Jesus intend to *destroy* (*apollymi*) him (3:6). The liturgical reader of Mark would be especially attentive to this mounting danger that will eventually end up destroying Jesus on the cross, the cosmic chaos out of which will come resurrection and new creation. The controversies here, therefore, are at the center of understanding the purpose of the Gospel. Simply put, the more the reader of Mark understands on what basis the opponents of Jesus actually oppose his ministry, the more that same reader understands what Mark is trying to persuade his readers to support.

Following the deliberate movement from synagogue to house in the story of Peter's mother-in-law (1:29–31), the stories in this section of Mark are transparent to a time in the life of the church in which the early Christian house churches continued to be separated from the synagogues. The issue, as Mark portrays it here in the narrative, concerned the legitimacy and extent of the Gentile mission at the heart of this separation. Beginning here and throughout the remaining narrative, Mark carefully constructs the portrayal of Jesus around both the divine authorization behind the mission to include the Gentiles and the resistance to that inclusion coming from both the Jewish leadership (Jewish synagogues) *and* the Jewish disciples (Jewish Christians). For the liturgical reader, this way of understanding Mark centers the purpose of the Gospel in an understanding of the inclusive nature and significance of the Christian rituals of baptism and the Lord's Supper. Mark understands these rituals as the means by which Gentiles and women are brought into and sustained within the Christian house churches of his time.

In sum, the narrative drama of Mark, the story of cosmic destruction and resurrection, is at the heart of how Mark attempts to persuade his community toward his way of understanding the proper performance and meaning of the rituals of baptism and meal.

27. For commentary on the structure of these five stories and references to secondary literature, see Donahue and Harrington, *Mark*, 96–100.

The Gentile Paralytic

And he came again into Capernaum, and after a few days it became known that he was in the house [*oikos*]. And many [*polys*] were gathered, so that there was no longer any room, not even by the door. And he spoke the word [*logos*] to them. And there came to him a paralytic carried by four [*tessares*].[28] And when they were not able to bring the paralytic to him because of the crowd, they unthatched the roof where he was. When they had dug through, they lowered the bed upon which the paralytic lay. When Jesus saw their faith [the faith of the four], he said to the paralytic: "Child [*teknon*], your sins are forgiven."

And there were some scribes sitting there and debating in their hearts [*kardia*]: "Why does this man speak this way? It is blasphemy. Who is able to forgive sins but the one God?"

And immediately Jesus knew in his spirit that they were debating among themselves.

And he said to them, "Why do you debate these things in your hearts? What is easier? To say to the paralytic, 'Your sins are forgiven'; or to say, 'Resurrect [*egeirō*] and take your bed, and walk'? But so that you may know that the Son of Man has authority to forgive sins upon the earth"—he said to the paralytic—"I say to you, resurrect [*egeirō*], take up your bed, and depart to your house." And he resurrected [*egeirō*] and immediately took up his pallet and went out [*exerchomai*] before them all, and they all were amazed and glorified God saying, "We have never seen anything like this." (2:1–12)

The initial outreach to all of Galilee is here apparently completed. Jesus remains outside of the towns in the *wilderness* (*erēmos*) places with people coming to be with him from *everywhere* (*pantothen*; 1:45). Then Mark tells us: "He [Jesus] came again to Capernaum" (2:1). This is the place of the first exorcism in the synagogue (1:21). This time, however, Jesus does *not* go to the synagogue. Mark carefully tells us that "after a few days it became known that he was in the house [*oikos*]." The time period indicated (a few days) would allow those who were coming to Jesus *from everywhere* to arrive at the house, as apparently they did. Elsewhere in Mark the reference to many (*polys*) signals the inclusion of Gentiles (10:45; 14:24), as it might to the liturgical reader here. The number of people was so great that the door to the house was blocked.

---

28. Literally, "the paralytic was carried by four." It is significant that the text simply states the number four, instead of, for example, "four men" or "four persons." Mark does the same thing with this number at another key moment in the narrative. In 8:9, at the second meal narrative, simply *four thousand* are fed (not four thousand *men* or four thousand *people*). Both cases call the readers' attention to the number four, which, I will argue, is the main point of both stories: the inclusion of the Gentiles.

The *word* (*logos*) being spoken to *many* (*polys*) takes the reader to the parables of chapter 4 as well as to Jesus's passion prediction at 8:32. In the parables of Mark 4, the *word* is the seed (4:14), the proclamation of the necessary death of Christ (8:32), which has been planted in different soils.[29] In certain soil—and here it is easy for the liturgical reader to equate the soil with the throng of Gentiles who have gathered in the house—the proclamation takes root and leads to an extraordinary harvest: thirty-, sixty-, and a hundredfold (4:20).[30]

Just as the striking allusion to Naaman the Syrian brings the liturgical reader to think that the leper touched and cured by Jesus was a Gentile, so here the reference to the *four* who carried the paralytic brings the reader to consider these men and the paralytic as Gentiles. The narrative detail Mark provides would be difficult to miss for the liturgical reader. The paralytic, who is identified by Jesus as apparently needing the forgiveness of sins,[31] is carried by *four*, and they are having difficulty getting into the *house*. More important, the number four is the plain number of Gentiles, *four* thousand, who were fed in a Gentile place at the second meal narrative (8:9).

The narrative would appear to be transparent both to the difficulty that some Gentiles would experience in joining Christian house churches and their eagerness to overcome that difficulty. Here they take off the thatch, dig through the roof, and lower the bed of the paralytic to where Jesus was teaching inside (2:4). Jesus sees the faith of the four and then addresses the paralytic as "child" (*teknon*). Later in the narrative Mark will tell the story of the Gentile Syrophoenician woman (7:24–30), and there the point at issue will be specifically whether a Gentile *child* (*teknon*) can receive the loaves, that is, can eat the *loaves* in the second ritual meal about to take place in the wilderness (7:27; 8:1–9). So when Jesus here addresses the paralytic as "child," it is yet another indication to the reader that the paralytic is a Gentile carried by *four* Gentiles of very persistent faith.

What Jesus says to the child is also unexpected. The obvious reason the paralytic has been brought through the roof is to gain the healing for which

29. In some, Satan takes the word/seed away (4:15), while in others the word/seed takes root, but soon persecution causes the rocky soil (*petrōdēs*) to reject it (4:16). The allusion to Peter, the rock (*Petros, petra*), at 3:16 is reasonably obvious here: Peter rejects the *word* of the necessary death of Christ (8:32) and denies Jesus out of fear of persecution in the passion narrative (14:54–72). Other soil rejects the seed when there is a turn to wealth or other worldly affairs (4:19).

30. For a thorough discussion of the relationship of this parable to the overall narrative structure of Mark, see Tolbert, *Sowing the Gospel*.

31. Paul, of course, can quite naturally assume Gentiles are sinners precisely in a discussion of inclusion in the ritual meal (Gal. 2:15). Matthew, of course, places *Gentiles* together with tax collectors (18:17).

Jesus is now famous. Jesus has resurrected Peter's mother-in-law, cleansed the leper, and healed various sorts of diseases (1:34, 45). The audience within the narrative and the reader of Mark would both expect Jesus immediately to heal the paralytic. So to portray Jesus as instead saying to the paralytic, "Your sins are forgiven," without even a hint of a physical healing, directly introduces and isolates the controversy at the heart of the story: Does Jesus, who has died in ritual baptism and risen to receive the creative Spirit of God, and who has healed Gentiles of physical maladies and demonic possession, also have the capacity to forgive the sins of the Gentiles and thereby include them with the Jews in a new Genesis humanity?

The scribes now debate "in their hearts [*kardia*]" (2:8), introducing a broader theme in Mark but one which ties directly to how the present story of the paralytic fits into Mark's overall narrative purpose. Questioning "in the heart [*kardia*]" of both opponents and disciples is how Mark understands resistance to Jesus's mission to the Gentiles throughout the narrative. In Mark, *hearts*

1. cause the failure to comprehend Jesus's power to forgive the sins of the Gentile paralytic (2:6);
2. ironically plot to kill Jesus because of his inclusive meal practice (3:5–6);
3a. fail to understand the link between walking on the water, rising (resurrection) into the boat, and the feeding of the Gentiles with the five thousand Jews (6:52);
3b. miss the sign of the one loaf of the ritual meal for both Jews and Gentiles (8:14–21).

Hence the overall pattern of how Mark understands the heart is transparent to Mark's overall theological purpose in putting together the narrative of the Gospel. The *heart* causes

1. the failure to understand the link between the claim to forgive the sins of the Gentiles,
2. rooted in the necessary death of Christ enacted in baptism,
3. and the welcoming of the Gentiles to join with Jews at the Lord's Supper.

Here, as elsewhere, the narrative of Mark is transparent to Mark's overall theological purpose, at the center of which was the capacity of the death of Christ, enacted in ritual baptism, to bring the Gentiles to full inclusion at the ritual meal of the Lord's Supper.

The scribes' charge of *blasphemy* in Mark 2:6 takes the reader directly to consideration of Jesus's trial in Mark 14. The accusation of blasphemy there begins with the question of the high priest—"Are you the Christ, *the Son* of the Blessed?"—followed by Jesus's response, "I am, and you will see the Son of Man sitting at the right hand of power and coming on the clouds of heaven." So in his response to the high priest Jesus affirms the baptismal vision of Mark 1:11 ("You are my beloved *Son*") and the resurrection (Transfiguration) vision of Mark 9:7 ("This is my beloved *Son*"). In the midst of his trial and passion, Jesus, the Son of Man, testifies that out of his death, in the narrative enacted in baptism, the resurrection has begun, and that it will soon be completed "on the clouds of heaven."

So it is that the scribes' internal hesitation and consideration of blasphemy concerning Jesus's claim to forgive the sins of the paralytic bring the liturgical reader back to the opening baptismal scene of Mark in order to recall that the purpose of baptism is the forgiveness of sins (1:4). There Jesus himself moved through ritual death and forgiveness (1:4), rising from the water to the acclamation of resurrection ("You are my beloved Son"). And now here on the basis of his own ritual death, Jesus, the Son of Man, claims this same authority on the earth to forgive sins. On this basis he can command the Gentile paralytic: "Resurrect [*egeirō*],[32] take up your bed, and depart to your house" (2:11). And just as Jesus had previously *resurrected* and had *come out* (*exerchomai*) to the cities of Galilee (1:35–38), so now the narrative reports that the paralytic *resurrected* and *came out* (*exerchomai*) before them all (2:12). In Mark's narrative Jesus, baptized and raised, does have the capacity to forgive the sins of Gentiles and restore them to the perfection of the original creation, the body of the resurrection, the body of Christ. In the story of the raising of the Gentile paralytic Mark teaches his community: the baptismal death and forgiveness of the Gentiles in Mark's house church place them at the Lord's Supper, the restored creation, the body of Christ (14:22).

The following four controversy stories in Mark (2:14–17, 18–22, 23–28; 3:1–6) are also constructed to be transparent to Mark's overall narrative purpose: to convince the readers and hearers of the Gospel that the Gentiles, on the basis of their baptismal death, are to be included with Jews at the Lord's Supper. In this series of narratively constructed controversies the opponents' opposition to Jesus is transparent to opposition to Mark's church practice from within the Jewish community. After the last of these controversies, resulting in the plot to *destroy* Jesus (3:1–6), Mark will introduce further opposition

32. See Mark 16:6.

from within the Jewish Christian community (3:31–35). Then, finally, Mark will introduce even the disciples' ignorance and hesitation concerning Gentile inclusion (6:36). The attack of chaos on the creation, the restored body of Christ, is building within the narrative of Mark.

Levi

And he came out again along the sea. And the whole crowd came to him, and he taught them. And passing by [*paragō*] he saw Levi, son of Alphaeus, sitting at the tax office. And he said to him, "Follow [*akoloutheō*] me." And he resurrected [*anistēmi*] and followed him. (2:13–14)

Following the notice of Gentile resurrection in the story of the paralytic, the entire crowd, presumably those who had gathered about the house of Jesus in Capernaum, follows Jesus out to a place beside the sea. Though the sea is not named, Jesus is again at the place where the ministry started and the first disciples were recruited (1:16).[33] Just as in the call of the first disciples (1:16), Jesus is passing by (*paragō*) when he notices Levi, son of Alphaeus. But instead of the honorable profession of fishing, Levi does the dishonorable work of collecting taxes and is sitting at his tax office. Nevertheless, Jesus commands him to *follow* (*akoloutheō*), just as earlier Peter and Andrew *followed* Jesus (*akoloutheō*; 1:18). So Levi resurrects (*anistēmi*) and *follows* Jesus (2:14).[34]

Eating with Many

And he was reclining for a meal in his house.[35] And many tax collectors and sinners were reclining to eat with Jesus and his disciples. For there were many [*polys*], and they followed him. (2:15)

Transparent to the house churches and meal ritual of Mark's time, the next scene has Jesus at his house sharing a meal, perhaps with his original

33. This is the same place from which he will teach the crowd parables about the mysterious inclusion of Gentiles in Mark 4:8, 20 and the place from which he will cross the sea to the Gentiles in 4:35–41.

34. The careful juxtaposition of the two Markan words for resurrection in these two stories is deliberate: the Gentile paralytic *resurrects* (*egeirō*; 2:9, 11; 16:6), and the tax collector *resurrects* (*anistēmi*; 2:14; 8:31).

35. Whose house is not exactly clear in the narrative, either Jesus's house (2:1) or the house of Levi. Many commentators favor the latter (Donahue and Harrington, *Mark*, 101). In either case the liturgical reader would read this as a movement of undesirable persons into the house church.

27

four disciples along with *many tax collectors and sinners*. In a rather odd grammatical construction, Mark also writes, "For they were *many*, and they followed him" (2:15). The liturgical reader of Mark is immediately drawn to Mark 10:45, "The Son of Man came also not to be served but to serve, and to give his life as a ransom for *many* [*polys*]," and 14:24, "my blood of the covenant being poured out for *many* [*polys*]." If, as every indication points, the immediately preceding story of the paralytic concerns the restoration of a *Gentile* sinner on the basis of the faith of the four who brought him, then the sinners here in the narrative are most likely Gentiles, and they, along with the Jewish tax collectors,[36] are the *many* present at the Lord's Supper with Jesus and his disciples. The price of their admission has been paid by the baptismal death of Christ for the forgiveness of sins (1:4).

Opposition to the Inclusive Meal

And the scribes of the Pharisees, seeing that he was eating with sinners and tax collectors, said to his disciples, "Why does he eat with tax collectors and sinners?" Yet Jesus heard and said to them, "Those who are healthy do not need a physician, rather those who are sick. I did not come to call the righteous but the sinners." (2:15–17)

At this point, the opposition shown by the *scribes of the Pharisees*[37] is expressly directed against the inclusive practice of the ritual meal eaten with Jesus. They now challenge his disciples rather than confront Jesus directly: "Why does *he* [Jesus] eat with tax collectors and sinners?" The reader of Mark might well understand the Jewish synagogue of Mark's time addressing the Christian community through the narrative characters of the disciples: "Why have Christian house churches allowed unconverted Gentiles [sinners] to become part of their community?" And to this Jesus in Mark responds: "I did not come to call the righteous but sinners" (2:17). The reader's attention is again drawn to the previous healing and resurrection of the sinner, the Gentile paralytic. And so from this point in the narrative Mark makes it even clearer that the purpose of Jesus's mission is the conversion and welcoming of the Gentiles to the meal. These are the sinners who, along with despised Jews, gather as the body of Christ, the new creation, brought to life out of the baptismal death of Christ.

---

36. It may well be that tax collectors, who worked on behalf of the Roman administration and regularly came into contact with idolatrous coins, would also have been considered persona non grata in the Jewish synagogue. For Mark, Gentiles and tax collectors both represent God's acceptance of the unacceptable.

37. This is the first appearance of this group in Mark.

The Fast

And the disciples of John and the Pharisees were fasting. They came and said to him, "Why do the disciples of John and the disciples of the Pharisees fast [*nēsteuō*] but your disciples do not fast?" And Jesus said to them, "The sons of the wedding are not able to fast while the bridegroom is with them. But the days will come when the bridegroom is torn away from them, and then they will fast on that day." (2:18–20)

For the liturgical reader, the question about fasting at a wedding celebration might will be read as transparent to a description of the Lord's Supper in Mark's house church. As John 2:1–11 (the wedding at Cana) demonstrates, the wedding feast was a common metaphor for the eschatological banquet enacted in the Lord's Supper.[38] Mark here divides the time within the narrative—the divine authorization of the Gentile mission so that Gentiles are gathered with Jews at the eschatological banquet—from an overt reference to the later time in which Mark is actually writing ("They will fast on that day"). The effect is to portray the foundation of the Gentile mission within the time of the narrative. As becomes clear with a similar reference to the Gentiles at the second wilderness meal narrative in Mark 8:3—"If I send them away to fast [*nēstis*], they will faint on the way"—the time of Jesus and his disciples' eating with the Gentiles in the Lord's Supper is within the time of the narrative. Thus, the narrative again functions as the divine authorization for the inclusive practice of the Markan house church. Jesus and the disciples do not fast. Rather, they eat the Lord's Supper with sinners (Gentiles) and tax collectors.[39]

Cloth

No one sews an unshrunken patch on an old garment lest the new patch tear away from the old garment and cause a bad tear. And no one puts new wine into old wine skins lest the wine tear apart the skins and the wine and the skins be destroyed [*apollymi*]. But new wine is for new wine skins. (2:21–22)

38. The wedding banquet is the celebration of God's triumph at the end of history; compare, e.g., Luke 14:15; 22:29–30; Matt. 8:11; Rev. 19:9. The symbolism of the wedding feast in John is also distinctly eucharistic, extensively discussed in Cullmann, *Early Christian Worship*. I use the term *eschatology* here to refer to the hope, shared by ancient Jews and Christians, that God would soon act to restore Israel and the entire creation to its original, pristine condition. See Madigan and Levenson, *Resurrection*, 5. For further references, see Marcus, *Mark 1–8*, 236–37.

39. It would appear, therefore, that Mark has taken a traditional controversy about fasting and transformed it to fit his overall narrative purpose. For fasting as a controversial topic between the early Christian churches and the Jewish synagogues, see Did. 8.1.

In 2:21–22 Jesus is speaking from inside the newly emerging house church (2:15). In this narrative context the liturgical reader of Mark understands Mark to be turning to two traditional sayings about new patches and new wine to explain why the Lord's Supper, the new eschatological banquet of misfit Jews and Gentiles, is no longer part of the structure of the "old" synagogue and has instead moved to the new location of the house church.

To Make a Way

It happened on a Sabbath that he was passing through grain fields. His disciples began to make a way [*hodos*], plucking heads of grain. And the Pharisees said to him, "See, your disciples are doing what is not permitted on the Sabbath." And he said to them, "Have you never read what David did when *he was in need and he was hungry* [*peinaō*], *and also those with him*? How he entered the house of God when Abiathar was high priest and ate the loaves [*artos*] of offering—which only the priests are permitted to eat—and gave [the loaves] to those who were with him?" And he said to them, "The Sabbath was given for humanity and not humanity for the Sabbath, so that the Son of Man is Lord also of the Sabbath." (2:23–28)

The fourth controversy in this series depicts Jesus and his disciples on the Sabbath passing through grain fields. The story is often referred to by scholars as a Sabbath controversy, and very often, especially in some Protestant commentaries, the legalism of the Pharisees is contrasted with the humanitarian impulse of Jesus.[40] In a liturgical reading, however, understanding the story hinges on who Jesus's disciples are in verse 23 and who Mark has in mind when he recalls the story of David giving the loaves "to those who were with him" in verse 26.[41] Such a reading understands the disciples to have been the original disciples called out in Mark 1:16–20 along with Levi the tax collector and the other tax collectors and sinners, the *many* who followed him at this point in the narrative and who had been invited to eat with Jesus and the disciples (2:15–20). When the story makes the unexpected turn at Mark 2:25, from the depiction of an accusation against the disciples about doing what is not lawful on the Sabbath—making a way (*hodos*)—to a story about

---

40. Gundry, *Mark*, 139–49, and sources cited there. Boring, *Mark*, 91–92, emphasizes that Jesus in Mark does not set aside the law or abrogate the Sabbath, but rather affirms it as the gift of God to humanity subject to the authority of the Son of Man. Boring also points to the humanitarian interpretation of the Torah in Hellenistic Judaism (91n37).

41. Jesus, having been proclaimed *Son of David* by Bartimaeus (10:47–48), will later be hungry (*peinaō*) and enter the temple and proclaim the temple to be a "house of prayer for all of the Gentiles" (11:17). It is, of course, also the Gentiles who have "nothing to eat" in the second ritual meal at 8:2.

King David eating the *five loaves* of offering in the house of God and giving the loaves to those who are with him,[42] the intended analogy with the Davidic story suddenly is centered not on the legality of making a way (*hodos*) by plucking grain on the Sabbath but on the question of who has the prerogative to eat the five loaves of offering in the house of God.

In other words, this fourth controversy follows the line of argument established in the first three controversies and, for the liturgical reader, makes yet a further claim: Jesus, Son of David (10:47–48), is able to consecrate those who were with him on the way (*hodos*) and so give the five sacred loaves (*artos*) to those with him. In other words, the story does not at all center on what is permitted or not permitted on the Sabbath, but on whether Jesus is able to consecrate (*hagnizō*) those with him (Gentiles and sinners) and so allow them to eat the sacred loaves (grain) by his hand. The narrative affirms that Jews (the original disciples, Levi, and the Jewish tax collectors) and Gentiles (the paralytic sinner) are now given the (five) loaves by Jesus (David) and belong at the Lord's Supper.

Further, the liturgical reader of Mark notes that the narrative makes clear that those who were with David were hungry and in need and that David himself ate the loaves and gave the loaves to those who were with him. Such a reader is immediately drawn to the later scene in Mark 8:1–9, the second wilderness feeding narrative, where there is another group of Gentiles who hunger and have nothing to eat (8:1), who cannot fast (*nēstis*), and who have need of sustenance for their journey (8:3). In the present story the Pharisees are opposed to Jesus feeding "those who are with him," and in the later meal narrative the Jewish disciples will have similar reservations: "How can one feed *these people* with loaves here in the wilderness?" (8:4). In both stories the issue is, Who belongs at the table, the wedding feast, the Lord's Supper, with Jesus?

In Mark's narrative arrangement the story of making a way (*hodos*) by plucking grain on the Sabbath is not a sudden right-angle turn to a completely new topic of Jesus somehow overturning Sabbath law. Rather, this is a story about whether these new disciples of Jesus, the Gentile sinners and misfit Jewish tax collectors, are to be fed the five loaves of the Lord's Supper. Just as

---

42. The story is based on 1 Sam. 21:1–6 (LXX), and in that story there are of course five loaves (*artos*) of sacred (*hagios*) bread which can be shared with David's men if they are purified (*hagnizō*), that is, having had no sexual relations with women. David's response, that they have been with him on the way (*hodos*) for three days (*tritē hēmera*) and are made pure because (*dioti*) they are with him (21:6), places the liturgical reader of Mark squarely within the context of the second ritual meal narrative of Mark 8:1–9. There the crowd has been with Jesus for "three days," and if they are sent away to their own house hungry (i.e., without the loaves, *artos*), they will faint on the way (*hodos*).

David entered the house of God and ate the five sacred loaves and gave some to those who were *his* disciples, so also Jesus, the Son of David (10:47–48), will be hungry (11:12) and enter the house of God and declare it to be a house of prayer for the Gentiles (11:17) and then give the one loaf (*artos*) to his Jewish and Gentile disciples (8:14–21; 14:22).

Finally, the concluding refrain of this story, "The Sabbath was given for humanity, not humanity for the Sabbath" (2:27), is not, for the liturgical reader of Mark, about the abrogation of Sabbath law in favor of a general humanitarian consideration. Rather, the saying is about the Gentiles' (humankind's) rightful place in honoring the Sabbath, the day of the restoration of creation, to what it was always meant to be. On the Sabbath all are fed; all are provided for by God. For Mark, the Sabbath is no longer just for the Jewish synagogue (humankind for the Sabbath) but now includes the Christian gathering of the house church, Jews and Gentiles, in the Lord's Supper. This is the resurrected Lord's banquet that enacts the eternal continuation of the Sabbath (1:35). The Sabbath was given for humankind. Jesus as Lord of the Sabbath authorizes this new humanity in the in-breaking of the eschatological age.

Mark 3

The Withered Hand

And again he came into the synagogue. And there was there a man who had a withered hand. And they observed him as to whether he would heal on the Sabbath so that they might accuse him. And he said to the man who had the withered hand, "Resurrect [*egeirō*] into our midst [*mesos*]."
And he said to them, "Is it permitted on the Sabbath to do good or to do evil? To save life or to kill?" But they were silent. And looking around at them with anger, deeply grieved at the hardness of their hearts, he said to the man, "Stretch out your hand." And he stretched it out and his hand was restored [*apokathistanō*]. And the Pharisees went out immediately with the Herodians and held council against him, how they might destroy [*apollymi*] him. (3:1–6)

The fifth and final controversy in this section of Mark is about Jesus's raising and restoration of a man with a withered hand in the midst of the synagogue.[43] The story about a Jewish man resurrected (*egeirō*) and restored (*apokathistanō*) in the middle (*mesos*) of the synagogue forms the perfect

43. This is the second time Jesus has been in the synagogue (1:21), and a close reading of Mark 3:1 indicates that the setting is probably again the synagogue in Capernaum, though it is not specifically named. In both cases, the synagogue in the narrative of Mark is transparent to the Jewish community in the time of Mark's writing.

bookend to the initial controversy story about a Gentile paralytic man resurrected (*egeirō*) in the middle of the house (2:4). Both stories present a central Christian claim followed by the noted resistance of the opponents and concluding with a final healing. For the liturgical reader, the disputed claim in the story of the Gentile paralytic was whether the Son of Man, having himself been crucified and raised in baptism, had the authority to forgive the sins of a Gentile and so allow him to become part of the resurrection body of Christ. In that story Jesus told the Gentile paralytic to *resurrect* and *come out*. Gentile sinners are forgiven and become part of the Christian community. The disputed claim in the story of the Jewish man with a withered hand is whether Christian resurrection, enacted and experienced in the ritual meal, is the restoration (*apokathistanō*) of the Genesis creation, the in-breaking of the eternal Sabbath. Jesus tells the man with the withered hand, "Resurrect into our midst," and, after a description of the Sabbath as the doing of good and saving life, restores the hand of the man to its original Genesis condition (3:5).[44] The Gentile paralytic is forgiven and raised. The Jewish man with the withered hand is raised and restored. The Gentiles are to be joined to the faithful Jews in the ritual meal that is the enactment of the eternal Sabbath.

This fifth and final controversy story also gives the liturgical reader the first notice of the plot to destroy (*apollymi*) Jesus: "And the Pharisees went out immediately with the Herodians and held council against him, how they might destroy [*apollymi*] him" (3:6). In these five controversy stories from 2:1–3:6 Mark's narrative is transparent to a certain level of general Jewish resistance to the Christian eschatological claim that the Gentiles are now to be restored in a new creation through ritual participation in the sacrificial death and resurrection of Christ. In Mark's church this claim was enacted in the rituals of water baptism and the eating of the one loaf of the Lord's Supper. In addition, these five controversy stories set up the main irony of Mark's entire narrative: resistance to this claim by the Jewish opponents of Jesus (scribes, scribes of the Pharisees, Pharisees, and Herodians) eventually will destroy Jesus. Yet it is that very cosmic destruction (*apollymi*) and the resulting resurrection which establishes both the rationale and the ritually enacted reality of the new and inclusive creation in the Lord's Supper. That is why the Jewish man of this final controversy story *resurrects* into their midst and has his hand *restored* (3:5). In the narrative and in Mark's house

---

44. The word Mark uses here, *apokathistanō*, often translated as "recapitulation," will later become technical Christian theological language for the return of the created universe to harmony with the uncreated Divine. See A. Scott, *Origen and the History of the Stars*.

church, this ritual meal with tax collectors and sinners quite literally enacts the wholeness of the restored creation.

The End of the Galilean Mission

The Galilean mission of the resurrected Christ begun at 1:38 is now drawing to a close. The narrative here seems to be transparent to the origins of Mark's house church in the initial call of the Jewish disciples (1:16–20) being joined by faithful and forgiven Gentiles in the Lord's Supper (1:40–42; 2:1–11), although the narrative also apparently reflects the early Christian movement as part of the Jewish synagogue (3:1–6). The liturgical reader of Mark's narrative is aware that Jesus is faced with opposition to the Gentile mission (2:1–28) and threatened with destruction by the Pharisees and Herodians on the basis of the eschatological claim presented by the resurrection of the Jewish man in the synagogue and the restoration of his withered hand.

A New Community

And again Jesus withdrew with his disciples to the sea. And a great many from Galilee and Judea followed. And also from Jerusalem and Idumea and beyond the Jordan and from the regions of Tyre and Sidon, a great number, having heard the things he had done, came to him. And he told his disciples to have a boat ready for him because of the crowd, so that they might not crush him. And he healed many, so that as many as had diseases fell upon him so that they might touch him. And the unclean spirits, whenever they beheld him, prostrated themselves before him and cried out, "You are the Son of God." And he rebuked them mightily, lest they make him known. (3:7–12)

Jesus now withdraws from the synagogue to gather the new and inclusive community of Jews and Gentiles, again beside the sea (2:13; 3:7). The cleansed leper from earlier in the narrative has indeed proclaimed (*kēryssō*) and spread enthusiastically (*diaphēmizō*) the *word* (*logos*; 1:45). A large crowd of followers, who are perhaps, in the narrative, transparent to Jews who have withdrawn from the synagogue, now come from Galilee and Judea to be with Jesus and the disciples. They are joined by a large crowd that quite obviously includes Gentiles from the Gentile lands beyond the Jordan as well as from the Gentile region of Tyre and Sidon (3:8). The pressing nature of the crowd (3:10), echoing the earlier reaction to the healing power of Jesus (1:33–34, 45), surely signals the desire and importunity of those coming to Jesus, especially Gentiles, to enter the community. That Jesus healed many of these Gentiles—presumably on the model of the healing of the leper and the paralytic—creates the fervent desire among many others with illnesses to touch him (3:10). It would appear that among the Gentiles Jesus's mission achieves great success.

As previously in Mark, when Jesus encounters unclean spirits they identify him (1:24). Yet at this point in the narrative the expansion of the mission to the Gentiles is noted in the new title given to Jesus by these unclean spirits. Earlier in the narrative the unclean spirits in the synagogue at Capernaum identified Jesus as "the Holy One of God" (1:24), a specifically Jewish title.[45] Now as the Gentiles gather to Jesus, the unclean spirits, after prostrating before him, declare that he is "the Son of God" (3:11). Whether or not Mark opens his Gospel with this title "Son of God,"[46] this is how "the voice from heaven" identifies Jesus as he rises from the waters of baptism to begin his mission to Jews and Gentiles (1:11) and, more importantly, how the *Gentile* centurion at the foot of the cross publicly identifies Jesus at the moment of his death and the release of his Spirit (15:39). Here Jesus orders the unclean spirits not to make him known (3:12).[47] Within the narrative Jesus's full identity is not to be revealed until he accomplishes his death as a ransom for the *many* (10:45), the Gentiles, and thereby releases from the cross the Spirit of the new creation (15:37), which forms the gathered community of Jews and Gentiles: it is the Gentile centurion who publicly proclaims Jesus as Son of God (15:39).

Jesus ascends a mountain at Mark 3:13. Though unnamed in the narrative, the mountain reminds the liturgical reader of both Sinai and the temple. But given the structure of the narrative here, this is undoubtedly also the mountain of the eschatological vision of Isaiah:

> And the foreigners who join themselves to the Lord, to serve him, to love the name of the Lord, and to be manservants and maidservants for him, all who keep my Sabbath and do not profane it and hold fast my covenant, I will lead them unto my holy mountain, and they will rejoice in my house of prayer, and their whole burnt offerings and their sacrifices will be acceptable upon my altar, for my house shall be called a house of prayer for all the nations. (56:6–7 LXX)

The foreigners described in Mark 3:8 as coming from beyond the Jordan and as far away as Tyre and Sidon are present here as Jesus ascends the mountain. The careful construction of the story of plucking grain (2:23–28) ensures

---

45. Focant, *Mark*, 69.

46. Some of the more important manuscripts of Mark do not have the title "Son of God" in the first verse. See A. Y. Collins, *Mark*, 130–32, for extended discussion.

47. On the many roles of Satan and the demons in the Gospel of Mark, see Garrett, *Temptations of Jesus*.

that the reader understands that the Gentiles with Jesus have indeed kept the Sabbath. Here also the liturgical reader is pointed forward in the narrative to the story of the cleansing of the temple (11:11–25): the Christian ritual meal in the house church will become a house of prayer for all the nations.[48] This ritual meal, created in the sacrificial death of Christ (14:23), is now the fulfillment of Isaiah's prophecy here: it is the house of prayer for all the nations (Isa. 56:7). The twelve Jewish disciples' reluctance to accept their role with respect to this inclusive community of Jews and Gentiles forms a great deal of the narrative intrigue from here forward.[49]

The House Again

And he came to the house [*oikos*]. And a crowd came together again, so that they were not able to eat the loaf [*artos*]. And when those around him heard this, they went out to seize him, for they said, "He has lost his senses [*existēmi*]." And the scribes coming down from Jerusalem said that he was possessed by Beelzebub, and, "By the prince of demons he is able to cast out demons."

And he called them and spoke to them in parables. "How is Satan able to cast out Satan? And if a realm is divided against itself, that realm is not able to stand. And if a house is divided against itself, that house is not able to stand. If Satan has risen against himself, he is not able to stand and is finished. But no one is able to enter a strong man's house to plunder his goods unless he first binds [*deomai*] the strong man, and then he can plunder his house.

"Amen, I say to you that all sins will be forgiven the sons of men, sins and blasphemies as many as they blaspheme. But whoever *blasphemes* against the *Holy Spirit* has no forgiveness unto eternity, but is guilty of an eternal sin." For they had said, "He is possessed by an unclean spirit." (3:20–30)

Mark 3:19, "And he came to the house [*oikos*]," is the sudden transition back to what is apparently the house church of 2:1. And again a gathering of a crowd is noted. Now, however, the twelve Jewish disciples have been called out by Jesus and are present with the crowd in the house. And just here Mark includes a singular yet potent change from that earlier narrative

48. Given the clear allusion to Isa. 56:6–7, Mark 3:13 is most likely a reference to both Jewish and Gentile disciples being gathered around the base of the mountain as Jesus ascends the mountain: "He went up on the mountain and called those whom he wished to call, and they came to him." The selection of twelve "to be with him and to be sent to preach and have authority to cast out demons" is then a reference to their place and function as Jewish leaders within the larger Jewish-Gentile community around Jesus.

49. The number twelve here undoubtedly refers to the reconstitution of the twelve tribes of Israel, to whom the Gentiles are joined to form the final gathering of humanity signaled by Isa. 56:6–7. See Focant, *Mark*, 130.

description of the crowd at the house: this time "they were not even able to eat the loaf."

So we are at the point in the narrative of Mark where the Gentile sinner has been forgiven in the midst of this same house (2:1–11). Jesus, as David, has claimed the right to eat "the loaves of offering" and the power to sanctify and give the *loaves* to "those that were with him" (2:26). And now the crowd at this same house includes those who have come from the Gentile lands "beyond the Jordan and Tyre and Sidon" (3:8). Here the liturgical reader of Mark understands that the present narrative circumstance is remarkably similar to the first ritual meal narrative (6:30–44), in which the twelve Jewish disciples complain about feeding *loaves* to the large crowd (6:37). Both stories can be read as transparent to the issue of whether the Gentiles are to be fed the Lord's Supper along with Jews in the house church.

To read the narrative as presenting Jews and Gentiles gathered in the Lord's Supper according to the eschatological vision of Isaiah 56:6–7 signals as well that those featured in these controversies (other Jews and the Jewish family of Jesus) are transparent to an early Jewish resistance to the presence of Gentiles at the meal. After all, in Paul's account of the incident in Antioch in Galatians 2:11–16 it was the "men from James," the brother of Jesus, who apparently came down from Jerusalem to oppose Gentile participation with Peter, Paul, and other Jews at the Lord's Supper in Antioch. In Mark "those near to Jesus" (3:21) hear about the crowd of Jews *and Gentiles* at the house, apparently gathered to eat the ritual meal (*loaf*) but unable to do so (3:20). They have come to drag Jesus away from the house. Indeed the rationale given in the narrative for their desire to take Jesus away from the house is that Jesus has lost his senses. That is, Jesus has lost his senses because the ritual meal, the Lord's Supper, is about to take place. For these Jews, Jesus's desire to eat this meal with the Gentiles is quite simply crazy.

This is also what explains the immediate narrative shift here to the "scribes coming down from Jerusalem" (3:22).[50] Their concern must also be that Jesus is about to eat with the Gentiles who are part of the crowd pressing in on Jesus in the house. Their accusation here (that he was possessed by Beelzebub and "By the prince of demons he casts out demons") is clearly linked by Mark to the previous scene, Mark 3:7–12, where Jesus healed many Gentiles, and the unclean spirits, apparently noting Jesus's association with the Gentiles, truthfully acclaimed Jesus to be "Son of God." These unclean spirits cast out from the Gentiles apparently have it right: Jesus is the Son of

50. The reader again recalls that in the Antioch incident reported in Gal. 2:11–14 the men from James are Jewish Christians who most likely came from the Jerusalem church.

God. The Jewish scribes from Jerusalem have it wrong: Jesus himself cannot be possessed by the unclean spirit Beelzebub because he has control over these unclean spirits. So it is that the liturgical reader of Mark knows that at his baptism Jesus is infused with the creative *Spirit of God* (Gen. 1:1), and that he is on that basis declared to be "Son of God," the one who rises from death (*anabainō*) to new creation (Mark 1:10). In fact Jesus's exorcisms, his power over the unclean spirits,[51] are what authorizes the Gentile mission. The liturgical reader sees the new creation ritually enacted in the Lord's Supper of Jews and Gentiles.

Mark 3:27 explicitly ties together Jesus's exorcisms with the Gentile mission. The saying "But no one is able to enter a strong man's house to plunder his goods unless he first binds [*deomai*] the strong man" refers the liturgical reader to Jesus's first voyage by sea to a specifically Gentile area. Jesus arrives at the Gentile country of the Gerasenes at Mark 5:1 to encounter an "unclean spirit," actually a legion of unclean spirits, who is so strong that no one can *bind* (*deomai*) him even with chains and fetters (5:3). And in that place also, just as in the present circumstance, the unclean spirits know that Jesus is the Son of God (5:7). The Spirit of God in Jesus, whom Jesus received at his baptismal death and who contends with them throughout the narrative of Mark, rules them (5:13).[52]

For the liturgical reader, the charge of *blasphemy* to which Jesus refers at Mark 3:28 therefore has to do with the scribes' denial that Jesus does in fact have power over, meaning the capacity to *bind* (*deomai*), the unclean spirits of the Gentiles and so permit Gentiles their rightful place at the Lord's Supper. And this is also the substance of Jesus's harsh reply to the scribes' charge: "Whoever *blasphemes* against the *Holy Spirit* has no forgiveness unto eternity, but is guilty of an eternal sin" (3:29). The scribes' accusation, that Jesus is possessed by an unclean spirit (Beelzebub), speaks directly against the Holy Spirit in Jesus, given to him through his baptismal death (1:10; 15:37), the Spirit of creation in Genesis, which gives him the capacity to rule over the unclean spirits of the Gentiles and thereby to include the Gentiles in the new creation enacted within the ritual meal gathering of the house church.

> And his mother and his brothers came and were standing outside [*exō*]. They sent to him and called to him. And the crowd sat around him and said to him, "See, your mother and your brothers [and your sisters] are outside seeking you." And he answered them and said, "Who are my mother and brothers?" And having looked at those sitting round about him, he said, "See my mother

51. As David in 1 Sam. 21:5–6, Jesus sanctifies those who are with him.
52. Garrett, *Temptations of Jesus*, 19–49.

and my brothers. For whosoever should do the will of God, this person is my brother, sister, and mother." (3:31–35)

It is just at this moment that Jesus's family arrives at the house asking for Jesus to come out (*exō*) of the house. In the narrative context, apparently what is at stake is a pending ritual meal with the Gentiles gathered *inside* the house with the Jewish disciples (3:20). For the liturgical reader, the family of Jesus is here transparent to the traditional Jewish ethnic ties of family and synagogue, the family members who remain explicitly *outside* (3:32). The narrative signals here that the transition to a new family identity based on the gathering of the house church rather than the familial ties of the synagogue has taken place. Jesus deliberately contrasts his Jewish biological family (mother and brothers) with "those sitting round about him." This is the Jewish and Gentile gathering now around Jesus *inside* the house. Indeed the Gentiles gathered inside now have a new eschatological ethnic identity according to the vision of Isaiah. They are the manservants and the maidservants gathered in the house of prayer for all the nations (Isa. 56:6–7). In the narrative they are now the mother and brothers and sisters of Jesus. Moreover, Mark intends this new ethnic and family identity to include both this crowd and the crowds of Jews and Gentiles yet to come as the Christian mission continues to expand within the narrative:[53] "See my mother and my brothers. For whosoever should do the will of God, this person is my brother, sister, and mother" (3:35).[54] These people will eat the Lord's Supper with the Jews inside the house.

Mark 4

The Parables

And again he began to teach by the sea. And a large crowd [*ochlos*] gathered to him, so that he got into a boat to sit upon the sea. The whole crowd was beside the sea upon the land. (4:1)

Mark 4 marks the transition of the Christian mission beyond the synagogue and newly formed house church in Galilee in which Jesus has gathered with Gentiles and Jews (3:20). Again the mission travels of Jesus are transparent

---

53. The new ethnic identity will be sorely challenged by the active persecution of Christians from both synagogue and Roman authorities depicted in 13:9.

54. On the familial language of belonging within the early Christian house churches, see Meeks, *First Urban Christians*, 85–94. On Christians co-opting the ethnic identity of the Jews through the ritual of baptism, see Levenson, *Death and Resurrection*, 213–19.

to the exigencies and tensions within the early Christian house churches as they emerged from the Jewish synagogue.

The liturgical reader notices that the parables of Mark 4:1–34 form a sort of interlude in the narrative movement of the story up to this point. Understanding the parables depends on the knowledge this reader has gained from the previous narrative. That Jesus is teaching a large crowd again (*palin*) by the *sea* (4:1) recalls the previous large gathering *by the sea* of Jews and Gentiles, the latter from as far away as the Gentile lands of Tyre and Sidon (3:8). The fact that the narrative has Jesus climb into the very boat that will carry him across the sea to the Gentile Gerasenes at the conclusion of these parables must indicate that the parables function to prepare the reader to understand the journey across the sea. Jesus teaches these parables in this boat on the sea, a position from which he dominates the primeval chaos that the sea represents. This domination will be shown spectacularly in the story of the storm crossing at Mark 4:35–41. Hence the domination of chaos is demonstrated in both teaching (4:1–34) and narrative action (4:35–41).

The liturgical reader knows that a Jewish and Gentile crowd has gathered to listen to Jesus. What this reader does not know is the explicit rationale or explanation for such an unlikely event. How did this happen, and what does it all mean? These are the questions the parables seek to address. The parables function within the narrative to give inside knowledge to the community that has gathered with Jesus, and as they do so, the narrative gives this knowledge to the readers of Mark.

The Sower

He taught them many things in parables. He said to them in his teaching: "Listen, behold a sower went out to sow. And when he began to sow, some of what he sowed fell upon the way [*hodos*]. The birds came and devoured it. Some fell upon the rocks, where there was not much earth. And immediately what was sowed sprang up because there was not much depth of soil. And when the sun bore down, what was sowed withered because it had no root. And some fell into thorns, and the thorns rose up and choked it and it bore no fruit. What remained fell into good soil [*epesen eis tēn gēn kalēn*] and, having risen [*anabainō*], produced fruit and increased. One brought forth thirty-, one sixty-, and one a hundred-fold." And he said, "Whoever has ears to hear, let that person listen." (4:2–9)

The liturgical reader of Mark would see an immediate connection with what was sown and the word. This reader would understand the connection between the death of Christ (what was sown having fallen into the good soil of the Gentiles) and the resurrection (*anabainō*) of the Gentiles into the house church (2:11–12). This is the amazing efficacy of the death of Christ, ritually enacted in baptism (1:10), to bring Gentiles into the Lord's Supper.

For the liturgical reader, the parable *is* the narrative. Jesus will die in the narrative to become what is sown and gathered in the parable: the body of Christ, Jews and Gentiles in the Lord's Supper. That is why the placement of the first parable in the sequence of Mark 4 is crucial: it allows the reader to understand both what has happened in the narrative up to this point and the narrative yet to come. What is not often noted by commentators on this parable is that the success of the mission depends on its burial.[55] In the first three soil conditions, what is sown encounters hard path, rocks, and thorns. Here there is no burial *into the good earth (eis tēn gēn kalēn)* of what is sown. There is therefore no germination, no harvest.[56] Only in the fourth condition does Mark write that what was sown "fell into the good earth." Here the narrative uses the same word that describes Jesus *rising* from the baptismal water at 1:10 *(anabainō)* to describe the *rising* of the plant to produce its abundance. The liturgical reader reads the parable as a description of the ritual baptismal death of Jesus, who has risen into the astoundingly large harvest of thirty-, sixty-, and a hundredfold of those, Jews *and Gentiles*, who have joined the movement (4:8). This is the great crowd which is being taught by Jesus by the sea. Yet Mark insists that some are fated not to understand this parable. They will not understand the connection between the *necessary* death of Christ and its ritual enactment, which creates the eschatological community of Jews and Gentiles (4:11–12).[57]

Interpreting the Parable

And he said to them, "Do you not understand this parable? How are you to understand all the parables? The sower sows the word.

"And these are those beside the way [*hodos*] where the word is sown. And whenever they hear immediately Satan comes and snatches the word that was sown into them.

"And these are the ones that are sown upon rocky ground [*petrōdēs*]. And when they hear the word they receive it immediately with joy. But they do not

---

55. Van Iersel, *Mark*, 176–87; Culpepper, *Mark*, 131–36; Marcus, *Mark 1–8*, 294–97; Donahue and Harrington, *Mark*, 143–44.

56. Crucial here is the literal translation of Mark 4:5: "Some fell upon the rocks, where there was not much earth. And immediately what was sowed sprang up because there was not much depth of soil. And when the sun bore down, what was sowed withered because it had no root." What was sown does not actually get buried.

57. The reader recalls here the scribes (2:6), the scribes of the Pharisees (2:16), Pharisees (2:24), and Pharisees and Herodians (3:6).

have root [*rhiza*] among them and last for a time. Then tribulation or persecution comes, and they are immediately scandalized.

"Others are those sown among the thorns. These are those who hear the word, but concerns about worldly matters and the love of wealth and desire for other things enter in and choke the word, and no fruit comes of it.

"But these are the ones sown on good soil, who hear the word and accept it and produce fruit by thirty-, sixty-, and a hundredfold." (4:13–20)

Here Jesus in the narrative goes on to explain the foregoing parable. The explanation expands on the conditions in which the seed finds itself when it is sown. This expansion points the reader to upcoming events within the narrative: the reference to Satan and rocky ground (*petrōdēs*) might well presage both Peter's refusal to accept the necessity (*dei*) of the death of Jesus (8:31) and the flight of Peter (*petras*) and the disciples at the arrest of Jesus (14:50). Concern for worldly matters and for wealth describes the wealthy man who turns away from Jesus at 10:22–23. Finally, the parable appears to take the liturgical reader beyond the time of the narrative into the church of Mark's day, describing the great number of Gentiles who accept the word and who have joined the body of Christ, buried and risen in baptism, and so constitute a large part of the burgeoning Christian movement.

Mark 4:20 therefore places a capstone on this liturgical reading of the parable: "But these are the ones sown on good soil, who hear the word and accept it and produce fruit by thirty-, sixty-, and a hundredfold." The success of the mission to Jews and especially to Gentiles is endangered by both persecution and confiscation (8:34–38; 10:28; 13:9), yet perseverance unto death (burial), both with Jesus and the seeds—the martyrs, who are the Christian community of Mark's time—brings forth astounding growth in the churches: thirty-, sixty-, and one hundredfold. In this narrative the ritual enactment of the death of Christ in baptism must be followed by the actual execution of Christ to provide the means for this great influx of Gentiles to the house churches. So too the original readers and audience of Mark, Jews and Gentiles in the house churches, now threatened with confiscation and persecution, must enact their own baptismal death (10:38–39) to bring about the final consummation of Jesus's mission in his return and gathering of the church (13:11–13, 27).

The remaining parables of Mark 4 describe the mysterious growth of this mission (4:21–32). The narrative thus anticipates (1) Jesus's arrival in a Gentile place where there are already believers (7:24) and (2) the disciples' encounter with a Christian exorcist whom they do not recognize (9:40). The parable also alludes to the churches' miraculous growth (4:32) with respect to the synagogue (4:25). More important to the present study is the notice to the liturgical reader that Jesus spoke only in parables to the larger crowd but that in private he explained everything to the disciples (4:11). These disciples, apparently the twelve disciples who came to be with Jesus at 3:13, are therefore set in the following narrative to understand the unexpected and large growth of the Gentile mission. Yet, as the continuing narrative story makes clear, they often do not.

In the narrative that follows the parables of chapter 4, the lack of understanding centers on the legitimacy of the Gentiles eating the Lord's Supper with the Jews (6:52; 8:17). So Mark here deliberately creates narrative tension between what the disciples should understand about the Gentile mission on the basis of understanding the parables and what they actually do understand as the narrative unfolds. The liturgical reader of Mark is therefore drawn into the tension. How will the disciples, and therefore the church of Mark, come to full acceptance of the rightful place of the Gentiles at the Lord's Supper? In other words, how will the subsequent narrative enact the parables of chapter 4?

2

Baptismal Death and Resurrection

The First Mission to the Gentiles

4:35–5:20

Mark 4

The Crossing of the Sea

On that day when it was evening [*opsia*], he said to them, "Let us cross to the other side." And leaving the crowd, they took him as he was into the boat. And other boats [*alla ploia*] were with him. And there came a great gale of wind [*anemos*], and the waves were crashing into the boat, so that the boat was already filled. And he was in the stern, sleeping [*katheudō*] on a cushion. And they resurrected [*egeirō*] him and said to him, "Teacher, do you not *care* [*melei*] that we are being destroyed [*apollymi*]?" And having been resurrected [*diegeirō*], he *rebuked* [*epitimaō*] the wind and said to the sea [*thalassa*], "Silence! Be still!" And the wind ceased, and there was great calm. And he said to them, "Why are you *timid* [*deilos*]? Do you not yet have faith?" And they feared with great fear and said to one another, "Who is this, that the wind and the sea obey him?" (4:35–41)

45

With the teaching in parables completed, Mark 4:35–41 returns the liturgical reader to narrative drama: the crossing of an angry sea (chaos). The drama depicts a second death and resurrection of Christ (the first was the baptismal scene) that provides the foundation for the mission to the Gentile Gerasenes. This prepares the reader for the following two crossings that mark Jesus's active mission to the Gentiles *on Gentile soil* within the narrative (6:48–51; 8:13–22).

The scene begins with a notice that it was "on that day," that is, the conclusion of the Sabbath day that began all the way back at Mark 2:23–28 with the story of the disciples' plucking of the grain to make a path. That story, as I argued previously, was centered on Jesus's prerogative to include the Gentiles at the Lord's Supper (Jesus as David gives five loaves to those who are with him). In that story the warrant for their inclusion is provided in the concluding pronouncement: "The Son of Man is Lord also of the Sabbath" (2:28). The movement of the narrative is now to cross the *sea* toward those very Gentiles.

The journey begins on that same Sabbath when it is evening (*opsia*; 4:35). Here Mark draws on what is perhaps the earliest Christian understanding of the death and resurrection of Christ as the eternal continuation of the Sabbath day, that is, the seventh day and the final triumph of God's act of creation over the forces of primeval chaos (darkness and water).[1] In addition the liturgical reader is aware that the end of the Sabbath day is also the time of the Lord's Supper, depicted in the first wilderness meal narrative (6:2, 35), and that Mark repeats this time reference to the "evening" when Jesus walks upon the water, dominating chaos and *resurrecting* into the boat, immediately following that evening ritual meal (6:47).[2] Gentiles eating with Jews on the Sabbath in the wilderness enact the resurrection as the continuation of the Sabbath, the new creation emerging from primeval chaos, darkness, and water: What does the liturgical reader not understand about the loaves (6:48–52)? Here Jesus and the other boats with him (*alla ploia*), surely to be

---

1. In Mark, the two Marys and Salome come to the tomb exceedingly early, before sunrise (16:2). The resurrection of Jesus has happened during the night: the Sabbath has not ended. The Gospel of John also places resurrection appearances in the midst of both sides of the darkness surrounding the first day of the week. It is dark—before dawn—when Mary Magdalene arrives on Sunday (John 20:1), and Jesus appears to the disciples after sundown on that same day (Sunday), and exactly the same time one week later (20:19; 26). Thus John develops in his own narrative fashion the early Christian understanding of the resurrection as the continuation of Sabbath, that is, from Sabbath to Sunday ad infinitum. On the Sabbath as the experience of the world to come, see Madigan and Levenson, *Resurrection*, 251.

2. When Jesus in Mark speaks about what is to happen at the end of days in Mark 13, often referred to as the "eschatological discourse," evening (*opsia*) marks the time when the master may return (13:35). This is an obvious reference to the imminent return of the resurrected Christ.

understood as filled with Gentiles, embark into the darkness upon the water. And just as surely the liturgical reader will "see" baptism, resurrection, and the dominance of chaos that follows.[3]

The narrative depiction is again one of the inner circle of disciples (the Twelve?) in the boat with Jesus *just as he was*,[4] and a larger crowd of disciples who also followed Jesus in *other boats that were with him* (4:36). Given the unfolding of the narrative to this point, there is no reason to doubt that the larger group includes both Jews and Gentiles. The liturgical reader is aware that whatever happens to the boat with Jesus and the disciples (the attack of chaos in wind and sea) is also happening to those who are in these other boats.

The presentation of water as chaos is first. The apocalyptic setting is made plain by the oft-noted depiction of storms at sea that mark the final battle between chaos and creation.[5] The near-defeat of the boat by the wind and waves surely reminds the earliest readers of Mark that persecution often accompanies the movement of Christian churches into new areas.[6] But more precisely, Mark notes that "the waves were crashing into the boat, so that the boat was already filled" (4:37). In other words, the boat is under water. Meanwhile Jesus is *sleeping* (*katheudō*) on the cushion (4:38). The liturgical reader immediately grasps that once again, as in his baptism, Jesus has been covered (buried) by water chaos. In Mark sleep is the Christian state of death immediately prior to resurrection (5:39).[7] The disciples then resurrect (*egeirō*) Jesus. They want him to *care* (*melei*) that they, along with the others in the boats around them, are being *destroyed* (*apollymi*). This is the same word Mark uses for the potential cosmic destruction of Jesus within the narrative (3:6; 11:18). Their being *timid* (*deilos*; 4:40), therefore, is owing to their concern that this destruction is all there is; that out of this cosmic destruction

---

3. The narrative pattern is clear enough. The reference to a Sabbath meal of Jews and Gentiles at Mark 2:26 is followed by Jesus's domination of chaos (water) in the depiction of resurrection here (4:39) and then the mission to the Gentile Gerasenes. The reference to a Sabbath meal of Jews and Gentiles at Mark 6:30–41 is followed by Jesus's domination of chaos (water) in a resurrection scene (6:47–52) and the following Gentile mission to Tyre and Sidon (7:24).

4. Both here and in the stories of Jesus walking on the water (6:49–51) and the Transfiguration (9:8), the liturgical reader is guided to understand that the resurrected Christ is corporeal rather than a spirit or apparition. Whether to understand the resurrection of Christ as a spiritual or a bodily phenomenon was at the forefront of doctrinal controversy in the early churches (John 20:25–28; Ignatius, *Smyr.* 3–4). For extensive discussion, see my recent article, "Our Opinion Is in Accordance," 79–90.

5. See, e.g., Dan. 7:2–3; Dead Sea Scrolls, 1QH 3:6–18; 6:22–25; 7:4–5.

6. See Mark 13:9; Acts 16:19–24; 17:5; 18:12; the tension caused by Christian mission activity is well documented in the early-second-century letter of Pliny, governor of Bithynia, to the Roman emperor Trajan (Pliny, *Ep.* 10.96).

7. Eph. 5:14; 1 Thess. 4:15.

(death and chaos) there will be no resurrection and restoration of creation.[8] Jesus then *resurrects* (*diegeirō*; Mark uses a strengthened form of the word for resurrection) and *rebukes* (*epitimaō*) the contrary wind. Mark uses the same word he uses to refer to Jesus's rebuking of both the unclean spirits (1:25; 9:25) and, later in the narrative, Peter (8:33).[9] Jesus then calms and silences the raging sea (chaos), and there comes about a great calm (4:39).[10] The resurrected Christ creates the Sabbath peace, the new creation without conflict. From the baptismal waters of chaos rises the new creation of resurrection.

Yet even though the disciples on the boat have witnessed the defeat of chaos in the resurrection of Christ, they are still timid (*deilos*; 4:40). They fear with great fear because they do not understand who Jesus is, the man in the boat with them "just as he was," who rises out of death to defeat chaos and enact the peace of an ordered creation (4:41). The liturgical reader, however, immediately connects the mission to the Gentiles (the boat crossing the sea to the Gentile Gerasenes) with the resurrection of Christ. It is because Christ died that chaos is defeated and the new creation, Gentiles and Jews at the Lord's Supper, comes into being. Further, the liturgical reader begins to understand that Christ must be destroyed (he must die) in order for the Gentiles to come into the community through ritual baptism into his death.

On the other hand, it is just here that the Jewish disciples are timid (*deilos*) and lack faith (4:40). As later with their spokesman Peter (8:32–33), they fail to see the link between the death of Christ, the defeat of chaos, and the resurrection enacted in the Jewish-Gentile meal. For Mark, in other words, the story of the storm provides for these hesitant Jewish disciples the meaning of their ritual practice, the movement from chaos to creation, from baptism (death) to the Lord's Supper (resurrection). And the liturgical reader begins to

8. The waiting of the dead to be raised by the general resurrection (inaugurated in the events of the passion) surely underlies the apocalyptic sequence of Mark 13:35–37 followed by Gethsemane at 14:32–42. The reference to the return of the Lord (13:35) during the night at three separate times prior to dawn (14:32–42) signals the resurrection at the final moment of chaos/darkness. The disciples (Peter, James, and John) are not to sleep (*katheudō*, 13:36; 14:37) but to watch (*grēgoreō*, 13:37; 14:34). At Gethsemane Jesus enters into *death* (*thanatos*, 14:34), and the disciples (Peter, James, and John) in Gethsemane are found *sleeping* (*katheudō*) at three separate times during the night on which Jesus gives them the command to watch (*grēgoreō*). The command *let us resurrect* (*egeirō*) at 14:42 implies that at that moment (the final moment of betrayal and darkness) Jesus is resurrected along with his disciples. The climactic moment of chaos is at once the moment of its cosmic defeat.

9. Peter, of course, is rebuked for his denial that it is necessary (*dei*) that the Son of Man suffer and be rejected and killed prior to his resurrection (8:31).

10. Levenson, reading Weinberg, suggests that in the Second Temple period the Sabbath was considered the day of God's enthronement, with the "rest" that is associated with enthronement elsewhere in the ancient Near East. See the discussion in *Creation*, 108.

see that ritual practice, rightly understood, provides a deep symbolic understanding of the narrative.

Here the wind and sea obey not the divine man but the resurrected man.[11] Jesus is the one who enacts again the Sabbath creation on the basis of his victory over chaos. Those who are *with him* (4:36), both Jewish disciples and Gentiles in the other boats, have gone into the water with him and become part of the resurrection. The only path to this triumph is through death (the very waters of baptism). The story of Jesus is set to become the real story of the earliest readers of Mark, who suffer persecution and martyrdom from both Jewish and Roman authorities (13:9). Like the disciples in the boat with Jesus, in the darkest hour of death and destruction they would cry out for the return of Jesus on the clouds (13:27). They cry out for Christ to rise and to save them. And even though they proclaim the resurrection and enact its reality in their ritual meals, in this horrific hour they too are very afraid (16:8).

Finally, the liturgical reader would consider the words of Jesus here—"Why are you timid? Do you not yet have faith?"—not as a question of faith as that term is often understood in our day, that is, as a reference to a moment of individual faith in Jesus. Rather, for the liturgical reader the question is one of faith in the physical reality of the new creation enacted in ritual baptism and meal, the means by which the liturgical reader comes to be part of the reality revealed in the narrative. Thus, the readers of Mark are brought to understand their own fear and suffering within the reality created by the ritual of baptism—immersion into the waters of chaos, persecution, and estrangement from the world—as well as by the redemption of the Lord's Supper, which is a communal participation in the resurrection and restoration of peaceful creation.

And in a similar way, the consternation of the disciples—"Who is this, that the wind and the sea obey him?"—is about the connection between Jesus *just as he was* (4:36) and the resurrected Christ, who is able to order creation out of chaos. Mark has implicitly told the liturgical reader that it is the human and corporeal Jesus who rises in the resurrection to rebuke the wind and silence the sea. The corporeal nature of the rituals of baptism (water) and meal (loaf), Gentiles and Jews physically present together at the Lord's Supper, is affirmed in the corporeal nature of the resurrection itself and its relation to

11. Marcus, *Mark 1–8*, 75–79, discusses and then critiques modern scholarship that understands the purpose of Mark to be a "corrective Christology," namely, that Mark was written to correct an understanding of Jesus that focused on his divine power rather than the necessity of his passion and death. It should be obvious that a liturgical reading, focusing on the in-breaking of a restored creation following the struggle with chaos, has very little in common with such readings.

the restored creation. Hence the very physical reality of suffering and physical redemption are both here offered to the reader of Mark.[12]

Mark 5

The Gerasene Demoniac

And they came to the other side of the sea to the region of the Gerasenes. And when they got out of the boat, immediately a man with an unclean spirit from the tombs met him. He dwelled among the tombs, and no one was able to bind him [deomai], even with a chain. For he had often been bound [deomai] with fetters and chains, but he ripped apart the chains around him and smashed the fetters, and no one had the strength [ischyō] to subdue him. (5:1–4)

Following the baptismal death and resurrection of Jesus in the storm at sea, Jesus and the disciples (and the other boats?) arrive on the other side of the sea. For the first time the mission comes to the Gentile land of the Gerasenes (5:1). The description here of the man possessed by demons is carefully tied to what Jesus declared at 3:27: "But no one is able to enter a strong man's [ischyros] house to plunder his goods unless he first binds [deomai] the strong man [ischyros], and then he can plunder his house." The man here among the Gerasenes is indeed strong, there is no one strong enough (ischyō) to subdue him (5:4), and he is apparently growing stronger. Previously he had been held with chains and fetters, but now he is so strong he has destroyed these, so that nothing can bind him (deō; 5:4). Coming across the sea to this Gentile place, Jesus enters the dwelling of the strong man among the tombs, the place of the demons who possess him, and will bind this man and the demons. He will plunder his house by sending the demons into the herd of swine grazing nearby.

For the liturgical reader, both the words and narrative action here are linked to the earlier scene surrounding Mark 3:27. The primary accusation there by the Jewish scribes who had come down from Jerusalem was that Jesus was using the power of Beelzebub, the prince of demons, to cast out demons. Jesus's response, "No one is able to enter a strong man's house to plunder his goods unless he first binds the strong man," was therefore looking forward to his entry into this Gentile territory and the exorcism of the demonic presence here. What ties together the narrative pattern of 3:7–35 is Jewish resistance, among both the Jewish leadership and then the family of Jesus, to the Gentile

---

12. The corporeal nature of Jesus's resurrection is directly tied to the validity and necessity of corporeal suffering in the Christian communities. See, e.g., Ignatius, *Smyr.* 4.2.

mission. In overcoming this resistance Jesus declares he has power over the unclean spirits that possess the Gentiles (much as he has power to forgive the sins of Gentiles, 2:5) and also power to create a new community, a new family of mother, brothers, and sisters, based not in ethnic identity (i.e., being part of the synagogue) but in doing the will of God (*thelēma*; 3:35) within the house church. This means following Jesus as he yields to what the Father wills (*thelō*; 14:36), submitting to martyrdom.

The exorcism of the legion demoniac among the Gentile Gerasenes signals to the liturgical reader that all of Jesus's exorcisms, his confrontations with the demons throughout the narrative to this point, have to do with the establishment of the Gentile mission. When Jesus resurrects from the baptismal waters to confront Satan in the *wilderness* and overcome him (1:10–12), this reader is pointed toward the *wilderness* of Mark 6:35, wherein a great crowd of Gentiles has gathered with the Jews to be fed by the Jewish disciples and Jesus. And again the liturgical reader is directed toward the *wilderness* of 8:1–9, somewhere in the Gentile Decapolis (7:31), where the Gentiles will be fed with the Jews by Jesus and the twelve disciples (8:8).

The exorcism of a legion of unclean spirits here among the Gerasenes also helps the liturgical reader to better understand the odd reaction of those present to the exorcism in the synagogue in Mark 1:27. Their exclamation there—"What is this? A new teaching?"—might now be seen as the new teaching proclaiming this Gentile mission. Such a reading might well explain the otherwise enigmatic detail of a switch to the plural in the dialogue there:

> And immediately in their synagogue there was *a man with an unclean spirit*, and he cried out, saying, "What have you to do with *us*, Jesus of Nazareth? Have you come to destroy *us*? I know who you are, the Holy One of God." (1:23–24)

In this case the exorcism of demons (plural) would confirm the truth of the new teaching and point the reader to the saying about binding the strong man (3:27) and to the exorcism of the legion of demons here among the Gentile Gerasenes (5:9).

The pattern of the so-called messianic secret, wherein the demons recognize Jesus of Nazareth to be the Holy One of God (1:24) or Son of God (3:11), followed by Jesus's command not to make him known, fits the pattern that these demons recognize who Jesus is and his power over them.[13] He is the strong man who can bind Satan and free the Gentiles for full inclusion in the

---

13. The demons inhabiting the Gerasene man bend the knee (*proskyneō*) before Jesus (5:6).

Christian house churches. Yet the characters within the narrative, perhaps best symbolized by Peter at 8:29, must first come to realize that Jesus's power over the demons springs from his baptismal death (1:13). Along with the liturgical reader, they must learn that this is the necessary confrontation with chaos out of which comes the resurrection, the new creation. In Mark this is the place of the ritual meal gathering of Jews and Gentiles, a wilderness free of demonic chaos.[14]

The Pigs

There was next to the mountain a large herd of pigs feeding. And they called Jesus and said to him, "Send us to the pigs so that we might enter them." And he gave them leave, and the unclean spirits went out and entered into the pigs, and the herd rushed down a steep bank into the sea, two thousand in number, and drowned in the sea. (5:11–13)

The strange incident in which the demons ask for and receive permission to enter a herd of swine followed by the suicidal rush of the herd down an embankment into the sea may foreshadow Jesus's later declaration that, with respect to the ritual meal, all foods are clean (7:19). In any event, both Paul (Gal. 2:11–12) and Mark (7:1–23), as well as Acts (10:9–16; 11:19–29), indicate that there was intense disagreement surrounding the role Jewish food laws should play in the Lord's Supper of the earliest house churches.[15] Most important, however, is the fact that both demons and swine have been eradicated from a Gentile land. The mission of the early church has now reached Gentile lands, where the Lord's Supper will be celebrated (8:1–9).

The Gerasene Demoniac Restored

And they came to Jesus and beheld the demon-possessed man clothed [himatizō] and sitting soberly, the one who was possessed by legion, and they were afraid. (5:15)

14. The idea of the space of the Lord's Supper as a space without chaos is supported by a reading of 1 Cor. 11:17–34. There Paul decries unethical ritual practices that have allowed chaos to enter the community: "Because of this many among you are weak and ill, and many of you are falling asleep" (11:30).

15. The eradication of the swine here might well be transparent to an early stage of the controversy, one in which pork was at first eliminated in the ritual meals of the Gentile mission. Later, and perhaps depending on location, these restrictions were either eliminated (7:19) or modified (Acts 15:29). Marcus, *Mark 1–8*, 351–52, apparently sees no relationship between the destruction of the swine and Jewish food laws (he highlights both the military and comedy aspects of the story); for extensive discussion and references to the scholarly discussion of this aspect of the story, see Moloney, *Gospel of Mark*, 104.

For the liturgical reader of Mark, there is an allusion to baptism in this story of exorcism. When the townspeople come out to see what has happened (after all, two thousand pigs have rushed over a cliff into the sea), the possessed man is there "*clothed* [*himatizō*] and sitting soberly." This notice suggests he was *not* clothed before this and has now received a new (baptismal) garment.[16] He is not unlike the young man sitting in a white robe in the tomb of Jesus, perhaps the same young man who dropped his clothing at the scene of the arrest of Jesus (14:51–52). In any event this man now sits soberly with Jesus in the same way the Gentiles sat with Jesus at his house in Mark 3:34.

The obvious reason Jesus is asked by the townspeople to depart is that he has threatened their prosperity with the destruction of the herd of pigs (5:13). On a deeper level this may also be transparent to an initial failure of the Gentile mission in the early Christian church.[17] The demoniac, however, wants to stay with Jesus, but Jesus sends him away to his house, that is, to become the first missionary to the Gentile area of the Decapolis (5:19). This moment is crucial to the narrative structure of Mark: Gentiles are now evangelizing other Gentiles (9:38–40). When Jesus finally does arrive in the Gentile Decapolis later in his mission, there are already believers there (7:31), evangelized by Gentiles such as the one here. These are the Gentiles who will join with Jesus and the disciples in the second ritual wilderness meal (8:1–9).

16. For the many allusions to unclothing and clothing in the early Christian ritual practice of baptism, see Meeks, *First Urban Christians*, 150–57.

17. Marcus, *Mark 1–8*, 352–53.

3

Conclusion of the Jewish Mission and the Inclusion of Gentiles

The First Ritual Meal Narrative and Explanation

5:21–7:23

Mark 5

Jesus Leaves the Gerasenes

Jesus again crossed [in the boat] to another place [*peran*]. And a great crowd gathered to him again. And he was beside the sea. (5:21)

The geographic marker at Mark 5:21 is not certain. Most modern English translations follow one version of the Greek text that has Jesus "crossing again in the boat to another place." In that case what follows would seem to take place back in Galilee at the place, beside the sea, where Jesus had taught in parables (4:1). However, there is also a strong witness in some Greek texts of Mark that leave out any mention of a boat. In that case the text would translate

"Jesus again crossed to another place. And a crowd gathered to him again."[1] The setting for what follows might then be part of the Jewish diaspora, Jewish communities in Gentile lands. As I will explore below, there are good reasons why, for the liturgical reader at least, a diaspora setting makes more sense for the two intercalated stories that follow: the raising of Jairus's daughter and the saving of the woman with the hemorrhage (5:21–43).[2]

The Weaving of Two Stories: The Daughter of Jairus and the Woman with a Hemorrhage

And one of the leaders of the synagogue approached. His name was Jairus. And seeing Jesus, he fell upon the feet of Jesus. And he beseeched him, saying, "My daughter is about to die. Come and lay your hands upon her so that she might live and be saved." And Jesus went with him, and a great crowd followed him and gathered around him.

And there was a woman who had a flow of blood for twelve years. She suffered a great deal under many physicians and had spent everything she had. But she had gained nothing, but rather the condition worsened. When she heard about Jesus, she came into the crowd behind him and touched his cloak. For she said, "Even if I might touch his cloak, I will be saved." Immediately her flow of blood dried up. And she knew in her body that she had been healed of the disease. And immediately Jesus knew in himself that power had gone out. So he turned to the crowd and said, "Who touched my cloak?" But his disciples said to him, "You see the crowd gathered around you, and you say, 'Who touched my cloak?'" And he turned to see who had done this. And the woman in fear and trembling knew what had happened to her. She came and knelt before him and told him the whole truth. And he said to her, "Daughter, your faith has saved you. Depart in peace and be healed of your disease."

And just as he was saying this, they came from the synagogue, saying, "Your daughter has died; why bother the teacher anymore?" But Jesus overheard what they were saying and said to the ruler of the synagogue, "Do not fear [*phobeomai*], only believe." And he allowed no one to follow him except Peter, James, and John, the brother of James. And they came into the house [*oikos*] of the ruler of the synagogue, and he saw distress and weeping and great wailing. And having entered the house, he said to them, "Why are you distressed and weeping? The child is not dead but sleeping [*katheudō*]." And they ridiculed him. And he threw all of them out. And he took the father and mother of the child and

---

1. The vague geographical and modal reference at 5:21—"in the boat"—is missing from important uncial and minuscule manuscripts; see R. J. Swanson, *New Testament Greek Manuscripts*, 72.

2. Placing one story within another (intercalation) is part of Mark's unique narrative style. For discussion and analysis, see Edwards, "Markan Sandwiches," 193–216; T. Shepherd, "Markan Intercalation," 522–40; ibid., *Markan Sandwich Stories*.

those who were with him and entered the place where the child was. And he grasped the hand of the child and said to her, "Talitha koum," which translated means, "Little girl, I say to you, resurrect [*egeirō*]." And immediately the little girl resurrected [*anistēmi*] and walked. For she was twelve years old. And they were amazed and greatly confused. And he expressly told them that no one was to know about this. And he told them to give her something to eat. (5:21–43)

Other than Jesus's twelve disciples, Jairus is the first and only Jewish leader in Mark to be named.[3] And unlike the Jewish leaders who challenge Jesus (2:7, 16, 24; 3:6, 22), Jairus, a leader of the synagogue (*archisynagōgos*), falls down at Jesus's feet (5:22). So also the woman with a hemorrhage makes an extraordinary effort to approach Jesus and desires merely to touch his cloak.

The liturgical reader of Mark is aware that both stories bring into prominence physical touching and being touched as integral to the manner in which the stories are told. In the first part of the Jairus story, the leader of the synagogue implores Jesus to come and "lay hands upon her *so that* she might be saved and live" (5:23). Then at the conclusion of the story Jesus grasps the hand of the child in order to resurrect (*egeirō*) her from death (5:41). In the intercalated story of the woman with a hemorrhage, the woman has faith that if she touches the cloak of Jesus she will be saved.[4] In these stories the salvation offered and received is physical salvation, restoration of body and life in the new creation.

Carefully intercalated healing stories that feature the physicality of touching and healing most likely emerged from the early Christian sense of the sacred space surrounding the Lord's Supper. One notes, for example, that in Mark the second wilderness meal narrative is prefigured by the healing of the deaf and mute man (7:34–37) and postfigured by the healing of the blind man (8:22–26). From its earliest inception as the place which ritually enacted the resurrected *body of Christ*, the meal enacted in time and space the resurrection of Christ as the restored creation. Paul even goes so far as to claim that

3. Depending on how one understands Mark 5:21, that is, whether this narrative scene is located within the Jewish diaspora or Galilee, the unusual naming of the character Jairus, along with his religious title (*archisynagōgos*), may reflect the Christian missions' success in the diaspora synagogue. Such a reading, as well as the allusion to the unnamed woman with the hemorrhage, would suggest a prominent place for Jewish women in the Christian house churches outside of Galilee and Judea. The unexpected prominence given to the number twelve in these intercalated stories (the young girl is *twelve* years old; the woman has had her flow of blood for *twelve* years) also jibes with the diaspora setting. The early Christian mission sought to reconstitute the *twelve* tribes of Israel. See, e.g., the prayer in Did. 9.4.

4. Scholars have long noted the striking number of women involved in the early Christian mission; see Scroggs, "Paul and the Eschatological Woman"; "Paul and the Eschatological Woman: Revisited."

the reason physical maladies and death have affected certain members of the Corinthian congregation is their neglect of the norms governing the social practices that constitute the cultic reality of the *body* of Christ, the Lord's Supper (1 Cor. 11:28–30).

In these intercalated stories Jesus, the crucified and physically resurrected Son of God, restores the wholeness of body of the woman with a hemorrhage. As with the man with the withered hand (3:4–5), she is restored to the wholeness of the new creation and full participation in the Lord's Supper. It is perhaps also intentional that Jesus, using the ancient Aramaic Christian proclamation of the resurrection (*talitha koum*; 5:41), brings the little girl to life just as she enters into her womanhood (twelve years old). She, along with the hemorrhaging woman, is now fully part of the community of Jews and Gentiles, males and females (Gal. 3:28; Col. 3:11). Jesus instructs his disciples (Peter, James, and John) who are present with him to give her something to eat. Not only is she physically raised from the dead (*egeirō*; *anistēmi*) by the grasp of Jesus; she is now served and presumably eats the Lord's Supper *with* the male Jewish disciples in the ritual enactment of the restored creation (5:43).

Mark 6

Jesus Returns Home

He went out from there and came to his home village [*patris*]. And his disciples followed him. And when it was the Sabbath, he began to teach in the synagogue. And many who heard him were astonished, saying, "From where does he possess these things? What wisdom is given to him? And what mighty works come about through his hands? Is this not the child, the son of Mary, and the brother of James and Joses and Jude and Simon? And are not his sisters here among us?" And they were scandalized by him. And Jesus said to them, "A prophet is not without honor except in his home village [*patris*] and among his family and in his house [*oikos*]." And he was not able to do a mighty work [*dynamis*] there except to lay his hands upon a few sick people and heal them. He was amazed at their unbelief. And he went around in the villages teaching. (6:1–6)

If Jesus is still somewhere in the Jewish diaspora for the resurrection of Jairus's daughter and the healing and saving of the woman with a hemorrhage, then Mark 6 signals a return by Jesus to either Nazareth, or more likely Capernaum, the place from which his mission began (1:21; 2:1). The geographic reference at Mark 6:1, "he . . . came into his *home village* [*patris*]," ties the rejection of Jesus by the townspeople and his family to the saying that

Jesus pronounces at 6:4: "A prophet is not without honor except in his *home village* [*patris*] and among his family and in his house."[5]

As in Mark 1:21, Jesus again teaches in the synagogue on the Sabbath. At that earlier time also there was a sense of wonder among his audience: "And they were astonished at his teaching. For he was teaching them as one with authority and not as the scribes taught" (1:22). Since that time, both the reader of Mark and the characters in the narrative know that a great deal more has taken place. To the authority of this initial teaching Jesus has added both wisdom (4:1–34) and numerous mighty deeds.[6]

The issue for the members of the synagogue here in chapter 6—"*From where does he possess these things?*"—clearly reminds the reader of the earlier opposition to Jesus among the scribes who had come down from Jerusalem to challenge him. There they had charged that Jesus received his power not from God but from being possessed by the prince of demons, the unclean spirit Beelzebub (3:22). The earlier narrative places the controversy between the notice that "those around him" (perhaps his relatives in his home village) said "He is crazy" (3:21) and the notice that his mother and brothers were outside and calling for him to come out of the house (3:31). Clearly, therefore, the narrative is carefully constructed to refute the opponents' claim that Jesus's power does not come from his relationship to God. While the opponents of Jesus imply that he is not Son of God but Son of Mary along with her other children (3:31), Jesus, the Son of God who binds Beelzebub (1:11), gathers in the house with the true sons and daughters of God (3:35).

The scene at Mark 6:1–6 follows similar lines. Here the consternation of members of the synagogue—"From where does he possess these things?"—is again followed by a reference to Jesus as the child of Mary along with his siblings (3:32; 6:3). In each scene, the contention from opponents (that Jesus is the Son of Mary in the same way that Jesus's siblings are the children of Mary) implies that his power and status do not come from being the Son of God because he is the Son of Mary. And so again the liturgical reader is drawn to the baptismal scene to recall that Jesus *is* the Son of God (1:11), the very claim that creates scandal (6:3; cf. 3:21) and also the juridical conviction at his trial before the Jewish Sanhedrin (14:61–62).

The liturgical reader further notes that the designation of Jesus as "Son of God," besides framing the beginning and end of the entire Gospel narrative

5. This appears to be a general wisdom saying, the source of which is not known. It seems clear that the use of the word *patris* (instead of the word for house, *oikos*) in the unknown wisdom saying is what dictates its use at Mark 6:1, 4.

6. Healings (1:29–30, 34, 40–44; 3:1–6; 5:25–34) and resurrections (1:29–30; 2:1–12; 5:35–42) and the defeat of cosmic chaos (4:35–41) along with the casting out of demons (1:21–27; 5:1–20).

(1:1; 15:39), is proclaimed by God at the *baptismal* scene. Jesus rises (*anabainō*) from ritual death, and this is followed immediately by the descent of the Spirit into Jesus (1:10–11). Jesus, as the Son of God, possesses not Beelzebub but the Holy Spirit of God (1:8) and is able, as the demons themselves know, to drive them away (1:24; 5:12–13). This capacity of Jesus as Son of God to cast away unclean spirits by the Spirit of God, or to perform acts of restoring the physical body and life itself, is, for the liturgical reader of Mark, the capacity to create the new family and the sacred space of the ritual meal in the new house churches of the community (3:34–35; 6:1).[7] Those who are restored to their original creation—Peter's mother-in-law, the Gentile leper and paralytic, the Jewish man with the withered hand in the midst of the synagogue, the Gentile legion demoniac, the Jewish daughter of Jairus, and the woman with a hemorrhage—are all part of the restored creation emerging from the ritually enacted death of Christ. This is the sacred spatial and temporal reality enacted in the inclusive Lord's Supper ritual in the house churches of Mark's time.

The two narrative depictions of Jesus's family and relatives in opposition to his mission (3:31–35; 6:1–6), especially his mission to the Gentiles (3:32; 6:4), can be read as an allusion to the perceived opposition in the Jewish Christian community and in the Jewish synagogue community to the inclusive house churches for whom Mark is writing.[8] With respect to the latter, it appears that official Jewish opposition to the churches at times led to martyrdom within Mark's community (13:9). And within the narrative it is this opposition which brings about the trial (14:53–65) and eventual condemnation of Jesus (15:8–15). Moreover, through the depiction of the narrative character of Jesus, Mark appears to be genuinely mystified by the failure of the contemporary Christian mission to the synagogue: "He [Jesus] was amazed at their unbelief" (6:6). But just as the apostle Paul earlier was convinced that the mysterious purpose of God in bringing in the Gentiles was being furthered by this failure in the mission to the Jews (Rom. 11:25),

---

7. This, of course, closely follows Paul's understanding of the antithesis between demons and the Lord's Supper, e.g., in 1 Cor. 10:21: "You cannot drink the cup of the Lord and the cup of the demons; you cannot partake of the table of the Lord and the table of the demons."

8. Moloney, *Gospel of Mark*, 113–14, as well as other commentators (e.g., Focant, *Mark*, 222–27), does not see this opposition to Jesus as an allusion to the opposition experienced by Mark's house churches; not surprisingly, the thorny theological issue of Jesus's *biological* brothers and sisters is taken up in several commentaries; see Donahue and Harrington, *Mark*, 186–89; Culpepper, *Mark*, 189–92. It is worth noting that if this section and the previous mention of family (3:31–35) are in fact transparent to Jewish Christian and Jewish opposition to the Gentile mission, then what we can safely glean about the family of the historical Jesus is brought into doubt.

so also Mark uses this moment in the narrative to finalize the mission to the Jews in Israel and the diaspora and look forward to a more successful mission to the Gentiles.

Twelve Disciples in Mission

And he called the twelve and began to send them two by two. And he gave to them authority over the unclean spirits. And he commanded them to take nothing on the way [hodos] except for a staff: not a loaf, not a satchel, and no money in their belts. They were, however, to wear sandals but not to wear two tunics [chitōn]. He said to them, "Whenever you enter into a house [oikos], remain there until you go out from there. And when a place does not receive you and does not listen to you, go out from there and shake the dust from under your feet as a witness to them." So they went out and preached repentance. And they cast out many demons and anointed with oil many who were sick and healed them. (6:7–13)

On the heels of the rejection at the Jewish synagogue, the final mission to the Jews in Israel and the diaspora begins in earnest (6:7). The Twelve are sent out on mission with Jesus's authority over the unclean spirits (3:27). This is the authority given to Jesus following his baptismal death and resurrection with the descent of the Spirit and the declaration of Jesus as Son of God (1:10–11). Perhaps more important, it is the spiritual authority by which Jesus, following his baptismal death and resurrection in the storm (4:35–41), cast the legion demons of Gerasa into the swine and thereby created the possibility of the sacred space of the Lord's Supper even within Gentile areas (5:1–20). The disciples' mission will establish the possibility of the sacred meal, Gentiles with the Jews, which is to be enacted in both Jewish and Gentile places on their return (6:30–44; 8:1–9).[9]

In the sequence of the narrative, it is important that the Twelve are sent out on this mission at Mark 6:7, a good while after they were first selected for the mission at Mark 3:12–14. At Mark 3:15 they are given authority to cast out demons but are not actually sent anywhere. Now at 6:7 Jesus actually sends them out two by two with this authority. What has taken place in the meantime in the narrative of Mark? Quite simply, Mark has taken the opportunity to defend the argument that the Spirit within Jesus (1:10), far from being the unclean spirit of Beelzebub (3:22), is actually the Spirit that can bind Beelzebub. Jesus's Spirit can enter the strong man's house and bind

---

9. In a moment of true transparency to the time of his own writing, Mark not only describes the establishment of the still-ongoing mission; he also describes the contemporary ritual of anointing the sick with oil (6:13; cf. James 5:14).

him (3:27; 5:4). Hence the reign of Beelzebub in the land of the Gentiles and the Jewish diaspora is finished. The strong one can be bound (5:1–20), and the churches can be established among those Jews and Gentiles who do not reject the disciples' mission (6:10–11). The twelve Jewish disciples now being sent out in Mark 6:7 have Jesus's authority, the Spirit of the Son of God, to bind the unclean spirits in the entire earth (2:10), even the ones as strong as legion.

Twelve disciples are sent out, and the number is important. For Mark the number twelve represents the Jewish core of the mission, the center from which the mission to the Gentiles proceeds and to which the Gentiles are added.[10] This is most dramatically represented by Mark's featuring of the number twelve in the intercalated stories of 5:21–43 (the woman has the hemorrhage for *twelve* years; the little girl is *twelve* years old) and the gathering of *twelve* baskets in the first feeding narrative (6:43; 8:19). In Mark's narrative purpose, the Jewish mission was in fact first, and *only after the inevitable rejection of that mission* by some Jews and their leaders (4:11–12; 3:6) was the successful mission to Gentiles and Jews in the lands of the diaspora begun (5:1). What is uniquely important to Mark's narrative purpose, however, is that the leaders of his own Christian community come to understand, accept, and nurture the Gentiles who have joined the church through ritual baptism as a result of the church's mission to the Gentiles.[11] These Gentiles are to join with the Jews and together, as the restored community of Genesis,[12] eat the one loaf of the Lord's Supper.

After the story of the death of John the Baptist, which, whatever other purpose Mark had in mind,[13] serves as a warning of the possible fate of the twelve disciples who have been sent out on mission (10:39), the disciples return to Jesus and report to him all that they have done and taught (6:30). It is not clear in the narrative how far they have gone and how many house churches they have founded ("Whenever you enter into a house [*oikia*], remain there until you go out from there"; 6:10). But if, as the liturgical reader might suppose, they are acting in imitation of what Jesus has done in the narrative up to this point, then they have brought into the community both Jews and Gentiles from Israel and the lands of the diaspora. It is this group of people who now form the large crowd featured in the first ritual meal narrative. This meal apparently takes place somewhere in Galilee (6:1).

10. Following the fulfillment of Isa. 56:6–7. See the discussion of Mark 3 above.

11. One is reminded here of Mark 6:37: "You [twelve disciples] give them something to eat."

12. This is the implication of the implied and explicit use of the number seven in the two ritual meal narratives (6:38; 8:5, 8).

13. Mark 6:14–29; for extensive commentary, see Marcus, *Mark 1–8*, 391–404.

The First Ritual Meal in the Wilderness

And the apostles gathered together with Jesus and told him all that they had done and taught. And he said to them, "Come away by yourselves to a wilderness [*erēmos*] place and get refreshment." For there were many [*polys*] coming and going, and they did not have the opportunity to eat. And they departed in the boat to a wilderness [*erēmos*] place by themselves. Yet when the many [*polys*] discovered them leaving, they ran there by land from all of the cities and got to that place ahead of them. And when he disembarked, he saw a great crowd [*ochlos*] and had pity [*splanchnizomai*] upon them, for they were as sheep without a shepherd. And he began to teach them many things. And the hour [*hōra*] was already getting late.

His disciples came to him and said, "This is a wilderness [*erēmos*] place, and already the hour [*hōra*] is getting late. Dismiss them so that they might go into the fields and villages round about and purchase for themselves something to eat." But he answered and said to them, "You give them something to eat." And they said to him, "Are we to go and buy two hundred denarii of loaves [*artos*] so that we might give them loaves to eat?" And he said to them, "How many loaves [*artos*] do you have? Go and see." And when they found out, they said, "Five, and two fish."

And he commanded them all to recline for a meal, eating group [*symposion*] by eating group [*symposion*], upon the green grass. And they reclined group [*prasia*] by group [*prasia*] by hundreds and by fifties. And taking the five loaves [*artos*] and the two fish, he looked up [*anablepō*] to heaven. He blessed [*eulogeō*] and broke [*kataklaō*] the loaves [*artos*] and gave [*didōmi*] them to the disciples so that they would distribute them. And the two fish he [Jesus] divided for them all. And they all ate and were satisfied [*chortazō*]. And there were twelve baskets [*kophinos*] utterly filled [*plērōma*] with the broken bread pieces [*klasma*] and with the fish. And those who ate the loaves [*artos*][14] were five thousand males [*anēr*]. (6:30–44)

For the liturgical reader, the narrative purpose of the first feeding narrative, with unmistakable allusions to the biblical story of God's provision of manna to Israel in the wilderness,[15] is to place the Gentiles within that story and so to root the meaning of the Lord's Supper ritual in a new understanding of the story of the exodus-Passover centered on the death of Jesus. Mark

14. The reference to the loaves here is a strong variant in the manuscript tradition which, in my reading, makes sense as part of the text. See the comments on this passage in R. J. Swanson, *New Testament Greek Manuscripts*.

15. Exod. 16:15 (LXX): "It is the loaf [*artos*] which the Lord has given you to eat." There are also clear allusions to the Exodus description of the encampment of Israel in the wilderness: Mark 6:40; Exod. 18:21. Commentaries also point to the biblical story of Elisha the prophet feeding one hundred men with twenty barley loaves as a model for this story (2 Kings 4:42–44).

depicts Jesus as overcoming the reluctance of his Jewish disciples to include the Gentiles in the wilderness meal.

For the liturgical reader, there are several hints that Mark is drawing out an allusion to some Jewish-Christian resistance to this inclusion in the churches of Mark's own time. The disciples complain, but Jesus responds by commanding the disciples to feed everyone gathered. Meanwhile Jesus himself distributes the fish, the symbol of the Gentile mission, to all who are gathered. All of this should become clearer as Mark's ritual meal narrative is here carefully unpacked.

Mark does not tell us how far the twelve disciples' mission, commissioned by Jesus at 6:7–13, extended. But given that Jesus himself had previously encountered and welcomed Gentiles in Jewish areas (3:8) and had crossed the chaotic sea to reach the Gentiles (5:1), it is safe for the reader to assume that Gentiles as well as Jews of the diaspora lands had been the object of the disciples' mission. The day of the twelve disciples' return from mission is apparently the Sabbath (6:2). After the interlude of the story of the death of the Baptist, Jesus invites the Twelve to the wilderness (*erēmos*). For the liturgical reader, this is the same wilderness (*erēmos*) that Jesus experienced following his ritual baptismal death and in which he was tempted by Satan (1:12–13). Mark here invites the reader to understand this story of Jesus, the disciples, and the crowds as a retelling of Israel's exodus through the Red Sea to the wilderness (Exod. 13:18), the Israelites' temptation to turn away from Moses (Exod. 16:2–3), and God's provision of the loaves (manna) to satisfy them (Exod. 16:12). In the narrative of Mark, formed and informed by the rituals of baptism and Supper, time collapses. The story of Israel's emergence out of the chaos and death of the Red Sea (Passover) is at once the story of Jesus's emergence from death in resurrection enacted within the meal ritual in the house churches of Mark's time.

Also within the careful narrative sequence of Mark 6:31–32, it is hard not to see that the story in Mark is transparent to the desire of some Jews within the newly formed house churches of Mark's time to eat the Lord's Supper separately from Gentiles. Mark tells us here that initially Jesus and his twelve disciples *withdrew* from the many (*polys*) who were coming and going in order to eat their own meal in the wilderness (6:31). They cross the sea in a boat, quite likely an allusion to the exodus of Israel through the Red Sea. Here in the wilderness Jesus and the twelve Jewish disciples would, presumably, be able to eat this ritual meal by themselves. The eager crowd, at this point including Gentiles who have been the object of both Jesus's and the disciples' missionary efforts, sees them leaving in a boat and yet travels *by land* to the wilderness. Hence these Gentiles arrive not by way of the Red

Sea, as in the story of Israel, but by dry land. They therefore follow the way (*hodos*) proclaimed in the wilderness (*erēmos*) at the outset of the narrative by John the Baptist. This is the way (*hodos*) of Isaiah's proclamation that opens Mark's Gospel. In Mark's narrative the way (*hodos*) of the death of Christ is now ritually enacted in the waters of baptism (1:2–3, 9; 2:23; 10:52).[16] So now *baptized* in the new exodus, the new way, proclaimed at the outset of the Gospel, the way of the death of Christ, these Gentiles arrive from all the cities at the place of *wilderness*. The new path to the wilderness is one of repentance and baptism. By different means, the death of Christ ritually enacted in baptism, a number of Gentiles have now joined with the Jewish disciples in the *wilderness*, eager to be part of the ritual meal of loaves (manna), eager to be fed by God.

As in the story of compassion (*splanchnizomai*) for the Gentile leper (1:41), compassion (*splanchnizomai*) for the *Gentile* crowd gathered in a Gentile place in the second wilderness feeding (8:2), and compassion (*splanchnizomai*) for the *Gentiles* who bring a possessed boy to Jesus (9:22), Jesus has *compassion* (*splanchnizomai*) on the Gentile crowd gathered here (6:34). The allusion to sheep without a shepherd and in need of teaching would be a particularly apt description of Gentiles.[17] The reference to the lateness of the hour at 6:35 is, within the narrative, a notice of the end of the Sabbath day. Yet the use of the specific term *hour* (*hōra*) here must also be understood as an overt reference to the impending apocalyptic hour of the death of Christ and the hour of Christian martyrdom (13:11; 14:35, 41; 15:25). Thus the narrative connects the impending meal with the death of Christ (the new Passover on dry land), a connection already made explicit by Paul in his letters (1 Cor. 10:1–33; 11:17–34). From Jesus's death and the surrounding darkness come life and new creation. The meal which enacts the resurrection, the body of Christ, takes place at that *hour*. And it takes place in the *wilderness*. So when the twelve Jewish disciples announce this obvious fact to Jesus ("This is the wilderness"; 6:35), it is not to inform Jesus of where they are but to claim that they want to eat in the *wilderness* without the Gentiles. The liturgical reader might read this complaint in paraphrase:

> This is the *wilderness*! The hour is now late, and it is time for the Lord's Supper. Send these Gentiles away, for we cannot eat with them. These Gentiles do

16. The blind Gentile man Bartimaeus throws off his garment in a baptismal gesture and follows Jesus "on the way [*hodos*]" (10:50–52).

17. The Christian community is the reconstitution of Israel scattered and brought together by the Lord (Num. 27:17; 1 Kings 22:17; 2 Chron. 18:16).

not belong in *this* place, Israel's wilderness, to be fed the loaf [manna] in the Lord's Supper.

Once again the narrative of Mark is transparent to what Mark hopes to accomplish by telling the story of Jesus in just this way. In Mark's house churches there was Jewish-Christian resistance to the idea of eating the Lord's Supper with the Gentiles, and more than a small part of Mark's narrative purpose is to overcome that resistance. Hence the unexpected response by Jesus, given as a blunt command to his twelve disciples: "You give them something to eat" (6:37). In a fell swoop Jesus defeats the intention of the disciples to send the crowd out of the wilderness to eat. Rather, the crowd is invited by Jesus to join the restored Israel in the new Christian wilderness of the Lord's Supper. And so it is that the response of the disciples, "Are we to go and buy two hundred denarii of loaves [*artos*] and give the loaves to them to eat?" (6:37), is not a claim of poverty but rather both an indication of the size of the crowd and a repeated attempt to avoid eating with any Gentiles who are part of it.

The question and command posed by Jesus at 6:38, "How many *loaves* do you have? Go and see," takes the liturgical reader again deeply into the story of Israel in the wilderness. The response this reader might expect is given: the Jewish disciples go out and find five loaves. These would be symbolic of Torah, the five books of Moses, and so would root the meal of loaves exclusively within the story of Israel and symbolize the gathering of the elect of Israel.[18] Jesus had only asked about the loaves. The twelve disciples, however, discover what Jesus does not ask for: five loaves *and two fish*. This wilderness meal will be changed. Two fish will be added to the five loaves, and the reader begins to understand the allusion.

The liturgical reader of Mark, sensitive to the symbolic meaning of the elements of the meal, realizes immediately that Jesus's earlier prediction to the two disciples, Peter and Andrew, has in fact come true: "Follow me and I will make you fishermen of people" (1:17). The disciples have just returned from their initial mission, two by two (6:7), and as a direct result of their mission, a great crowd of Jews and Gentiles has gathered for this meal in the wilderness. The Gentiles have joined the new Israel by the way (*hodos*) of dry land: there are here five loaves *and two fish*. And now the implicit number seven is present in the meal, a number which represents the eschatological gathering

18. See Acts 4:4, where the Jews who choose to join the "way" are five thousand. See the discussion in Marcus, *Mark 1–8*, 407: "The five loaves of bread may be related to the Law of Moses, the Pentateuch . . . means five part book. Following the lead of Proverbs 9:5 (cf. Deut. 8:3), post-biblical Judaism developed bread or manna into a symbol for the Torah."

of humanity, Jews and Gentiles, in a return to the original seven-day creation.[19] This wilderness is the new Eden.[20] The Sabbath will continue, and, just as the sun does not set on the seventh day of creation (Gen. 2:3), darkness will not fall on this meal of the resurrection.

Jesus tells the reluctant disciples to command the people to recline into separate eating groups upon the green grass. They now recline group by group, in hundreds and in fifties (6:39–40). This rather loose allusion to the camp of Israel in the wilderness (Exod. 18:21, 25) is surely to be read as transparent to some of the churches of Mark's time. The narrative seems to indicate some degree of separation between Jewish and Gentile groups assembled for the Lord's Supper (*symposion*, *prasia*; 6:39–40). This is a separation which will be overcome in the second ritual meal narrative, where the separation of the community into groups is absent (8:6).

Early Christian ritual practice forms the heart of the narrative description of what Jesus does with the loaves at 6:41 ("blessed . . . broke . . . and gave"), a nearly identical ritual practice described in the next two ritual meal narratives (8:6; 14:22). The description at 6:41 is precise:

And taking the five loaves [*artos*] and the two fish, he looked up [*anablepō*][21] to heaven. He blessed [*eulogeō*] and broke [*kataklaō*] the loaves [*artos*] and gave [*didōmi*] them to the disciples so that they would distribute them. And the two fish he [Jesus] divided for them all. (6:41)

The ritual blessing is said only over the five loaves, and Jesus commands the disciples to distribute these loaves to all who are present. In other words, the disciples may have been reluctant to feed Gentiles along with the Jewish people in this wilderness, but now the narrative utilizes the narrative character of

19. Despite the objections of Marcus, *Mark 1–8*, 489, there is ample reason to conclude that the number seven has a special connotation in the early Christian church, suggesting the ingathering of the Gentiles in the eschatological age (exactly what is enacted in liturgy and exactly the number of loaves distributed to Gentiles in the second ritual meal in the Gentile wilderness and gathered into baskets; Mark 8:5, 8). In the Old Testament there were *seven* commandments of the Noachic covenant binding on Gentiles (Gen. 9:4–7); all of the nations of the world are symbolized by the *seventy* nations of Gen. 10:2–31; in the New Testament the *seven* Hellenists (Gentiles) are chosen as deacons as a result of complaints by Greeks (Gentiles) within the community (Acts 6:1–6); there are also *seven* churches in Revelation, which undoubtedly symbolize the worldwide church (Rev. 2–3).

20. The biblical theme of the wilderness as the seventh day of creation as well as the garden of Eden is discussed at some length in Levenson, *Sinai and Zion*, 89–184.

21. It is worth noting that Jesus "looks up" at the cure of the Gentile deaf mute (7:34) and the cure of the Gentile blind man (8:24). These are the two healings that fall on either side of the second ritual meal narrative, where the Gentiles are fed the Lord's Supper on Gentile soil. A ritual gesture indicating the acceptance of the Gentiles?

Jesus to overcome directly this reluctance, and the Jewish disciples serve the entire community, eating group by eating group. The liturgical reader might see here the situation in the house churches of Mark's own time: Gentiles must be fed with the Jews at the Lord's Supper. Jesus himself distributes the two fish among them all, and this is followed by the emphatic statement of the narrative, "They *all* ate and were satisfied [*chortazō*]" (6:42). Both groups, Gentiles and Jews, ate their fill of the five loaves (manna) and of the two fish. The narrative points toward the expected ritual acceptance of the Gentiles by the twelve Jewish disciples and the other Jews gathered for the meal. The narrative also points to the final gathering of the remnant of Jews in the twelve tribes (twelve baskets) who have been brought into this Christian community: "Those who ate of the loaves were five thousand males" (6:44).[22]

Mark's careful ending to the ritual meal notes that there were gathered *twelve* small baskets (*kophinos*) utterly filled (*plērōma*) with the pieces (*klasma*) of the *five* loaves ritually broken by Jesus and which included the *two* fish (6:43). Again the liturgical reader understands that the restored creation, the seventh day, has been established in this meal on the Sabbath. The elect, the reconstituted twelve tribes of Israel, five thousand men,[23] have now been gathered into the twelve baskets.[24] Yet here there are also the pieces of the two fish in the twelve baskets, Gentiles who have now been brought into the community, also elect, and who are also part of the restored creation (13:27).[25]

The pattern of mission at this point in the Markan narrative is now clear, and it prepares the reader for what is about to take place as the disciples are sent out by boat toward Bethsaida.

---

22. The use of the specific word for males here (*anēr*) may reflect the biblical manner of counting the population by heads of households (Harrington and Donahue, *Mark*, 207). Focant (*Mark*, 261) suggests the fullness of Israel in the five loaves and the five thousand men. The use of the specific term for males here must also be contrasted with the absence of that term in the description of those attending the second ritual meal in the wilderness. The movement in Mark seems to be toward the full inclusion of women (cf. the story of the Syrophoenician woman, 7:24–30), indicated by the fact that in the second meal four thousand (people) are fed (8:9).

23. Acts 4:4.

24. This is of course how the Gospel of John also understands the symbolism of the baskets, as referring to the ingathering of those who remain in the community (John 6:12).

25. The resurrection story in John 21:1–13 indicates that Mark is working with common Christian symbolism of equating fish eaten within ritual meal with people gathered into the church. In the story in John, the disciples, and especially the beloved disciple, who is the first to recognize the resurrected Christ (John 21:7), bring in 153 large fish. Jesus, however, is already eating loaves (*artos*) and fish with Peter on the shore and specifically commands that the fish caught by the disciples be added to the meal (John 21:10). Clearly different early Christian communities are being combined (most notably the communities beholden to Peter as their founder and those beholden to the beloved disciple as their founder). Jesus feeds them all the bread (*artos*) and the fish (John 21:13).

In the first crossing by boat toward the Gentile Gerasenes (4:35–41), the ritual death (sleeping, *katheudō*) and resurrection (*diegeirō*) of Jesus had mastered the chaos of the impending evening (*opsia*), wind (*anemos*), and sea (*thalassa*) and resulted in binding the demons that held the strong man, the legion demoniac, a Gentile in a Gentile land (5:8). Yet these Gentiles of Gerasa had rejected the mission there (5:17), and so it came to pass that the healed demoniac was sent by Jesus to begin the Gentile-to-Gentile mission in the Decapolis (5:19–20). The resurrected Christ had then gone on to restore (*sōzō*) the woman with the hemorrhage of *twelve* years and to resurrect (*egeirō*) Jairus's *twelve*-year-old daughter from the dead (5:21–43). Clearly the narrative indicates that the final gathering of Israel (*twelve* tribes) was now taking place. Then back in Israel the rejection by kindred Jews of the claim that this Jesus was the Son of God rather than the Son of Mary (6:1–6) led immediately to the sending out of the *twelve* disciples, perhaps to the lands of the diaspora, to gather the final elect of Israel; to the feeding of *five thousand males*; and to the gathering of *twelve* baskets of the ritual loaves in the *wilderness*. Along with these would be gathered some Gentiles—the two fish—and on this basis the Gentile mission now begins in earnest (6:30–41).

Jesus Walks upon the Water

And he [Jesus] immediately forced his disciples to get into the boat and to go out before him, toward Bethsaida, while he dismissed the crowd. And when he parted from them he went away to the mountain to pray. And when it was evening [*opsia*], the boat was in the middle of the sea [*thalassa*], and he was alone upon the land. And he saw that they were rowing only with great difficulty, as the wind [*anemos*] was against them. It was about the fourth watch of the night [*nyx*]. He came toward them walking on the sea [*thalassa*], and he wanted to press on by them. And when they saw him walking upon the sea [*thalassa*], they thought it was an apparition [*phantasma*], and they cried out. For they all saw him and were disturbed. And immediately he spoke with them and said to them, "Have courage, I am [*ego eimi*], do not fear." And he rose [*anabainō*] toward them into the boat, and the wind abated. And among themselves they were amazed, for they did not understand [*syniēmi*] about the loaves [*artos*], but their heart was hardened.

And crossing over to land, they came to anchor at Gennesaret. And when they got out of the boat, immediately they recognized him. And that whole region came running, and when they heard where he was, they began to bring to him the diseased upon beds. And wherever he would enter a village or a city or a rural area, they brought the diseased to the marketplace and begged him that they might touch even the fringe of his garment—and as many who touched it were saved. (6:45–56)

Now, as it grows dark, Jesus forcefully sends his disciples over the sea (*thalassa*) directly toward Bethsaida and the Gentiles beyond. As once before in the crossing to the Gerasene Gentiles in a boat (4:35–41), the resurrection of Christ will confront chaos in the form of wind (*anemos*), darkness (*nyx*), and sea (*thalassa*). Now, however, Jesus is not in the boat with them.

At the fourth watch of the night after the Sabbath day, at the time just before dawn and exactly the time of the resurrection (*lian prōi*; 16:2), Jesus, the resurrected Son of God, comes to them walking upon the sea (*thalassa*), dominating chaos.[26] And he wants to press on by them. All of the disciples see Jesus but think he is a phantom. They are troubled and cry out. Jesus then identifies himself and tells them not to be afraid. He rises (*anabainō*) into the boat with them, and the wind ceases. They could go on to Gentile Bethsaida if they understood the connection between Jesus, his resurrection, the domination of the sea (chaos), and the loaves.[27] But the disciples do not yet fully understand this connection, and so some education, for the disciples and for the liturgical reader of Mark, must first take place.

At this point in the narrative the question for the liturgical reader centers on what Mark hopes to show about the reality of the early Christian Lord's Supper with this narrative portrayal of resurrection. To answer this question it is valuable to work back from the end of the story, that is, from Mark 6:52: "For they [the disciples] did not understand [*syniēmi*] concerning the loaves, but their heart was hardened."[28] Immediately before this the Jewish disciples had resisted feeding the Gentiles with the Jews in the wilderness (6:36). Indeed they only did so at the express command of Jesus (6:37). Here the disciples fail to comprehend the connection between Jesus's walking on the water and calming the wind, on the one hand, and a proper understanding of the

26. That the story takes the general form-critical category of resurrection appearance (the domination of chaotic opposition in the form of turbulent seas as well as the epiphanic statement "I am" (*egō eimi*; Exod. 3:14) cannot be doubted. See Marcus, *Mark 1–8*, 433; Donahue and Harrington, *Mark*, 213. The resurrection appearance here forces the reader to ask whether the young man's directive at 16:7, "Go and tell his disciples and Peter that he goes before you to Galilee; there you will see him," is meant to direct the reader to this appearance in Galilee. If so, then the liturgical reader has one more reason to encounter the relationship between the loaves of the Eucharist and the resurrected Christ (6:52).

27. They will in fact arrive at Bethsaida, but not until another sea crossing by boat (8:22).

28. Mark 6:52 is often cited by scholars as a key verse in the disciples' overall misunderstanding of Jesus and his mission. But beyond the extended discussion of the ritual of Eucharist in Quesnell, *Mind of Mark*, there is not much focus on the ritual of the Lord's Supper itself. See Marcus, *Mark 1–8*, 427; Taylor, *St. Mark*, 331; Henderson, "Concerning the Loaves," 4, writes about the disciples' misunderstanding of "their active participation in the in-breaking, eschatological kingdom of God" without reference to the actual liturgical context (*artos*) of that "in-breaking."

loaves—that is, the feeding of the five loaves (and the two fish) that has just taken place—on the other. In the ritual feeding narrative the Gentiles have joined with Israel (five loaves and two fish) in the *wilderness* in the final restoration of Israel (five loaves taken up in twelve baskets) and humanity. For the liturgical reader, the connection Mark is making by portraying Jesus walking on the water is between this ritual meal of Jews and Gentiles (*loaves*) and the domination of chaos in the new creation of the resurrection of Christ.

This reader recalls that in Jesus's previous healings, as well as in the resurrection of Jairus's daughter, there has been a distinct emphasis on the *body*: Jesus resurrects (*egeirō*) Peter's mother-in-law by grasping (*krateō*) her hand, and she serves a meal which, one supposes, would have been eaten (1:31); Jairus's daughter is physically resurrected (*anistēmi*) and then eats (5:42–43); the woman with a hemorrhage touches (*haptō*) Jesus's clothing to be saved (5:28–29). Hence it is not unreasonable to assume that the contrast intended in the resurrection scene here is between portraying Jesus's resurrection as a spiritual apparition (*phantasma*) and portraying it as a corporeal, bodily resurrection. Hence for the liturgical reader of Mark the words of Jesus at Mark 6:50, "Take courage, I am [*egō eimi*], have no fear," would not be a statement of so-called high Christology (the idea that Jesus is God)[29] but rather a statement about the identity of the resurrected Jesus as a physical body. Such a reading is supported by what Jesus then does in the narrative: he "*rose [anabainō]* toward them into the boat" (6:51). It was only then that the wind (chaos) died down. The liturgical reader immediately sees the connection to Jesus who rose (*anabainō*) from the waters of baptismal death (chaos) to receive the Spirit (dove) of the new creation (1:10).[30] As Jesus rises (*anabainō*) into the boat with the disciples, chaos is defeated: the wind that was against their voyage physically calms down (6:51). The embodied, resurrected Christ, who dominates chaos and restores creation, is now in the boat with the disciples. So what should the disciples—and the reader—now understand about the loaves (6:52)?

The liturgical reader of Mark would be guided by the narrative to understand (*syniēmi*) the ritual meal (the loaves) of Jews and Gentiles as the enactment of the resurrected *body* of Christ—the Christ who dominates chaos (walking upon the sea and calming the wind)—and to understand the ritual gathering of restored and healed Jews and Gentiles as the physical enactment of the new creation. The narrative emphasis in the description of the ritual

29. Many modern commentators read the statement in this way. For references, see Moloney, *Gospel of Mark*, 134n94.

30. As I noted previously in the discussion of 1:10, the allusions to the Noah story (boat, chaos, dove, and the emergence of new creation from chaos) are part of Mark's narrative design.

meal in the wilderness is on the *eating* by *everyone* gathered (6:42). This description signals the physical nature of the ritual elements as themselves part of the new creation, a theme dramatically picked up in Mark 14:22 ("This loaf is my body") and then later in the Gospel of John (John 6:55–56). This equation of the corporeal nature of the ritual meal with the corporeal nature of the resurrected Christ, the new creation, is the basis of Irenaeus's theology of the Eucharist in the later second century.[31]

But there is more to the liturgical reading of this story. Mark adds the curious detail that Jesus, walking upon the water, "wanted to press on by them." In the narrative this can only mean that Jesus wanted to lead them to where he was forcing them to go, the stated goal of reaching Bethsaida, the predominantly Gentile town on the far side of the lake (6:45; 8:22). In other words, Jesus here desires to lead them toward the Gentile mission and the second meal on Gentile soil, the meal in which Jesus will command the disciples to distribute seven loaves (*artos*) and take up an overabundance (*perisseuma*) of bread pieces, seven very large baskets (*spyris*), after feeding four thousand people (8:1–9). Hence when Mark, after depicting Jesus rising into the boat (*anabainō*) and the headwind calming (6:51), reports that the disciples "did not understand [*syniēmi*] about the loaves [*artos*]" (6:52), the liturgical reader of Mark does understand the narrative connection Mark is making.

Jesus "wanted to press on by them," because it is not enough that the Gentiles have joined with the remnant of Jews (five loaves in twelve baskets feeding five thousand) in the first wilderness meal (6:41–44). The Twelve must now follow Jesus despite persecution (the wind against them)[32] and press on toward Gentile Bethsaida. On the way they will gather Gentiles to the second ritual meal in the wilderness, where the Twelve will distribute *seven* loaves (*artos*) to *four* thousand and take up *seven* baskets (8:1–9).

This, then, is what the disciples do not understand about the loaves. The mission is more than just gathering the Gentiles to the remnant of Israel in the wilderness; it is the expansion of the mission toward Bethsaida, toward the gathering of the Gentiles to the Lord's Supper in Gentile lands. To understand the loaves as the first wilderness feeding of five loaves and twelve baskets is not fully to understand the loaves.[33]

---

31. Bobertz, "Our Opinion Is in Accordance," 79–90.
32. On rowing (*elaunō*) against the wind denoting persecution, see Marcus, *Mark 1–8*, 423.
33. Marcus, *Mark 1–8*, 426, is wrong to dismiss Mark 6:48 ("[Jesus] wanted to press on by them") as depicting Jesus's desire to lead the disciples toward the Gentile mission and Bethsaida. He does so claiming that the Markan community is already predominantly Gentile and situated outside of Palestine. In this he fails to grasp the *narrative* purpose of Mark: to legitimize the mixed (Jewish and Gentile) house churches of the Markan community. In Mark's narrative the Jewish disciples resist this inclusion of Gentiles. This is exactly why Jesus must "force

The cogency of this liturgical reading of the story of the resurrected Jesus walking upon the sea (chaos) is confirmed by how Mark concludes the story. The boat, now with Jesus and the disciples in it, lands not at the original destination of Bethsaida but at Gennesaret on the western shore of the Sea of Galilee. His reputation having preceded him here (the disciples' mission at 6:7?), Jesus apparently extensively evangelizes the area (6:56). And here once again the emphasis is on the healing power of Jesus in *physical* contact. As the diseased here attempt simply to touch Jesus's garment in order to be saved (*sōzō*; 6:56), the reader is reminded again of the woman with a hemorrhage, who also sought only physically to touch Jesus's clothing in order to be saved (*sōzō*; 5:27–29). The corporeal resurrection of Jesus, the body of Christ, is the physical restoration of creation enacted in the ritual meal of Gentiles gathered with Jews. This is what the liturgical reader should understand about the loaves.

Mark 7

Eating Together

And the Pharisees were together with him. And some of the scribes came from Jerusalem. And they noticed that some of his disciples ate the loaves with unclean hands, that is, unwashed. For the Pharisees and all the Jews do not eat unless they wash their hands in a fist [*pygmē*], holding to the tradition of the elders. And they do not eat in the market unless they wash. And there are many other things that they have received and hold to, washing cups and pitchers and bronze vessels. And the Pharisees and scribes asked him, "Why do your disciples not walk according to the tradition of the elders, but eat the loaf with unclean hands?" And he said to them, "Well did Isaiah prophecy concerning you hypocrites, as it is written, 'This people honors me with their lips but their hearts are far distant from me. They worship me in vain, teaching the precepts of men as teachings. They let go the commandment of God to hold fast to the tradition of men.'" And he said to them, "How nicely you reject the commandment of God in order to stand by your tradition. For Moses said, 'Honor your father and your mother,' and, 'Let the one be executed who curses father or mother.' But you say if a man says to his father or mother, 'Any gift you would have received from me is Corban'—you no longer allow him to do anything for his father or mother. You revoke [*akyroō*] the word of God by maintaining your tradition. And you do many things similar to this." And again he called the crowd and said to them, "Listen all of you and understand [*syniēmi*]: nothing

---

[*anankazō*]" the disciples to go toward the Gentile mission here (6:45) and why the disciples question the feeding of the Gentiles in the two ritual meal narratives (6:37; 8:4).

that is outside of a man when it enters into him is able to make him unclean. But those things that come out of a man make him unclean." (7:1–15)

At the beginning of Mark 7, Jesus and the disciples have landed by boat somewhere in the vicinity of Gennesaret. They had been heading toward Bethsaida (6:45), which destination they now will not reach until after the second ritual meal in the wilderness and a following journey by boat (8:22). People from the entire region of Gennesaret have come running to bring to him sick people on pallets. Mark tells us that "as many as touched even the fringe of his garment were saved" (6:56). For the liturgical reader, there are clues that this group that has come running to Jesus includes both Gentiles and Jews. The eagerness with which these people pursue Jesus and the pallets upon which the sick are brought remind the reader of the extensive efforts of the *four* men who brought the Gentile paralytic to Jesus on a pallet (2:1–12). The fact that "as many as touched even the fringe of his garment were saved [*sōzō*]" places the reader again into the story of the Jewish woman with a hemorrhage, who was also saved (*sōzō*) after she managed to touch Jesus's clothing (5:24–34).

If both Jews and Gentiles are being saved by Jesus in the region of Gennesaret, then the remarkable scene at 7:1 can be better explained. Apparently there are Pharisees who have gathered with Jesus, along with scribes who have come from Jerusalem. In other words, these are Jews who have "gathered to him," and, as in Mark 3:22, some of these Jewish scribes have come down from Jerusalem. In the earlier story the scribes had come down from Jerusalem because Jesus, having cast out demons from Gentiles, was about to eat with these Gentiles in his house. Now here some of the disciples are eating the loaves with unwashed hands; that is, their eating ritual is apparently at odds with the eating ritual of other Jews. These scribes then prompt the Pharisees to address concerns over the disciples' ritual meal practice (7:5). Here again the narrative of Mark resembles the episode in Paul's Letter to the Galatians in which Peter and other Jews withdrew from eating the Lord's Supper with Gentile Christians when "certain men from James" came down from Jerusalem to question Christian meal practice (Gal. 2:11).

What best explains the abrupt narrative transition here, from the restoring of Jews and Gentiles in the region of Gennesaret to the sudden appearance of "scribes [who] came down from Jerusalem," is the overall narrative concern of Mark to negate the influence of any ongoing Jewish opposition to the inclusive table fellowship within the Christian community at the time Mark was written. Within the narrative Jews and Gentiles have just eaten together in the wilderness. As a result the narrative depiction of the scribes is likely transparent to certain Jewish opposition to the emerging ritual practice within the churches of Mark's time. So in the narrative the scribes suddenly come down from Jerusalem to address an immediate issue concerning the ritual meal. They too have hardened hearts and do not understand about the loaves (6:52), that is, about the ritual meal of Jews and Gentiles in the wilderness that has just taken place (6:31–44). The ensuing dialogue between Jesus and these Jews points to Mark's intended resolution of this issue in the churches of Mark's time: certain ritual requirements should not prevent Jews and Gentiles from eating the ritual meal together in the churches.

Earlier in the narrative of Mark, in the controversy over making a way (*hodos*) on the Sabbath (2:23–28), the Pharisees pointed out how Jesus's disciples were "doing what is not permitted on the Sabbath." Here, however, the concern about what Jesus's disciples are doing centers not on the written law but on the interpretive tradition that grew up alongside the written law, the authoritative interpretation of Torah, the Oral Torah, that was a particular hallmark of Pharisaic Jews.[34] Perhaps this is also why the scribes, professional legal interpreters, are present in the story.

Here the heart of the story is not a denial of the validity of the Oral Torah. Rather, the Pharisees and scribes simply neglect the first principle of the Oral Torah: it cannot revoke (*akyroō*) the written Torah (7:13). The addendum here, "You do many things similar to this," alerts the readers in Mark's churches that Jewish leaders are apt to be wrong in their pronouncements of Oral Torah. The way is now clear for Jesus, in the narrative transparent to the community situation in Mark's churches, to proclaim valid Oral Torah with respect to ritual meal practice. In the narrative Jesus now calls together the crowd (undoubtedly the Jews and Gentiles who have been saved by touching even the fringe of his garment, 6:56) and pronounces his own Oral Torah: "Listen all of you and understand [*syniēmi*]: nothing that is outside of a man when it enters into him is able to make him unclean. But those things that come out of a man make him unclean" (7:15). Jesus's pronouncement of Oral Torah here concerns whether particular Jewish ritual washing with hands in a fist (*pygmē*; 7:3) is necessary when the churches gather to eat the loaves (the Lord's Supper). The ritual practice of the house church, with the influx of Gentiles, is being established. The narrative is here preparing its ancient readers for the active inclusion of the Gentiles on Gentile soil in the next narrative portrayal of the ritual meal in the wilderness (8:1–9).[35]

34. For extensive discussion of the role of oral tradition in Pharisaic Judaism of the Second Temple period, see A. Y. Collins, *Mark*, 343–63.

35. Within the larger context of Christian house churches at the time Mark was written, this saying of Jesus would lessen the impact of Jewish Oral Torah with respect to ritual meal

And he came into the house away from the crowd. His disciples asked him about the parable [*parabolē*]. And he said to them, "Are you also without understanding? Do you not comprehend that everything outside passes into a man and cannot make him unclean? For it does not enter the heart but the stomach and goes out into the latrine. All foods are made clean." And he said, "What comes out of a person, that is what makes a person unclean." (7:17–20)

Just what "house" Jesus enters here in the area of Gennesaret is unclear. The narrative move to include additional private teaching to the disciples (with the readers of the narrative listening in) likely signals that the narrative here is directly transparent to the churches of Mark's time. The issue is disagreement and hesitation over changes in the ritual meal practice of the house churches.[36] Hence the narrative focus is on the Jewish disciples' potential *resistance* to what Jesus is teaching concerning particular practices at meals ("His disciples asked him about the parable"; 7:17). Jesus's further teaching of these Jewish disciples, transparent to elements of the Jewish community in the house churches of Mark's day ("Are you also without understanding?" in 7:18), is meant to overcome any hesitation about what is emerging as the new ritual pattern within these churches. At such moments the modern reader of Mark literally gets a glimpse into the transformation of the ritual practices in the earliest Christian house churches.

What follows at this juncture in the narrative is the bold claim, in the face of opposition from the Jewish community outside (Pharisees and scribes), as well as hesitation from the Jewish Christian community inside (the disciples), that Jesus has the capacity to adjudicate and pronounce new Oral Torah. At Mark 7:19 Jesus declares that food does not enter the heart but the stomach and so comes out into the latrine. The process of digestion does not intrinsically change the food: it does not make the food clean. Hence the logic of Jesus's new Oral Torah is clear: washing the hands in a particular way, with the fist (*pygmē*), does not change the food: it does not make the food clean. All food, whether clean or not clean, kosher or not kosher, is intrinsically the same at the beginning and at the end.

Jesus's new Oral Torah would stipulate that whether one washes hands or does not wash hands in a particular way (*pygmē*) before food preparation is a matter of indifference. This Jewish ritual does not change the food, and

---

practice. Many modern readers of Mark overlook the fact that Jesus's pronouncement here may have nothing to do with Jewish food laws, which were only gradually let go in many house churches (Acts 15:29), but rather has to do with the manner and extent of ritual washing.

36. Earlier in the narrative, the additional explanation in private had to do with the expansion of the mission to the Gentiles (4:10). It follows that particular ritual meal practices would be an immediate and pressing concern in mixed (Jewish and Gentile) house churches.

so the ritual's absence or presence is of no concern. In the context of Mark's narrative purpose the Jews in the house churches can and should eat the Lord's Supper with the Gentiles without this particular Jewish meal ritual and without other ancient Jewish rituals that remain unknown to us (7:3). What Jesus says here about conduct—to attend to what enters the heart, for the same as what enters will come out (7:19)—fits this reading of the narrative entirely. If vices enter into the heart, they will come out unchanged, and so a person will be defiled by the same vices that entered into his or her heart (7:20–23).

In modern studies of Mark, stemming ultimately from theology emerging in the sixteenth-century Reformation, this particular story in Mark has far too often been read as an attack on external ritual in favor of internal ethical attitude.[37] A close liturgical reading of Mark disputes such a reading. In Mark's narrative purpose the story reflects the very real situation of the house churches of Mark's time, in which some Jewish Christians were anxious to maintain certain Jewish rituals in relation to the Lord's Supper while some Jews in the synagogue saw the absence of such rituals in Christian meal practice as a reason to oppose the Christian mission. Far from being a disparagement of ritual practices, the overall narrative purpose of Mark, to bring Gentiles and Jews together in the Lord's Supper, was itself driven by an appreciation for the substance and reality of the ritual performance of the Lord's Supper. Jews and Gentiles in the ritual meal enact by their eating the meal together the domination of chaos (6:48) and the restoration of a new humanity and creation intended by God from the very beginning (10:6). This is what is to be understood about the loaves (6:52).

37. For extensive discussion of this tendency within modern scholarship, see my article "Prolegomena to a Ritual/Liturgical Reading."

4

The Gentile Mission and the Second Ritual Meal Narrative

The One Loaf

7:24–8:26

Mark 7

The Gentile Woman of Tyre

From there he resurrected [*anistēmi*] and came into the district of Tyre. And when he came into a house [*oikia*], he wanted no one to know about it. But there was no way he could escape notice. But immediately a woman [*gynē*] whose little daughter [*thygatrion*] was possessed by an unclean [*akathartos*] spirit heard about him. She entered and prostrated herself [*prospiptō*] at his feet. And the woman was a Greek, a Syrophoenician in ethnicity. And she asked him to cast out a demon from her daughter [*thygatēr*]. And he said to her, "The children must first be allowed to eat and be satisfied [*chortazō*]. For it is not good to take the loaf [*artos*] from the children and cast it to the small dogs." And she answered and said to him, "Lord [*kyrios*], the small dogs [*kynarion*] under the table also eat from the crumbs of the children." And he said to her, "Because of this word [*logos*], depart; the demon has gone out from your daughter." And having departed to her house, she discovered the child cast upon the bed, and the demon exorcised. (7:24–30)

For liturgical readers, it is the *risen Jesus* (*anistēmi*) who now travels north from Gennesaret to the Gentile land of Tyre. They recall how earlier Jesus *had risen* (*egeirō*) from sleep/death (*katheudō*) under the waters of the sea/chaos (*thalassa*) to come to the Gentile land of the Gerasenes and exorcise the unclean spirit from the legion demoniac (4:35–5:1). Now in Tyre the risen Christ will perform another exorcism for a Gentile, the daughter of a Greek woman, a Syrophoenician. The narrative is enigmatic at this point: "And when he came into a house [*oikia*], he wanted no one to know about it. But there was no way he could escape notice" (7:24).[1] Apparently even Jesus is at first reluctant to be discovered in a house (a house church?) by the Gentiles in this Gentile land. In fact, it will take an argument with this Syrophoenician woman to convince him that Gentiles ought to be fed here in the house![2]

Given Mark's overall narrative purpose to bring Gentiles and Jews together in the Lord's Supper of the early house churches, it is likely that the narrative here is transparent to just how difficult this transition to inclusive meal practice was within these churches, and perhaps especially within the diaspora (Tyre), wherein Jewish identity might have been especially prized and guarded. The narrative here might express keenly Jewish hesitation toward table fellowship with Gentiles. As a result, Jesus in this story has to be convinced of the rightness of inclusive table fellowship by this Gentile woman, a woman who seeks him out in a house and prostrates herself at his feet.

The liturgical reader notices that the earnest faith of this Gentile woman, prostrating (*prospiptō*) herself at the feet of Jesus, matches exactly the express ritual of obeisance of the Jewish leader Jairus (*piptō*; 5:22) and the Jewish woman with a hemorrhage (*prospiptō*; 5:33). And just as it is Jairus's *daughter* (*thygatrion*; 5:23) who is raised, and the woman with a hemorrhage is addressed by Jesus as *daughter* (*thygatēr*; 5:34), so also here the woman's request is on behalf of her *daughter* (*thygatrion*; *thygatēr*). The Gentile woman's request to be part of the community, using the language of family, children (*teknon*), and daughter (*thygatēr*), reminds the reader as well of the earlier story of

1. The reader is reminded of Mark 4:22 with reference to the meaning of the parable of the sower ("for there is nothing hidden except to be made manifest, nor is anything secret but that it might become plain"), a parable which points toward the remarkable success of the coming Gentile mission (4:20).

2. Marcus, *Mark 1–8*, 468; see Donahue and Harrington, *Mark*, 235–38, for affinities with the Elijah and Elisha narratives in the Old Testament (1 Kings 17:8–24; 2 Kings 4:18–37). As commentators have many times pointed out, the Gentile woman in this story is the only person in the entire Gospel to best Jesus in an argument.

the inclusion of Gentiles as family, mother, sister, and brother, at the house in Jewish Capernaum (Mark 3:34–35). Clearly the Gentiles now match the eagerness of the Jews to be part of the new humanity, the new family identity, enacted in the ritual meal of the house church.

The argument begins with the request from the woman to Jesus to cast out an unclean (*akathartos*) spirit from her daughter. Here the reader is immediately brought back to the charge made by the scribes who had earlier come down from Jerusalem to challenge Jesus: "By the prince of demons he is able to cast out demons" (3:22). Jesus's response there, that the *strong* (*ischyros*) man, Beelzebub, must first be bound (*deō*), and then his house plundered (3:27), comes to pass when Jesus casts out the legion demon who had bound (*deō*) the *strong* (*ischyō*) Gerasene Gentile (5:4). Now again here in Tyre, Jesus will cast out a demon from a Gentile on Gentile soil. Yet the result this time is different. The Gentile Gerasenes apparently reject Jesus's mission to them (they beg him to leave their territory, 5:17), while other Gentiles gather with Jesus in the Jewish wilderness for a ritual meal (6:30–44). Here the unclean spirit is exorcised from the Gentile woman's daughter, and many Gentiles will join in a ritual meal with Jesus and the Jewish disciples in a Gentile place (Mark 8:1–9). Following an initial rejection in Gerasa, the mission to the Gentiles in Gentile lands will now be successful.

But the narrative purpose of this exorcism and dialogue between the Gentile woman and Jesus goes further. Mark is careful to introduce a *woman* (*gynē*) to the dialogue with Jesus. Jesus has come to this Gentile place immediately after he has made the correlation between his domination of chaos/water in the resurrection (walking upon the water) and the ritual meal of the wilderness: "For they did not understand about the loaves" (6:52). The *loaves* Jesus referred to there had been the inclusive wilderness meal of Jews and Gentiles (five loaves and two fish), but specifically refers to five thousand Jewish *males* (*anēr*), the final gathering of the elect of Israel, who were gathered with the Gentiles in the twelve baskets (6:43–44). Now here among the Gentiles in Gentile places the understanding of who should participate in the Lord's Supper is set to expand.

In the forthcoming second ritual meal in the wilderness and in Gentile Decapolis (8:1–9), Mark will drop the exclusive reference to only males being present and, coupling that story with that of the Gentile Syrophoenician *woman* here, will indicate to the liturgical reader that both Jews and Gentiles, men and women, are now gathered to eat the Lord's Supper (8:1–9). Following Mark 4:22, what was present but implicit (hidden) within the first ritual meal narrative—the restored creation of five loaves and two fish—will now become manifest in the second ritual narrative. In the second ritual meal the reader sees that the implicit five loaves and two fish (seven) have become the explicit *seven loaves*. The reconstitution of the elect of Israel (five loaves and five thousand men) with some Gentiles will now become the manifest restored creation and new humanity (seven loaves and four thousand men *and women*, 8:9). For the liturgical reader, it cannot be incidental to the purpose of the narrative that a demon is exorcised from the Gentile woman's daughter immediately before this more inclusive meal takes place with the Gentiles on Gentile soil.

In particular the dialogue between Jesus and the Gentile woman, ostensibly about whether Jesus should exorcise a demon from this woman's daughter, goes directly to the heart of who can eat the Lord's Supper. Rather than a disagreement about from whom a demon can be exorcised, the argument immediately turns specifically to a consideration of who can eat the loaf (*artos*). And beyond entirely changing the subject, Jesus's response to the woman refers directly to the first ritual meal narrative: "Let the children first be *satisfied* [*chortazō*]" (7:27). Here the liturgical reader recalls the exact description of that earlier meal: "They all ate and were *satisfied* [*chortazō*]" (6:42). Apparently Jesus's initial argument hinges on what has previously taken place in the narrative. Jesus's claim is that here in the Gentile diaspora first the Jews must be gathered to the Lord's Supper (they must be *satisfied* first), and only then might the Gentiles be added to table fellowship. It is not good to take the loaf from the children and too soon throw it to the small dogs (7:27).[3] Yet given the overall apologetic thrust of Mark's narrative, it is difficult to take this rejoinder from Jesus at face value. It is more likely that Mark has the character Jesus set up the argument in order for the argument to be defeated. Put differently, the narrative here sets up the argument emerging from some Jewish Christians against the inclusion of Gentiles with Jews in the Lord's Supper ("It is not good to take the loaf from the children . . .") in order for the Syrophoenician woman to defeat the initial argument ("Lord, the small dogs under the table also eat").

The Syrophoenician woman's response to Jesus merely states a fact: the small dogs eat the children's crumbs under the table; that is, the children and the small dogs under the table eat the loaf at the same time! More directly, her point is that both the children and the small dogs, Jews and Gentiles, eat the loaf at the same time, and, as in the ritual meal in the wilderness, both are *satisfied* (*chortazō*). And while it is hard not to read this exchange as highlighting the superior status of Jews at the table of the Lord's Supper, it

3. Recall here that narratively Jesus remains hidden, alone with this woman in the house in Tyre.

might also be just a straightforward statement about both men and women, Jews and Gentiles, belonging at the ritual meal in the same house church. Surely Jesus's response to the *woman* indicates the possibility of such a reading: "Because of this word [*logos*], depart; the demon has gone out from your daughter" (7:29). The word (*logos*), of course, is that here in Tyre and in the other lands in the diaspora the Gentiles too belong at the Lord's Supper. And for the liturgical reader especially, the word (*logos*) is the death of Christ, the seed buried in good soil (the Gentiles) and providing an unexpectedly bountiful harvest (4:14–20, 33).

The story of the Syrophoenician woman indicates beyond a doubt that the narrative of Mark intends to advocate for the inclusion of Gentile women in the ritual meal of the Lord's Supper. The earlier stories of saving (*sōzō*) the Jewish woman with a *twelve*-year hemorrhage (5:24–34), of resurrecting (*egeirō*) Peter's mother-in-law (1:29–31), and of resurrecting (*egeirō*) the *twelve*-year-old daughter of the synagogue leader Jairus (5:41) all indicate that in the first ritual meal in the wilderness Jewish *women* were to be counted within the restoration of Israel indicated by the presence of five thousand males as head of each house. Now at this point in the narrative the story of the Syrophoenician woman and her daughter indicates the presence of Gentile women within the four thousand present in the second ritual meal of seven loaves in the Gentile wilderness (8:1–9). In the early Christian house churches, with respect to both Jewish and Gentile members, women were to be a part of the ritual meal, the ritual enactment of the restoration of creation and the new humanity.

The Deaf and Tongue-Tied Gentile

And again he went out from the region of Tyre and came through Sidon to the Sea of Galilee, up to the midst of the region of the Decapolis. And they brought to him a deaf man whose tongue was tied [*mogilalos*]. And they called to him so that he might lay his hand upon him. And he [Jesus] took him away from the crowd by himself [*idios*]. He placed his fingers into the man's ears [*ōtos*] and spit, and he touched his tongue. And looking up to heaven, he groaned and said to him, "*Ephphatha*," that is, "Be opened." And his ears were opened and the bonds of his tongue were loosened and he spoke plainly. And he ordered them to tell no one. But the more he ordered them to say nothing, the louder they proclaimed it. And astonished beyond all measure, they said, "He has done all things well; he has made the deaf to hear and the dumb to speak." (Mark 7:31–37)

Say to those who are discouraged, be strong! Do not fear! Behold, your God pays back with judgment. He will pay back and he will come to save [*sōzō*] you. Then the eyes of the blind will be opened, and the ears [ōtos] of the deaf will hear. The lame shall leap like a deer, and the tongue that is tied [mogilalos] will be loosened. For water will gush in the wilderness [erēmos] and create a ravine in the thirsty earth. The dry place will become a marsh, and a fountain of water will come to the thirsty earth. The joy of birds will find a home in the reeds and marsh. It will be called a clean [katharos] way [hodos], a holy way [hodos], and the unclean [akathartos] will not come there. It will not be the way [hodos] of the unclean. And those who are scattered [diaspeirō] will come upon it and will not be led astray from it. (Isa. 35:4–8 LXX)

In one of the most discussed verses in the Gospel of Mark, Jesus appears now to arrive "in the midst of the region of the Decapolis" (7:31).[4] The narrative now directly echoes part of Isaiah, that the ears of the deaf will hear and the one who is tongue-tied will proclaim (35:5–6). The people of the Decapolis, who in the narrative were most likely to have been evangelized by the former legion demoniac,[5] bring to Jesus a deaf and tongue-tied man and ask Jesus to "lay his hand upon him" (7:32). In this request the physical restoration of creation is to be brought to Gentile soil. Jesus takes the man aside from the crowd who has brought him there and very *physically* touches his ears and tongue. The Aramaic proclamation, *ephphatha*, translated by Mark for his Greek readers, "Be opened," signals the Gentiles' hearing the gospel and proclaiming it further in this Gentile area.

Here the opening of the *ears* (ōtos) is aimed directly at the liturgical reader of Mark. It signals the proper understanding of the parable of the sower and seed in Mark 4: "Whoever has ears [ōtos] to hear, let that person listen" (4:9). The seed of the parable of the sower has here in the Decapolis fallen on good soil, Gentile soil, and has taken root, yielding thirty-, sixty-, and a hundredfold (4:8–9). What was hidden (Jesus in the house where the Syrophoenician woman finds him; the deaf and tongue-tied man having been pulled to a private place by Jesus) has become manifest; what was secret has come to light (4:22–23), namely, the success of the Gentile mission. Indeed it was on account of the "word [logos]" that the demon left the Syrophoenician woman's daughter, the word which in the parable is the buried seed that springs forth in abundance

4. Contra A. Y. Collins, *Mark*, 369, who places Jesus somewhere near the Sea of Galilee in a Jewish area, I would agree with Donahue and Harrington, *Mark*, 239, "Mark wants to have Jesus move north, then east, and finally south to compass the whole of the southern Phoenician (Gentile) territory prior to his journey to Jerusalem in 8:22–10:52." This would indicate that the second ritual meal in the wilderness is meant to be the gathering of the Gentiles (four thousand, with seven baskets) with the Jews previously gathered (five thousand, with twelve baskets) prior to the *way* (hodos) of the passion.

5. The reader recalls here that the Gerasene demoniac was not allowed to follow Jesus but was sent to his friends at home in the Decapolis (5:20).

(4:8), the death and resurrection of Christ now manifest in the success of the Gentile mission on Gentile soil. What is more, the hidden presence of the Gentiles (the fish discovered among the loaves) in the first feeding of the five thousand is now revealed as the narrative moves toward the second ritual meal of seven loaves feeding the four thousand (8:1–9).

In addition, the narrative sequence here, the exorcism of the Syrophoenician woman's daughter, who is unclean (*akathartos*) and so made clean (*katharos*) by exorcism, followed by the cure of the Gentile deaf man whose tongue was tied (*mogilalos*), is undoubtedly influenced by Mark's understanding of Isaiah 35:4–8 in the Septuagint (translated above). Here Isaiah provides an eschatological description of the final redemption of Israel in the wilderness (*erēmos*) and the restoration of creation to its original and pristine origin. Isaiah prophecies that there will be "a clean way [*hodos kathara*], a holy way [*hodos hagia*], and the unclean will not come there. It will not be the way of the unclean [*hodos akathartos*]" (Isa. 35:8).[6]

At the beginning of the Gospel, Mark had declared from Isaiah that this way (*hodos*) of Jesus was being prepared by John the Baptist (1:2).[7] Through his baptism into death, the way (*hodos*) of the passion (10:38; 10:52), Jesus is given the Spirit of the restored creation (1:10). So with the exorcism of the unclean spirit from the Syrophoenician woman's daughter and the restoration of the Gentile deaf and tongue-tied man, Christian Gentiles have been made clean. Following Isaiah's prophecy, both Jews and Gentiles who have been scattered in the diaspora can now join Jesus on the way (*hodos*), that is, the way of the passion. They will now be included in the wilderness (*erēmos*) meal of 8:1–9. They will not grow weary on the way (*hodos*; 8:3). They will not be led astray. In sum, the eschatological vision of Isaiah is being realized within the narrative of Mark. So here in the narrative of Mark the Gentiles themselves proclaim from Isaiah: "He has done all things well; he has made the deaf to hear and the dumb to speak" (7:37).

---

6. The liturgical reader now realizes that the inclusion of both Jews and Gentiles on the way (*hodos*) in Mark is especially marked by Jesus's domination of the unclean spirits, that is, the creation of the clean way (*hodos kathara*), the holy way (*hodos hagia*) of Isa. 35:8. This takes place in two stages. The first is the exorcism of the unclean spirit (*pneuma akatharton*) in the Jewish synagogue (1:26). The extension of this way (*hodos*) for the Gentiles is prepared for in the confrontation with the scribes over the meaning of Jesus's casting out of the unclean spirits (*pneuma akatharton*; 3:22–30). Jesus is able to bind the strong one, the unclean spirit (*pneuma akatharton*) of the Gentile Gerasene (5:8), and so also the unclean spirit (*pneuma akatharton*) from the Gentile Syrophoenician woman's daughter (7:25). The way (*hodos*) of the Gentiles and women for participation in the Lord's Supper in Mark 8:1–9 has been established.

7. Perhaps an allusion to his martyrdom, which takes place in Mark 6:17–29.

Mark 8

Gentiles at the Meal

And in those days again [*palin*] a great crowd was there. And they did not have anything to eat. So he called his disciples and said to them, "I have pity on the crowd, for they have already [*ēdē*] been with me for three days, and they do not have anything to eat. And if I send them to their house [*oikos*] to fast [*nēstis*], they will grow weak [*eklyomai*] on the way [*hodos*], and some of them have come from a great distance [*makrothen*]." And his disciples answered and said to him, "How can *these people* eat their fill [*chortazō*] of loaves here in the wilderness [*erēmia*]?" And he asked them, "How many loaves do you have?" And they said, "Seven." And he commanded the crowd to recline for a meal upon the earth [*gē*]. And taking [*lambanō*] the seven loaves, he gave thanks [*eucharisteō*]. He broke [*klaō*] and gave [*didōmi*] [the loaves] to his disciples so that they might distribute them. And the disciples distributed them. And they had a few small fish [*ichthydion oligon*]. Having blessed [*eulogeō*] these, he [Jesus] said that they should be distributed. And they ate and were satisfied [*chortazō*]. They gathered an overabundance [*perisseuma*] of bread pieces, seven very large baskets [*spyris*]. There were four thousand present. And he dismissed them. (8:1–9)

The casting out of the unclean spirit from the Syrophoenician woman's daughter (7:25–30) and the physical cure of the deaf and tongue-tied Gentile (7:32–37), that is, the way (*hodos*) made holy and clean (*hagia, kathara*) and the creation restored to its original condition (Isa. 35:5–8), is the prelude to the inclusion of women and Gentiles at the Lord's Supper. This second major ritual meal immediately follows in the narrative. The setting is still the Gentile Decapolis (7:31), and the time is nondescript, "in those days" (8:1).[8] And here Mark could hardly be more transparent to his theological motive for writing the narrative: "Again a great crowd was there. And they did not have anything to eat" (8:1). The "again" signals to the reader that the crowd constitutes those same Gentiles who had so eagerly brought the deaf and tongue-tied man to Jesus to be restored and the same crowd who stubbornly refused to be silent about Jesus's restoration of the man (7:36). Now these Gentiles are here in the wilderness (8:4), cleansed, restored, and proclaiming Jesus, *and they have nothing to eat* (8:2)! Will they be invited to the Lord's Supper?

Jesus now summons his Jewish disciples to tell *them* that he has compassion on the crowd of Gentiles and then *repeats* the fact that these Gentiles

8. The first feeding narrative on Jewish soil had taken place on the Sabbath (6:2).

have nothing to eat.[9] At the literal level of the narrative, the indication that these folks have been with Jesus for three days means nothing more than their supply of food has apparently run its course. But the Markan narrative is more careful with time references than such a reading will allow. *Three days* plays a pivotal role in how Mark understands the passion of Christ, and in how the liturgical reader understands the manifestation of the resurrection that takes place in the context of the ritual meal.[10]

In the forthcoming passion narrative, at the pivotal moments in the trial by night before the Sanhedrin and his execution on the cross, Jesus is accused of saying that he would destroy the temple made by human hands and, *during the course of three days* (*dia triōn hēmerōn*), build another temple not made with hands (14:58; 15:29). And though the readers of Mark are aware that the literal accusation is false (the temple was destroyed by the Romans, not Jesus), they also know the accusation to be ironically true in a different way. The church of Jews and Gentiles, the temple not made with hands, the house of prayer for the Gentiles (11:17), has indeed been built during the way (*hodos*) of the three days of Jesus's passion. The Gentiles are baptized into the death of Jesus and with the Jews have come to form the new temple, the body of Christ, the church gathered in the Lord's Supper.

In each of the three passion predictions in Mark Jesus declares that the Son of Man will rise *after three days* (*meta treis hēmeras*; 8:31; 9:31; 10:34). These predictions prove true within the narrative: Jesus dies and is placed into a tomb prior to sundown on the day prior to Sabbath (Friday, 15:46). This is day one. Jesus remains in the tomb on the Sabbath, that is, day two. Jesus rises sometime after sundown on the Sabbath (16:2), and so the resurrection takes place *after three days*. Here in the second feeding narrative the Gentile crowd has been with Jesus for three days, and it is after three days that Jesus, according to the predictions within the narrative, will rise. As a result, Mark's careful use of time here, "They have already [*ēdē*] been with

9. Here again the narrative appears to be transparent to the time of Mark's church: Jesus has to tell his Jewish disciples that he has compassion on this crowd because they cannot eat. The statement implies the reluctance of the Jewish disciples to do anything about the situation, that is, the reluctance of some Jewish Christians of Mark's time to include the Gentiles within a common ritual meal.

10. Here again is the importance of Mark 6:52 ("For they did not understand about the loaves"), a reference to the manifestation of the resurrection: Jesus walks upon the sea. Also, within the tradition being used by Mark here there is an apparent adaptation of the story in Exod. 3:8, 18 (LXX): "I came down [*katabainō*] to deliver them from the hand of the Egyptians and to lead them out [*exagō*] of that land . . . to proceed on the way [*hodos*] for three days [*treis hēmerai*] into the wilderness [*erēmos*] so that we might sacrifice to our God." In Mark the Gentiles have joined with Jews in the way (*hodos*) of the exodus to the wilderness, the three-day passion (sacrifice) of Christ.

me for three days," places the liturgical reader of Mark on notice to expect the resurrection to manifest itself in the ritual meal about to be celebrated.[11]

Here the fundamental purpose of Mark's narrative is brought to the fore: in response to some Jewish Christian reluctance to include the Gentiles at the one table (one loaf for Jews and Gentiles), Mark points to the fact that the Gentiles deserve to be at the table through (*dia*) the death of Christ enacted in the ritual of their baptism.[12] They are here akin to the blind Gentile Bartimaeus, whom Jesus meets *immediately* after declaring that the Son of Man came to give his life as a ransom for *the many* (10:45). In that story Bartimaeus, literally "the son of Timaeus,"[13] throws off his cloak in a type of baptismal disrobing (*apoballō*), having been called to rise (*egeirō*) and follow Jesus on the way (*hodos*; 10:50–52).[14] So in the present context, when Mark reports that the Gentiles here have already been with Jesus on the way (*hodos*) for three days, the liturgical reader senses a strong allusion to their baptismal death and rightful place at the Lord's Supper.

The declaration by Jesus here, "And if I send them to their house [*oikos*] to fast [*nēstis*], they will grow weak [*eklyomai*] on the way [*hodos*], and some of them have come from a great distance [*makrothen*]" (8:3), takes the liturgical reader back to 2:18–20, where the question is posed: Why do the disciples of John and the Pharisees fast (*nēsteuō*) while the disciples of Jesus do not fast? Jesus's response there, "The wedding guests are not able to fast [*nēsteuō*] while the bridegroom is with them" (2:19), would now apply to these Gentiles gathered with Jesus and the disciples in the wilderness: these Gentiles are the wedding guests, and the bridegroom is here. These Gentiles cannot be sent *a great distance* (*makrothen*) back to their house to fast. In the early formation of the Markan house churches, this is the distance of social, civil, and religious separation that these Gentiles have traversed to become part of the Christian community. Previous ties with family and city have been severed, and now these Gentiles must be fed by the disciples.[15]

---

11. The connection of the Lord's Supper (the loaves) to the manifestation of the resurrection is also present at Mark 6:52.

12. This is quite possibly the meaning of the reference to "the other boats" (4:36) that are part of the sea crossing in Mark 4:35–41. These boats would include Gentiles (3:8) and would have found themselves under the sea in the storm.

13. Bartimaeus is quite literally "the son of Timaeus." The *Timaeus*, Plato's dialogue about the origin of the universe, was one of the most widely read treatises in the ancient world. See Lathrop, *Holy Ground*, 25.

14. The stubborn faith of this Gentile, the son of Timaeus, is demonstrable: having been told to go (*hypage*), he instead follows Jesus on the way (*hodos*; 10:52, cf. 1:18).

15. In the Septuagint those who have come a great distance (*makrothen*) are Gentiles (Josh. 9:6; Isa. 60:4). This is also the usage in Acts 2:39; 22:21; Eph. 2:11–12: see Donahue and Harrington, *Mark*, 244.

Here also the peculiar use of the singular word *house* (*oikos*) is likely transparent to Mark's narrative purpose at the time of the Gospel's writing.[16] The Gentiles should not be dismissed to a Lord's Supper in a separate house church but belong gathered with the Jews for the ritual meal. In the narrative they are to eat with Jesus and the Jewish disciples (*oikos*; 3:20, 32–35). The clear implication is that separate ritual meals in separate house churches create the danger of apostasy—growing weak (*eklyomai*)—with respect to the *way* (*hodos*). Mark will from here on increasingly emphasize the call to follow Jesus to the cross—that is, the way (*hodos*)—in the face of constant temptation to deny Jesus and save one's own life and property (8:34, 38; 14:72). For Mark, the persecution the community is suffering in his own time comes at the hands of both Jewish and Gentile authorities (13:9) and is directly tied to the suspect practice of inclusive ritual meals. Those who will be gathered and saved from the *wind* (*anemos*; 4:37; 6:48) of persecution, the chosen ones (*eklektos*), will come from the *four* (*tessares*) winds, from the boundary of earth to the boundary of heaven (13:27). Separate house churches for Jews and Gentiles would erase the scandal of the cross and the need to take up the cross in the time that Mark is writing his Gospel.[17]

The question that is now asked by the Jewish disciples in response to Jesus tends to confirm this reading of Mark's narrative purpose: "How can *these people* [Gentiles and women] eat their fill [*chortazō*] of loaves [*artos*] here in the wilderness [*erēmia*]?"[18] The liturgical reader is now made aware that the issue is not simply food, but the *loaves* (*artos*) of the Lord's Supper. And of course the location is now specified as the wilderness (*erēmia*). Though the narrative location is somewhere in the Gentile Decapolis (7:31), the reader is again brought to the same ritual space of the Lord's Supper, the wilderness (*erēmia*) that marked the earlier ritual meal (*erēmos*; 6:35).

Many modern interpreters of Mark understand the dialogue here as highlighting the ignorance of the disciples.[19] They have seen Jesus feed people once before in the wilderness, so how is it they would doubt it could be done again?

---

16. The literal text, of course, defies logic: a large crowd (*polys ochlos*) would not fit into a single house.

17. We know of this tension already from Paul's Letters. From the structure of the argument in Galatians it appears that Paul's initial persecution of the Christian church was based on the practice of inclusive table fellowship (1:13; 5:11). This is the ritual practice he strives so mightily to defend in his letter, what he describes as the very heart of his gospel (2:11).

18. The use of the nonspecifically gendered term "these [*houtos*]" (translated here as "these people"), as well as the word for eating their fill (*chortazō*, to be satisfied) points to the inclusion of the Syrophoenician woman and her daughter, those who will be satisfied (*chortazō*) with loaves (*artos*; 7:27). See Marcus, *Mark 1–8*, 492; Donahue and Harrington, *Mark*, 244.

19. E.g., Focant, *Mark*, 312; Marcus, *Mark 1–8*, 495; Moloney, *Gospel of Mark*, 153–54.

Such readings fail to take into account Mark's consistent narrative purpose. The *Jewish* disciples again pose the question. These disciples are *again* reluctant to include the Gentiles at the same meal with the Jews. With reference to Isaiah's exodus event that the Lord's Supper enacts in ritual (1:3–4), the Jewish disciples here claim that the Gentiles are not to be fed manna (loaves) by God in the wilderness, especially wilderness in a Gentile place.

For the liturgical reader of Mark, the answer to the Jewish disciples' question has just been given: these Gentiles have already been with Jesus *for three days*. They have been entombed with Christ in the ritual of baptism. They were present—marked implicitly as the fish who were unexpectedly found to be there with the loaves—in the first ritual meal in Jewish Galilee. Now they are here explicitly present in the seven loaves in the second wilderness ritual in Gentile Decapolis. In narrative terms what happens now is the manifestation of Jesus's earlier statement: what was hidden has become plain (4:22).

So in response to the disciples' question—"How can *these people* [Gentiles and women] eat their fill of loaves here in the wilderness?"—Jesus asks yet another question: "How many loaves do you have?" Again, on a literal level the implication behind the question is whether there are enough loaves to feed the crowd that has gathered. The literal answer from the Jewish disciples would at first indicate an insufficient number: seven loaves. Yet for the liturgical reader tuned to the symbolism in the narrative, this is the perfect answer with the perfect number. This is the provision given by God in the first seven-day creation. The Lord's Supper now provides the fulfilled meaning of the story of God's provision of the manna in the exodus wilderness. Here is the return to the intended seven-day creation, the world prior to the first human disobedience and its consequences.[20] Here in the ritual meal of this Genesis garden, humanity is unified, Jew and Gentile, male and female, and provided for by God.

So for the liturgical reader, *these people* can be fed in the wilderness *because* there are *seven* loaves. This is not the five loaves (Israel) and the two found fish, Gentiles, implicit in the first feeding (6:38), but an explicit seven *loaves*. Gentiles and Jews, men and women, together in the wilderness of the new Eden. Moreover, the setting no longer recalls the camp of Israel, as in the first feeding narrative (Exod. 18:21; Mark 6:40), but rather these Gentiles are commanded by Jesus to recline on the earth (*gē*) itself, the Genesis garden.

Jesus himself performs the ritual action of the meal. He *takes* the seven loaves and *gives thanks* (8:6).[21] Then, in a deliberative ritual action Jesus gives

---

20. Gen. 3:19 (LXX): "From the sweat of your face you shall eat the loaf."
21. The ritual action changes here from the first ritual meal narrative. In the Jewish context of the first ritual, and commensurate with Jewish meal practice, Jesus *blesses* the loaves (6:41); in the Gentile context of the second ritual narrative, and commensurate with the ritual

the seven loaves to his disciples "in order that they [the Jewish disciples] might serve the loaves to the crowd." And Mark tells us that the disciples "served the loaves to the crowd" (8:6). In this Gentile setting the Jewish disciples serve seven loaves in the wilderness to a Gentile crowd reclined upon the earth. The liturgical reader of Mark understands that Jesus himself, in these ritual actions, has overcome the hesitation of the disciples to feed *these people*. They are now part of the inclusive Lord's Supper, and the Jewish disciples have become the servants of these Gentiles. They are now beginning to understand the imitation of the Son of Man, who came not to be served but to serve (10:45). Indeed this call to service is the foundation of the Christian community in Mark (9:35; 10:43).

In a deliberate change from the earlier ritual meal description, the narrative now reports that they "had a few small fish [*ichthydion oligon*]" (8:7).[22] In the first ritual meal, in a Jewish context, the disciples found exactly two fish (*ichthys*) to go with the five loaves. The implicit number seven (five plus two) revealed the unexpected presence of Gentiles at the meal. Here in the second ritual meal, in a Gentile context, the number of the loaves, seven, is explicit from the beginning. Hence there is no number of fish given. In the first feeding narrative there was no ritual action over the fish. Yet in a particularly demonstrative lesson on Jewish soil, as if to say that the Gentiles are indeed present, *Jesus himself* distributes the fish to both Jews and Gentiles who were there (6:41). In the second feeding narrative the fish have become part of the ritual meal of the seven loaves. Jesus *gives thanks over the fish* and commands *the disciples* to distribute the fish (8:7). The Jewish disciples are to ritually include and care for the Gentiles. Put differently, for the liturgical reader, the Gentiles, now in Genesis (seven loaves), are fully included in the elements of the ritual meal itself: both loaves and fish are served and so present at the table.

The earlier question of the Jewish disciples to Jesus—"How can *these people* eat their fill [*chortazō*] of loaves here in the wilderness?"—has now been answered. Mark tells us that "they *all* [including the Gentiles] ate their fill [*chortazō*]." Moreover, the fact that the Gentiles are now included takes the reader back to the parable of the seed in Mark 4: the one able to hear the

---

practice of the emerging diaspora house churches, Jesus *gives thanks* (the word *Eucharist*) for the loaves. As will be explored in detail below, the final meal scene in Mark, the so-called Last Supper, integrates both these ritual actions: Jesus *blesses* the bread and *gives thanks* over the cup, the latter being explicitly associated with the death of Christ and baptism (9:38; 14:22–23).

22. In a change from the description in the first ritual meal narrative—two fish (*ichthys*)—Mark uses the diminutive of the Greek word for fish here, "small fish [*ichthydion*]." The use of the diminutive here matches the use of the diminutive for dog (*kynos*), that is, "small dogs [*kynarion*]," and the use of the diminutive "small daughter [*thygaterion*]" in the story of the Syrophoenician woman. The parallel points the reader to the Gentiles in both stories.

parable (4:9), the one whose deafness has been overcome (7:35), now realizes that here is the superabundance of the Gentile mission: thirty-, sixty-, and a hundredfold yield (4:8). In this ritual meal in the Gentile Decapolis, the disciples take up not just the full (*plērōma*) regular baskets (*kophinos*) of loaf pieces (*klasma*),[23] as they did in the first ritual meal in Galilee (6:43), but now rather a *superabundance* (*perisseuma*) in seven very *large baskets* (*spyris*)[24] of loaf pieces (*klasma*). The reader who can now hear and *understand* (*syniēmi*; 6:52; 8:21) realizes that the laws of *kashrut*, a separation of Jew from Gentile, no longer apply to the loaves of the Lord's Supper (7:14–15): an astounding number of Gentiles have been joined at the meal with the Jews in the restoration of the seven-day creation.

The second ritual meal narrative concludes by reporting that there were four thousand present. Besides the obvious reference to the Gentiles with the number four,[25] the telling omission here is the specific reference to males from the first feeding narrative: "Those who ate the loaves were five thousand *males*" (6:44). What Mark had implicitly indicated in the earlier narrative, that the Gentiles were in fact present within the ritual gathering (6:40; Exod. 18:21, 25), has now been made manifest (Mark 4:22). Even Jesus's own reluctance to include Gentile men and women at the common table, demonstrated in the story of the Syrophoenician woman (7:24–30), has been overcome. More important, the reader now begins to understand the inevitable logic of the ritual enactment of the Lord's Supper: from wilderness to the restoration of the Genesis garden, the redemption of Israel (twelve baskets) is the unification of humanity in Genesis (seven baskets), Jews and Gentiles, male and female.[26]

23. In the early Christian churches *klasmata* becomes a technical term for the loaf pieces of the Lord's Supper (Did. 9.4; John 6:12).

24. In Acts the basket, *spyris*, is large enough to carry a person! (Acts 9:25).

25. The reader is reminded of the *four* Gentiles who, having lowered the paralytic through a roof opening, are commended for their faith (2:1–12). As I noted in the discussion of that story, in both stories the number four is specially noted: the paralytic is carried by "four" (rather than, e.g., four *men*), while here four thousand are fed (rather than, as in 6:44, five thousand *males*). For the universal connotations to the number four, see the discussion of the calling of the four disciples (1:14–20) and the story of the paralytic (2:1–12) above.

26. Here there is an interesting convergence with Fowler's careful redactional study of the two Markan feeding narratives. *Loaves and Fishes* concludes, on the basis of vocabulary and context, that the second feeding narrative (8:1–9) is taken from a pre-Markan source and the first feeding narrative (6:30–44) is a Markan composition based on the story of 8:1–9. While my interpretation of the symbolism present in both stories diverges widely from Fowler's study, it is worth noting how Fowler's study supports what I argue here. If Mark is attempting to explain the origin and nature of the inclusive ritual meal symbolized fully in 8:1–9, then the composition of 6:30–44 gives us the "hidden" presence of the Gentiles in the two fish that produce the *unspoken* number seven and the tie-in to the commandment to "fish" for people at the very beginning of the narrative (1:17). Indeed the corresponding feeding cycles (6:30–44;

Loaves and Boat

And he immediately compelled [*anankazō*] his disciples to get into the boat and to go out before him, toward Bethsaida, while he dismissed the crowd. (6:45)

He dismissed the four thousand and immediately got into a boat. He came with his disciples to the region of Dalmanutha. And the Pharisees came out and began to dispute with him. They sought from him a sign from heaven [*ouranos*], for they wanted to test him. And groaning deeply in his spirit, he said, "Why does this generation seek a sign? Amen! I will tell you if this generation will be given a sign." He dismissed them and again he got into the boat and came to the other side. (8:9–13)

In a narrative parallel to the conclusion of the first ritual meal description, the second ritual meal is followed by the description of another boat journey. In the earlier narrative Jesus *compelled* (*anankazō*) the disciples to begin the journey toward Bethsaida (that is, toward the Gentiles), while he stayed back to dismiss the crowd (6:45). The obvious reason to compel the disciples to move toward the Gentile mission was so that the disciples could be brought to understand that the success of the mission in the face of persecution (the chaos of the waters and strong contrary winds) depended on the presence of the resurrected Christ in the ritual of the Lord's Supper. The resurrected Christ dominates the powers of chaos by walking upon the sea and shutting down the wind (6:51). After rising from the water (*anabainō*) into the boat, he asks the incredulous disciples what they do not understand about the loaves (6:52).

Now at the end of the second ritual meal there is no reason to force the disciples to journey toward the Gentile mission; that mission has already been established in the feeding of the four thousand Gentiles (men and women) in a Gentile land (Decapolis). So here Jesus gets into the boat with the Jewish disciples and comes to the district of Dalmanutha.[27] Apparently they are back within a Jewish context, and the Pharisees come out of nowhere to dispute with Jesus. They seek a sign from *heaven* (*ouranos*) in order to test Jesus. At the same time the reader is aware that in the first ritual meal narrative the Gentiles were present as Jesus looked up to *heaven* (*ouranos*) at the very moment he blessed the loaves and performed the ritual actions of the meal

8:1–9), lake crossings (6:45–56; 8:10), controversies with Pharisees (7:1–23; 8:11–12), stories of bread or leaven (7:24–30; 8:13–21), and healing stories (7:31–37; 8:22–26) also point to this understanding of the narrative. Mark is explaining the hidden presence of the Gentiles in the story of Israel, a presence that has now become manifest in the new creation (Genesis) enacted within early Christian ritual.

27. Dalmanutha or Magdala? The manuscripts are divided as to the location.

(6:41).[28] The first ritual meal in the wilderness was therefore the manifestation of a sign from heaven. The reader would also presume that within the second ritual meal the deaf and tongue-tied Gentile was present, his restoration having been accomplished as Jesus looked up to heaven (*ouranos*; 7:34). So when the Pharisees here request a sign from heaven (*ouranos*), the liturgical reader is fully aware of the irony. Had they eyes to see and ears to hear (4:12), they would realize, along with the readers of Mark, that the sign from heaven had just been given in the inclusion of the Gentiles at the Lord's Supper. In Mark's narrative the presence of the Gentiles, now at the ritual table with the Jews, and indeed the Jewish disciples serving the Gentiles through the distribution of the loaves (8:6), comprise the greatest of all possible signs from heaven.

The declaration that a sign may not be given to this generation (8:12)—set in the immediate context of the Pharisees' seeking of a sign—must indicate that in the narrative there is now a shift away from an active mission to the Jews. These Jews will not share in the sign of the inclusive Lord's Supper. So Jesus immediately departs to the "other side [*peran*]," namely, now toward the Gentiles.

For any reader of Mark, the simple narrative sequence here is hard to follow. At 8:10, after the gathering of the seven baskets from feeding the four thousand, Jesus crosses with his disciples to Dalmanutha but then oddly appears to cross back again by himself (8:13). Yet Mark 8:14 implies that the disciples are in fact there on the boat with Jesus for the return voyage, and this sets up the context for the dialogue which follows between Jesus and his disciples. Understanding this next dialogue between Jesus and the disciples is pivotal for understanding the overall narrative purpose of Mark.

> Now they [the disciples] had neglected to bring loaves; and they had only one loaf with them on the boat. He took his disciples aside and said to them, "Watch and be aware [*blepō*] of the leaven of the Pharisees and the leaven of Herod." And they [the disciples] talked among themselves, saying that they did not have any *loaves* [*artos*]. And knowing this, he [Jesus] said to them, "Why are you saying among yourselves that you do not have any loaves? Do you not yet discern or understand [*syniēmi*]? Is your heart hardened [*pōroō*]? Having eyes do you not see [*blepō*], and having ears do you not hear [*akouō*]? And do you not remember? When I broke [*klaō*] the five loaves for the five thousand, how many baskets [*kophinos*] full [*plērēs*] of loaf pieces [*klasma*] did you gather?"

28. The liturgical reader notes as well that it is the *voice from heaven* (*ouranos*) at the baptism that declares Jesus to be the Son (1:11), a title which Mark carefully ties to the Gentile mission: it is the Son of Man who has the authority on earth to forgive the sins of the Gentile paralytic (2:10), and the Son of Man who gives his life as a ransom for the *many*, a reference to the salvation of the Gentiles (10:45).

And they said to him, "Twelve." "When I broke the seven loaves for the four thousand, how many very large baskets [*spyris*] abundantly filled [*plērōma*] with loaf pieces [*klasma*] did you take up?" And they said to him, "Seven." And he said to them, "Do you not yet understand [*syniēmi*]?" (8:14–21)

Even the casual reader of Mark 8:14 can become confused. Here is my literal translation of the verse compared with two major modern translations:

Now they [the disciples] had neglected to bring loaves [*artous*]; and they had only one loaf [*arton*] with them on the boat. (my translation)

Now the disciples had forgotten to bring any bread; and they had only one loaf with them in the boat. (NRSV)

They had forgotten to bring bread, and they had only one loaf with them in the boat. (NAB)

So did the disciples bring bread aboard the boat or not? What is obscured in both modern translations (and others that could be consulted) is Mark's careful attention in the Greek original to the distinction between the plural *loaves* (*artous*) and the singular *loaf* (*arton*). On that score the statement is really quite literal: the disciples did not have loaves, but they did have one loaf. The ensuing dialogue crucially hinges on this difference between loaves (plural) and loaf (singular).[29]

Jesus's warning to the disciples to look out for the yeast of the Pharisees and the yeast of Herod brings the liturgical reader back to Mark 3:6, where, following the restoration of the man with the withered hand, the Pharisees *and the Herodians* conspire to destroy Jesus. Once again the reader is reminded that the first notice of the plot to destroy Jesus comes on the heels of a series of five controversies in which the inclusion of the Gentiles in the Lord's Supper is the main point of tension (2:1–3:6). As a result of that threat, Jesus withdrew from the synagogue toward the sea, followed by a large crowd of Jews and *Gentiles* (3:7–8).

Hence the warning at 8:15, "Watch and be aware of the leaven of the Pharisees and the leaven of Herod," for the reader of the narrative as well as

29. The resonance here is all the way back to the story of the loaves at 2:23–28, the loaves of the first ritual meal in the wilderness (6:31–44), and the disciples' failure to understand the loaves at 6:52. The Septuagint version of the story of David and the priest Abimelech, in which David is able to make clean the five loaves of offering and so able to give the five loaves to his men, features a wordplay on one loaf as opposed to five loaves of offering. In the temple on that day there was not one loaf but five loaves, and David apparently ends up giving one warm loaf to each of his men (1 Sam. 21:1–6).

the disciples in the story, is obvious: the Pharisees and Herod want to destroy Jesus. But for many of the disciples here, who were chosen by Jesus only after the controversies of 2:1–3:6 and after the threat of the Pharisees and Herodians to destroy Jesus (3:6), this warning comes out of the blue. That is, from these disciples' perspective in the narrative a warning about Pharisees and Herodians makes little sense. As a result they conclude the warning must be about the fact that they have do not have loaves (plural) and have only one loaf. In other words, they would have heard Jesus as saying, watch and be aware of the leaven of the Pharisees and Herodians with respect to the one loaf you have with you on the boat.

As a result the dialogue at this point centers on what sort of leaven inhabits the one loaf on board the boat: Is it symbolic of opposition to the inclusion of Gentiles at the Lord's Supper? And what about the other option?

"And they [the disciples] talked among themselves, saying that they did not have any *loaves* [*artous*]" (8:16).[30] For the casual reader of the usual English translation the disciples appear to be troubled because they have no bread on the boat (and therefore no leaven). But the Greek text does not say this. Rather the Greek text says clearly that they do have one loaf on the boat. So they are obviously reacting to Jesus's concern about the leaven with a concern that they do not have with them loaves (plural). But here they miss Jesus's point entirely: they do have one loaf with them, and *that loaf* could in fact be spoiled by the leaven of the Pharisees and the leaven of Herod.

Jesus's response to the disciples recognizes the interior conflict among these Jewish disciples precisely on this point. Mark tells us that Jesus knows and understands their reaction and asks them, "Why are you saying among yourselves that you do not have any loaves?" (8:17). Jesus's challenge here concerns the reality of the one loaf on the boat and the disciples' apparent concern about not having loaves with them on the boat.

Once again what Jesus says in response to the disciples brings the liturgical reader back to an earlier point in the narrative:

Do you not yet discern or understand [*syniēmi*]? Is your heart [*kardia*] hardened [*pōroō*]? Having eyes do you not see [*blepō*], and having ears do you not hear [*akouō*]? (8:17–18)

30. At this point in the narrative the disciples' response has caused consternation in the manuscript tradition, almost evenly divided between "*We* have no loaves" and "*They* have no loaves." The first reading here, "*We* have no loaves," makes more narrative sense given Jesus's response to the disciples, "Why are *you* saying among yourselves that you do not have any loaves?" (8:17).

The challenge of whether the heart is hardened brings the reader to two specific moments in the narrative. First, when the Pharisees and Herodians (thus the overt connection to the narrative here) in the synagogue desire to accuse Jesus for restoring the man with the withered hand on the Sabbath, Jesus becomes angry and grieves "at the hardness [*pōrōsis*] of their hearts [*kardia*]" (3:5). They fail to accept that Jesus's mission is the restoration of the Sabbath and creation itself, the restoration that includes Gentile sinners (2:1–12) and gives to them the loaf (*artos*) on the way (*hodos*; 2:23–28). Second, the Jewish disciples themselves fail to understand (*syniēmi*) the connection between Jesus walking upon the water, the resurrection,[31] and new creation—the domination of chaos (water and wind)—and understanding what has become manifest in the meal of the *loaves*: "For they [the disciples] did not understand [*syniēmi*] about the *loaves*, but their heart [*kardia*] was hardened [*pōroō*]" (6:52). In both earlier instances there is Jewish resistance, among the Jews of the synagogue and among Jewish Christians, to what the narrative sees as the proper enactment of the Lord's Supper, that is, the inclusion of the Gentiles with the Jews at the one ritual meal.

The challenge to the disciples concerning the loaves also brings the reader back to the parables of Mark 4 and Jesus's emphasis there on seeing (*blepō*), hearing (*akouō*), and understanding (*syniēmi*) the parable of the planted seed. The parable tells the story of how the death of Christ (the planted seed) brings about the unexpected large harvest of grain, the Jews *and Gentiles* at the Lord's Supper. It is meant to hide the truth from those outside, "so that they may *see* [*blepō*] but not see, and hearing not *hear* [*akouō*] and not *understand* [*syniēmi*]" (4:12).

So on the boat, and not like those outside (the Pharisees and Herodians), the disciples are supposed to see (*blepō*), hear (*akouō*), and understand (*syniēmi*) that they now have the one *loaf* on board with them (8:14). The sign of the great harvest has taken place in the two ritual meals in the wilderness, the first common meal of the five thousand gathering twelve baskets and the second common meal of the four thousand gathering seven *very large* baskets. Yet in those places the Jews and Gentiles were fed with five *loaves* and seven *loaves*, respectively: How is it now to be understood that there is in reality only one *loaf* from which all are fed?

Jesus now makes clear exactly what the disciples should see, hear, and understand. The reality of the ritual of the Lord's Supper is that there are

---

31. Jesus rises (*anabainō*) into the boat from the waters just as he rises (*anabainō*) from the waters of baptism (1:10; 6:51).

not two separate meals (five loaves and seven loaves), but one meal for both Jews and Gentiles, the one loaf.[32]

In addition, Jesus's statement "Do you not *remember* [*mnēmoneuō*]?" (8:18) invokes for the liturgical reader of Mark the ritual setting of the Lord's Supper. That *memory* literally creates the reality of the ritual setting for the early Christians is made clear in how Paul describes the ritual meal in 1 Corinthians:

> For I received from the Lord what I passed on to you, that the Lord Jesus, on the night in which he was handed over, took [*lambanō*] the loaf [*artos*], and having given thanks [*eucharisteō*], he broke [*klaō*] the loaf [*artos*] and said, "This is my body for you; *perform this in my memory* [*anamnēsis*]. So likewise with the cup following the supper . . . "*Perform this, as often as you drink it, in my memory* [*anamnēsis*]." For as often as you eat this *loaf* [*artos*] and drink the cup, you proclaim the death of the Lord until he comes. (11:23–26)[33]

Under different yet similar circumstances (factionalism within the Lord's Supper), Paul invokes memory to create the ritual reality of the one loaf, which, thanks having been given and the loaf having been broken, enacts the sacred space of the resurrected body of the Lord.

So here in Mark the disciples are commanded by Jesus *to remember*, that is, to bring into reality the rituals of the two previous feeding narratives and through this invocation of memory in ritual performance to now understand the reality of the one loaf they have on board. Jesus here *remembers* the ritual performances that took place earlier in the narrative:

> "When I broke [*klaō*] the five loaves for the five thousand, how many baskets [*kophinos*] full [*plērēs*] of loaf pieces [*klasma*] did you gather?" And they said to him, "Twelve." "When I broke the seven loaves for the four thousand, how many large baskets [*spyris*] abundantly filled [*plērōma*] with loaf pieces [*klasma*] did you take up?" And they said to him, "Seven." And he said to them, "Do you not yet understand [*syniēmi*]?" (Mark 8:19–21)

The five loaves and twelve baskets, the seven loaves and the seven baskets—these have now become the one loaf, Jesus, who is on board the boat with the

32. On the importance of the "one loaf [*heis artos*]" in the continuing ritual practice on into the second century, see Ignatius, *Eph.* 20.1. The practice of separate ritual meals appears to be at the center of the dispute between Paul and Peter in Gal. 2:11–13. It is possible to argue that the main subject of Paul's Letter to the Galatians is not the abstract sense of the gospel vis-à-vis the law, but concrete ritual practice: whether Gentiles, women, and slaves are to be included with the Jews in the ritual setting of the Lord's Supper as "one" in Christ Jesus (3:28).

33. Paul's emphasis on the single loaf (*artos*) throughout the ritual description matches Mark's concern for the one loaf (*artos*) here.

disciples. It is through a correct understanding of the ritual reality created in the two previous meals that the Jewish disciples, and of course the liturgical reader of Mark, can now *understand* (*syniēmi*) this. The disciples in the narrative and the reader of the narrative realize now that indeed "they had neglected to bring loaves; and they had only one loaf with them on the boat" (8:14). When Jesus tells them to beware of the leaven of the Pharisees and the leaven of Herod, he is referring to the disciples' potentially incomplete understanding of the one loaf within the narrative, that is, the potential failure to grasp the inclusion of Gentile men and women at the common table. In other words, Jesus's warning about leaven is transparent both to Jewish resistance to this new Christian ritual practice and to a potential lack of understanding among Jewish Christians. There is one loaf, one common table, of Jews and Gentiles, men and women.

For Mark, the Jewish disciples in the narrative—and so his readers—should now have eyes to see and ears to hear and come to understand that the five loaves of the first ritual meal in a Jewish place and the seven loaves of the second ritual meal in a Gentile place are in fact the ritual reality of the one loaf, that is, the one loaf they have on board the boat (8:14). The twelve baskets of the Jews and the seven baskets of the Gentiles have been gathered together into one community at one table, where the one loaf is broken and distributed. Through the lips of Jesus, Mark asks his readers: Do you not yet understand about the one loaf? Already at the time Mark was written, the narrative character of Jesus is transposed with the loaf. The liturgical dynamic of the story—for readers immersed in the ritual reality of the loaf as the body of Christ—could not be more plain.

The narrative now also breaks open and completes what should have been understood by both disciples and liturgical readers concerning Jesus's walking upon the sea following the first ritual meal (6:45–52). It was only after he rose (*anabainō*) into the boat from the waters, just as he rose (*anabainō*) from the waters of baptism (1:10), that the contrary winds died down (6:51). What the disciples should have understood about the loaves then is what they should understand now, namely, that the one loaf, Jesus, is on the boat with them. The many loaves, Jews and Gentiles, men and women, are indeed to share in the one loaf at the one common table. They are all to eat and be satisfied (*chortazō*).[34]

---

34. The relationship with 1 Cor. 12:12–13 is distinct: "For just as the body is one and has many parts, all of the parts are of the body. The many parts are one body and this is Christ. For we are all in one spirit, baptized into one body, whether Jew or Greek, slave or free; all are given to drink of one spirit." The reference to an inclusive table ritual here is unmistakable (one body, Christ, spirit, drink).

To understand this, the liturgical reader of Mark is now drawn far ahead in the narrative to the description of the Last Supper in Mark 14:22–26. There in the narrative is the enactment of Paul's famous description of the Lord's Supper, "on the night in which he was handed over" (1 Cor. 11:23). Mark's description of this ritual meal reads as follows:

> And while they were eating, he took [*lambanō*] the (one) loaf [*artos*] and blessed [*eulogeō*] the loaf and broke [*klaō*] the loaf and gave [*didōmi*] the loaf to them and said, "Take [*lambanō*], this [one loaf] is my body."
>
> And he took [*lambanō*] the cup and gave thanks [*eucharisteō*] and gave [*didōmi*] it to them. And they all drank from it. And he said to them, "This is my blood of the covenant which is poured out on behalf of the many [*polys*]." (14:22–24)

The one loaf here at the Last Supper is the loaf on board the boat at 8:14. This is the ritually enacted *body of Christ*. It is the one loaf formed from the two ritual meals that have gathered the Jews (five loaves in twelve baskets) and Gentiles (seven loaves in seven baskets), men and women, into the one loaf: *"This* is my body" (14:22). Moreover, in the description of this meal ritual Mark combines the primary ritual action of the first ritual meal narrative, blessing,[35] with the primary ritual action of the second ritual meal narrative, giving thanks.[36] The combined ritual action creates a narrative depiction of the Lord's Supper that enacts the ritual reality of an inclusive community (one loaf, the one body of the Lord) along with the act of sacrificial death that brings the community into being, that is, blood poured out for the many.

The Healing of a Blind Man

And they came to Bethsaida. And they brought to him a blind man and they beseeched him that he might touch him. And taking hold of the hand of the blind man, he brought him outside the village. And he spit into his eyes and laid his hands upon him. And he asked him, "Do you see [*blepō*] anything?" And he looked up and said, "I see [*blepō*] men; I see [*oraō*] them like trees walking." And again he [Jesus] laid hands upon his eyes. And he [the blind man] saw clearly [*diablepō*] and was restored [*apokathistanō*]. And he looked

---

35. In the first ritual meal, Mark 6:31–44, Jesus *blesses* the five loaves, that is, uses a Jewish form of prayer (blessing) with a number that signifies the final eschatological gathering of the Jews (five loaves and five thousand males).

36. In the second ritual meal, Mark 8:1–9, Jesus *gives thanks* over the seven loaves, that is, uses a Gentile form of prayer (giving thanks) with a number that signifies the final eschatological gathering of Gentiles with the Jews (seven loaves and four thousand).

at [*emblepō*] all things distinctly. And he sent him into his house [*oikos*] and said, "Do not even go into the village." (8:22–26)

"And they came to Bethsaida" (8:22). One is tempted to read into Mark's narrative here and say that "they *finally* came to Bethsaida!" For that journey had been a long one, having begun in a boat after the first ritual meal in the wilderness (6:45) with a stop in between at Gennesaret (6:53), followed by the second ritual meal in the Decapolis (8:1–9) and again another boat journey and stop at Dalmanutha (8:10). But at this point in the narrative the inclusion of the Gentiles into the one loaf of the inclusive Lord's Supper has been accomplished (8:21). Now the cure of the blind man is meant to open the eyes not only of the man from Bethsaida but as well the readers of Mark's Gospel. And while many modern commentators link this cure of a blind man with the cure of the blind Bartimaeus in 10:46–52,[37] my sense is that the liturgical reader would see this cure as the culmination of the *movement* of the Lord's Supper from a Jewish gathering in a Jewish place (6:45)—partial sight—to the inclusion of the Gentiles with the Jews in a Gentile place (Decapolis)—clear vision. And indeed this is the only miracle of Jesus in Mark's Gospel that itself shows movement. The blind man here moves from partial sight to full vision along with the reader of Mark, who now *sees clearly* (*diablepō*) and *understands* (*syniēmi*) about the one loaf for Jews and Gentiles.

The inclusion of the Gentiles into the one loaf at the second ritual meal fulfills the vision of Isaiah: "The eyes of the blind will be opened, and the ears of the deaf will hear" (35:5 LXX). Immediately prior to that meal the deaf man was made to hear (7:32–37), and now, after the meal (8:1–9) and the proclamation of the one loaf (8:14–21), the eyes of the blind man are opened (8:22–26). For Mark, the way (*hodos*) of Isaiah 35:8 is the death of Christ that brings Gentiles and Jews together in the final restoration (*apokathistanō*) of humanity (8:25). And as with the stopover at Gennesaret, the people once again recognize the healing power of touching Jesus (6:53–56). They bring to him the blind man and ask Jesus to touch him (8:22). Once again Mark links the reality of the ritual meal of Jews and Gentiles, the one loaf which is the enactment of the new creation from chaos, to the physical saving and restoration of the physical body (6:53; 8:25).

In addition, it may well be that Mark intends the reader to understand that Jesus and his disciples have, after their meal with the Gentiles, arrived again in a Jewish village (Bethsaida) and that the reference to the people

---

37. Donahue and Harrington, *Mark*, 258; Marcus, *Mark 1–8*, 589–92; Moloney, *Gospel of Mark*, 163; A. Y. Collins, *Mark*, 395.

there, "And *they* brought to him a blind man and they beseeched him that he might touch him" (8:22), is a reference to the Jewish people of Bethsaida. A narrative frame for the two feeding narratives would then be suggested. On one end is the cure of the Gentile deaf-mute in a Gentile place (Decapolis), who then proclaims his salvation openly, which in turn leads to Jesus being proclaimed by the Gentiles (7:32–37). On the other end is the cure of a Jewish blind man in a Jewish place (Bethsaida). Jesus grasps the blind man by the hand (the reader here recalls the grasping and raising of Peter's mother-in-law, 1:31). But instead of performing the miracle there, Jesus leads the man out of the (Jewish) place and, after he can "see" everything clearly, sends him to "his house" with the command to no longer enter the (Jewish) village. Those Jews who can now see are separated from the ordinary course of Jewish religious life. They are now part of their own house church, where Jews and Gentiles share the one loaf.

The strange, two-stage healing, therefore, has everything to do with this Jewish man coming to *see* the initial mission to the Jews (the first ritual meal in the wilderness) made complete with the acceptance of the Gentiles at the Lord's Supper (the second ritual meal in the wilderness). The liturgical reader is even tempted to see the water from Jesus's mouth (8:23) as baptismal, and so Jesus's question at that point ("What do you see?") is neither curiosity on Jesus's part nor a demonstration of Jesus's initial failure as a healer. Rather, this is a real question that expects a real answer: if one sees only the Jews as part of the Lord's Supper, then one does not see clearly. The man answers truthfully: he does not see clearly; he sees men walk like trees. The second stage of the healing—with the implication of spittle being again applied to the man's eyes—brings this Jewish man not only to see clearly but to be "restored [*apokathistanō*]" (8:25). To see the inclusion of the Gentiles in the second feeding brings this Jewish man from darkness to light, that is, to become part of the ritual enactment—Jews and Gentiles at the common table—that is, the restoration (*apokathhistanō*) of creation itself. He is sent by Jesus to become part of this new house church.

5

The Necessity of the Death of Christ

8:27–10:52

Mark 8

The Confession of Peter

And Jesus and his disciples went out into the villages of Caesarea Philippi. And on the way [*hodos*] he asked his asked his disciples, saying to them, "Who do people say that I am?" And they said, "John the Baptist, and others Elijah, and still others one of the prophets." But he asked them, "Who do you all say that I am?" And Peter answered and said to him, "*You* are the anointed one [*christos*]." And he warned them that they should say nothing about him to anyone.

And he began to teach them that the Son of Man must suffer greatly and be rejected by the elders, chief priests, and scribes, and be killed and after three days rise. And he proclaimed the word [*logos*] boldly.

And Peter took him aside and began to rebuke [*epitimaō*] him. And Jesus, turning [*epistrephō*] and seeing [*horaō*] his disciples, rebuked Peter and said, "Get behind [*opisō*] me, Satan! For you are not thinking the things of God but the things of humans."

And he called the crowd [*ochlos*] with his disciples and said to them, "If anyone wishes to follow behind [*opisō*] me, let that person deny himself, take up his cross, and follow me. For whoever wishes to save [*sōzō*] his life will destroy [*apollymi*] it; but whoever would destroy [*apollymi*] his life on account of me and the gospel will save [*sōzō*] it. For what does it profit a man to gain the whole world and suffer the loss of his life? For what would a man give in exchange for his life?

"Whoever is ashamed of me and of my words in this adulterous and sinful generation, of this person the Son of Man will be ashamed when he comes in the glory of his Father with the holy angels." (8:27–38)

In many scholarly commentaries on Mark, the dramatic scene of Peter's acclamation of Jesus as the Messiah (8:29) is read as the absolute climax of the Gospel.[1] For these interpreters, it is a sort of virtuoso performance in which Peter's statement of faith in Jesus encapsulates the entire message of Mark (and often Christianity itself). The liturgical reader of Mark might, on the other hand, think such a reading to be at the very least insufficient, but perhaps as well tone-deaf to the liturgical context of this part of the narrative of Mark.

For the liturgical reader of Mark, the climax of the Gospel has just taken place. The reader now *understands* that the many loaves, Jews and Gentiles, men and women, have been gathered into the one loaf, the common table of the early Christian house church. The confession of Peter that Jesus is the Messiah is not, therefore, an isolated realization of faith but an affirmation of Jesus as the one loaf, the community of Jews and Gentiles gathered in the ritual enactment of the restoration of the creation itself.

After the second ritual meal narrative and the lesson of the one loaf aboard the boat, and after the establishment of a Jewish house church of Jews and Gentiles eating the Lord's Supper together (8:26), Jesus and his disciples are *on the way* to a Gentile place, the villages of Caesarea Philippi. The particular use of the term *way* (*hodos*) resonates deeply with the way of the passion that has been part of the story since John the Baptist was introduced as the messenger of the *way* (*hodos*) of Isaiah at the very beginning of the Gospel (1:2–3). Here the liturgical reader understands the way (*hodos*) to be ritually enacted in the baptismal death (immersion in water and chaos) and resurrection (*anabainō*) of Christ from the water as the proclaimed beloved Son (1:10–11). Now in the narrative Jesus and the Jewish disciples are *on the way* when Jesus, seemingly out of nowhere, asks, "Who do people say that I am?"

The question is not meant to ascertain public opinion concerning Jesus, but rather to ask how these Jewish disciples understand the identity and mission of Jesus now that Jews and Gentiles are sharing the one loaf of the Lord's Supper. Have these Jewish disciples, like the blind man of Bethsaida (8:22–26),

1. Typical is Donahue and Harrington, *Mark*, 264: "Jesus' question to Peter in Mark 8:29 ('Who do you say that I am?') is the central theme of the entire gospel." See also Focant, *Mark*, 331 (high point); Moloney, *Gospel of Mark*, 165 (climax).

been brought to see the identity of Jesus as the Messiah, the anointed one, who brings Jews and Gentiles together in the ritual restoration of the new creation?

Here the liturgical reader is brought to consider carefully a sequence of events earlier in the narrative. After successfully binding the demon who possessed the strong man in the Gentile place of Gerasa (5:8), Jesus had apparently come to an unspecified location, perhaps the Jewish diaspora (5:21). There he was sought out by Jairus, a Jewish synagogue leader, and an unnamed woman with a hemorrhage of twelve years, also presumably Jewish. The dynamic saving (*sōzō*) of the woman's body (*sōma*; 5:29) from merely touching the fringe of Jesus's garment (5:28), as well as the grasping of the twelve-year-old girl's hand followed by her undeniably corporeal resurrection (5:41), provide the basis for Jesus's reputation when he returns to his home synagogue (6:1–6). The three questions posed by the Jews in the synagogue— "*From where* does he possess these things? *What wisdom* is given to him? And *what mighty works* come about through his hands?"—all point to the earlier accusation from the scribes that it was by the prince of demons (Beelzebub) that he drove out demons (3:22). In other words, the implied accusation of these Jews is that Jesus's power and wisdom come from Satan (Beelzebub) and not from God. He is an ordinary man doing the bidding of the higher demonic power, and so his Jewish kinsmen are scandalized by him (6:3). As a result the Jewish mission is not successful (6:5–6), *and it is on the basis of this unsuccessful mission* that Jesus sends his disciples out two by two *with authority over the unclean spirits*.

Jesus does have power over these spirits (he has bound the strong one), especially as they have bound the Gentiles (5:13; 7:29). Now that power is given to the Twelve sent out on mission. Whomever they encounter, Jews or Gentiles, should accept the message and repent (6:8–12). On this mission the Twelve cast out many demons and anointed with oil many who were feeble and healed them (6:13). It is just at this point, the success of the mission among Jews and Gentiles, that Jesus's name becomes known to King Herod. Those around Herod offer a three-part speculation concerning the identity of Jesus: some say he is John the Baptist raised from the dead (and so has power), some say he is Elijah, and others say he is a prophet like the prophets of old. Herod then agrees with those who say Jesus is the resurrected John the Baptist (6:16). Mark then narrates the story of how John the Baptist had been executed at the hands of Herod (6:16–28).

When the disciples return from their mission—casting out demons and anointing and healing the sick in the name of Jesus—the question for the liturgical reader of the narrative is whether King Herod is correct: Is Jesus the resurrected John the Baptist? The reader then follows the story through the two ritual meals performed by Jesus, the restoration of Israel in the first ritual meal gathering (five thousand males and the gathering of twelve baskets) and the inclusion of the Gentiles in the restoration of creation itself in the enactment of the second ritual meal (four thousand and the gathering of seven baskets), and learns that these two meals are then to be understood in actuality as the one loaf, Jews and Gentiles, men and women, at the common table of the house church (8:14–21).

It is this same reader who now listens to the question posed by Jesus *on the way*: "Who do people say that I am?" (8:27). Again, the alternatives which were first expressed to Herod, *prior to the two ritual meals being enacted and explained*, are offered: some say John the Baptist, some say Elijah, and others one of the prophets. The difference now in the narrative is that the reader has been told the story of the *beheading* of John the Baptist: Jesus cannot be John resurrected, because John's head was severed from his body. And indeed John the Baptist was, in his ministry, the return of Elijah (1:6; 9:13). So if John was Elijah, then Jesus is not Elijah.[2] So is Jesus one of the prophets (8:28)?

The repetition of the threefold speculation about Jesus's identity (6:15; 8:28)—is he John the Baptist? Is he Elijah? Is he one of the prophets?—frames the question at 8:27: "Who do people say that I am?" This is not some moment of faith that suddenly comes to Peter. Rather the question is now posed in light of the enactment of the two ritual meals and the boat journeys that followed each meal. For the liturgical reader, Jesus is the one who answers the question—"Who do people say that I am?"—by celebrating the Lord's Supper in the two feeding narratives as the ingathering of Jews and Gentiles into one community, the one loaf who is on board the boat following each meal ("For they did not understand about the loaves" in 6:52; "Do you not yet understand?" in 8:21). This therefore is what Peter *understands* when he makes his famous declaration at 8:29: "You are the anointed one [*christos*]." Peter is identifying Jesus as Messiah on the basis of what the liturgical reader has already surmised: Jesus has brought the Jews and Gentiles to the same table, to the one loaf of the Lord's Supper. Peter's declaration is about who Jesus is (the one loaf), but on the basis of what he has done (gathering Jews and Gentiles to the common table of the Lord's Supper).[3]

2. The narrative carefully marks the fact that all of Jesus's early ministry up to the time of the first ritual meal narrative in the wilderness takes place while John the Baptist is locked up in Herod's prison (1:14–6:30). Jesus's ministry is not that of either John the Baptist or Elijah.

3. It should also be noted that Mark carefully constructs this scene to challenge the reluctance of the Jewish disciples to accept this as the foundation of Jesus's identity: Jesus poses the question first to all of the disciples—"Who do you all say that I am?"—and it is only then that Peter responds with the declaration that Jesus is the Messiah (8:29).

What follows next in the narrative would seem to be unexpected for the reader: Jesus admonishes all of the disciples to tell no one about him. That is, these Jewish disciples must first be taught that the Messiah, the Son of Man, who brings Jews and Gentiles together to share in the one loaf, must also suffer many things and be rejected by the elders, chief priests, and scribes and be killed and after three days resurrect (8:31). Mark tells the reader that Jesus spoke the word (*logos*)—the necessary suffering, rejection, death, and resurrection of the Messiah—boldly (8:32). Yet Peter, the same disciple who proclaimed Jesus to be the Messiah, begins to rebuke him. Peter does not accept Jesus's bold word, that the Messiah and Son of Man must suffer, be rejected and killed, and then rise after three days. He hesitates to affirm that Jesus's power to restore the creation in the Lord's Supper must come *as a consequence of* his death. Peter does not yet understand what the liturgical reader now comes to understand: the manifestations of Jesus's power over demons, disease, storms, and death come from the ritual enactment of his death and his rising from the waters to receive the Spirit of the new creation (1:9–11). Put differently, Peter here hesitates to accept the deep truth expressed in the narrative to this point: the true mission of Jesus, raised from the waters of death and chaos (1:10; 4:39; 6:51), is to bring the Jews and Gentiles together in the Lord's Supper as the ritual manifestation of his resurrection, the restoration of the new creation.

Peter, however, is not alone in his hesitation. The narrative carefully tells the reader that Jesus deliberately turns (*epistrephō*) toward his disciples and sees (*horaō*) them (8:33). Only then does he rebuke Peter: "Get behind [*opisō*] me, Satan! For you are not thinking the things of God but the things of humans" (8:33). Jesus's rebuke of Peter as Satan and his command to "get behind [*opisō*]" echoes for the liturgical reader the role that Satan and the demons have played throughout the narrative to this point.[4] They too have known who Jesus is—"the Holy One of God" (1:24), "Son of the Most High God" (5:7)—and they too have been rebuked and commanded by Jesus (1:25; 5:13). The reader now knows that all of the titles given to Jesus thus far in the narrative—Holy One of God, Son of the Most High God, Messiah, Son of Man—depend on the necessary suffering, rejection, and death of Jesus.

In addition, the reader now better comprehends the falsity of the accusation leveled at Jesus by the scribes at 3:22, namely, that Jesus was possessed by the prince of demons and by this means was able to cast out demons. In fact Jesus

4. There is at least a hint in the narrative here that Peter rejects the purpose of Jesus's death as the means by which the Gentiles come in the church: at Mark 1:17, Peter and Andrew had been commanded to "get behind [*opisō*]" Jesus in order to become fishermen of persons, a reference to the Gentile mission.

was possessed by the Spirit of God at his baptism (1:10), his ritual entry into the way (*hodos*) of suffering, rejection, and death. It is only on the basis of the enactment of his ritual death and resurrection at the outset of the narrative that he is able to defeat chaos; exorcise demons from Jews, Gentiles, men, and women (1:24; 5:7; 7:29); heal the bodies of both Jews and Gentiles, men and women (1:31; 5:34; 7:35; 8:22–26); and quiet the unruly creation (4:39; 6:51). Peter and the other Jewish disciples, if they are to lead the churches, must accept this reality and themselves follow on the way (10:38–39).

At 8:34–38 the narrative takes a dramatic turn. Jesus now summons the crowd (*ochlos*) along with the Jewish disciples. This is the crowd of the second ritual meal in the wilderness (8:1), the Gentiles who were with Jesus for the three days (the passion), who have gathered with the Jewish disciples to break the one loaf. This new community of Jews and Gentiles, men and women, must now be taught that to "get behind [*opisō*]" Jesus is to follow him in the *way* (*hodos*) to the cross. And so Mark establishes the central irony of the narrative, which will carry the story to its conclusion: the necessary suffering, rejection, and death of the Messiah, his apparent defeat at the hands of his enemies, is the means by which, through ritual baptism and subsequent persecution, the Gentiles are brought together with the Jews to share the common table, the one loaf of the Lord's Supper.

The mission to include the Gentiles in the ritual gathering, the enactment of the new Genesis creation, elicits again the primordial cosmic battle between God's creative Spirit and the forces of chaos that oppose that creation. When Jesus with his disciples ventures out to bring this gospel to the Gerasenes, the waters of chaos rise in opposition. They seemingly *destroy* (*apollymi*) Jesus, only to have him rise (*diegeirō*) and calm the waters (4:39). Jesus then establishes the new creation on Gentile soil by exorcising the legion demon. The formerly possessed man is sent out to bring the mission to Gentile Decapolis (5:20). When Jesus sends the disciples across the waters on the way to bring the mission to Bethsaida (6:45), the forces of chaos again oppose them (6:48), only to be calmed when Jesus rises (*anabainō*) from the waters into the boat. The one loaf who brings together the loaves is in the boat with them (6:51–52).

It is on the same water that the disciples are taught that the loaves of the Jews (twelve) and loaves of the Gentiles (seven) are the one loaf of the Lord's Supper (8:14–21). At the beginning of creation itself, chaos (waters and darkness) resists the Spirit of God. Yet God defeats the enemy, and creation itself is born. So now out of this very chaos, the waters of darkness and death, the resurrection of Christ establishes the Lord's Supper, the ritual enactment of the new Genesis creation.

The effect of this story on Mark's original readers, themselves gathered at the ritual meal of a house church and subject to persecution (13:9), would have been enormous. The narrative speaks to who they are, Jews and Gentiles, men and women, gathered to break the one loaf, a community ritually formed by and within the death of Christ. Especially the Jewish members of the house churches would be brought by this narrative to a new understanding of the reality of the ritual, the legitimacy and *necessity* of Gentile presence with them in the ritual enactment of the restored creation emerging from the death of Christ.

The remaining narrative will challenge this fledgling community to a new ethic, one founded on following Jesus on the way (*hodos*) of death and resurrection. The paradox that is the heart of the narrative of Mark emerges from this relationship of ritual practice and communal ethic. The Messiah must be rejected, suffer, and die in order to rise as the restored creation of God. It is this killed and raised Messiah in the narrative who both creates the ritually inscribed community of Jews and Gentiles and establishes the basis of their ethical practice rooted in sacrificial love (10:45). Now Jews and Gentiles, united at table, must follow the way (*hodos*) of the cross in order to create their ritual identity and communal practice experienced in the restored creation. All of the members of this new house church must take up the cross and follow Jesus (8:34).

In sum, the narrative of Mark is meant to teach the liturgical reader, then and now, about the reality of the ritual of baptism and Lord's Supper and the communal ethic that emerges from it. This is the community in which members give of themselves—in status, possessions, and life itself—in order to find themselves within the new Genesis creation.

Mark 9

The Transfiguration

And he said to them, "Amen, I say to you that there are some here standing who will not taste death until they see the kingdom of God coming in power." And after [*meta*] six days Jesus took Peter and James and John and brought them to a high mountain by themselves. And he was transfigured before them. His garment [*himation*] became radiantly white [*leukos lian*], as no fuller on earth could make white. And there was seen with them Elijah with Moses, and they were talking with Jesus. And Peter responded and said to Jesus, "Rabbi [*rabbi*], it is good for us to be here. Let us make three tents, one for you, one for Moses, and one for Elijah." For he did not know how to respond, for they were all very afraid [*ekphobos*]. And a cloud came overshadowing them, and a voice came from the cloud, "This is my beloved Son; hear [*akouō*] him." And suddenly, looking around, they no longer saw anyone but Jesus alone with them. And when they came down from the mountain, he commanded them not to discuss what they had seen with anyone before the Son of Man resurrects [*anistēmi*] from the dead. And they kept the matter to themselves, wondering what resurrection [*anistēmi*] from the dead meant. (9:1–10)

The lesson begins at the outset of Mark 9. The story most often referred to as the Transfiguration features three Jewish disciples, called out by Jesus at the very beginning of his ministry (1:16–20). Peter, James, and John, who previously had witnessed the resurrection of the twelve-year-old Jewish girl (5:37–43), are now to be shown the meaning of the resurrection for the Gentile mission.[5] The time of the episode is carefully constructed, "*after* six days" (9:2), so that this scene of resurrection takes place on the seventh day, the Jewish Sabbath. The place of the narrative is also carefully constructed: the high mountain recalls Mount Sinai, the place from which God spoke to Moses and gave to him the laws of Israel. Yet this mountain, like the wilderness of the second ritual meal, is now located in a Gentile place: Caesarea Philippi (8:27). Again the narrative places the ancient story of Israel, the revelation of God to Moses at Sinai, into a Gentile setting.

The narrative detail that Jesus takes Peter, James, and John by themselves to witness the Transfiguration on a high mountain in this Gentile place again indicates to the reader that the setting (Gentile Decapolis) and content (Mount Sinai), as well as the characters (the main Jewish disciples), of the narrative are carefully constructed to convince the original Jewish readers of Mark of the intimate relationship between the resurrection and the Gentile mission. This reading of the narrative purpose of the Transfiguration story is also indicated by the placement of the story immediately following 8:38: "Whoever is ashamed of me and of my words in this adulterous and sinful generation, of this person the Son of Man will be ashamed when he comes in the glory of his Father with the holy angels." It is most likely that Peter's rebuke of Jesus's proclamation of his *necessary* (*dei*) suffering, death, and resurrection (8:31–32) is the shame referred to by Jesus here. And so within the narrative, the scene of the glory of the Transfiguration is pointed most directly at Peter, and through him at the other Jewish disciples, and serves as a strong warning of the need for a change in attitude concerning the necessary death of Christ as prelude to the imminent return of the resurrected Christ and the judgment that will follow (9:1; 13:27).

5. The story appears to be based on an early Christian midrash of Exod. 24. Detailed discussion of this relationship can be found in Marcus, *Mark 9–16*, 635–42.

The description here of Jesus's glistening white garment (*leukos lian*; 9:3) immediately takes the reader to the scene at the empty tomb following the crucifixion of Jesus, in which the young man (*neaniskos*) who greets the women is also clothed in a white (*leukos*) garment (16:5).[6] So here the resurrected Jesus is upon a high mountain in a Gentile place, and Elijah, who represents the Prophets, and Moses, who represents the Law, appear with the resurrected Jesus and converse with him. It is hard to escape the conclusion that the Jewish disciples in the narrative, and by inference the original Jewish readers of Mark, are now being directed to see that this resurrected Jesus is the summation of the Law and Prophets:[7] after speaking with Elijah and Moses, Jesus stands by himself (9:8).

The reader knows that Peter's attempt to address Jesus is entirely wrong: he calls Jesus merely "rabbi [teacher]," an utter failure to recognize the status obviously given to the resurrected Jesus on the mountain. In clearly ironic understatement, the narrative has Peter proclaim, "It is good for us to be here," followed by his suggestion that the three Jewish disciples build three booths for the three figures on the mountain.[8] In other words, to build the *three* booths would be to understand Jesus as a teacher (*rabbi*) on a par with the Prophets (Elijah) and the Law (Moses).[9] But of course in Mark's narrative Jesus, resurrected, now surpasses these earlier figures.

As in two earlier episodes of encounter with the resurrected Jesus, the Jewish disciples are here very fearful (*ekphobos*). When Jesus *resurrects* (*diegeirō*) to still the storm in the boat crossing to the Gentile mission to the Gerasenes, the Jewish disciples have "great fear [*phobos*]" (4:41). And then when the hidden inclusion of the Gentiles is indicated in the first ritual meal in the wilderness (6:38, five loaves *and two fish*), the resurrected Jesus walks upon the chaotic waters (6:48) and invokes fear among the disciples in the boat (*phobos*; 6:50). Jesus's response to the Jewish disciples at that moment—"For they did not understand about the loaves"—highlights the connection between the resurrected Christ and the inclusion of the Gentiles in the Lord's Supper.

6. There might be more than a faint allusion to the ritual practice of baptismal disrobing and reclothing, as it is also a young man (*neaniskos*) who leaves his garment behind and runs away naked at the scene of the betrayal and arrest of Jesus (14:51–52).

7. Focant, *Mark*, 355.

8. The reference to booths (*skēnē*) associates the story with the Jewish feast of Sukkot (Tabernacles) and messianic expectations attached to the weeklong religious festival that celebrated the wilderness experience of Israel. Moloney, *Gospel of Mark*, 180n38, is skeptical of a link to the Markan narrative. Given the prominence of the wilderness theme in Mark, however, I would not share the skepticism.

9. In Jewish tradition both Elijah and Moses were thought to have been translated to heaven (Focant, *Mark*, 355).

111

Now on the mountain of the Transfiguration Peter and the other Jewish disciples are again fearful (*ekphobos*), and again the fear is brought on by a manifestation of the resurrected Jesus. In each instance the reader encounters the disciples' fear generated by a lack of understanding concerning the death and resurrection of Jesus and its connection to the Gentile mission. Here the narrative carefully places the resurrection scene on a mountain in a Gentile place immediately after Jesus tells all disciples who would follow him that every disciple must be willing to suffer and die on a cross (8:31–38). The Gentile mission brings potential persecution and death (13:9), and this is the meaning of the story about to be told of Jesus's passion and death. In Mark Jesus teaches his disciples, and especially the Jewish disciples, that his death is for the purpose of the Gentile mission, the resurrection of the body of Christ of Jews and Gentiles, men and women, gathered at the one table.

Jesus transfigured is not merely teacher (*rabbi*), but the resurrected Christ who brings together Elijah and Moses, the Prophets and the Law. In the narrative a cloud appears which mirrors the cloud that covered Mount Sinai when Moses spoke with God to receive the commandments (Exod. 24:15–18). Yet instead of speaking in thunder (Exod. 19:16), a voice from the cloud declares that *Jesus* is the beloved Son.[10] For the second time in the narrative Jesus is declared the beloved Son. The first time followed Jesus's baptism by John in the Jordan, the ritual enactment of his suffering, death, and resurrection. No characters in the earlier story hear the voice, and so only the reader of Mark knows this truth. Only now in the narrative, after the Gentiles have been gathered with the Jews in the one loaf and Jesus has taught them all that the Son of Man must suffer greatly and be killed and resurrect after three days, *only now* do the disciples as characters within the story hear this declaration that Jesus is the Son of God. They must be taught, and through them the liturgical readers of Mark, that the suffering and death of Jesus, the divine Son, provides the very meaning of the ritual of baptism and the ritual of the Lord's Supper that follows, the gathering at table of both Jews and Gentiles, men and women, the resurrected body of Christ.

As with the earlier resurrection appearance of Jesus walking on the water (6:47–52), there is here an abrupt return from the resurrected Jesus to the more "ordinary" Jesus of the narrative. In the earlier story Jesus rises into the boat with them, and the contrary wind dies down (6:51). Here Jesus is suddenly alone and no longer in dazzling white (9:8). As they descend from

10. More than *rabbi*, he is the Son of God, able to teach the Jewish disciples concerning the discipline and ethical basis of the newly gathered community. It is this divine authority that is, for the remaining narrative, the basis of Jesus's teaching concerning the ethical practices of the community.

the mountain, Jesus tells his disciples not to relate what they have seen (the resurrection appearance) to anyone until the Son of Man rises from the dead (9:9). The readers of the narrative and the crowd within the narrative all know what Peter and the other Jewish disciples have up to this point resisted: the Son of Man must suffer greatly and be rejected by the elders, the chief priests, and the scribes, and be killed before he can be resurrected (8:31). These disciples in the narrative still must learn the connection between the suffering and death of Jesus and his resurrection and what that means for the foundation and life of the restored creation, the one table of the house church.

John the Baptist

And they asked him, "Why do the scribes say that it is necessary for Elijah to come first?" And he said to them, "Elijah does come first and restores all things. And how is it written that the Son of Man must suffer greatly and be despised? But I say to you, Elijah has come, and they did to him as they wished, as it is written concerning him." (9:11–13)

Jesus commands the three Jewish disciples to say nothing of their experience on the mountain of the Transfiguration "until the Son of Man resurrects from the dead" (9:9). Within the narrative this command appears to be linked to the potential of the characters within the story to mistake the resurrection of Jesus with claims about the resurrection of John the Baptist. Within the narrative Herod first made that mistake (6:14), so Mark related the story of the death of John the Baptist in order to make clear to the readers that Jesus was not John raised from the dead. Jesus's ministry had in fact begun while John was still in Herod's prison (1:14). Later, others whom the disciples encountered made the mistake of saying that Jesus was actually the return of Elijah (8:28). So, coming down from the mountain upon which Elijah had appeared with Jesus, Jesus clarifies that John the Baptist was indeed Elijah,[11] and that he had indeed suffered martyrdom. The baptism of Jesus by John had indeed restored all things (9:12). Now Jesus, as the Son of Man who follows the return of Elijah, must also suffer martyrdom as the necessary foundation of the resurrection and restoration of the Genesis garden.[12] Later in the narrative Mark will make it clear that this suffering is enacted in ritual baptism

11. This is clear to the reader from the description of John's clothing and food at Mark 1:6 (cf. 2 Kings 1:8).

12. This is the importance of the narrative depiction of Jesus on the cross in 15:35–36. Elijah (John) has come to bring in the messianic age through the ritual enactment of the suffering and death of Jesus (baptism). His role is completed, and he has suffered martyrdom at the hands of Herod. Jesus must now on the cross complete the movement of chaos to creation, death to

113

and that baptism forms the basis for the ritual inclusion of Gentiles into the community (10:38–39).

The Exorcism and Resurrection of the Gentile Boy

When they came to the disciples, they saw a great crowd around them and the scribes disputing with them. And then the entire crowd saw him and was amazed. And they ran to greet him. And he asked them, "What are you discussing among yourselves?" And a person from the crowd answered him, "I brought [pherō] my son to you. He has a mute spirit. And whenever it possesses him it throws him down, and he foams and gnashes his teeth and withers. And I spoke to your disciples about casting it out, but they were not strong [ischyō] enough." And he answered and said to them, "O faithless generation! How long will I be with you? How long must I endure you? Bring [pherō] him to me." And they brought him to Jesus. And when the spirit saw him, immediately he convulsed him, and he fell to the earth and rolled around foaming. And he [Jesus] asked the father, "How long has this been affecting him?" And the father said, "Since childhood. And often it [the demon] casts him into the fire and into water so that it might destroy him. But if you are able, help us and have compassion on us." And Jesus said to him, "If you are able? All things are possible for those who believe." And immediately the father of the child cried out and said, "I believe, help my unbelief." And Jesus, seeing that the crowd had again come together, rebuked the unclean [akathartos] spirit, saying, "Dumb [alalos] and deaf [kōphos] spirit, I command you to come out of him and to no longer enter him." And he cried out and greatly convulsed him, and he became as dead, so that many said that he had died. And Jesus grasped [krateō] his hand and raised [egeirō] him, and he resurrected [anistēmi].

And when he came into the house [oikos], his disciples asked him in private, "Why were we not able to cast it out?" And he said to them, "This kind cannot be cast out by anyone except through prayer." (9:14–29)

Jesus and the three Jewish disciples now return to the other disciples, who are with a large crowd and in a dispute with the scribes (9:14). The content of the dispute as specified within the narrative apparently has to do with the nine disciples' inability to cast out a demon from the son of a man within the crowd (9:17–18). The liturgical reader is immediately reminded of the scribes' earlier contention that Jesus drives out demons because of an alliance with the prince of demons, Beelzebub (3:22). Jesus had refuted this claim by stating that no one can enter the strong (ischyros) man's house to take his property unless he first binds (deō) the strong man (3:27). Then Jesus proceeds to bind

---

resurrection, and thereby complete in narrative what is enacted in the rituals of the inclusive house churches of Mark's time.

(*deō*) the strong (*ischyō*) demon of the Gentile Gerasene (5:4) and cast him out (5:12–13) and commissions the Twelve to also cast out demons on their own mission (6:7).

The nine disciples here, in a Gentile place and without Jesus, now appear unable to bind the strong (*ischyō*) demon (9:18). With this the narrative signals that the Jewish disciples do not fully embrace the Gentile mission. Jesus even goes so far as to refer to them here as a "faithless generation," difficult to endure (9:19). At the same time the narrative here appears to speak directly to the churches of Mark's time: there will be areas in which the Gentile mission fails initially and so requires the missionaries' perseverance in prayer (9:29).

The Gentile father with the son possessed by a demon is the narrative twin of the Gentile mother, the Syrophoenician woman, with the daughter possessed by a demon (7:24–29). The description of the physical maladies caused by the possession are similar to those described for the Gentile legion demoniac (9:18; 5:4–5). The description of the boy as unable to speak (*alalos*) reminds the reader of the exorcism of the Gentile deaf man whose tongue was tied, a man whose ears are opened and tongue loosened immediately prior to the second wilderness meal and the inclusion of the Gentiles (7:32–35).[13]

The difference with this exorcism is also dramatic. It takes place after the second ritual meal in the wilderness and Jesus's explanation of the one loaf, the unity of Jews and Gentiles at the Lord's Supper (8:21). And it is the culmination of a pattern of exorcisms of Gentiles in Gentile places that moves through the exorcism of the legion demoniac and the Syrophoenician woman's daughter without physical contact (5:13; 7:30) to the definitive touching of the deaf and tongue-tied man as well as the blind man (7:33; 8:23). Here in this story is the culmination of the Gentile mission, which matches features of the earlier Jewish mission. Jesus not only physically grasps (*krateō*) the hand of the Gentile boy as he did earlier with the Jewish mother-in-law of Peter (1:31), but also raises him from the dead (*egeirō*; 9:27) as he previously raised the Jewish girl from the dead (*egeirō*; 5:41). The pattern of resurrection and restoration (Jewish girl, Gentile boy) is now brought to both Jews and Gentiles, women and men. The liturgical reader of Mark would see the narrative intention to show that the pattern of the two feeding narratives—Jews in a Jewish place in the first ritual meal (five thousand males and twelve baskets, 6:43–44), Gentiles and women in a Gentile place in the second ritual meal (four thousand people and seven very large baskets, 8:8–9)—is also the pattern of these two acts of resurrection. The raising from the dead of Jairus's daughter is emphatically

13. The exorcism itself, with the Gentile crowd gathering around, brings the reader again to Isa. 35:5–6: the ears of the deaf will be opened, and the tied tongue will sing for joy.

Jewish in tone and description, utilizing the Aramaic proclamation of the resurrection (*talitha koum*) as well as the description of the girl as *twelve* years old. In contrast, the raising of the Gentile father's son from the dead is emphatically Gentile in tone and description, the setting in a Gentile place and utilizing two early Christian Greek terms for resurrection: *egeirō* and *anistēmi* (9:27). Such sequencing of the narrative, Jewish female to Gentile male, makes it clear to the reader that both Jew and Gentile, female and male, together constitute the community of the resurrection, the restoration of the Genesis creation.

The narrative purpose of presenting the necessity and legitimacy of the Gentile mission may also be hinted at by a small detail in the way the story here is told. At 9:22 the dialogue between the father and Jesus suddenly switches from singular to plural: "And often it [the demon] casts him into the fire and into water so that it might destroy him. But if you are able, help *us* and have compassion on *us*." The plea here, "Help *us* and have compassion on *us*," might be a reference to the father with the son, but it might also be a general plea from the Gentiles who are gathered here in the narrative. After all, Jesus's response to the father, "All things are possible for those who believe" (9:23), reminds the reader of the saying of Jesus concerning the Gentiles with him in the house at 3:35, "For whosoever should do the will of God, this person is my brother, sister, and mother." In that instance the Gentiles are declared to belong with Jesus not through prior ethnic identity, by being part of his Jewish family, but by doing the will of God. Here the intense plea of the Gentile father, "I believe, help my unbelief" (9:24), shows the readers, and especially Jewish Christian readers at the time of Mark's writing, even more convincingly that the Gentiles, in a manner akin to the paralytic being lowered through a roof (2:1–12), are eager to overcome any and all obstacles to belong to the Christian community.

The conclusion of the exorcism of the demon from the Gentile's son has an air of finality to it: "Dumb [*alalos*] and deaf [*kōphos*] spirit, I command you to come out of him and to no longer enter him." The Gentile boy, and by implication all of the Gentiles gathered into the church, are now free to hear and understand (4:11) and to proclaim Christ openly (5:20; 7:35). The word (*logos*) that was hidden has been revealed (4:22) and now, with the understanding of the necessity of the suffering, rejection, and death of Jesus (8:31), can be proclaimed among Jews and Gentiles alike.

The Second Prediction of the Passion

And he left there and passed through Galilee, and he did not want anyone to know this. And he taught his disciples and said to them, "The Son of Man will be betrayed [*paradidōmi*] into the hands of human beings [*anthrōpos*], and they will kill him, and when he is killed after three days he will resurrect [*anistēmi*]." They [the disciples] did not understand what he said, and they were afraid to ask him. (9:30–32)

Jesus and the disciples now return from the Gentile mission to Jewish Galilee, and here Jesus predicts for the second time that he will be killed and resurrect after three days. The earlier prediction (8:31) took place as they moved within the Gentile villages of Caesarea Philippi (8:27) and stated that Jesus would suffer much and be rejected by the Jewish elders, chief priests, and scribes. Here in Jewish Galilee Jesus tells them that he will be betrayed into the hands of human beings (*anthrōpos*) and they will kill him. Now the picture of the upcoming passion narrative is more complete: after a night trial and scourging by the Jewish Sanhedrin, Jesus is betrayed (*paradidōmi*) to the Romans (the hands of human beings) the following morning (15:1). It is these Romans who kill Jesus (15:15). The Jewish leadership and the Romans are complicit in the forthcoming execution of Jesus. In the narrative, however, the notice of Jesus's impending death constitutes the ethical foundation of the inclusive Christian house churches. Yet the Jewish disciples still do not completely understand this (9:32).

> And he came to Capernaum. And when he was in the house [*oikia*], he asked them what they were discussing on the way [*hodos*]. And they were silent. For they had been discussing among themselves on the way [*hodos*] who was the greater.
> And Jesus sat down and called the twelve. "If any of you wishes to be first, let him be the least and the servant [*diakonos*] of all." (9:33–35)

Returning now to Jewish Galilee from the mission to the Gentiles, the narrative setting once again becomes the house in Capernaum (9:33; cf. 2:1, 15; 3:20). As in the narrative events in this setting previously (2:1, 15; 3:20), the ensuing dialogue between Jesus and the Jewish disciples has everything to do with encouraging the ancient readers', especially Jewish Christian readers', acceptance of the Gentiles within the house churches of Galilee. And within the narrative here irony abounds. After predicting his passion and death (the way, *hodos*), Jesus asks the Jewish disciples what they were discussing "on the way [*hodos*]." The reader realizes the unmistakable reference to the "way [*hodos*] of the Lord" proclaimed by the voice (*phonē*) in the wilderness (*erēmos*) at the opening of the Gospel (1:3). This is the way (*hodos*) of the exodus on dry land for the Gentiles, how they are indeed to come into the *wilderness* (6:31–33; 8:4). This way (*hodos*) is the death of Christ (8:3) enacted in ritual baptism. This death enacted in ritual accomplishes the forgiveness

117

of sins (1:4) and thereby the inclusion of the Gentiles at the Lord's Supper. Thus at the baptismal death of Jesus the initial voice (*phonē*) declaring the way (*hodos*) of the passion (1:3) announces, as Jesus rises from the water, that Jesus is the beloved Son (1:10–11).

The disciples' silence in the face of Jesus's question mirrors the silence of the Jews gathered in the synagogue when the man with the withered arm was restored. Such silence cues the liturgical reader to both the disciples' discomfort and their increasing awareness of what the rejection and death of Christ means for the status of the Gentiles. The narrative here directly addresses the Jewish leadership of the house churches of Mark's time: Jesus sits down (a position of teaching authority)[14] and specifically calls the twelve Jewish disciples to himself. Jesus then teaches the Jewish disciples that they must humble themselves and become the servant (*diakonos*) of *everyone* (*pas*). The liturgical reader is again reminded of the two ritual meals. These same disciples are commanded by Jesus to set out the loaves for both Jews and Gentiles gathered in the wilderness for the Lord's Supper (6:41; 8:6). Instead of favoring their own Jewish identity, the disciples are taught by Jesus to serve everyone, including the Gentiles. Indeed the use of the word "servant [*diakonos*]" reminds the readers of ritual meal settings (1:31).[15] The Gentiles are to be included at the Lord's Supper in the house churches.

> And taking a child, he stood the child in their midst and embraced the child. "Whoever receives one of these children in my name receives me. And whoever receives me receives the one who sent me." (9:36–37)

To be sure the Jewish-Christian readers in Mark's churches do not miss this purpose of the narrative, Jesus stands up a child (*paidion*) in their midst. The liturgical reader immediately recalls the Jewish "child [*paidion*]," Jairus's daughter raised from the dead and given something to eat (5:39–41), and the "child [*paidion*]" (7:30) of the Greek Syrophoenician woman from whom a demon was expelled so that she might be able to eat the loaf with the children (7:28). Jewish and Gentile females were raised from the dead, exorcised, and allowed to eat the ritual meal, the Lord's Supper. For the liturgical reader of the narrative, the child here (*paidion*) is both Jew *and Gentile* and perhaps even beyond gender.[16] In an extraordinary act of acceptance and inclusivity within the house, Jesus places his arms around this *child* (9:36).

14. Focant, *Mark*, 379.
15. Explicit also at Acts 6:2.
16. The child holds a status prior to the expression of gender, and there is good reason to assume that the early Christians thought about the imminent messianic age as one in which there

The teaching which follows this act of acceptance appears to be directed squarely at the Jewish Christians within the house churches of Mark's time: "Whoever receives one of *these* children in my name receives me. And whoever receives me [i.e., this child] receives the one who sent me [God]." Here in the narrative setting of Jesus's house (*oikia*), with Jesus sitting for a formal pronouncement directed at the twelve Jewish disciples, there could be no stronger message to the churches of Mark's time: "You give them something to eat" (6:37). Gentiles are to be embraced and served the one loaf with the Jews at the Lord's Supper.

> John said to him, "Teacher, we saw someone casting out demons in your name, and we stopped him because he does not follow us." And Jesus said, "Do not stop him. For there is no one who does a mighty deed in my name and then is capable of speaking ill of me." (9:38–39)

Finally, not only are Gentiles to be accepted within the Jewish house churches; these same churches are to accept the legitimacy of other, perhaps Gentile, house churches. John informs Jesus that the disciples have seen someone driving out demons in the name of Jesus and that they tried to stop this person because he was not a member of their group. The spread of Christianity, in the time of Mark's writing, is not only from the Jewish core outward, but also from group to group: most likely the Gentile mission to other Gentiles (5:20). Even these Gentiles are to be accepted by Mark's community. The narrative calls for optimism rather than skepticism at this turn of events.

Mark 10

Divorce

And from there[17] he rose [*anistēmi*] and came into the region of Judea beyond the Jordan. And a crowd [*ochlos*] gathered to him again, and, as was his custom, he again taught them.

And the Pharisees came to ask him if it was permissible for a man to divorce a woman. They asked this to test him. And he answered and said to them, "What did Moses command you?" And they said, "Moses permitted a certificate of divorce to be written and to divorce."

And Jesus said to them, "On account of your hardness of heart he wrote this command.

---

would be a radical transformation of gender (Gal. 3:28: "There is not male and not female"). For extensive discussion, see Meeks, "Image of the Androgyne," 165–208.

17. That is, from the house in Capernaum (9:33).

"From the beginning of creation he created them male [*arsēn*] and female [*thēlys*].[18] On account of this a man leaves his father and mother. And the two become one flesh. So they no longer are two but one flesh. What God therefore has joined together let not humans separate."

And again in the house [*oikia*] his disciples asked him about this. And he said to them, "Whoever divorces his woman and marries another commits adultery against her. And if she divorces her man, she commits another adultery." (10:1–12)

Again Jesus "rises [*anistēmi*]," leaves the house in Capernaum (9:33), and comes for the first time into the area of Judea beyond the Jordan. And again a crowd, most likely including Gentiles as well as Jews, gathers to be taught by Jesus. What follows, therefore, is teaching transparently directed to the inclusive house churches of Mark's time, churches that find themselves suffering from persecution by both Jewish and Roman authorities (13:9) and so find themselves *on the way* with Jesus toward his death and resurrection.

The challenge here comes from the Pharisees—most likely transparent to the Jewish community in opposition to the Christian house churches—who ask Jesus a question concerning the Jewish law of divorce in order to test him. The liturgical reader can sense that the Jewish Christians of Mark's community would be keenly interested in Jesus's response to a challenge concerning the proper observance of the law of Moses.

The liturgical reader also knows the response here will be from the resurrected (*anistēmi*) Jesus (10:1), who speaks for a community that understands itself to be, especially in its ritual practices, enacting the restoration of the Genesis creation itself. And when Jesus tells the Pharisees that the commandment to allow divorce was given because of their "hardness of heart," this reader is quickly drawn to the role the proper attitude of heart plays earlier in the narrative: the Jewish scribes resist *in their hearts* the idea that the Gentile paralytic could be forgiven and raised (2:8); the Jewish Pharisees and Herodians resist *in their hearts* the idea that the Jewish man's body ought to be restored in the synagogue on the Sabbath (3:5); the disciples fail to understand *in their hearts* the connection between Jesus's domination of chaos in the resurrection and the inclusion of the Gentiles in the first wilderness meal (6:52). In each of these instances, and in the present narrative circumstance, opposition and resistance to Jesus's mission are a reaction to the Christian claim that the resurrection of Jesus is indeed the

18. Particular terms for male and female taken from the Septuagint version of Genesis. See Meeks, "Image of the Androgyne," 183–88.

in-breaking of the restored Genesis creation, the union of Gentiles with Jews, females with males.

As previously in Capernaum (9:33), the narrative abruptly switches the location of Jesus's teaching to the house.[19] And here again the narrative speaks to the Jewish-Christian leaders of the house churches of Mark's time. It is the reality created by the ritual enactment of the Genesis creation—unclean spirits defeated, bodies restored, and forces of nature calmed—that governs the more stringent norms of sexuality and marriage in the Christian community. It is within the reality manifested in ritual place (the one loaf), the restoration of Genesis in which God created them male and female (Gen. 1:27),[20] that the Christian house churches must understand sexuality and divorce differently from the Jewish community (10:10–11).[21] Not only can there be no separation (divorce) of the eschatological body (male and female) joined in sexual union—the Genesis body created in marriage (Gen. 2:24)—but also both male and female are bound by this new reality (10:11).[22]

Allow the Children

And they brought to him children [*paidion*] so that he might touch them. And the disciples rebuked them. And when Jesus saw this, he became indignant and said to them, "Allow the children to come to me, and do not stop them. For such as these are the kingdom of God. Amen, I say to you, whoever does not receive the kingdom of God like a child [*paidion*] will not enter it." And taking them into his arms, he blessed them and laid his hands upon them. (10:13–16)

Mark now turns to an echo of Jesus grasping the hand of the Gentile father's son in order to raise him from the dead (9:26–27) and embracing the child (*paidion*) in 9:36–37. From one child (*paidion*) to many children (*paidia*), here beyond the Jordan the number of Jews *and Gentiles* to embrace

19. This house (*oikia*) is somewhere beyond the Jordan (10:10).

20. The narrative uses the specific language of the Septuagint here, male (*arsēn*) and female (*thēlys*).

21. Paul too understands norms governing human sexuality, marriage, and divorce as part and parcel of the experienced reality of the resurrection wherein "the two become one flesh" ("body"; Gen. 2:24). See, e.g., 1 Cor. 6:18; 7:1–4, 10–11, 14, 39. For detailed discussion, see Meeks, "Image of the Androgyne," 165–208.

22. Commentators often point to the injunction against divorce by the woman as an indication of the Hellenistic context of the Markan narrative (outside of the Jewish community and within the Roman world generally, women were allowed to divorce men). This may be, but the peculiar language used by Mark here, "And if she divorces her man and marries another, she commits another adultery," might point rather to the fact that either male or female leaving the one eschatological "body" of Genesis destroys the unity of the one body. See the discussion in Marcus, *Mark 9–16*, 707–13; Donahue and Harrington, *Mark*, 295–98; A. Y. Collins, *Mark*, 459–65.

in the house churches has increased (4:8).[23] Those who bring the children to Jesus—"*they* brought to him children so that he might touch them"—can be understood in the narrative as Gentiles. So again there is here an indication of the purpose of the narrative: Jesus accepts (literally embraces) the success of the Gentile mission (10:16).

And once again the Jewish disciples resist the acceptance of these (Gentile) children and proceed to warn them away. Jesus, however, becomes indignant and issues the strong pronouncement: "For such as these are the kingdom of God" (10:14). The Gentiles' faith is exemplary and must be emulated by the Jewish disciples (10:15–16). As previously, the narrative appears to mark both the eagerness of the Gentiles to enter the community (2:1–12; 7:25–30) and the Jewish disciples' resistance to their inclusion (6:36; 8:4).

The Wealthy One

And he went out on the way [*hodos*]. And someone came running and prostrated himself and asked him, "Good teacher [*didaskalos*], what must I do so that I might inherit eternal life?" And Jesus said to him, "Why do you call me good? No one is good but God. You know the commandments: do not murder, do not commit adultery, do not steal, do not bear false witness, do not defraud, honor your father and mother." And he said, "Teacher, all of these commandments I have kept since my youth." And Jesus looked at him and loved him, and said to him, "One thing you lack: go, and as much as you have, sell it and give to the poor. You will have treasure in heaven, and then come and follow me."

And his countenance fell at the word, and he departed in grief, for he had many possessions. (10:17–22)

As Jesus sets out on the way (*hodos*), the reader is aware that the narrative has now begun a transition to bring Jesus, the twelve disciples, and the Gentile crowd toward Jerusalem and the passion. Martyrdom will require the willingness to lose everything, and so Mark begins this section of the narrative with the story of an anonymous person, quite possibly a Gentile who fears God,[24]

23. The narrative here has a strong affinity with Paul's understanding of marriage and the ritually gathered "body of Christ." Paul repeats a teaching of Jesus about divorce (1 Cor. 7:10–11) and then discusses the status of children born to what are apparently mixed marriages between Christians and non-Christians (1 Cor. 7:14). It is possible that the narrative here indicates a similar acceptance of the children of "mixed" marriages, though the narrative does not provide much direct evidence of that concern.

24. He addresses Jesus as "good teacher [*didaskalos*]" and is rebuked by Jesus for calling him "good" when only God is good. Would a Jew have made such a mistake? His willingness to follow the Jewish commandments perhaps places him into the category of Gentiles who fear God (Acts 10:2, 22; 13:16, 26).

who asks Jesus what he must do to inherit eternal life. As with the Gentile children, Jesus is willing to accept this person who fears God into the community (10:21). But at this point the exchange revolves around the man's apparent unwillingness to sell his many possessions for the benefit of the poor and then to follow Jesus on the way to martyrdom (10:21). The reader is immediately aware of the cost of discipleship. Persecution by Roman authorities included the potential confiscation of one's property as well as torture and execution.[25]

> And Jesus looked at his disciples and said, "How difficult it is for those who have wealth to enter the kingdom of God." And the disciples were amazed at his words. So Jesus again responded and said to them, "Children [*teknon*], how hard it is to enter the kingdom of God. It is easier for a camel to pass through the eye of a needle than for a rich person to enter the kingdom of God."
> And they were utterly astonished, saying among themselves, "So who can be saved?" And Jesus looked at them and said to them, "With humans this is not possible, but with God all things are possible." And Peter began to say to him, "See, we have left everything and followed you." And Jesus said, "Amen, I say to you, no one who has left brothers or sisters or father or mother or lands on account of me or on account of the gospel will not receive now, in this time, a hundred times houses and brothers and sisters and mothers and children and lands, with persecution, and in the age to come eternal life. For many who are last will be first, and the first will be last." (10:23–31)

Here on *the way* Jesus now makes two pronouncements about the danger of wealth to discipleship, first to his Jewish disciples and then more generally to the Gentile crowd. The disciples' reaction to what Jesus says is amazement. The narrative is silent concerning why they were amazed. As generally in ancient society, perhaps they would have considered wealth to be a sign of God's favor.[26]

Jesus now doubles down with his disciples on the price of following him on the *way*: "Children [*teknon*],[27] how hard it is to enter the kingdom of God. It is easier for a camel to pass through the eye of a needle than for a rich person to enter the kingdom of God" (10:25). The collective astonished response of the Jewish disciples—"So who can be saved?"—prompts Jesus to assure all of them that "with God all things are possible " (10:27). The disciples are now aware, as is the reader of the narrative, that the *way* of suffering and martyrdom will be utterly difficult but not impossible.

25. The earliest and best description of this sort of persecution is captured in Pliny the Younger's letter to Trajan (Pliny, *Ep.* 10.96–97).
26. Moloney, *Gospel of Mark*, 201.
27. These "children" are the Jewish Christians at the table of the Lord's Supper (7:27).

Mark now turns to the response of the disciples. Peter's statement here, "We have left everything and followed you," brings the reader back to the beginning of the mission, where he and Andrew left their nets to follow Jesus while at the same time James and John left their father and the other hired men (1:16, 20). Jesus's command there, "Come after me and I will make you fishers of persons" (1:17), comes to fruition in the Gentile mission symbolized by the two fish found at the first ritual meal narrative. Now these Jewish disciples, transparent to the community of Mark's time, face the reality of confiscation and execution as they follow Jesus along the way of the passion.

Jesus's words of assurance at Mark 10:29–30—"No one who has left brothers or sisters or father or mother or lands on account of me or on account of the gospel will not receive now, in this time, a hundred times houses and brothers and sisters and mothers and children and lands, with persecution, and in the age to come eternal life"—are specifically inclusive not only of the Jewish disciples but all of the first readers of Mark's Gospel, Jews, Gentiles, men and women, themselves quite possibly subject to confiscation, persecution, and martyrdom (13:11–13). As the example of Peter and the other Jewish disciples' flight and betrayal of Jesus during the passion shows (14:50, 72), the Gentiles might be even more willing to suffer for the gospel than the Jewish disciples: "For many who are last will be first, and the first will be last" (10:31).

And they were on the way [*hodos*] rising up [*anabainō*] to Jerusalem. And Jesus went before them, and they were amazed [*thambeomai*], and those who followed were afraid [*phobeomai*].

And again taking the twelve aside he began to tell them of the things about to happen to him. "Behold, we are rising up [*anabainō*] to Jerusalem, and the Son of Man will be betrayed to the chief priests and the scribes,[28] and they will condemn him to death[29] and betray [*paradidōmi*] him to the Gentiles.[30] And they will mock him, spit upon him, and scourge him.[31] They will kill him,[32] and after three days he will rise [*anistēmi*]." (10:32–34)

As Jesus rises up (*anabainō*) from the waters of baptism to confront the power of Satan (chaos) in the wilderness (1:10–13),[33] so here he rises up

28. Cf. Mark 14:1, 43.
29. Cf. Mark 14:64.
30. Cf. Mark 15:1.
31. Cf. Mark 15:19–20.
32. Cf. Mark 15:37.
33. The baptismal death of Jesus thereby defeats the powers of chaos (Satan) and opens the wilderness to the Gentiles to join with Jews at the two ritual meals in the wilderness (6:35; 8:4). The narrative itself, once famously called a passion narrative with an extended introduction,

(*anabainō*) to confront the powers of Satan in the passion in Jerusalem.[34] To begin the way (*hodos*) of the passion, the crowd (Gentiles) from 10:1 seems to reappear with the Jewish disciples; one group is amazed and the other fearful as Jesus leads them.[35] The reader of Mark immediately recalls "the way [*hodos*] of the Lord" (1:3) of John the Baptist, who suffered martyrdom at the hands of Herod (6:27). So also just before this in the narrative the disciples were amazed (*thambeomai*) at Jesus's statement of how difficult it would be, when property was at stake in persecution, for the wealthy to suffer confiscation rather than to apostatize (10:24). As the way is set for actual martyrdom, they are again amazed.

Jesus now pulls the twelve Jewish disciples aside and, for the third time, predicts his passion and resurrection. This third prediction in the narrative is even more detailed than the previous two predictions (8:31; 9:31) and follows closely the events which are about to unfold in the passion. Jesus will be condemned by the chief priests and scribes and be handed over to the Romans for prisoner scourging and execution. It is only after the condemnation, torture, and death—for the liturgical reader the battle with chaos—that Jesus will rise after three days.

James and John

And James and John, the sons of Zebedee, approached him and said to him, "Teacher, we wish that whatever we ask of you, you will do for us." And he said to them, "What do you wish that I do for you?" And they said to him, "Grant to us that one of us may sit [*kathizō*] on your right hand and one on your left hand in your glory."

And Jesus said, "You do not know what you are asking. Are you able to drink the cup that I drink or to be baptized with the baptism with which I am baptized?" And they said to him, "We are able." And he said to them, "The cup which I drink you will drink; and the baptism with which I am baptized you will be baptized with. But to sit at my right and at my left is not given to me but is for whom it is prepared."

And when the ten heard this, they began to be indignant toward James and John. And calling them, Jesus said to them, "You know that those who appear to rule the nations lord over them, and their great ones exercise authority. It is not to be that way among you. Whoever wishes to be great will be the servant

is rather on the whole an extended baptismal narrative, that is, the defeat of chaos extended from the baptismal death of Jesus to the death of Jesus on the cross.

34. Irony abounds! As the scribes accuse Jesus of defeating the demons using the prince of demons (3:22), it is they who act on behalf of demonic powers (chaos) that will destroy Jesus (14:1).

35. Jesus has again to pull his disciples aside from this main group here (10:32).

of all [*pas*]. And whoever wishes to be first will be the slave of all. For the Son of Man came not to be served but to serve and to give his life as a ransom on behalf of the many [*polys*]." (10:35–45)

When James and John ask to sit (*kathizō*) on either side of Jesus when he comes into his glory (10:37), they are asking to sit in places of prominence at the messianic banquet to be held when Jesus appears in final glory.[36] Yet it is obvious that they have failed to consider that condemnation, suffering, and death are the necessary precursors to the resurrection and Jesus's final gathering of the community. The liturgical reader is again brought to consider why Jesus, in all three predictions of his necessary passion (8:31; 9:31; 10:34), aimed each prediction specifically at the twelve Jewish disciples. They appear reluctant to accept the death of Christ, the way of the Lord, and so seem reluctant to accept the means by which the Gentiles are brought to share the Lord's Supper. Following the first prediction and Peter's denial of the necessity of Jesus's suffering, Jesus teaches the crowd (*ochlos*), inclusive of both the Jewish disciples and the Gentiles, that they must take up the cross and follow.[37] Following the second prediction, the disciples outright do not understand what Jesus is saying when he predicts that he will be betrayed, be killed, and resurrect after three days (9:32). Jesus then teaches them that they must accept the children, the Gentiles, as he accepts them into his embrace (9:36–37).[38] Now following the third and most detailed yet of the passion predictions, the disciples do not grasp what it means that condemnation, suffering, and death precede the resurrection and the final coming of Jesus. And again Jesus's response has to do with the inclusion of the Gentiles.

Here Jesus makes distinct allusions to the place of the Gentiles at that ritual meal. When he refers to the cup (*potērion*) that he will drink (10:38), the reader is drawn to the second part of the description of the Last Supper in the passion narrative: "And he took the cup [*potērion*] and gave thanks [*eucharisteō*] and gave it to them. And they all drank from it [the cup]" (14:23). The ritual of the Last Supper combines ritual language from the two earlier meal rituals. In the first ritual meal in a Jewish place, Jesus *blesses* (*eulogeō*) the five loaves before the breaking and distribution of the ritual food (6:41);

36. The meal would be associated with the final appearance of the resurrected Christ, the gathering of the church from the four winds (Did. 9.4; Mark 13:27). The Lord's Supper celebrated in the house churches would have been, to some large degree, proleptic celebrations of this event (Did. 10.6).

37. Cf. 8:34: "And calling together the crowd [*ochlos*] with his disciples, he said to them, 'If *anyone* [*tis*] wishes to follow behind me, let him deny himself, take up his cross, and follow me.'"

38. Again the reader notes that the "child [*paidion*]" of the Gentile woman is cleansed of a demon (7:30), and the child (*paidion*) of the Gentile man has also been cleansed of a demon (9:24).

in the second ritual meal *in a Gentile place*, Jesus *gives thanks (eucharisteō)* over the seven loaves before the breaking and distribution of the ritual food for the Gentiles (8:6). Then in the final ritual meal, Jesus *blesses* (Jewish) the one loaf and *gives thanks* (Gentile) over the cup (14:22–23). Giving thanks *(eucharisteō)* over the cup *(potērion)* as part of the description of the ritual is therefore indicative of the presence of Gentiles at the meal (8:6; 14:23). In the final ritual meal in Mark, Jesus and the disciples eat the one loaf *(artos)* and drink of the one cup. The one loaf encompasses those gathered to participate in the ritual as the one body of Jesus (14:22). To drink the blood of the covenant from the one cup signals that all of the participants, Jews and Gentiles, came to be part of the gathering by means of the death of Jesus. His blood will be poured out for the many *(polys;* 10:45; 14:23–24).

In Mark, therefore, the ritual of the drinking of the cup signals Gentile inclusion at the meal of the Lord's Supper. When Jesus challenges James and John to drink the cup that he drinks and to be baptized with the baptism in which he is baptized, he refers directly to the Gentiles' presence at the meal through baptism, their entry into the passion and death of Jesus, which must be accepted by all Christians in the current circumstance of persecution and martyrdom.

And even given that both James and John will in fact undergo martyrdom (10:39), these Jewish disciples are not *entitled* to an *exclusive* place at the ritual meal of the resurrection. Others who suffer and die for the church, those who drink the cup, may also be seated at the table. Mark carefully signals to the reader that these others may in fact be Gentiles whom these Jewish disciples must serve at the final banquet (6:37; 8:6; 9:35).

At this point Jesus broadens the point made to include the other ten Jewish disciples. They must be willing to be the servant of one another and, more important to the narrative purpose of Mark, of the Gentiles. The Jewish disciples are to exercise their authority by being the servant of all *(pas)*, that is, to the Gentiles in the community. The death of Jesus, the narrative now makes clear, was necessary for the final gathering of humanity, Jews and Gentiles (13:27). Jesus came not to be served *(diakoneō)* but to serve *(diakoneō)*[39] and to give his life as a ransom on behalf of the many (10:45). On the cusp of the story of the passion in the narrative, a story which is given its very meaning by the description of the final ritual meal (14:12–31), the only possible meaning for this pregnant assertion within the narrative of Mark is the inclusion of the many *(polys)*—the Gentiles who have entered the community through the death of Christ (8:2)—within the ritual meal space of the community.

39. Again the allusion: to serve *(diakoneō)* is to serve at the table of the final ritual banquet.

The saying of Jesus at Mark 10:45 sets out the narrative purpose of Mark as a whole: the *way* of the Lord (1:2) is the way of the passion, and the way of the passion is the means by which chaos is defeated and the Gentiles are joined with Jews in the new creation ritually enacted in the Lord's Supper of the house churches.

> And they came to Jericho, and he and his disciples and a large crowd [*ochlos*] went out from Jericho. Bartimaeus, the son of Timaeus, a blind beggar, sat by the way [*hodos*]. And when he heard [*akouō*] it was Jesus of Nazareth, he began to cry out [*krazō*] and to say, "Son of David, have mercy on me." And many rebuked him so that he might be silent. But he cried out [*krazō*] all the more, "Son of David, have mercy on me." And Jesus stood and said, "Call him." And they called the blind man, saying to him, "Have courage, rise [*egeirō*], he calls you." And casting off his mantle, he sprang up and came to Jesus. And Jesus responded to him and said, "What do you wish that I do for you?" And the blind man said, "Rabbi [*rabbouni*], that I might see [*anablepō*]." And Jesus said, "Go, your belief has saved [*sōzō*] you." And immediately he saw and followed him on the way [*hodos*]. (10:46–52)

To make clear to the reader that Jesus's life given as a ransom for the many (10:45) is the meaning of the passion narrative about to take place, Mark now tells the story of the saving of the blind beggar Bartimaeus, that is, "son of Timaeus." This character is the only named recipient of a healing miracle from Jesus in the entire Gospel.[40] The name therefore matters. But how? Surely Gordon Lathrop is correct in pointing out that here Mark is making a direct comparison to the Platonic dialogue *Timaeus*, which was the most widely known and influential creation narrative in the ancient world. In the course of this philosophical and mythological account of the origin of all things, there occurs a short speech in praise of sight. Specifically it is sight that leads to observation, and observation allows one to see the intelligence displayed in the fixed motion of the heavenly bodies. And so our observation leads us to the natural truth of reason. We then can "imitate the unerring courses of God and regulate our vagaries."[41]

Timaeus tells the story of sight for its own purpose, that is, to accomplish the imitation of the unerring courses, the *way* (*hodos*), of God. In the story of sightless Bartimaeus, son of Timaeus, Mark deliberately picks up the theme of sight and the *way* (*hodos*). In Mark, however, the importance of the story lies

40. See the provocative discussion of Bartimaeus in Lathrop, *Holy Ground*, 30–45.
41. Ibid., 28. Lathrop provides Jowett's translation of the *Timaeus* (Hamilton and Cairns, eds., *Collected Dialogues of Plato*).

in who is brought to see and how the person responds to the offer to follow on an entirely different *way* (*hodos*), the way of Jesus and Christian martyrdom.

Yet the name Mark uses here, *Timaeus*, is more than an important reference to Plato's dialogue. The narrative oddly names the blind man twice; he is at once the Greek "son of Timaeus [*huios Timaiou*]" and the Aramaic (Jewish) "son of Timaeus [*Bartimaios*]." In the context of bringing Jews and Gentiles together at the Lord's Supper through the death of Jesus, we have here a dual name and quite possibly a dual identity: Greek Timaeus and Aramaic (Jewish) Timaeus (10:46). The story therefore aims at both Jews and Greeks in the ancient world who would be attracted to the philosophical way (*hodos*). For Mark, this way is to remain in blindness. Rather, Jesus here offers true sight (*anablepō*) to observe and then follow on the way (*hodos*) of martyrdom and resurrection (10:52).

The sightless son of Timaeus, who is sitting "by the way [*hodos*]," hears (*akouō*) that it is Jesus of Nazareth and cries out to him as the Son of David asking for mercy. This blind person, symbolic of both Jews and Greeks who might join the way, obviously hears and understands the word (*logos*; 4:12) and is about to become an insider, a member of the community (4:11). His cry (*krazō*) to Jesus echoes the cry of the disciples the night they thought the resurrected Jesus was a phantom walking on the water (*anakrazō*; 6:49). There Jesus had told the disciples who he was and to have courage (*tharseō*) and not to fear. Jesus, who had provided the loaves for the Jews and the Gentiles in the wilderness, is the one who dominates the waters of chaos and brings a new creation. Jesus baptized and risen (*anabainō*) is the one who *rises* (*anabainō*) into the boat with them (1:10; 6:51). In the story here Bartimaeus's cry (*krazō*) is not out of fear but recognition: Jesus of Nazareth is the Son of David. At this point many rebuke the blind man who sits on the way (*hodos*) and ask him to be silent (10:48). Why? Is there palpable fear that a royal claim, Son of David, will lead them all to martyrdom at the behest of the Roman authorities in Jerusalem? Surely both the many who rebuke him and the son of Timaeus, Bartimaeus, are aware of this reality. But Bartimaeus cries out even louder a second time to the *Son of David* that he might have mercy upon him (10:48).

Here the liturgical reader realizes that the title "Son of David" (that is, a Davidic king) is a new title for Jesus but that earlier in the narrative Jesus referred to the example of King David in the temple, who "ate the loaves [*artos*] of offering . . . and gave them to those who were with him" (2:26). Now Jesus, Son of David, who has given the loaves to his disciples to feed both Jews and Gentiles in the wilderness meals (6:41; 8:6), is about to enter the temple to perform the act—the symbolic destruction of the temple—that foreshadows his own destruction and resurrection (11:15–16; 14:58). This is

129

the Jesus who feeds his body, the one loaf, to Jews and Gentiles (14:22). He is the temple, the body of Christ, who will become a house of prayer for the Gentiles (11:17).

Bartimaeus will now move from sitting "by the way [*hodos*]" to following "on the way [*hodos*]" of martyrdom. Jesus stands and directs that they summon the blind man. Instead of rebuking the blind man to silence, these followers now obey Jesus and tell the blind man to have courage and to resurrect (*egeirō*), for Jesus is calling him (10:49). At the word of Jesus the blind man springs up and throws off his mantle, perhaps the traditional cloak of the philosophers (son of Timaeus), but for the liturgical reader easily a reference to baptismal disrobing.[42] The *way* of the Lord has been prepared (1:2), baptism and martyrdom, for all those, Jews and Greeks, who would follow on the way (*hodos*) as Jesus enters Jerusalem.

Bartimaeus springs up (*anapēdaō*). The eagerness of faith again strikes the reader. He comes to Jesus, who asks him, "What do you wish that I do for you?" This is not an easy question for Bartimaeus, or any disciples or readers at this point in the narrative. To say that he desires to no longer be blind is potentially to see (*anablepō*) and to follow Jesus, Son of David, on the *way* (*hodos*) to Jerusalem and all that will transpire there. This is not sight aimed at the observation of the intelligence of the heavenly bodies in order to imitate the unerring courses of God and regulate one's vagaries, but sight that sees the connection between the resurrected Christ, the unified table of Jews and Gentiles, men and women, and the way of martyrdom that is both the result and the genesis of the life of Mark's Christian community. Even so, Bartimaeus responds by addressing Jesus as "rabbi [teacher]." The philosopher's cloak has been thrown off, and the teacher of this Jewish and Gentile character is no longer Plato (Timaeus), but Jesus of Nazareth. And again the narrative extols the faith of this new disciple. When Jesus responds to his request to see, he also commands him to depart with his sight. The eagerness of his belief has given him his physical sight, or, in the words of the narrative, it has saved him. Bartimaeus is able to see (10:52). Yet Bartimaeus does not desire to use his sight to go his own way but rather to see and to follow Jesus on the *way* (*hodos*). So it is that the narrative makes Bartimaeus, son of Timaeus, transparent to all Jews and Gentiles in the house churches of Mark's time. In the narrative they now *see* that the way of Jesus in their own time is the way of suffering and death, and through this way their own resurrection (13:27).

42. The allusion to the young man who disrobes at the scene of the arrest (14:51–52) and the young man who is "wrapped in a white robe" in the tomb of Jesus (16:5) lends credibility to the notion that the stripping and reclothing of the early Christian baptismal ritual informs the narrative here. See the discussion in Lathrop, *Holy Ground*, 32–33.

6

The House of Prayer
for All the Gentiles

11:1–12:44

Mark 11

Jesus Enters Jerusalem

And when they drew near to Jerusalem, to Bethphage and Bethany, near the Mount of Olives, he sent out two of his disciples and said to them, "Go into the village opposite. Immediately when you enter the village, you will find a colt tied up there, a colt that has never been sat upon by anyone. Untie it and bring it. And if anyone says to you, 'Why are you doing this?' say the Lord [*kyrios*] has need of it and he will immediately again send it back here." And they went out and found a colt tied up near a door, outside on the street, and they untied it. And some of those standing there said to them, "Why are you untying the colt?" And they [the disciples] told them what Jesus had said, and they [the bystanders] permitted the disciples to untie the colt. And they brought the colt to Jesus and they cast their garments upon it, and he sat upon it.

And many [*polys*] spread their garments on the way [*hodos*], while others cut leafy branches from the fields. And those going ahead and those following cried out [*krazō*], "Hosanna, blessed is the one who comes in the name of the Lord. Blessed is the coming kingdom of our father David. Hosanna in the highest." (11:1–10)

131

Bartimaeus, the son of Timaeus, is now with Jesus on the way (*hodos*) to Jerusalem and martyrdom along with the Jewish disciples and crowd (10:32, 52). As the group comes near to Jerusalem, the liturgical reader might easily identify the two unnamed disciples who are sent out to find and bring back a colt as Gentile followers of Jesus. After all, Bartimaeus, son of Timaeus, a figure who must represent both Gentiles and Jews, can now *see* and has just been added to the company of followers (10:52). These two disciples are told to go into the village opposite and there to find and bring back a colt upon which no one has ever sat (11:2).[1] What they are told to say by Jesus when confronted by the bystanders (11:3)—"The *Lord* [*kyrios*] has need of it"—brings the liturgical reader again to the story at Mark 2:23–28. The example Jesus used in that story, King David eating the loaves (*artos*) of offering in the temple and giving them to those who were with him (2:26), an obvious reference to the Gentiles with Jesus, is what leads Jesus to make the pronouncement that the Son of Man is Lord (*kyrios*) of the Sabbath (2:28). Now these two (Gentile) disciples proclaim Jesus as Lord (*kyrios*) to the Jewish villagers and are allowed to bring the colt to Jesus.

As Jesus gives his life as a ransom for the many (*polys*; 10:45), many (*polys*) now take off their robes and spread them on the way (*hodos*; 11:8). With the stripping of the garments the liturgical reader cannot miss the allusion to the way (*hodos*) enacted in the baptismal ritual for Gentiles (1:2–4), even as the story of Jesus's passion begins in earnest. Those ahead of Jesus and those who follow all proclaim him as the one who comes *in the name of the Lord* (*Kyrios*), the *Lord* who provides for both Jews and Gentiles (2:28), the *Lord* who bound the strong one and cast out the demon from the Gentile demoniac (5:19). They also proclaim the new Davidic kingdom just as Bartimaeus, son of Timaeus, had proclaimed Jesus Son of David and now follows him on the way (*hodos*). As Jesus enters into Jerusalem on the way of the passion, there can be no doubt for the reader that this is indeed the way (*hodos*), the enactment of the baptismal death of Jesus that establishes the new Davidic kingdom, the community of Jews and Gentiles gathered to eat of the one loaf.

Three Days at the Temple

And he came into Jerusalem to the temple and looked around at everything [*pas*]. And since it was already the hour [*hōra*] of the evening [*opsia*], he went out to Bethany with the twelve.

1. The narrative is quite obviously constructed on the basis of fulfilling the prophecy of Zech. 9:9 (see Matt. 21:9).

The next day they left Bethany, and he was hungry [*peinaō*]. And seeing a fig tree in leaf from a distance, he came to it to find out if he could find anything on it. When he got there, he discovered nothing but leaves, for it was not the season for figs. And he reacted and said to it, "From here on, may no one eat any fruit from you ever again!" And his disciples heard it.

And he came to Jerusalem and entered the temple. He began to cast out the buyers and the sellers in the temple, and he overturned the tables of the money changers and the seats of the dove sellers. And he did not permit anyone to carry vessels though the temple. And he taught and said to them, "Is it not written, my house [*oikos*] shall be called a house [*oikos*] of prayer for all the Gentiles? But you have made it a den of thieves." And the chief priests and the scribes heard this and sought how they might destroy [*apollymi*] him. For they were afraid because the crowd was amazed by his teaching.

And when it was evening they went out from the city.

And passing by early [*prōi*], they saw the fig tree withered [*xērainō*] to its roots. And Peter remembered and said to him, "Rabbi, see, the fig tree which you cursed is withered." And Jesus responded and said to them, "Have faith in God. Amen, I say to you, whoever says to this mountain, be taken up and cast into the sea, and does not doubt in his heart but believes what he says will happen, then it will. For this reason I say to you: All things that you pray and ask for, believe that you have received, and it will come to pass.

"And whenever you stand to pray, forgive whatever you might have against another person, so that your Father in Heaven might forgive your own trespasses." (11:11–25)

What strikes the liturgical reader about the story of Jesus coming to the temple in Jerusalem is that the story is carefully divided into *three days*. On the evening of the first day Jesus comes into the temple and looks at everything and departs prior to sundown. On the second day Jesus curses the fig tree and halts the sacrificial atonement ritual of the temple. Early on the third day (the exact time of the resurrection, *prōi*, 16:7) Peter notices that the fig is cursed, and Jesus declares that forgiveness is now located within the Christian community. There can be little doubt that the three-day sequence here foreshadows the Friday-to-Sunday sequence of the passion story about to be narrated. More important, it provides for the reader *the* interpretive clue to the meaning of the death and resurrection of Jesus in Mark: the resurrected body of Christ, the inclusive house church meal of the one loaf, is now the sacred space of the temple.

The story of Jesus in the temple begins with the time notice that it is evening (*opsia*). For the liturgical reader, the apocalyptic implications of the pending darkness are clear. In the story of Jesus and the disciples crossing the Sea of Galilee toward the Gentile Gerasenes, it is *evening* (*opsia*; 4:35).

Jesus dies (sleeps) beneath the waves of the wind-driven sea (chaos) and resurrects (*diegeirō*) to rebuke the wind and silence the sea. The baptized and resurrected Jesus then binds the strong man, the Gentile Gerasene demoniac, who becomes a disciple (5:20).

The first ritual meal narrative takes place late in the day.[2] It is the meal in which the two (Gentile) fish are discovered amid the gathering of the twelve tribes symbolized in the five loaves and the gathering of the twelve baskets of broken bread pieces. And after this meal, still in the *evening* (*opsia*; 6:47), Jesus sends the disciples out alone to confront the wind and waters of chaos (6:45). Then, at the fourth watch, the time of resurrection on Sunday, the resurrected Jesus walks upon the water and dominates chaos (darkness, wind, and water). Noting the fear of the disciples as Jesus rises (*anabainō*) from the water into the boat, Mark suggests that the disciples do not understand about the *loaves*. The inclusion of the Gentiles in the ritual meal of the five thousand and of the four thousand is the one loaf who has risen from the water into the boat with the disciples (8:14–21). His body is the one loaf of Jews and Gentiles, men and women, that is broken and eaten in the ritual meal that interprets his death (14:22–25). It is the ritual enactment of the inbreaking of the new creation, the resurrection and the domination of chaos.

So in the present narrative when Jesus enters the temple for the first time, Mark notes not only that it is evening (*opsia*), but also that it is the hour (*hōra*) of the evening. Surely this is the hour of apocalyptic judgment that comes with the crucifixion and death of Christ in the third and ninth hour (*hōra*) of Friday (15:25, 34), the necessary death of Christ prior to the resurrection (8:31). And for the reader in Mark's community, this is also the hour (*hōra*) of potential judgment and death in martyrdom, which is unexpected and may come at any time (13:11). This is the way (*hodos*) that followers of Jesus must be ready to endure in order to join with Jesus in the resurrection (8:34–35).

On the second day (Sabbath), the narrative tells us that Jesus, leaving Bethany with the twelve Jewish disciples, was hungry (*peinaō*). And now of course the liturgical reader realizes that earlier in the narrative, as Jesus defends the disciples' creating a way (*hodos*) on the Sabbath (2:23), he tells the story of what David did long ago in the temple when he was in need and hungry (*peinaō*), *as were the people with him*. David ate the loaves (*artos*) of offering (and so acted as priest) and *gave the loaves to those who were with him* (2:25–26). The story of making a way (*hodos*) through the grain is not about humanitarian concerns overriding ritual requirements, but about the prerogative of *David*. Here in the narrative Jesus has just been proclaimed

2. The time of day, late and toward the evening, is mentioned twice in one verse (6:35).

Son of *David* (10:47–48), who brings the kingdom of *David* (11:10). He will occupy the temple and give the loaves to those who are with him. The Jewish disciples and the Gentiles with Jesus (Bartimaeus and the crowd) can be fed in the new temple, the sacred space of the Christian ritual meal, because Jesus is Lord (*kyrios*) of the Sabbath (2:28) and comes here to the temple in the name of the Lord (*kyrios*; 11:10).

Jesus is Lord and the one who brings in the kingdom of David (11:9–10). He is hungry (*peinaō*) and about to enter the temple. He sees from a distance a fig tree and approaches it in order to eat from it. He does not find a fig, because it is not the season for figs. Jesus then directly curses the plant: "From here on, may no one eat any fruit from you ever again!" So either Jesus in the narrative is unaware of what time of year this is, or the fig tree is symbolic of the temple. The season of the temple is passed. The temple will no longer produce fruit. The temple is no longer the place of holiness, the original and pure creation which has the capacity, through the ritual system of atonement sacrifice, to enact the sacred space of the original Genesis creation.[3]

Mark notes that the Jewish disciples heard the curse given to the fig tree (temple). The detail here is aimed at the second encounter with the fig tree a day later (Sunday), when these same disciples notice, after Jesus has acted to disrupt the sacrificial rituals of the temple, that the fig tree has in fact "withered" according to Jesus's curse (11:20). The narrative is again leading the Jewish disciples, transparent to the Jewish Christians in the house churches of Mark's time, to a new understanding of the destruction of the temple by the Romans in AD 70 and the relocation of that sacred space to the ritual gathering of Jews and Gentiles in the Christian Lord's Supper.

As David exercised his authority in the Jerusalem temple by eating the loaves of offering and giving them to those who are with him (2:26), so now Jesus, with his Jewish disciples present, exercises his authority over the temple. By interrupting the exchange of idolatrous money (imperial coins stamped with the likeness of the Roman emperor or the gods of the empire)[4] for temple coins used by Jews to purchase sacrificial offerings, and as well interrupting the carrying of such offerings through the temple precincts, Jesus here effectively ends ritual atonement, daily sacrifices, in the Jerusalem temple.[5]

The liturgical reader would take into account that the narrative is aimed not simply at the temple in Jerusalem, the temple that was undoubtedly destroyed at the time of Mark's writing (13:2), but at inculcating the idea of new sacred

3. On the understanding of the temple as the ritual space of the original Genesis creation, see Levenson, *Creation*, 85–86.
4. Donahue and Harrington, *Mark*, 327.
5. Focant, *Mark*, 456.

space, the ritual meal of the house church, that was surely a large part of the self-understanding of the early Christian house churches. When Jesus teaches *them* at this point in the narrative, it might well be a teaching aimed at both the buyers and sellers in the temple *and* at the twelve Jewish disciples. When Mark has Jesus quote Isaiah 56:7 (LXX), "My house [*oikos*] shall be called a house [*oikos*] of prayer for all the Gentiles," he surely has the ritual space of the Christian house church in mind. Simply put, the ritual meal of the house church, the new sacred space and the restored creation, the body of Christ, now includes Gentiles.

In the symbolic action of Jesus in the narrative, the sacred space of the temple sustained by ritual sacrifice as atonement for sin has been rebuked and replaced. The new temple, inclusive of Gentiles, is the body of Christ, the ritual space of the Lord's Supper (14:22). What follows in Mark's narrative is the story of the death of Jesus. But now this story is told for a purpose. As the Jerusalem temple is destroyed (*apollymi*), so Jesus is destroyed (*apollymi*) by his enemies (3:6; 11:18). Yet from that very destruction the new temple of the body is raised in the ritual meal of the house church (14:58). From death to resurrection, both Jew and Gentile now eat of the one loaf at the table of the Lord.

The chief priests and the scribes hear the teaching of Jesus and seek to destroy (*apollymi*) him (11:18). Earlier the Pharisees and Herodians sought to destroy Jesus when he restored the man with the withered hand in the midst of the synagogue (3:6). There Jesus was grieved at the hardness of heart, in Mark an unwillingness to accept the Gentiles as part of the full Sabbath restoration of a unified humanity. Here the chief priests and the scribes hear the teaching of Jesus about the temple becoming a house of prayer for the Gentiles and also react with a desire to destroy (*apollymi*) Jesus. The liturgical reader again notes the deep irony embedded in the Gospel: to destroy Jesus for his teaching concerning the inclusion of the Gentiles is to bring about the means of their baptismal inclusion at the ritual meal.

The chief priests and the scribes, though they desired to destroy Jesus, were afraid to act because the crowd was amazed at his teaching (11:18). The liturgical reader understands that this is the teaching about the new temple, the house of prayer for all the Gentiles. Apparently many within the Jewish community of Jerusalem were willing to hear. Ultimately, however, they would hear and not understand. This crowd in Jerusalem will at a later point in the narrative turn against Jesus as the events of the passion unfold (15:13).

"And when it was evening they went out from the city" (11:19). The narrative thus creates the third day of this prefigured passion story (the destruction of the temple is the destruction of Jesus), by noting the third day at the exact time of resurrection: "And passing by early [*prōi*],[6] they saw the fig tree withered [*xērainō*] to its roots" (11:20). The temple, the fig tree, has dried up and *withered* on the third day. In its place has emerged a new sacred space, the restored creation and eternal Sabbath. From the destruction of the temple (Jesus) has come the new house of prayer for the Gentiles, the Lord's Supper.

The liturgical reader is here drawn to the earlier story of the Jewish man with the withered (*xēros*) hand in the synagogue, who is told by Jesus to *resurrect* (*egeirō*) and come to the midst of the synagogue for all to witness. Jesus then restores (*apokathistanō*) the withered hand of the man in the synagogue (3:1–6). The reader notes that the hardness of heart of those in the synagogue is similar to those resistant to the forgiveness of the sins of the Gentile paralytic (2:8). The resurrection (*egeirō*) of the Gentile paralytic (2:11) and the resurrection and restoration of the *withered* hand of the Jewish man within the synagogue (3:2, 5) bring about the threat to destroy (*apollymi*) Jesus by the Pharisees and Herodians (3:6). Jesus is destroyed in the three days of the passion only to become the house of prayer for both Jews and Gentiles.

So in the present narrative the Jewish disciples, at the time of the resurrection on the third day, notice that the fig tree is *withered* to its roots. It is Peter who again goes beyond what the other Jewish disciples have discerned about Jesus.[7] While they notice the withered fig tree, Peter *remembers* that Jesus cursed the fig tree: "From here on, may no one eat any fruit from you ever again" (11:14). So Peter has apparently made the connection—and of course the reader of Mark also has made the connection—between the curse on the fruitfulness of the fig tree and Jesus's actions to end the fruitfulness of the rituals of atonement in the temple. Jesus's response to Peter, and apparently to the other Jewish disciples, indicates that the Jewish disciples now experience some fear and consternation concerning the connection Peter has just made between the withering of the fig tree and the withering of the temple. Here the narrative in its original setting most likely speaks to the Christian Jews of Mark's churches in the aftermath of the temple's recent destruction by the Romans (13:2). The temple has been destroyed, yet the place of atonement, its fruitfulness, has now been enacted in the new temple, the house of prayer for all the nations. This is the resurrection of Christ made present in the ritual meal, the one loaf, of the house churches.

6. In Mark 16:2, the women arrive at the tomb early in the morning (*prōi*).

7. At Mark 8:28 these disciples report how people have identified Jesus as Elijah, John the Baptist, or one of the prophets. It is Peter who goes beyond this identification of Jesus and declares him to be the Christ (8:29).

There is also the fear and consternation to which Jesus speaks at Mark 11:22: "Have faith in God." The one who has faith, the Christian, can command the temple (Mount Zion) to be consumed by chaos, thrown into the sea, and this will happen. So it should not concern Peter and the other Jewish disciples that the Jerusalem temple has indeed been destroyed by the Romans. The disciples and the readers of Mark have the new temple, the sacred space of the Lord's Supper in the house church. Atonement, forgiveness, is now located there. When these disciples stand to pray at the ritual gathering of the Lord's Supper, they are to forgive one another and receive the forgiveness of God.

In sum, for the liturgical reader, the three-day story describing Jesus's actions against the Jerusalem temple is a prefigured passion narrative. Within the story, the Jewish Christians of Mark's community are taught to understand the relationship between the recent destruction of the Jerusalem temple (AD 70) and the destruction of Jesus by his enemies. The Spirit of God, who once occupied the Jerusalem temple, now occupies Jesus, the Son of God (1:10). And whereas the Jerusalem temple was destroyed, Jesus cannot be destroyed. At his death, his baptism (10:38), the Spirit of God will be given to the Christian community (15:39) as John the Baptist had promised (1:8). The new temple, the new sacred space of the restored creation, is the gathering of the Lord's Supper in the house churches, the resurrected body of Christ, Jews and Gentiles, men and women, the one loaf.

Teaching in the Temple

And they came again to Jerusalem. He was walking in the temple, and there came to him the chief priests, the scribes, and the elders. And they said to him, "By what authority are you doing these things? And who gave to you the authority to do these things?" And Jesus said to them, "I will ask you one thing, and if I am given an answer, I will tell you by what authority I do these things. The baptism of John, is it from heaven or is it from humans? Tell me." And they disputed among themselves, saying, "If we say, 'From heaven,' then he will say, 'Then why did you not believe him?' But can we say, 'From humans'?" For they were afraid of the crowd, for all said that John was a prophet. So they said to Jesus, "We do not know." And Jesus said, "Then I will not tell you by what authority I do these things." (11:27–33)

On this same day, the third day and the day of resurrection, Jesus now teaches in the temple. And for the liturgical reader, it is apparent that the space of the temple in the narrative is now transparent to the sacred space of the house church. Here Jesus is challenged, this time by the three groups who will place him on trial and hand him over to the Romans: the chief priests, scribes, and elders.[8] So also the reader is now in a better position to understand that the role Peter plays in the narrative is transparent to the Jewish Christians in Mark's house churches. When Peter earlier in the narrative rebuked Jesus for teaching that the Son of Man must be rejected by the chief priests, scribes, and elders, be killed, and rise after three days (8:32), the narrative was pointing forward to the three-day story of Jesus's encounter at the temple with these same Jewish authorities. Peter's rebuke of Jesus at Caesarea Philippi, coming out of the experience of the two ritual meals in the wilderness, at first seems to be simply his reaction to Jesus's statement that the Son of Man must suffer and be tested and killed and only then resurrect.

But there is more to the development of the narrative here. Peter in the narrative has failed to see what the liturgical reader of the narrative has seen: Jesus dies in baptism and rises (*anabainō*) to begin his work as the Son of God (1:1–11); Jesus dies and rises (*egeirō*) to bring the word to the Gentile Gerasenes (4:35–5:1); Jesus dominates the waters of chaos and rises (*anabainō*) into the boat to bring the word to the Gentiles of Gennesaret (6:53) and eat the Lord's Supper with the Gentiles of the Decapolis (8:1–9). In sum, it is the destroyed (baptized) and resurrected Christ who authorizes the mission which at last brings the Gentiles and women with the Jews to the ritual space of the restored creation, the wilderness, to eat together the one loaf of the resurrected body of Christ (8:1–21). Hence Peter's resistance to the idea that Jesus *must* die is tied to his failure to understand the link between the necessary death of Jesus and the ritual gathering of the one loaf, one meal for Jews and Gentiles, men and women.

In the three-day story of Jesus's symbolic destruction of the rituals of the temple in Jerusalem (11:11–25), it is Peter who remembers on the third day the connection between Jesus's curse of the fig tree and what Jesus has done to end the ritual sacrifices in the temple. He and the other Jewish disciples must then be reminded to have faith in God (11:22). The meaning of the forthcoming passion narrative—the three-day suffering, rejection, and death of Jesus as the foundation for the sacred space of the inclusive house church, the house of prayer for all the Gentiles (11:17)—is becoming clearer for Peter and the Jewish disciples in the story. It is already clear to the liturgical readers of the story.

Jesus's response to the challenge from the chief priests, scribes, and elders centers on the baptism of John. Jesus asks them whether John's baptism comes from heaven or from humans (11:30). In the context of the narrative this must

---

8. Mark 14:53; in the first passion prediction Jesus declares that these same groups will reject the Son of Man, leading to his death and resurrection (8:31).

be a reference to the baptism of Jesus by John at the beginning of the Gospel (1:9). For the liturgical reader of Mark, the question again evokes the narrative purpose of the Gospel. It connects the death and resurrection of Jesus, enacted in his initial baptism, with what has just taken place in the temple. The purpose of the death and resurrection of Jesus is to unite Gentiles, Jews, and women in the Lord's Supper, the house of prayer for all the Gentiles. So for this reader the crowd is correct: John is a prophet (Elijah, 1:8) and so the baptism of Jesus is divinely sanctioned (the voice from heaven, 1:10–11; 11:32). When Jesus's Jewish opponents—scribes, chief priests, and elders—in the present context fail to answer Jesus's question, it is because they do not want to admit the link between the baptism of Jesus by John and what has just taken place in the action of Jesus to destroy symbolically the temple: the creation of the new sacred space of the house church. So it is quite possible that these characters within the narrative are transparent to Jewish opposition to the inclusive ritual practices of the house churches of Mark's day, that is, the inclusion of Gentiles and women in Christian house church meals on the basis of a ritual baptism into the death of Christ.

Finally, the story of the curse of the fig tree (11:14) and the parable of the vineyard (12:1–9) point to the failure of the temple to produce its fruits. Whether figs or grapes, it is clear to the reader of Mark that the subject of the challenge of Jesus to the chief priests, scribes, and elders at 11:27–33 is the *effectiveness* of John's baptism of Jesus (its fruits). The allusion to the death and resurrection of the beloved son (12:8) echoes the ritual baptism of Jesus by John to begin the Gospel (1:11) as well as the scene of resurrection on the mountain of the Transfiguration (9:7). In the parable of the vineyard, the death and resurrection of the beloved son leads immediately to the inclusion of the Gentiles (the "others" of 12:9) in a new sacred space, the new temple (cornerstone), which is, the reader now realizes, the house of prayer for the Gentiles (11:17).

The first passion prediction in Mark (8:31) has started to come to pass: the chief priests, scribes, and elders in the narrative ought to realize that the parable of the vineyard is about them. At the same time the liturgical reader now knows that the purpose of what is about to happen in the narrative, the death and resurrection of the beloved Son, is to bring Jews and Gentiles, men and women, together in the Lord's Supper.

Mark 12

Jesus now walks and teaches inside the temple (11:27). Within the narrative the temple has withered and no longer bears fruit even as Jesus has proclaimed the prerogative of forgiveness on behalf of the house church. He now confronts challenges by each of the major Jewish groups featured in Mark's Gospel. The chief priests, scribes, and elders challenge Jesus concerning the baptism of John (11:27–33), the Pharisees and Herodians ask about paying the temple tax (12:13–17), Sadducees challenge Jesus concerning the resurrection of the body (12:18–27), and a scribe described as "not far from the kingdom of God" asks Jesus about the commandments (12:28–34). By placing Jesus in the midst of the temple, which now cannot function, the narrative co-opts the sacred space of the temple in favor of the resurrected Christ. The ensuing dialogues between Jesus and his Jewish opponents are transparent to the dialogue between Jews and Christians in the aftermath of the destruction of the temple by the Romans in AD 70. Whether the temple tax should be paid (and if so, to whom), disputes over belief in the resurrection of the body, and a sense of how the primary commandments of the law should be understood are all topics that provide the narrative with the opportunity to establish a firm separation of the house church from the synagogue at the time of Mark's writing, that is, in the immediate aftermath of the fall of the temple.

Pharisees and Herodians

And they sent to him some of the Pharisees and some of the Herodians so they might trap him by what he said. And they came to him and said, "Teacher [*didaskalos*], we know that you are true and defer to no man. For you do not look at the surface of people, but you teach in truth the way [*hodos*] of God. Is it permitted to pay to Caesar the tax or not? Shall we pay or not pay?" But realizing their hypocrisy, he said to them, "Why do you test me? Bring me a coin and let me see it." And they brought it, and he said to them, "Whose image is this? And whose inscription?" And they said to him, "Caesar's." And Jesus said to them, "Give the things of Caesar to Caesar and the things of God to God." And they were amazed by him. (12:13–17)

The chief priests, scribes, and elders fail to arrest Jesus, because they fear a crowd that is supportive of Jesus's actions and teaching about the temple (12:12). They then send in the Pharisees and Herodians to challenge Jesus. Here the reader notes two details about the Pharisees and Herodians. These two groups are the first to react with a threat to destroy (*apollymi*) Jesus on the basis of what he has done in his ministry (3:6).[9] Yet these two groups are

9. The Pharisees in particular plot to destroy Jesus on the basis of two incidents. They accused Jesus's disciples of doing "what is not permitted on the Sabbath" when they are making a way (*hodos*) in the grain field (2:24), and they are the ones in the synagogue who want to accuse Jesus of healing on the Sabbath (3:2).

not mentioned in the three Markan passion predictions and do not play a role in the series of events that lead up to Jesus's death. Here their attempt to "trap him by what he said" (12:13) must be for the purpose of getting Jesus arrested and so fulfilling their earlier desire to destroy Jesus (3:6). Their effort utterly fails: Jesus provides a perfectly safe and rational answer to their question about paying taxes to Caesar. They leave the narrative at this point "utterly amazed" at Jesus (12:17). It is plausible that the narrative here is transparent to this part of the Jewish community divided in its attitude toward the early Christian house churches, some Pharisees supportive and others not.[10]

The only appearance of the Sadducees in Mark, to pose a question concerning the resurrection (*anistēmi*; 12:18–27), comes without a hint of hostility. There is no attempt to trap Jesus, but merely a straightforward dialogue about the corporeal nature of the resurrection body and the role of the body in the institution of marriage.[11] Apparently, as with angels, there will no longer be the need for propagation (12:25).[12] Both Jesus's teaching about the corporeal nature of the resurrection and his following statement about the "God of the living" (12:27) serve to establish the centrality of the idea of resurrection in the narrative immediately prior to the role it will play in Jesus's teaching about the imminent second coming (13:26–27) and serve as the main accusation against Jesus in his trial before the Sanhedrin (14:62). All of this should be heard in the context of ongoing martyrdom within the churches of Mark's time.

The Scribe Who Answered Well

And one of the scribes who heard the discussion came near. And seeing that he answered them well, he asked him, "What commandment is the first of all the commandments?" And Jesus answered, "The first is, 'Hear, O Israel, the Lord our God is one Lord. And you shall love your Lord God with your whole heart, your whole life, your whole mind, and all of your strength.' The second is, 'You shall love your neighbor as yourself.' There is no greater commandment than these." And the scribe said, "Well you have spoken, teacher; you speak the truth; he [God] is one and there is no other. And to love him with your whole heart,

10. The Pharisees shared with early Christians a belief in the resurrection of the body, and some of them are depicted in Acts as being early followers of Jesus (Acts 15:5). Given that the following dialogue with the Sadducees concerns the Sadducees' lack of belief in the resurrection of the body, it is quite possible that Mark is transparent to some range of Jewish attitudes toward the early Christian house churches.

11. The narrative of Mark has to this point repeatedly pointed to the corporeal nature of the resurrection: Jesus touches and is touched by others (1:31, 41; 5:27, 41; 7:33); there are references to the act of eating after being resurrected (1:31; 5:43).

12. Paul's preference for celibacy in the community at Corinth seems also to express this understanding (1 Cor. 7:38). See the discussion in Boring, *Mark*, 339–40.

your whole understanding, and all your strength, and to love your neighbor as yourself, this is superior to all whole burnt offerings and sacrifices." And Jesus saw that he answered wisely and said to him, "You are not far from the kingdom of God." And no one any longer dared to question him. (12:28–34)

In this story one of the scribes approaches Jesus. He acknowledges from the start that Jesus "answered [the Sadducees] well." This scribe then questions Jesus about which of the commandments is most important. After Jesus responds that love of God and neighbor takes priority, the scribe ends up in substantial agreement with Jesus. Yet at this point in the narrative the scribe *adds* that the twofold command to love God and neighbor "is superior to all whole burnt offerings and sacrifices."[13] Jesus responds by almost accepting the scribe as a disciple: "You are not far from the kingdom of God." The availability of atonement from temple ritual no longer exists; what does exist is the ritual practice and teaching of the Christian house churches expressed in the narrative here.

As a result of this sequence of dialogues (chief priests, scribes, and elders; Pharisees and Herodians; Sadducees; and the good scribe), the narrative carefully sets out a range of attitudes in the Jewish community toward the emerging Christian house churches at the time the Gospel was written. The chief priests and the scribes are openly hostile and desire to put Jesus to death (11:18). They will be the ones, along with the elders, to accuse Jesus and hand him over to the Romans for execution (15:1). The Pharisees and Herodians move from open hostility early in the narrative (3:6) to amazement here (12:17).[14] The Sadducees are not antagonistic at all but simply very wrong about the corporeal nature of the resurrection.[15] They leave the narrative as quickly as they came in (12:18–27). Finally, some of the scribes not only show no hostility to Jesus, but rather seem very close to becoming

---

13. Though often cast as a disparagement of ritual practice as normative for early Christianity, the scribe's statement has nothing to do with irrelevance of ritual practice per se. In the narrative context Jesus has just ended the sacrificial system of the temple and now stands and teaches as the resurrected Christ, the new sacred space of the Christian ritual meal. What Jesus teaches, love of God and love of neighbor, is at the heart of the new Christian self-definition. Historically, of course, at the time of Mark's writing the temple has recently been destroyed by the Romans, and the Christian house churches are in the midst of establishing their own ritual practices (baptism and meal). Burnt offerings and sacrifices are no longer possible in any event. For further discussion, see Bobertz, "Prolegomena to a Ritual/Liturgical Reading," 174–77.

14. In Mark, the word for amazement (*thaumazō*) seems to indicate a grudging respect. For example, Pilate is amazed (*thaumazō*) at the reticence of Jesus during the trial (15:5).

15. This, of course, would be of vital concern in the context of the active persecution and martyrdoms in the churches of Mark's time. It parallels Ignatius of Antioch's concern about those who would deny the resurrection of the body, a denial which would make senseless his own martyrdom (Ignatius, *Trall.* 10).

143

part of the Christian movement (12:34). A close reading of this section of the narrative, prior to the betrayal, trial, and execution of Jesus, reveals that at the time of Mark's writing perhaps only one part of the Jewish community, represented in the narrative simply as "the chief priests and the scribes," was in concerted opposition to the Christian house churches. At least as far as Mark's narrative story is concerned, it will not do to overly generalize and say that "the Jews killed Jesus."

The Son of David

And Jesus was teaching in the temple and said, "How do *the scribes* say that the Christ [anointed one] is the Son of David? For David himself said in the Holy Spirit, 'The Lord said to my Lord, "Sit at my right hand until I put your enemies under your feet."' If David himself calls him Lord, how is he his son?" (12:35–37)

The scribes now emerge as the main antagonists of Jesus as Mark prepares the reader to enter the detailed story of the arrest and crucifixion of Jesus. The narrative suggests that the scribes in the narrative and the reader of Mark should put to rest any notion that Jesus is merely the Jewish Messiah (the anointed one), the Son of David, and should also recognize Jesus as Lord (*kyrios*), the one who authorizes the Gentile mission.[16]

The liturgical reader now moves from an acknowledgment that Jesus is the Jewish Messiah (the anointed one), the Son of David, to the more complete understanding that Jesus is the Lord (*kyrios*) who gathers the Gentiles with the Jews in a new humanity. This is to go beyond what David did in the temple when he was in need and was hungry—eating the loaves of offering and giving them to those with him (2:26)—to becoming the Lord of the Sabbath and able to feed all who have come to him on the Sabbath (2:26–28; 6:42). This is to go beyond casting out the demon from the Jewish man in the synagogue (1:26) to being the Lord who binds the demon in the Gentile strong man and shows mercy upon him (5:1–19). And this is the Lord who, having been executed by his enemies, will come in judgment over all of humanity at the end of days (13:26–31).

---

16. As Lord (*kyrios*) of the Sabbath, Jesus has the authority to do what David did, namely, to eat the loaves of offering and give them to those who were with him (Gentiles, 2:28); Jesus as Lord (*kyrios*) exorcises the legion demon from a Gentile on Gentile soil (5:19); Jesus as Lord (*kyrios*) leads Jews and Gentiles on the way (*hodos*) into Jerusalem (10:52; 11:3); Jesus as Lord (*kyrios*) will give the wine from the vineyard to others (Gentiles, 12:9).

7

The Apocalyptic Discourse and the Death of Jesus

13:1–37

Mark 13

Like Mark 4, which is largely a break in the narrative action as Jesus gives a series of parables (4:1–34), Mark 13 is almost entirely a speech by Jesus about the persecution of the disciples and final judgment. In many modern studies of Mark it is referred to as the "apocalyptic discourse" because it depicts the persecution of Christians as part of the dissolution of creation and the triumph of chaos at the end of time. It is safe to say, however, that the real subject is a lesson given to the four primary Jewish disciples, Peter and Andrew, James and John—and so to the churches of Mark's time—concerning the proper understanding of the events surrounding the Roman suppression of the Jewish revolt which took place from AD 66 to 73.

For the liturgical reader, this understanding fits perfectly into the immediate narrative structure of Mark. In Mark 11:11–25, Jesus had entered the temple and, over the course of three days (the three days of the passion), disrupted the sacrificial system of the temple in favor of including the Gentiles in a new house of prayer (11:17). The temple there was symbolically destroyed, withered to its roots in the curse of the fig tree (11:21). The resurrected Jesus, the ritual enactment of the new house of prayer for the Gentiles, then teaches his disciples and takes on his antagonists in place of the withered temple. Meanwhile, within the narrative some of these antagonists, scribes and the chief priests, are ironically destined to *destroy* Jesus in the coming days of the passion (11:18).

Yet here also the narrative of Mark becomes complicated for the modern liturgical reader. Mark is writing at a time when the temple in Jerusalem has been, probably quite recently, destroyed by the Romans in AD 70.[1] Yet the narrative portrays the time of the ministry and death of Jesus, perhaps forty or so years before Mark put pen to papyrus. Mark is therefore using the narrative to explain to his readers, who have just experienced the circumstances surrounding the Roman war and the destruction of the temple, how they should understand these contemporary events. If these first readers of Mark truly understand the ministry of Jesus and his betrayal, suffering, and death, they will understand what has just happened in the recent fall of the temple and the persecution they are now experiencing at the hands of both Jews and Gentiles (13:9). Their suffering now as the body of Christ, the church, is joined to Jesus, the body of Christ, who has already suffered the passion. The narrative tells the reader that Jesus gathered Gentile men and women and Jewish men and women, and that this community, in the ritual of the Lord's Supper, became the body of Christ, the one loaf (8:14–21; 14:22). So when Jesus suffers and dies in the narrative, he suffers and dies as the one whose mission and purpose was to gather the body of Christ. And so too he rises from the dead as the body of Christ. So now the ancient reader of Mark, ritually joined to the body of Christ, Jews and Gentiles, men and women, in baptism and meal, understands his or her own potential passion and death as part of this story of Jesus. He or she now reads a narrative story made meaningful by both political reality and liturgical experience.

This means that in a certain way, most often practically ignored in contemporary scholarship, the narrative of Mark cannot be understood by modern readers without understanding the ritual setting within the narrative and the ritual setting of its originally intended readers. Jesus in the narrative becomes the resurrected Christ, the body of Christ, through the ritual of baptismal death at the opening of the narrative, and from there brings together the ritual meals in the wilderness, the one loaf, of Jews and Gentiles, men and women (8:14–21). And it is this resurrected Jesus who is also the body (*sōma*) of Christ created in the final ritual meal (14:22). It is this body, Jews and

---

1. Further discussion in Marcus, *Mark 1–8*, 37–39; A. Y. Collins, *Mark*, 11–14.

Gentiles, men and women, who also suffer and die with Jesus in the passion narrative. Modern studies of Mark that focus on the individual Jesus within the narrative miss the most crucial theological statement that Mark makes to his readers: just as the original creation was fashioned from chaos (Genesis), so now the new creation, the church, is again fashioned from chaos (death). The suffering and death of Jesus, both the original historical moment and its subsequent enactment in baptism, is the *necessary* chaos out of which the church, the new sacred space of the temple, the body of Christ, the one loaf, is created. In sum, Jesus, already *resurrected* within the narrative, must (*dei*) suffer and die in order to be the resurrected Jesus, the body of Christ, that is, the inclusive church ritually gathered then and now.

Put differently, the rituals of baptism (1:9–11) and the Lord's Supper (6:30–44; 8:1–21; 14:22–26) within the narrative present Jesus as himself the body of Christ who then brings together his own ritual body, the one loaf which is the body of Christ. The Jesus who then suffers, dies, and rises within the narrative also suffers, dies, and rises as the body of Christ, the ritually gathered community, now undergoing persecution and martyrdom in the time of Mark's writing. The ancient reader of Mark, baptized into the death of Christ and joined to others in the ritual meal as the body of Christ (14:22), would have read the narrative presentation of Jesus in Mark as part of his or her own ritual experience and historical context. As Paul teaches about the nature and identity of the ritual body in a letter (1 Cor. 12:12), so does Mark in his Gospel. The narrative was never intended to be read in the way most modern readers read it, as more or less some sort of historical account of events. It was rather created in a setting that presumed a particular ritual identity (Gentile men and women gathered with Jewish men and women in the house churches) and intended to communicate deeply, through symbolic movement, place, and action in narrative sequence, the proper identity of the ritual body in the face of the daunting circumstances of active persecution (13:9).

With all of this in mind, we can now return to a consideration of the narrative structure of Mark 13. The chapter comes immediately before and therefore interprets for the reader the meaning of the passion narrative about to unfold in the final chapters of Mark. The reader of Mark has to know how to interpret the apparent success of those who desire to destroy Jesus. Earlier in the narrative, in three separate predictions to his disciples (8:31; 9:31; 10:33), Jesus reiterated the fact that the Son of Man must be executed and after three days rise again. Mark now firmly links the death of Jesus in the narrative to the war with Rome and destruction of the temple in AD 70. Simply put, the destruction of the temple, as well as the vicious persecution of the Christian community in the years of the Jewish war, is in the narrative interpreted within the account of Jesus's passion.[2] Out of that destructive chaos—the destruction of Jesus, the temple, and Christian martyrs—will be born the resurrection of Jesus and with it the collective body of Christ, the house church as the new creation and temple. So the narrative Jesus who suffers and dies is not simply Jesus, but the church of Jews and Gentiles, men and women, which he gathers and encourages during the course of his mission in the Gospel. Put simply, within the narrative, Jesus is at once a narrative character and the manifestation of the inclusive house church of Mark's time. At the final ritual meal Jesus will declare this community, those who eat of the one loaf, to be his body. So it is this body—Jews, Gentiles, and women gathered throughout the course of the narrative—which dies and rises as Jesus dies and rises. Then and now the liturgical readers of Mark understand that they are the new house of prayer for the Gentiles (11:17). This is the ritual body in which the ancient Christian readers of Mark are called upon to suffer betrayal, confiscation, and martyrdom (8:33).

The Temple Destroyed

When he came out of the temple, one of his disciples said to him, "Teacher, see [horaō] what stones and what buildings!" And Jesus said to him, "Do you see [blepō] these great buildings? Here there will not be left a stone upon a stone which is not torn down [katalyō]." (13:1–2)

Chapter 13 opens with Jesus leaving the temple, a possible sign of condemnation (6:11). One of the disciples notes the stones and buildings of the temple. Jesus's response, "Here there will not be left a stone upon a stone which is not torn down [katalyō],"[3] has a double meaning for the liturgical reader: the temple has been torn down (katalyō; 13:2), and Jesus in the narrative will soon be challenged by bystanders near the cross to be the one who would tear down (katalyō) the temple and rebuild it in three days by coming down (katabainō) from the cross (15:29–30). The reader knows that Jesus can only build the new house of prayer for the Gentiles by not saving himself and coming down from the cross (11:17; 15:30).

2. Almost all of the modern commentaries cited throughout this book rehearse the controversy over the dating of Mark to either before or after the fall of the second Jerusalem temple (AD 70). It is obvious that I come down squarely on the side of dating Mark after the temple's destruction. I do so not only on the basis of reading Mark 13:2 and 12:9 as written after these historical events, but also on the carefully constructed theme of Jesus, the body of Christ, as the replacement of the temple. See, e.g., A. Y. Collins, *Mark*, 96–102.

3. The emphatic nature of the destruction, "not be left a stone upon a stone" (13:2), mirrors the destruction of the fig tree, "utterly withered" (11:21).

Out of the tearing down of the temple, in the narrative ritually enacted by Jesus in his cursing of the fig tree and his acting to end the cultic activity of the temple (11:11–25), will come the house of prayer for the Gentiles, the ritual gathering of the house churches. The ancient reader of Mark is now directed to understand the catastrophic events surrounding the tearing down of the temple by the Roman army and the passions stirred up in the wake of that event. Both the tearing down of the temple and the tearing down of Jesus in his death are the cosmic chaos out of which will soon come the resurrection, the imminent appearance of Jesus on the clouds to gather the elect in a new creation (13:27). As Jesus suffers and dies within the narrative to bring into being the ritually gathered body of Christ, so now in the time of Mark's writing the tearing down of the temple and the tearing down of Christian martyrs will bring about, at a time known only to God (13:32), the final redemption and gathering of the Christian community into the new creation, the resurrection, established by God (13:27). It is clear that the writer of the Gospel of Mark expects the imminent return of the resurrected Christ, his final judgment on those Jews responsible for the execution of Jesus, and the uplifting of the Christian community in the new creation established by him (12:1–11).

Four Jewish Disciples

And sitting on the Mount of Olives opposite the temple, Peter, James, John, and Andrew asked him in private, "Tell us when these things will be and what the sign will be when all of these things are about to be accomplished." And Jesus began to say to them, "See [blepō], lest someone cause you to be led astray. Many will come in my name, saying, 'I am,' and they will lead many astray. And whenever you hear of wars and reports of wars, do not be frightened, for this is necessary, but the end is not yet. For nation will rise up against nation and kingdom against kingdom; there will be earthquakes in some places, and there will be famine. These things are the beginning of the birth pangs." (13:3–8)

Having predicted the destruction of the temple for the anonymous disciple, Jesus now sits on the Mount of Olives opposite the temple and responds to a private question from the four Jewish disciples whom he had called at the very beginning of his mission (1:16–20): "Tell us when these things will be and what the sign will be when all of these things are about to be accomplished" (13:4). Through these narrative characters, who have been through the entire ministry of Jesus, who have heard what he has said, and who have seen what he has done to gather the community, Mark now teaches his readers, especially the Jewish Christians in the churches of his own day, what the events surrounding the Roman-Jewish war mean and how they are related to the death of Jesus.

149

Persecution by Jews and Romans

"See to yourselves! They will betray you to Sanhedrins and to synagogues to be beaten. And you will stand before governors and kings on account of me, as a witness [*martyrion*] to them. It is necessary that first the gospel be proclaimed to all the Gentiles.

"And whenever they lead you to be handed over, do not be anxious about what you might say. But whatever is given to you all in that hour [*hōra*], say it. For you are not the ones who speak, but the Holy Spirit.

"And brother will betray brother to death, and the father his child [*teknon*]. And children [*teknon*] will rise up against parents and have them put to death. And you will be hated by all because of my name. The one who endures to the end [*telos*] will be saved [*sōzō*]." (13:9–13)

The narrative equates the tearing down of the Jewish temple with the terrible persecution of the Christian community. These readers will here come to understand the relationship between the betrayal, suffering, and death of Jesus in the narrative and the betrayal, suffering, and death now taking place within the house churches. Jesus in the narrative gathered the house churches—Jews and Gentiles, men and women—for which he now gives his life (10:45; 14:24). This is the chaos—the death of Jesus and the death of the martyrs at the time of Mark's writing—out of which the new creation is to be born: "For there will be such persecution [*thlipsis*] as has not been since the beginning of the creation which God created until now and will not be again" (13:19).

These political events—nation rising against nation, and natural events of earthquakes and famine, as well as the persecution of Christians in Mark's time—are, in the perspective of the writer of Mark, the prelude, the birth pangs, of the imminent return of the resurrected Christ to gather the elect from the *four* winds (13:27).[4] But this end is not yet. The gospel must first be preached to all of the Gentiles (*ethnos*; 13:10), another indication that Mark's narrative is oriented toward a theological justification of that mission. Gentiles are to be joined with Jews in a new humanity marked by the one loaf and one cup of the Lord's Supper (14:22–24). Such missionary activity will be disruptive and will bring persecution in its wake. As Jesus was plotted against (3:6; 11:18), betrayed (14:18–20), and condemned (14:58) on account of his mission to the Gentiles,[5] so the missionaries of Mark's churches will

4. In Mark the wind (*anemos*) refers to active opposition to the mission toward the Gentiles (4:37, toward the Gerasenes; 6:48, toward Bethsaida); four (*tessares*) signals the inclusion of the Gentiles (2:3; 8:9, 20).

5. Both the plot against Jesus at 11:18 and the accusation against Jesus at 14:58 concern the building of a new house of prayer out of the death of Jesus (three days) for the Gentiles (11:17). It is also clear that Judas's betrayal has to do with a rejection of the express meaning

be betrayed and brought to martyrdom for their own mission activities. They are not to be anxious. Just as with Jesus, in their hour (*hōra*) of passion (6:35; 14:35) the Holy Spirit (*pneuma hagion*) will speak directly through them in testimony (13:11; 14:62).

More particularly, Jesus teaches these Jewish disciples in the narrative, plausibly transparent to the Jewish Christians in Mark's house churches, the meaning of persecution from their own Jewish community. Jewish Christians in the time of Mark now suffer the same fate as Jesus predicts here in the narrative. They will suffer as Jesus here in the narrative will suffer. They are to be betrayed to Jewish councils (*synedrion*; 13:9), as Jesus will be betrayed to the council (*synedrion*) and to the Romans (9:31; 14:41, 55; 15:1). They are to be beaten in synagogues (13:9), as Jesus will be beaten in his trial before Jewish authorities (14:65). They are to stand before Gentile authorities and kings and bear witness to them (13:9), as Jesus will stand before the Roman governor Pilate and bear witness to him (15:2).

As Jesus experienced in his own mission, these Jewish Christian disciples can expect their Jewish kin to resist the mission to include the Gentiles in the ritual gatherings of the house churches. When the family of Jesus, his mother and brothers, stood outside the house and called for him, Jesus refused to leave and instead named his Gentile kin as his new family (3:34–35). Later, members of his hometown synagogue close to his family were scandalized by him (6:1–4). Now in the course of the mission of Mark's churches one brother will betray another brother to be executed. A father will betray a child to be killed, and children will rise against their parents and kill them (13:12). The Jewish missionaries will be hated by all for the sake of the name of Christ. Those who endure unto the end—their own death or the imminent return of the resurrected Christ in judgment—will be *saved* (*sōzō*; 3:4; 5:34; 8:35).

Apocalypse Now

"When you see the abomination [*bdelygma*] of desolation standing where it is not necessary (let the one who reads understand) then those in Judea should flee to the mountains. The one on the rooftop should not come down or enter the house to take anything from it. The one coming in from the field should not return and get his cloak. Woe to those who are pregnant or suckling in those days. Pray that it might not be winter. For there will be such persecution

---

of the Last Supper as providing the one loaf, the body of Jesus, for Jews and Gentiles, men and women (8:14–21; 14:22). Judas is described as the "one eating with me [Jesus]" (14:18), who then betrays Jesus in the garden (14:43–45).

[*thlipsis*] as has not been since the beginning of the creation which God created until now and will not be again.

"And if the Lord had not shortened those days, all flesh would not be saved [*sōzō*]. But on account of the elect whom he chose he shortened the days. So if someone says to you, 'See, here is the Christ,' or, 'See, there [is the Christ],' do not believe him. For there will come false christs and false prophets, and they will give signs and wonders in order to lead astray, if it were possible, the elect.

"See [*blepō*]! I have told you all these things beforehand. But in those days with that persecution [*thlipsis*] the sun will be darkened, and the moon will not give its light. The stars will be falling from the heavens, and the powers of heaven will be shaken. And then you will see [*horaō*] the Son of Man coming on the clouds with great power and glory. And he will send out the angels to gather the elect from the four [*tessares*] winds from the heights of the earth to the heights of the heavens. From the fig tree learn the parable: when the branches are tender and put forth leaves, you know that the summer is near. And so when you see these things taking place, you know that he is near, at the very door. Amen, I say to you, this generation will not pass away until all of these things happen. Heaven and earth will pass away, but my words will not pass away." (13:14–31)

Mark 13:14 begins another description of the Jewish war and the desecration (*bdelygma*) of the temple by the Romans. Here the description of the catastrophic events surrounding the Roman conquest of Judea is closely intertwined with an apocalyptic description of the successful attack of chaos upon creation: the attack threatens to reverse the original ordering of chaos (darkness) to create light (Gen. 1:4, 14).[6] Here Mark describes the attack of chaos—in the form of Roman military devastation—as so intense that it threatened, as in the biblical time of Noah, the destruction of all flesh (*pasa sarx*; 13:20; Gen. 6:12 LXX). For the sake of the Christian elect[7]—those chosen by God and probably at the time of Mark's writing located somewhere in greater Galilee—the days are to be shortened, and creation to survive.[8]

For the second time Mark utilizes the narrative character of Jesus to describe the intensity of the war as the cause for an outbreak of religious fervor. False prophets and false messiahs are to arise and challenge the elect status

6. For the close parallels to the apocalyptic literature of the time of Mark's writing, see A. Y. Collins, *Mark*, 607–12.

7. Again the reference is to the LXX account of the Noah story (Gen. 6:8–14). God relents from the destruction of *all flesh* because of Noah's righteousness.

8. There is much debate in modern scholarship over the location of the Markan community. I place the community in Galilee, though the argument for Roman provenance is also often advanced. For discussion, see Black, *Mark*, 28–30; for references in the scholarly literature, see Donahue and Harrington, *Mark*, 41–47.

of the Christian community. They come with signs and wonders powerful enough to lead the elect astray, if that were possible. Here Mark appears to speak directly to his ancient readers. Jesus himself warns the readers of these conditions. The readers should not be led astray by the course of terrible events now taking place (13:23).

For the writer of Mark, the events of the Roman-Jewish war mark the imminent return of the resurrected Christ. Just at the moment of the apparent triumph of chaos over God's power to uphold creation, the opponents of the Christian house churches, perhaps those who have persecuted Christians and those who have attempted to lead Christians astray, will see the Son of Man, the resurrected Christ, return on the clouds. Now all of the elect in the whole world, in all of the house churches, Jews and Gentiles, men and women, will be gathered to Christ. He will send out his angels on the *four* (*tessares*) winds to the very heights of the earth to collect them into his body (13:27).

The reader of Mark hears again the example of the fig tree, that when it begins to bring forth leaves, the summer is near. When the events that Mark has described are happening within the Christian community, when persecution has reached its height both from Jewish communities and government authorities, when the families of Christians have begun to betray each other to these very authorities, when false messiahs have appeared and attempted to draw Christians away from the churches, when all of these things are in fact happening as they are now happening at the time of the Jewish war, the readers of Mark can expect the imminent return of the resurrected Christ. Indeed these readers will not pass away before this takes place (13:31).

Watch!

"But as to the day or the hour, no one knows. Not the angels in heaven, nor the Son, but only the Father. See [*blepō*]! Be alert [*agrypneō*]! For you do not know when the time is. It is as if a traveling man left his house and gave to each of his slaves the authority to do his work. And he commands the doorkeeper to watch [*grēgoreō*]. Watch [*grēgoreō*], therefore, for you do not know when the Lord [*kyrios*] of the house [*oikos*] is coming: evening [*opse*], midnight, cockcrow, or early morning [*proi*]. And when he comes suddenly, he might find you sleeping [*katheudō*]. And what I say to you all, I say to *all* of you: watch [*grēgoreō*]." (13:32–37)

But exactly when will Christ return on the clouds to gather the elect? The expectation of the readers of Mark, in the midst of war and persecution, must have been intense. Yet only the Father knows the exact time of the return of the resurrected Christ (13:32). In the narrative Jesus now relates the parable of the man who goes on a journey and leaves the servants with their duties along with a doorkeeper who is to keep watch (*grēgoreō*; 13:32–37).

Jesus begins the parable with a meaningful repetition of words: "See [*blepō*]! Be alert [*agrypneō*]!" (13:33). In the narrative there has been the constant juxtaposition of *seeing* (*blepō*) and understanding (*syniēmi*) the connection between Jesus's mission to the Gentiles and his necessary death. In the story of the one loaf on the boat (8:14–21), Jesus tells the disciples to "*see* [*blepō*]" in a different way than the leaven of the Pharisees and Herodians (8:15). What is this different way? "Having eyes do you not *see* [*blepō*], and having ears do you not hear?" (8:18). The bread fragments gathered in the two feeding narratives into the twelve baskets and the seven baskets are the one loaf (8:21). Yet this is still not complete *seeing*! In the very next story Jesus cures a blind man, who at first *sees* (*blepō*) indistinctly (people walk as trees, 8:24), and only on a second try with Jesus touching his eyes directly does he *see* (*diablepō*) with restored sight. The formerly blind man now *sees* (*emblepō*) all things clearly (8:25); that is, the Gentiles have joined the Jews to share in the one loaf (8:21).

How does this gathering of Jews and Gentiles, men and women, to share in the one loaf come about? Only through the suffering, betrayal, and death of Jesus (8:31; 9:31; 10:32). Bartimaeus, the son of Timaeus, the one who cannot see, calls upon Jesus as Son of David. He tells Jesus that he wants to "*see again* [*anablepō*]" and Jesus responds. Bartimaeus then *sees again* (*anablepō*) and immediately follows Jesus on the way (*hodos*), that is, to his suffering and death (10:46–52). Yet there is still more to this seeing (*blepō*).

In Jerusalem, upon coming out of the temple, Jesus tells his disciple to *see* (*blepō*) the great buildings, and to know that not one stone will be left upon another. The tearing down of the temple stones and the Christians' being torn down in betrayal and persecution are to be understood only within the story of the tearing down of Jesus: "See [*blepō*] to yourselves. They will betray you to Sanhedrins and to synagogues" (13:9).

So by beginning this small story of the Lord (*kyrios*) of the house who left on a journey with the command to *see* (*blepō*; 13:33), Mark teaches the liturgical readers that even in the present circumstance of betrayal and martyrdom they are to see and understand the meaning of the persecution and its relationship to the imminent return of the resurrected Jesus. They are to continue the work of mission (from which persecution rises). Each has authority to do his or her own work and to watch (*grēgoreō*) for the imminent return of Christ. Indeed Christ could return at any moment of this darkness: the evening, midnight, cockcrow, or the early morning prior to the rising of the sun (*proi*; 13:35). Even though they must be tired, they must hold on and not sleep. The darkness cannot last forever. They are to watch (*grēgoreō*) for the Lord.

Here Jesus's speech to the Jewish disciples ends. The characters in the narrative now teach the ancient readers of the Gospel to understand the persecution against the house churches of Mark's time by *seeing* (*blepō*) the relationship between the mission of Jesus to gather the inclusive church (*tessares*) and his own suffering and death. Out of his death and the subsequent ritual baptism enacting that death there was created the church of Jews and Gentiles, men and women, the church that now suffers his same fate. And just as the death of Jesus leads to his resurrection on the third day, so now the resurrection, the coming of Jesus on the clouds to gather the elect, must be imminent. The readers of Mark must now prepare to *see* themselves as the one loaf, the body of Christ (14:22–23) in the passion, death, and, in the gathering of the elect, the resurrection of Jesus and his imminent return to save them.

8

The Passion of Jesus

Meal and Garden

14:1–52

Mark 14

Seek to Kill

In two days it would be the Passover and the Feast of Unleavened Bread. And the chief priests and the scribes were seeking a way to arrest him by stealth [*dolos*] in order to kill him. For they said, "Not during the Feast, lest there be an uproar of the people." (14:1–2)

At the final verse of Mark 13, the narrative leaves both disciples in the narrative and the readers in suspense: "Watch [*gregoreō*]!" (13:37). The arrest, trial, suffering, and crucifixion of Jesus are about to take place in the narrative. The return of the resurrected Christ amid the crises of the Jewish war and the persecution of the church in Mark's time is about to take place: "Watch!"

Now the narrative returns to the story of Jesus with the notice that it was two days before Passover (14:1). Unlike many modern readers of the passion story, the ancient readers of Mark would not be reading *about* the arrest, trial, and crucifixion of Jesus but *with* the arrest, trial, and crucifixion. For these ancient readers, the tearing down of Jesus is the tearing down of the temple; the anticipated resurrection of Jesus (the empty tomb, 16:5) portends the imminent return of Jesus in glory to gather his church, the new house of prayer, in the midst of devastating persecution and suffering. Jesus has already taught the disciples that the Son of Man has come to give his life as a ransom for many (10:45), that the destruction of the temple and its ritual performance of atonement now takes place in the ritual performance of the destruction of Jesus (baptism), the ritual that opens up the way (*hodos*) for the Gentiles to join with the Jews in a new house of prayer (11:17). The readers of Mark have been told the story of Jesus's mission to gather Jews and Gentiles into the one loaf, the one ritual meal (8:14–21). These readers have noted the resistance to Gentile inclusion on the part of the Jewish disciples (6:37; 8:4) and even the family of Jesus (3:31), as well as outright hostility on the part of some Jews (3:6; 11:18). And now these readers are experiencing the suffering of many in their own churches at the hands of both Jews and Gentiles (13:9). Despite resistance and lack of understanding among the Jewish disciples in the narrative (8:32; 9:32), these readers realize from Jesus himself that it is necessary for Jesus to suffer and be executed and after three days rise (8:31; 9:31; 10:34). And so they are now prepared for the central irony of the Gospel to play out in the passion narrative: Jesus's mission to include the Gentiles has incited the hostility that leads directly to his execution; yet his death is the means by which, through ritual baptism, primeval chaos is defeated and the Gentiles are included in the sacred space of the ritual meal, the ritual meal that consummates the restoration of Genesis humanity. The resurrected Jesus will very soon come to defeat chaos (persecution) and gather the elect (13:27).

In Memory of Her

And when he was in Bethany at the house of Simon the leper, he was reclining at table. A woman came in with an alabaster jar of pure and very expensive ointment. She smashed the jar and poured [*katacheō*] it over his head [*kephalē*]. And there were some there who were indignant amongst themselves concerning why the ointment was destroyed [*apōleia*]. "This oil could have been sold for over three hundred denarii, and the money given to the poor." And they were angry at her.

But Jesus said, "Forgive her; why do you trouble her? She has done a good work for me. For you always have the poor with you, and whenever you wish you are able to do good toward them. But you will not always have me. She gave what she had [*echō*] and has anointed my body [*sōma*] now for burial. Amen, I say to you, wherever the gospel is preached in the whole world, what she has done will be told in memory of her." (14:3–9)

One aspect of the plot of the passion narrative is established immediately: the crowd is on the side of Jesus, and so the chief priests and scribes who desire to have Jesus executed must act in a way so as not to arouse the crowd (14:1–2). At 14:10 there is again notice of this plan to kill Jesus by stealth. In between these two notices of the plot to kill Jesus, Mark inserts the story of the woman who anoints Jesus for burial with nard and myrrh (14:3–9). As some of those around Jesus once again resist the notion that Jesus must die, this anonymous *woman* obviously understands and accepts that Jesus must die.

The liturgical reader would see Jesus reclining and preparing to eat the Lord's Supper in the house church of Simon the leper in Bethany (14:3). A woman comes into the room and crushes a flask of pure and costly nard and pours out (*katacheō*) the ointment over the head of Jesus. During the ritual of the Last Supper Jesus himself will pour out (*ekcheō*) the blood of the covenant for the *many* (*polys*; 14:24), which, along with giving his life as a ransom for the *many* (*polys*; 10:45) and the pouring out (*katacheō*) here, makes it clear that the purpose of Jesus's death is the inclusion of Jews and Gentiles, men and women, at the table.

Here the readers of Mark also note that this is the second time an anonymous woman has played a key role in the development of the narrative. Earlier the Syrophoenician (Gentile) woman successfully persuaded Jesus to include the Gentiles and women at the second ritual meal narrative: "Lord, the small dogs under the table also eat from the crumbs of the children" (7:28). As a result four thousand, including Gentiles and women, are fed at the ritual meal in the wilderness (8:9). The woman here who pours out (*katacheō*) the flask of pure and very expensive ointment has unexpectedly joined the other disciples at the meal and demonstrates an understanding, through her ritual performance, that her presence at the meal is grounded in the pouring out (*ekcheō*) of Jesus for the many (*polys*; 14:24).

Some of the participants at the meal are indignant. They are apparently not indignant over the fact that the woman has barged in, or that she has brought a flask of pure and very expensive ointment. They are indignant that the ointment was destroyed (*apōleia*). The readers are brought again to Mark 3:6, where, following a series of controversies that revolve around Jesus's acceptance, and inclusion, of Gentiles (2:1–3:6), the Pharisees and Herodians plot to *destroy* (*apollymi*) Jesus. And again these readers note that it is Jesus's statement about the temple, "My house shall be called a house of prayer for all the Gentiles," that incites the scribes and chief priests to seek to *destroy* (*apollymi*) Jesus (11:17–18). The liturgical reader of Mark therefore has every reason to conclude that these guests in the house church of Simon the leper, perhaps transparent to some Jewish Christians in Mark's time who are reluctant to include Gentiles and women, understand the connection with what the woman does in pouring out (*katacheō*) and destroying (*apōleia*) the ointment.

And if the guests do understand this connection between the pouring out and destruction of the ointment on the head of Jesus and the death he is about to suffer for the many (10:45; 14:24), their indignation is misguided. The woman could have sold the ointment for more than three hundred denarii, and the money have been given to the poor. Yet the liturgical reader knows that if this had been done, the oil would not have been "poured out" and "destroyed" here at this meal. The anonymous woman would not have been able to put into ritual form the connection between the inclusive ritual meal they were eating in the house of Simon the leper and the *necessary* death of Christ (8:31).

Jesus commands that those at the meal are not to trouble the woman. It is a good thing that this woman has literally enacted the connection between the death of Jesus and the ritual meal they are eating. Unlike Peter earlier in the narrative (8:32), she has not been resistant to Jesus's necessary death, nor has she been ashamed of Jesus's death (8:38). Unlike James and John (10:37), she has sought not the highest place at the table, but the lowest.[1]

The anonymous woman anoints for burial the body (*sōma*) of Christ at the ritual meal (14:8).[2] Hence she accepts that Jesus must die to become the resurrected body (*sōma*) of Christ enacted in the meal (14:22): the new humanity of Jews and Gentiles, men and women at the table. The narrative purpose of Mark, to advocate for an inclusive meal created by the death of Christ, is perfectly performed in this woman's ritual anointing of Jesus. The liturgical reader now remembers (*mnēmoneuō*) the five loaves of the five thousand in twelve baskets and the seven loaves of the four thousand in seven baskets (8:18), and now, "Wherever the gospel is preached in the whole world, what she has done will be told in memory [*mnēmosynon*] of her" (14:9).

Preparation for the Final Ritual Meal

And Judas Iscariot, one of the twelve, went to the chief priests in order to betray [*paradidōmi*] him [Jesus] to them. And when they heard this, they were glad

---

1. What the woman has done here does not mean that the poor should be neglected. Those at the meal have the means to attend to them. Rather they ought to realize that Jesus is about to be taken from them (14:7). And like the widow who cast her two cents into the temple treasury, all that she possessed (*echō*; 12:44), this woman too gave all that she possessed (*echō*; 14:8). For the liturgical reader, both women are figures of Christ within the narrative.

2. The reader would note the careful switch in language here. The woman enters and pours out the ointment on Jesus's head (*kephalē*; 14:3), and Jesus remarks that she has anointed his body (*sōma*; 14:8).

160

and promised to give him silver. And he sought to betray him at an opportune moment. On the first day of the Feast of Unleavened Bread, when they sacrifice [*thyō*] the Passover lamb, his disciples said to him, "Where do you wish that we should go to prepare for you to eat the Passover?" And he sent two of his disciples and said to them, "Go into the city, and you will meet a man carrying a vessel of water [*keramion hydatos*]: follow him. And wherever he enters, say to the householder [*oikodespotēs*], 'The teacher [*didaskalos*] says, "Where is my guestroom, that I might eat the Passover with my disciples?"' He will then show you a large upper room [*anagaion mega*], furnished and ready. Prepare for us there." His disciples went out and came into the city and found the situation as he had described. And they prepared the Passover. (14:10–16)

The reader of Mark already knows that Judas is one of the Twelve (3:19). So when Mark tells us that Judas, *one of the Twelve*, went to the chief priests in order to betray (*paradidōmi*) Jesus (14:10), the narrative is again linking what is happening in the passion of Jesus with the betrayals, even within families, that are taking place in the churches of Mark's time (*paradidōmi*; 13:9, 11). No motive is given for Judas's action. The chief priests, however, are glad of Judas's willingness to betray Jesus, because Judas might be able to accomplish this betrayal by stealth (*dolos*; 14:1), that is, at a time and place away from the crowd that favors Jesus (11:18; 14:11).

The narrative emphasis on the sacrifice (*thyō*) of the Passover lamb on the first day of Unleavened Bread brings the liturgical reader to consider carefully the relationship between the death of Jesus as a sacrifice (*thyō*) and the Passover meal Jesus is about to eat with his disciples (14:12). The disciples ask Jesus where they should go to prepare a place for him to eat the Passover. Just as at the meal in the house of Simon the leper, there appear to be more than just the twelve disciples accompanying Jesus here. He sends two of these disciples (they remain anonymous) to meet a man who carries a water jar.[3] They are to follow this man to a house and give to the householder (*oikodespotēs*) a message from the teacher: "Where is my guestroom, that I might eat the Passover with my disciples?" (14:14). The two disciples are to be shown a large upper room (*anagaion mega*) of the house, already set up for the ritual meal.[4] They

3. Here also the liturgical reader of Mark might note carefully the presence of a water vessel and its baptismal connotations—especially since there is no obvious rationale in the narrative for the man to be carrying a water vessel. Although the terms used for the water container are different in Mark and John (*keramion hydatos*; *hydria hydatos*; John 2:7), it might well be argued that the stone water jars in John's story of the wedding at Cana also possess baptismal connotations. See Cullman's discussion of John's symbolism in *Early Christian Worship*, 117–19.

4. The narrative implies that the location is apparently a house with a room in which the ritual Passover meal can be eaten. At the very least the room must be large enough to accommodate these two disciples along with the twelve Jewish disciples who will arrive with Jesus.

are to prepare for the arrival of Jesus and the twelve disciples. The narrative reports that these things all happened according to what Jesus had told them. So the two disciples prepare the Passover meal (14:16).[5]

The Disciples at the Meal

And when it was evening [*opsia*], he came with the twelve.[6] And when they were reclining at table eating, Jesus said, "Amen, I say to you, one of you will betray [*paradidōmi*] me, one eating with me." And they began to grieve and to say to him one by one, "Not I?" And he said to them, "One from the twelve, the one dipping with me into the dish. So it goes for the Son of Man as it is written concerning him, but woe to that man through whom the Son of Man is betrayed; it would be better for that man to not have been born." (14:17–21)

Mark begins the description of the Passover with a notice that it was "evening" (14:17). Throughout the narrative, Mark has already carefully linked the fall of darkness—the evening—with the in-breaking of the resurrection and restored creation. It is in the evening (*opsia*) after the sun has set on the Sabbath[7]—that is, Sunday[8]—that Jesus heals the many who are afflicted and casts out demons (1:32). After this, in the very early morning of Sunday (*prōi*), Jesus resurrects (*anistēmi*) and goes out to the wilderness (1:35). Again it is in the evening (*opsia*) that the disciples and Jesus set out in a boat on the sea traveling toward the Gentile Gerasenes (4:35). In that story Jesus will be baptized, dead (sleeping) under the sea, and then rise (*diegeirō*) to calm the waters of chaos (4:39). It is also in the evening (*opsia*) that the resurrected Christ walks upon the sea (on his way to the Gentile mission) and again calms the contrary wind (6:51). There is every indication, therefore, that this meal in the evening (darkness), besides being a normal Passover meal, alerts the liturgical reader that the resurrection, the body of Christ enacted in ritual (14:22), will emerge from the chaos of betrayal (*paradidōmi*) and darkness (*opsia*).

For the liturgical reader, the narrative indicates that more than just the twelve Jewish disciples are with Jesus for the Passover meal. The room is specifically designated as *very large* (*anagaion mega*; 14:15). The two anonymous disciples, whom the liturgical reader might see as Gentiles, are already

5. That the two disciples here are not part of the twelve is indicated in the next verse: "And when it was evening he came with the twelve" (14:17). The reader presumes that the two disciples are there at the very large upper room and then Jesus arrives with the twelve.

6. The reader notes that the two disciples who have prepared the Passover are not part of the Twelve.

7. Peter's mother-in-law was raised on the Sabbath after the exorcism in the synagogue (1:21).

8. Sunday—the first day of the new week—begins at sundown on the Sabbath.

present. In addition, the Jewish and Gentile Bartimaeus, son of Timaeus, has followed Jesus on "the way [*hodos*]," (10:52), and there is also the immediately preceding story of the anonymous woman who anointed Jesus while they were eating in Bethany (14:3).[9]

In addition to these suggestions, however, there is also a significant narrative signal that what is being described here is a larger and more inclusive ritual meal:

> And when they were reclining at table eating, Jesus said, "Amen, I say to you, *one of you* will betray [*paradidōmi*] me, one eating with me." And they began to grieve and to say to him one by one, "Not I?" And he said to them, "One [of you] from *the twelve*, the one dipping with me into the dish." (14:18–20)

From the description of a larger group, "one of you [plural]," the narrative moves to a deliberate contrast: "One [of you] from *the twelve*, the one dipping with me into the dish." Narratively, the second move to identify "one from the twelve" makes little sense without the contrast to a larger group present at the table. The narrative therefore suggests a larger group of disciples at the meal from which the Twelve, also at the meal, are distinguished. As with the situation of family and friends betrayal in the house churches of Mark's time (3:31–35; 6:1–4; 13:12), here also one of Jesus's closest companions will betray him.

The Ritual

And while they were eating, he took [*lambanō*] the loaf [*artos*] and blessed [*eulogeō*] it and gave [*didōmi*] it to them and said, "Take [*lambanō*] [the loaf], this is my body [*sōma*]."[10]

And he took the cup [*potērion*] and gave thanks [*eucharisteō*] and gave [*didōmi*] it to them. And they all [*pas*] drank [*pinō*] from it. And he said to them, "This is my blood of the covenant which is poured out [*echeō*] on behalf

9. The liturgical reader would note the narrative pattern here: the story of the Gentile Syrophoenician woman comes immediately before the second ritual meal narrative indicating that women are at that meal (7:25–8:9); the story of the woman who anoints Jesus comes immediately before this final ritual meal indicating that women are at this meal (14:3–26).

10. The Greek language marks gender, and as a result much is made of the fact that the word for "loaf [*artos*]" here is masculine, while the word for "this [*touto*]" (*this* is my body) is neuter. As such, the neuter word "this" cannot formally refer to the masculine loaf here. Indeed the reference here is most likely more general: "*this* is my body" refers, in the context of specific ritual action, to the larger group of disciples—Jews, Gentiles, and women—present at the meal. The more significant point here is that the single loaf ("he took *the loaf*"), which points to the one loaf aboard the boat at 8:21, signals the full unity of all those gathered at the one ritual meal, Jews and Gentiles, men and women.

of the many [*polys*]. Amen, I say to you, I will no longer drink from the fruit of the vine until that day when I drink it new [*kainos*] in the kingdom of God." (14:22–25)

As has often been noted by scholars, the ritual actions described here match almost perfectly the ritual actions described in the earlier ritual meal narratives. In all three rituals Jesus *takes* the loaves/loaf, *breaks* the loaves/loaf, and *gives* the loaves/loaf (6:41; 8:6; 14:22). The difference is in the prayer. In the first ritual meal narrative Jesus "blesses [*eulogeō*]" the loaves, associated with the Jewish context of that ritual (6:41), and in the second ritual meal narrative Jesus "gives thanks [*eucharisteō*]" for the loaves, associated with the Gentile context of that ritual (8:6).[11] Here in the final ritual meal those two ritual actions (blessing; giving thanks) are combined: Jesus "blesses [*eulogeō*]" the bread and then "gives thanks [*eucharisteō*]" over the cup (14:23). The Jewish context of the first ritual meal and the Gentile context of the second ritual meal have been combined in this one ritual of eating and drinking in the immediate context of Jesus's death (14:3–9). For the liturgical reader, the understanding of the first two meal rituals that emerges from the dialogue about the one loaf on the boat—that the five loaves feeding five thousand with twelve baskets left (Jewish), and the seven loaves feeding four thousand with seven (very large) baskets left (Gentile) is actually the one loaf on the boat with them (8:14–21)—is now fully expressed in the meal that sets out the meaning of the passion narrative itself: the blessing (*eulogeō*) of the one loaf is the Jewish and Gentile body of Christ; the giving thanks over the cup (*eucharisteō*) marks the death of Christ which is the means by which, through ritual baptism, the Gentiles, men and women, have come to be a part of that body. And here also the presence of a larger group of disciples beyond the twelve Jewish disciples signals well the overall purpose of the narrative of Mark: Jews and Gentiles, men and women, are to be present as the body of Christ to eat the one loaf and to drink the one cup.[12]

At 14:23, Mark furthers the description of the second act of the ritual with an emphatic statement: "And they all drank [*pinō*] from it [*potērion*, the cup]." Earlier in the narrative this ritual cup had been specifically linked to the baptismal death of Jesus. Jesus asks the question to James and John in a

---

11. Focant, *Mark*, 576; Marcus, *Mark 9–16*, 956–59; Donahue and Harrington, *Mark*, 391–401.

12. The remarkably similar language of Eph. 2:15–16 (cf. 3:6), Jews and Gentiles as one body created by the (baptismal) death of Christ, most likely also points to how the ancient liturgical reader would have understood the narrative description here. In the second century Ignatius of Antioch refers to Jews and Gentiles in the body (*sōma*) of the church (*ekklēsia*; *Smyr.* 1.1).

reference to their eventual martyrdom: "Are you able to drink [*pinō*] the cup [*potērion*] that I drink [*pinō*] or to be baptized [*baptizō*] with the baptism with which I am baptized?" (10:38). For the liturgical reader, then, drinking (*pinō*) the cup (*potērion*) points directly to the present martyrdom of Jesus as the fulfillment of ritual baptism, the way (*hodos*) of ritual death with which the narrative begins. This is the way (*hodos*) of death that brings about the unity of the house churches, the mission of Jesus to gather the inclusive churches, the body of Christ (14:8, 22) that now suffers persecution and martyrdom in the time of Mark's writing (13:9) and anxiously awaits the imminent return of the resurrected Christ on the clouds with his angels (13:26).[13]

Immediately after "they all drank from the cup," Mark adds to the intended meaning of the ritual: "This is my blood of the covenant which is poured out on behalf of *the many*" (*polys*; 14:24). The liturgical reader is brought again to consider Mark 10:45: "The Son of Man came not to be served but to serve and to give his life as a ransom on behalf of *the many* [*polys*]." The content of the cup is the blood being poured out now, the passion of Jesus about to be told, and it binds into covenant this larger group of disciples now together at the meal (*polys*, the many). By setting out the action and words of Jesus in this way, the narrative speaks directly to the ritual gathering of the churches in Mark's time: to acknowledge the death of Christ in the cup of the ritual meal is to acknowledge the express purpose of that death, namely, to establish in new covenant the inclusive community of Jews and Gentiles, men and women, as the body of Christ.[14]

Peter and Denial

And they sang a hymn and went out to the Mount of Olives. And Jesus said to them, "All of you will be scandalized [*scandalizō*], as it is written, 'I will strike the shepherd and the sheep will be scattered.' But after I am raised [*egeirō*],

13. The catechetical origins of the institution narrative are thoroughly discussed by McGowan, "Is There a Liturgical Text?," 73–87.

14. On the connotations of covenant from the Jewish Scriptures, see Donahue and Harrington, *Mark*, 391–401. Though using a different word for "new [*kainos*]," the final statement of Jesus regarding the ritual, "Amen, I say to you, I will no longer drink from the fruit of the vine until that day when I drink it new [*kainos*] in the kingdom of God" (14:25), reminds the liturgical reader of what Jesus had pronounced earlier in the narrative concerning the necessity of putting new (*neos*) wine into new (*neos*) wineskins (2:22). In that narrative context, with the demonstrated eagerness of Gentiles to be part of the community and Jesus's forgiveness of their sins (2:1–12), new wineskins might well be a reference to the establishment of the new Christian community in house churches. It is also undoubtedly a reference to the imminent coming of the resurrected Christ to this new covenant community: the death of Jesus in the narrative signals the imminent return of the resurrected Christ on the clouds to gather the elect (13:26–27).

I will go before you to Galilee." And Peter said to him, "Even if everyone is scandalized [*scandalizō*], I will not be." And Jesus said to him, "Amen, I say to you today, on this night before the cock crows twice you will deny me three times." But he [Peter] said insistently, "Even if it is necessary [*dei*] for me to die with you, I will not deny you." And they all said the same thing. (14:26–31)

After singing a hymn, Jesus and the larger group of disciples leave the large room of the Passover meal and go out to the Mount of Olives. Jesus's announcement, that all of these disciples will be scandalized, brings the liturgical reader to again consider the first ritual meal narrative. There Jesus taught the gathered group of Gentiles (sheep) as their scriptural "shepherd" (6:34), and here Jesus intones Zechariah 13:7 to predict that these same sheep will be scattered and then predicts his resurrection and appearance in Galilee (14:28), his imminent return to gather the (scattered) elect from the four winds and the ends of the earth (13:27).

The use of the plural *you* ("I will go before *you* to Galilee") here is matched by the statement of the young man in the tomb who greets the women in the morning of the resurrection: "Go, tell the disciples and Peter, he goes before *you* to Galilee" (16:7). Peter's resistance here, "Even if everyone is scandalized, I will not be" (14:29), indicates he now accepts that the Son of Man must suffer, be rejected and killed, and after three days rise (8:31), and that he intends to remain faithful. Jesus, however, predicts that Peter will in fact deny him three times before the cock crows in the morning. Peter's statement here apparently rectifies his earlier denial of the necessity (*dei*) of Jesus's suffering and death (8:32): "Even if it is necessary [*dei*] for me to die with you, I will not deny you" (14:31). Yet Peter famously fails to keep his promise here.

The narrative now brings the reader again to Jesus's description in chapter 13 of impending betrayal (*paradidōmi*), persecution, and resulting deaths within the Christian community, along with the assurance that "the one who endures to the end will be saved" (13:9–13). Therefore the narrative makes more sense if the point of contrast is between Peter and the larger group of disciples present rather than just the Twelve. Peter, as the lead spokesman for the *Jewish* disciples, will in fact fare no better in faithfulness than any of the disciples gathered for the final Lord's Supper. They will *all* scatter at the arrest of Jesus (14:50). Once again the narrative is transparent to Mark's churches. There will be both betrayal and martyrdom throughout the community, including both Jews and Gentiles, during the Roman war and the destruction of the temple (13:9–13). Those who hear the Gospel in Mark's churches are being taught to interpret this experience of betrayal and martyrdom and the temple's destruction as the story of the betrayal and destruction of Jesus, the cosmic chaos out of which will come the new creation, the resurrection of Christ and the building of a new temple, the body of Christ, Jews and Gentiles, men and women, the house of prayer for the Gentiles (11:17).

The Garden of Gethsemane

And they came to a place called Gethsemane. And he said to his disciples, "Sit here while I pray." And he took Peter, James, and John with him, and he began to be disturbed and troubled. And he said to them, "My soul is sad until death: remain here and watch [*grēgoreō*]." And he went a bit further and fell upon the earth and prayed that if it were possible, the hour [*hōra*] might pass from him. And he said, "Abba, Father, all things are possible with you; take this cup [*potērion*] from me, but not what I will but what you will."

And he came and discovered them sleeping [*katheudō*]. And he said to Peter, "Simon, are you sleeping? Do you not have strength to watch [*grēgoreō*] for one hour? Watch [*grēgoreō*] and pray that you may not come into temptation. The spirit is willing, but the flesh is weak."

And again he departed to pray in the same way. And again when he came back he discovered them sleeping [*katheudō*], for their eyes [*ophthalmos*] were weighed down and they did not know how to answer him.

And he came back again for the third time and said to them, "Will you sleep [*katheudō*] for the rest of the night and be refreshed? It is fulfilled. The hour [*hōra*] has come. Behold, the Son of Man is betrayed [*paradidōmi*] into the hands of sinners. Rise [*egeirō*], let us go. See, my betrayer [*paradidōmi*] draws near [*engizō*] to me." (14:32–42)

The story of the disciples with Jesus in the garden of Gethsemane serves the purpose of linking Jesus's passion and death to his imminent return as the resurrected Christ (13:27) amid the dire situation of the churches in Mark's time (13:9). Again the larger group of disciples is described, those who were with Jesus at the final ritual meal of Passover. From this larger group Jesus now selects the three Jewish disciples who have been with him from the very beginning of his mission (1:16–20). These three have witnessed the resurrection of Peter's mother-in-law in a house (1:29), the resurrection of Jairus's daughter in his house (5:41), the Transfiguration (resurrection) of Jesus on the mountain (9:2), and Jesus's long speech telling of the destruction of the temple, impending persecution, and his imminent return on the clouds (13:3–27). They have, in effect, been shown the reality of the resurrection of Christ and the fulfillment of Jewish apocalyptic expectations, the defeat of chaos and the dawn of new creation. They have been taught the link between the destruction of the temple, betrayals by family, and horrendous persecution, on the one hand, and the betrayal, persecution, and destruction of Jesus, on the other.

They now know and expect their suffering to be followed by the in-breaking of new creation: the church gathered from the four winds by the resurrected Christ (13:27). They have also been shown that the ritual meal of Jews and Gentiles, men and women, gathered together as the one loaf, is the inclusive community, the body of Christ, which will suffer persecution and martyrdom in the expectation of the imminent return of the resurrected Christ.

At the moment of this destruction, the moment of the death of the martyrs, the readers of Mark and these three Jewish disciples were told to *watch* (*grēgoreō*) for the return of Christ on the clouds of heaven (13:27, 37). And so the scene at Gethsemane is set. The story is about vigilance and endurance in the midst of betrayal (*paradidōmi*) and martyrdom. Once again the story of Jesus helps the reader in Mark's time to understand his or her own story. This ancient reader notes that Jesus has already told these three disciples that, at the destruction of the temple and the death of the martyrs, they are to *watch* (*grēgoreō*) for the return of the Son of Man (13:27). They are not to be caught sleeping (*katheudō*), as they know neither the day nor the hour of the return (13:32–37).

Now the narrative has brought these three disciples and the readers of Mark to the brink of the betrayal and death of Jesus. In the darkness Jesus is distressed and upset (14:33). Indeed his life is saddened unto death itself (*thanatos*; 14:34). And just here Jesus instructs the three disciples, and so also the liturgical readers of Mark, to "remain here and watch [*grēgoreō*]" (14:34). The destruction of the temple and the persecution and destruction of Christians in the time of Mark's writing are now to be understood within the story of Jesus's suffering and death. At the hour of betrayal and death the disciples in the narrative, and so the readers within Mark's church, are to "watch [*grēgoreō*]" for Christ's return (13:37; 14:34).

Modern readers of Mark often focus on the agony of Jesus in the garden and the moment of personal doubt Jesus has here about his own death. Certainly this display of emotion is integral to the narrative portrayal of Jesus in Mark. Yet there are two liturgical references in this scene which draw the attention of the liturgical reader of Mark as well. Jesus in the garden prays that if it were possible, the *hour* (*hōra*) might pass from him (14:35). The liturgical reader is brought back to the scene of the first ritual meal, where the Gentiles were unexpectedly present in the wilderness and where Jesus commands that they be fed by the disciples (6:37). There the narrative refers not once but twice to the lateness of the *hour* (6:35). In the second instance the disciples resist the idea of feeding the Gentiles: "This is a wilderness place, and already the *hour* is getting late." The dual notice of the lateness of the hour (*hōra*) signals that the following meal, the enactment of the resurrected body of Christ within the ritual meal

(14:22), will always take place within the context of the passion of Christ. It is here that the Gentiles and Jews, men and women, have been gathered at the table.

So when Jesus in the garden of Gethsemane utters the prayer that, "if it were possible, the hour [*hōra*] might pass," the liturgical reader is drawn once again to recall the meal of Jews and Gentiles in the wilderness made possible by the death of Jesus. Rather than focusing on the personal doubt implied in Jesus's statement about the ritual meal ("Abba, Father, all things are possible with you; take this cup [*potērion*] from me"), the liturgical reader might seize on the necessity of the connection of the ritual meal (*potērion*) to the death (baptism) of Christ. For this reader it is the necessary death of Christ (8:31) and martyrs (14:31) that creates the inclusive table fellowship.

The argument here between the Father (Abba) and the Son (from which the reader only hears one side) also reminds the liturgical reader of Jesus's argument with the Syrophoenician woman prior to the second ritual meal in the wilderness (7:24–30). Jesus there, at least for a moment, seemingly resists the inclusion of the Gentiles and women with the Jews at the Lord's Supper: "The children must first be allowed to eat and be satisfied [*chortazō*]" (7:27). Yet even so Jesus relents and casts the demon from the Gentile woman's daughter (7:24), and the Gentiles and women are satisfied (*chortazō*) at the subsequent ritual meal (8:8).

Here in Gethsemane Jesus also for a moment resists the necessity of his death, which will be the means by which the Gentiles, men and women, share in the one loaf of the Lord's Supper. His request that God might take the cup from him places the liturgical reader squarely within the context of the final ritual meal, wherein Jesus announces that the cup, over which he gives thanks, holds the blood of the covenant which will be *poured out* for the many (*polys*; 14:24). This is the death that ransoms the many (*polys*), the Gentiles and women (10:45). For the Jewish-Christian readers in Mark's churches, this would have been a powerful moment. Their own hesitation about the inclusion of Gentiles in the Lord's Supper is momentarily shared by Jesus himself. Yet here in the garden Jesus submits himself to the will of God: he must drink the cup and suffer the passion for the many (10:45; 14:24, 36).

Mark now directly links the drama taking place in Gethsemane to the ending of the temple discourse in chapter 13. In the earlier address to these same disciples Jesus stressed that, in the midst of persecution, they must not sleep (*katheudō*) as they kept watch (*grēgoreō*) for the coming of the Lord of the house (13:9–13, 37).

"But as to the day or the hour [*hōra*], no one knows. Not the angels in heaven, nor the Son, but only the Father. See [*blepō*]! Be alert! For you do not know when the time is. It is as if a traveling man left his house and gave to each of his slaves the authority to do his work. And he commands the doorkeeper to watch [*grēgoreō*]. Watch [*grēgoreō*], therefore, for you do not know when the Lord [*kyrios*] of the house [*oikos*] is coming: evening [*opse*], midnight, cockcrow, or early morning [*proi*]. And when he comes suddenly, he might find you sleeping [*katheudō*]. And what I say to you all, I say to *all* of you: watch [*grēgoreō*]." (13:32–37)

Now in Gethsemane, Jesus returns to find these three disciples *sleeping* (*katheudō*). The Lord of the house has returned! Jesus now addresses only Peter, apparently the doorkeeper who was commanded to watch, with the query, "Simon, are you sleeping [*katheudō*]? Do you not have the strength to *watch* [*grēgoreō*] for one hour?" (14:37). In the narrative, the doorkeeper Peter has temporarily failed, and will soon spectacularly fail, to keep watch, to have the strength to endure betrayal and persecution. And just here the narrative shifts away from particularly addressing Peter to include James and John and all readers of the narrative as well: "*You* [plural] *watch* [*grēgoreō*] and pray that you may not come into temptation. The spirit is willing, but the flesh is weak" (14:38). The ancient readers of Mark would again realize that the betrayals and persecution within the churches could be understood only in light of Jesus's own betrayal and persecution. The story of his betrayal and death in Mark signals that they now must not be caught sleeping but rather be watching for his imminent return to save them.

At Mark 14:39, Jesus withdraws again and prays in the same way; it is another powerful moment of hesitation and then acceptance of his death as the means by which the inclusive house church is established. When Jesus returns to the three disciples for a second time, he finds them sleeping, for, as the narrative explains, "their eyes [*ophthalmos*] were weighed down" (14:40). The reader is reminded of the blind man at Bethsaida, most likely a Gentile in that place, who came to see clearly when Jesus touched his eyes (*ophthalmos*; 8:25). His eyes came to see clearly what weighs down the eyes of these disciples in the garden: the death of Jesus results in the one loaf of the Lord's Supper for Jews and Gentiles, men and women (8:21).

Jesus now comes back to the disciples for a third time (14:41). He announces the hour of the passion: "Behold, the Son of Man is betrayed [*paradidōmi*] into the hands of sinners" (14:41). At this point the liturgical reader is made keenly aware that the Gethsemane narrative has been carefully constructed to convey *three* episodes of *sleeping* (*katheudō*) followed by the climactic moment of the betrayal and arrest of Jesus. For the liturgical reader of Mark, sleep (*katheudō*) conveys more than just inattentiveness on the part of the three disciples in the garden. It brings to attention the three days of death (*meta treis hēmeras*) and sleep (*katheudō*; 4:38; 5:39), followed by resurrection, which is integral to all three passion predictions (8:31; 9:31; 10:34). After three instances of *sleep* (*katheudō*), there is here the moment of betrayal and arrest. Jesus will rise after three days.

The ancient readers of Mark, in the midst of betrayal (*paradidōmi*) and martyrdom (13:12), can now expect to see soon the resurrection of Christ, the coming of the Son of Man on the clouds of heaven to gather his elect from the four winds (13:27; 14:62). So it is that at just this point in Gethsemane Jesus tells the disciples, "Rise [*egeirō*], let us go. See [*horaō*], my betrayer *draws near* [*engizō*] to me" (14:42). These readers now realize what Jesus said to these same disciples in the temple in the midst of predicting their betrayal and martyrdom: "When you *see* [*horaō*] these things taking place, you know that he *draws near* [*engys*], at the very door" (13:29). As the ancient readers of Mark enter into their own suffering and death, they should expect to see their redemption in the resurrection and imminent return of Jesus.

This interpretation of the Gospel also points to why the narrative ends so abruptly at 16:8 ("for they were afraid"). Mark ends the narrative immediately following the betrayal, suffering, and death of Jesus. After three days the women discover the young man at the tomb of Jesus. The young man tells the women to tell Peter and the other disciples that they will see (*horaō*) Jesus in Galilee (16:7). The ancient readers of Mark in Galilee would now understand what this means.[15] Jesus will soon appear on the clouds of heaven in the midst of their betrayals (*paradidōmi*), suffering, and martyrdom (14:62; 13:27). Those who endure to the end will be saved (8:34–38; 13:13). For Mark and his ancient readers, that moment—the arrest and betrayal of Jesus, his suffering, death, and the empty tomb—marks the imminent return of the resurrected Jesus, the moment that is now upon them in their own trials (9:1; 13:30).

The Betrayal

And immediately while he was still speaking, Judas, one of the twelve, came with his crowd with swords and clubs, and along with the chief priests, scribes, and elders. The betrayer had given them a signal, saying, "The one I will kiss [*phileō*] is him; seize him and lead him away securely." And immediately when he arrived, he approached him and said, "Rabbi!" And he kissed him. And they laid hands upon him and seized him.

15. The location of the original readers of Mark's Gospel is discussed at length in the major commentaries. For discussion see A. Y. Collins, *Mark*, 7–10; Focant, *Mark*, 7–9.

> One of the bystanders drew out a sword and struck the slave of the chief priest and cut off his ear. And Jesus said to them, "Did you come out with swords and clubs against a thief to arrest me? I was teaching every day in the temple amongst you, and you did not arrest me. But so that the scriptures might be fulfilled."
>
> And everyone abandoned him and fled. But there was a certain young man with a cloak wrapped about his naked body, who was following [synakoloutheō] Jesus; and they seized him. But he abandoned the cloak and fled naked. (14:43–52)

Here Mark draws out the correlation between the situation of Jesus in the narrative and the circumstances of the ancient churches amid trial and persecution. In the narrative, the new family of Jesus has been created, Jews and Gentiles, men and women in the house church: "And having looked around at those sitting round about him [in the house], he said, 'See my mother and my brothers. For whosoever should do the will of God, this person is my brother, sister, and mother'" (3:34–35).[16] And now this new family in the time of Mark's writing suffers horrific betrayal, suffering, and martyrdom: "Brother will betray [paradidōmi] brother to death, and the father his child. And children will rise up against parents and have them put to death [thanatoō]" (13:12).

In the narrative, Judas, one of the twelve Jewish disciples who was chosen to be with Jesus (3:19; 14:20), arrives with a crowd armed with swords and clubs along with the chief priests, scribes, and elders (14:43; 8:31). Judas is identified as the betrayer, and the one to be arrested will be the one to whom he shows overt affection, that is, a fervent kiss (phileō; 14:45). The liturgical reader recalls that Jesus's announcement of his pending betrayal took place at the Lord's Supper (14:18), so for the liturgical reader, the kiss might surely be understood as an ironic parallel to the kiss of peace, a central moment in both ancient and modern Christian liturgy.[17] As Jesus is betrayed by those closest to him, so also are the ancient readers of Mark betrayed by those closest to them.[18]

When the narrative portrays the Jewish disciples who are closest to Jesus in Gethsemane—Peter, James, and John—as abandoning him at the moment of his capture (14:50), it is difficult not to come to the conclusion that here Mark is addressing the situation in his own church, namely, the reluctance

16. A narrative version of the argument that Paul lays out at Rom. 9:8: "It is not the children of the flesh who are the children of God." At Rom. 9:3, Paul uses the same word for fellow Jews, syngenēs, that Jesus in Mark uses to describe his kinsmen (6:4).

17. For discussion and references, see McGowan, Ancient Christian Worship, 55–59.

18. Judas, the betrayer, addresses Jesus as rabbi (teacher). The reader knows that in his necessary death and subsequent resurrection Jesus is more than rabbi. In his mission to include Gentiles and women by means of his death he is Lord (1:3; 2:28; 12:36–37).

of some Jewish Christians to accept the necessity of the death of Christ as the means by which the Gentiles, men and women, are joined with the Jews to eat the one loaf of the Lord's Supper (cf. 8:32).[19] Any apparent shame in Mark's churches among Jewish Christians with respect to the manner of Jesus's death on the cross, perhaps similar to what Paul discusses in Galatians 3:13–14,[20] must now be overcome. It is this death, now being reenacted in the suffering and martyrdoms of Mark's churches, that brings resurrection and the imminent return of Jesus on the clouds in power and glory (13:26).

19. A liturgical reader might speculate here on the identity of the "young man [*neaniskos*]," who was a disciple (*synakoloutheō*), as being a Gentile follower of Jesus who contrasts with the Jewish disciples. He has a fine cloth around his naked body, and when he is seized along with Jesus, he leaves the cloth behind and runs away naked (14:52). We know that some early Christians were baptized naked, taking off clothes, then being immersed, and then being again clothed (cf. Gal. 3:27; 1 Cor. 12:13; Col. 3:11). On this reading, the "young man [*neaniskos*]" shows up again in the empty tomb clothed in a white robe (16:5). Has he been baptized into the death of Christ? For a full discussion of baptismal ritual in the earliest churches, see Meeks, *First Urban Christians*, 150–57.

20. Here it is worth noting that Paul makes the connection between the curse of crucifixion (hanging on a tree) and the Gentiles coming into the church in the context of a dispute over Gentile inclusion at the Lord's Supper (Gal. 2:11–13).

9

The Passion of Jesus

Betrayal and Trials

14:53–15:20

Mark 14

The Trial of Jesus

And they led Jesus to the high priest, and they all came together, the chief priests, the elders, and the scribes.

And Peter followed him from a distance as far as the inside of the courtyard of the high priest. And he was sitting with the servants and warming himself [*thermainomai*] by the fire.

And the chief priests and the entire Sanhedrin were seeking testimony against Jesus in order to execute him. But they found none. For many testified falsely against him, and their testimonies did not agree. And some rose and falsely testified against him, saying, "We heard him say, 'I will destroy this temple made with hands, and in the course of three days I will build another not made with hands.'" But even so, their testimony was not in agreement. And the high priest rose into their midst and questioned Jesus, saying, "Have you no answer to what these people testify against you?" But Jesus was silent and did not give an answer. And again the high priest asked him and said to him, "Are you the

Christ, the son of the blessed one?" And Jesus said, "I am [*egō eimi*]. And you will see the Son of Man sitting at the right hand of power and coming on the clouds of heaven."

And the high priest tore his cloak and said, "Why do we have need of witnesses any longer? You have heard the blasphemy. How does it appear to you?" And they all judged him to be liable to death. And some began to spit upon him and to cover his face and to strike him, and they said to him, "Prophesy [*prophēteuō*]!" And the servants received him with blows. (14:53–65)

The night trial of Jesus recalls the night of the boat crossings to the Gentiles in 4:35–41 and 6:47–52. The darkness powerfully symbolizes the threat of chaos that accompanies the trial and crucifixion of Jesus. The narrative construction of the trial scene itself features another of Mark's narrative sandwiches, juxtaposing Peter's relative warmth at the fire in the courtyard with the cruelty of the trial taking place, apparently within the house of the high priest.

The first scene is established with Peter warming himself by the fire with the servants. They are in the courtyard of the high priest. He is, at this point in the narrative, apparently comfortably sitting with the servants of the high priest (14:54). The narrative then abruptly shifts to the *inside* of the residence, where the high priest and the whole Sanhedrin (*synedrion*; 14:55; 13:9) have assembled to seek testimony in order to put Jesus to death (*thanatoō* in 14:55; *thanatos* in 13:12). The original audience of Mark would immediately recall Mark 13:9–12 and again be drawn into the narrative: "They will betray [*paradidōmi*] you to Sanhedrins [*synedrion*] and to synagogues" (13:9).

At first there is no agreement among those who testify against Jesus. Then some false witnesses, again without agreement, claim that Jesus said, "I will destroy this temple made with hands, and in the course of three days I will build another not made with hands" (14:58). The liturgical reader is now left in suspense: the charge that Jesus will destroy the temple and build another in the course of three days is not corroborated in the trial. Yet this reader knows that Jesus has symbolically destroyed the ritual effectiveness of the temple in the course of *three days*, carefully narrated in Mark 11:11–25, and that the rebuilding of the temple, the house of prayer for the Gentiles, will be completed in the ritual enactment of the death (baptism) and resurrection of Jesus in the ritual meal of the house church. He or she now anticipates the imminent return of the resurrected Christ to consummate history itself (13:27). Hence in the trial the high priest presses Jesus twice: "Have you no answer to what these people testify against you?" Jesus first remains silent (14:61). And only then does the high priest press a second question: "Are you the Christ, the son of the blessed one?" At this point Jesus does respond because the complete understanding of his mission in the narrative has been presented: "I am. And you will see the Son of Man sitting at the right hand of power and coming on the clouds of heaven" (13:26; 14:62).

Here the trial narrative has carefully laid out what the original readers of the narrative now should understand about the mission of Jesus. The recent tearing down of the Jerusalem temple in the Roman war (13:2) is made comprehensible by the three-day tearing down of Jesus in the narrative. What rises out of the death of Jesus is the resurrected body of Christ, the church of Jews and Gentiles, men and women, brought together through the ritual enactment of baptism into Jesus's death and the meal which brings participation in the resurrection as the body of Christ (14:22–24). Here in the narrative presentation of Jesus's trial, being read and heard amid the betrayals, trials, and martyrdoms within the inclusive house churches of Mark's time (13:9), the final resurrection and consummation of history is depicted as imminent. These readers are now to anticipate the return of Jesus on the clouds to gather the elect from all of the house churches suffering persecution (13:27).

The reaction of the high priest to Jesus's confession to be the "I am [ego eimi]," perhaps because he understood this to be a claim of the divine presence expressed in Exodus 3:14 (ego eimi, LXX), is to charge Jesus with blasphemy: "Why do we have need of witnesses any longer? You have heard the blasphemy. How does it appear to you?" (14:63–64).[1] For the reader of Mark, this response brings particular attention to Jesus's self-identification in the earlier resurrection scene in which Jesus walks upon the water following the first ritual meal in the wilderness (6:45–52). There too Jesus identifies himself as the "I am [ego eimi]" as he walks upon the sea, literally the divine domination of chaos (6:50). Had the disciples there understood the loaves (6:52), the inclusion of the Gentiles with the Jews in the first ritual meal of the wilderness (6:30–41), they would have understood, as the ancient readers of Mark now understand in the midst of the darkness (chaos) of this trial, that Jesus is the "I am [ego eimi]," the Son of the Blessed, who will dominate the chaos of death and return to gather the elect now suffering in the inclusive house churches (14:62).

The narrative now presents the substance of the charge of *blasphemy* that brings Jesus to the cross: "They all judged him to be liable to death" (14:64).

---

1. The reaction of the high priest to Jesus's pronouncement (after rending his garment in anguish) echoes the earlier charge of *blasphemy* from the scribes to what Jesus had done for the Gentile paralytic in pronouncing the forgiveness of his sins (2:7). Jesus, having risen from the waters of his baptismal death (1:10), now allows a Gentile into the community, the house church. Indeed Jesus commands the paralytic to "resurrect" and take up his mat and go to his own house (2:11).

The experience of Mark's readers in the context of the upheavals of the Jewish war is now made comprehensible by the story of Jesus within the narrative. In the narrative Jesus must die because he created the house churches of Jews and Gentiles, men and women, who share the one loaf (8:21; 14:22), the ritual place of forgiveness that replaces the place of atonement of the Jerusalem temple (11:11–25). And it is his death and resurrection which, in ritual enactment of baptism and meal, now creates the inclusive house churches of these readers. In the narrative Jesus dies as a ransom for the many (10:45), the readers of the narrative. These readers who endure to the end of the present persecution will find themselves within this story of Jesus; that is, those who are not ashamed of the cross and the inclusive churches it creates will soon be gathered by the resurrected Christ from the four winds (8:38; 13:27).

As the narrative scene shifts to the persecution of Jesus by those who have just condemned him to death (they spit upon him), a powerful irony is played out. These people cover the face of Jesus (so that he does not see) and strike him. Then they command him to *prophesy* (*prophēteuō*). The reader knows that Jesus had indeed *prophesied* this event on three separate occasions (8:31; 9:31; 10:34) and that to be able to really *see* is to see the reality of the gathered church willing to follow Jesus on the way (*hodos*) through this suffering to the cross itself (8:25; 10:52). The depiction of the persecution of Jesus allows the readers, themselves being persecuted, to *see* that the resurrected Christ draws near, that indeed he is at the door (13:29).

Peter at the Fire

And while Peter was down in the courtyard, one of the maids of the high priest came. And seeing Peter warming himself [*thermainomai*], she looked at him and said, "You were with the Nazarene called Jesus." And Peter denied it, saying, "I do not know nor do I understand what you are saying." And he went outside [*exō*] into the forecourt. But the maid saw him and began again to tell those standing there that he was one of them. And again he denied it. But after a little while those standing nearby said, "You really are one of them, for you are a Galilean." And he began to curse and to swear, "I do not know the man whom you are speaking about." And immediately a cock crowed for the second time, and Peter remembered the word Jesus had spoken to him, "Before the cock crows twice, you will deny [*aparneomai*] me three times." And he fell down and wept. (14:66–72)

The narrative sandwich—Peter, trial of Jesus, Peter—now comes back to Peter. As the trial commenced he had been *warming* (*thermainomai*) himself by the fire with the servants (14:54). Now the night trial at the residence of the high priest has ended with Jesus charged with blasphemy and deserving death.

Peter is seen again *warming* (*thermainomai*) himself by the fire (14:67). One of the maidservants of the high priest recognizes Peter as being *with* the Nazarene (14:66–67). Peter now discovers the full meaning of his earlier confession of Jesus to be the Christ (8:29) and Jesus's command to the disciples to keep the matter quiet (8:30). Jesus there gave the first of his three passion predictions, providing the detail of the trial that now has taken place here in the residence of the high priest (8:31; 14:53–65). Peter took Jesus aside and rebuked him for this bold proclamation (8:32), and in return Jesus rebuked Peter: "Get behind [*opisō*] me, Satan! For you are not thinking the things of God but the things of humans" (8:33). At that point Jesus turned to the crowd and to the disciples with the warning: "If anyone wishes to follow *behind* [*opisō*] me, let that person deny [*aparneomai*] himself, take up his cross, and follow me" (8:34). Peter, as well as the ancient readers of Mark, is learning that the Christ is the one who must suffer rejection and death. Peter here denies Jesus (*aparneomai*) not once but three times and so, for the moment at least, refuses to follow (*opisō*) Jesus on the way (*hodos*) of suffering, rejection, and death.

In the portrayal of Jesus as rejected, condemned, and tortured in the trial before the high priest, the narrative now moves to complete its understanding of Jesus as the Christ (8:29). Just as Peter earlier resisted the idea that it was *necessary* for the Christ to suffer and be rejected (8:31), now in the courtyard he chooses to deny the Christ who declares himself to be the "I am" in the midst of that very suffering and rejection. When the maidservant recognizes Peter to be *with* the Nazarene (3:14), Peter claims not to know or comprehend what she is saying (14:68). And instead of *following behind* Jesus by moving closer to him (8:33), Peter withdraws further *outside* (*exō*) into the forecourt of the residence (14:68). At this point the maidservant again recognizes Peter and says to those standing there that he is "one of *them*." For the Christians in the churches of Mark's time, the change to the plural here is significant: Peter has denied being with Jesus to the maidservant. Now he denies being a part of the *community* around Jesus and does so to the maid and to the bystanders (14:70). In the third movement of the narrative drama, the bystanders *collectively* accuse Peter of being part of the community: "You really are one of *them*, for you are a Galilean" (14:70). Peter then denies being part of the community by denying Christ. He curses and takes an oath: "I do not know the man whom you are speaking about" (14:71). The narrative here brings the reader to Peter's earlier confession of Jesus as the Christ (8:29) and Peter's rejection of what Jesus then taught about the necessity of the suffering, rejection, and death of the Son of Man. In that earlier episode, Jesus brought together the disciples and the crowd to warn them about the *necessity* of suffering as part of the community's experience prior to resurrection: "Whoever is ashamed of me and my words in this adulterous and sinful generation, of this person The Son of Man will be ashamed when he comes in the glory of his Father with the holy angels" (8:38).

For the ancient readers of Mark, perhaps located in the house churches of Galilee undergoing persecution and martyrdom, Peter's final and most adamant denial brings the narrative home. He has not only denied Jesus and failed to take up his cross (8:34); he has denied being a part of the churches of Galilee. He has denied the necessary connection of the suffering and martyrdom within these churches with the suffering and martyrdom of the Christ. Further, he has denied that Jesus's necessary death has given birth to these churches through ritual enactment of that death and that Jesus, as the Son of Man, will soon return to gather the elect, Jews and Gentiles, men and women, in the midst of their own suffering and death (8:38; 13:26–27).

The crow of the cock signals the end of the darkness and chaos of the night trial. Peter remembers what Jesus told him in the garden at Gethsemane: "Before the cock crows twice you will deny me three times" (14:30). He repents of his denial: he falls down and weeps (14:72). Yet however poignant the story of Peter here is, for the liturgical reader, it is more than just a story of personal crisis and moral failure. In the narrative, both in his earlier rebuke of Jesus (8:32) and his denials during Jesus's trial, Peter represents resistance to the very idea of suffering, rejection, and death as a necessary part of belonging to these inclusive house churches. Peter said at Gethsemane, "Even if it is necessary for me to die with you, I will not deny [*aparneomai*] you" (14:31). Here in the trial scene, Peter denies (*aparneomai*) Jesus. He refuses to become a martyr for the churches Jesus has established.

Finally, it would not have been difficult for the ancient readers of Mark to see Peter as transparent to the position of some Jewish Christians in their own time. When the family of Jesus is standing *outside* (*exō*) and calling Jesus to come out of the house (3:31), it might have been understood by these ancient readers as a bid from Jewish Christians to create a separate table, more than one loaf, distinct from the Gentiles. Indeed, for the Jewish population of the region (Galilee and Syria), separate house gatherings of Jews and Gentiles would be no cause for scandal and opposition. For Jews, a house church gathering of Jews would be Jewish; for the secular authorities, such a gathering would also be Jewish, that is, part of a community recognized as a legitimate religion in the empire.[2] It would have been only the particular practice of these Christian house churches, Jew and Gentile, men and women, at the one table, which brought them

2. For discussion and major references on the place of diaspora Judaism within the Roman Empire, see L. T. Johnson, *Writings of the New Testament*, 73–91.

to persecution from both Jewish synagogues[3] and Roman authorities (13:9).[4] It is this persecution which generated the unique narrative story line of Mark. The suffering of the Christian house churches, Jew and Gentile of the one loaf (8:14–21), finds itself caught up in the story of Jesus's mission to establish these inclusive churches and the opposition to that mission. Jesus's subsequent suffering, rejection, and death in the narrative is the result of opposition to that very *mission* (3:6; 11:18). The narrative ending of Mark (16:8), "for they were afraid," is the moment of expected resurrection and appearance to these churches of Galilee (16:7). It is the moment in which Jesus gathers this elect, the house churches of Mark's community, in the midst of their own horrendous suffering and persecution surrounding the events of the Jewish war (AD 66–73).[5]

So for both the ancient reader of Mark and the modern liturgical reader, the central irony of the narrative is the presentation of the resurrected Christ, the one who rose from the chaos/death of baptism and receives the Spirit of God (1:10), as the one who must suffer and be killed in order to be the resurrected Christ who will gather the elect and consummate history itself (13:26–27; 14:62). The readers of Mark now know that their experience of the body of Christ, the inclusive meal of the one loaf and the manifestation of the resurrection, depends on their own willingness to suffer and follow Jesus on the way (*hodos*) of martyrdom.

Mark 15

The Day Trial

And immediately in the early morning [*prōi*] the entire Sanhedrin, the chief priests with the elders and scribes, held council. They bound Jesus and led him away and betrayed [*paradidōmi*] him to Pilate. And Pilate questioned him, "Are you the king of the Jews?" And he [Jesus] answered, "You say so." And the chief priests accused him of many things. And Pilate again questioned him and said, "Have you no answer? See how earnestly they are accusing you." But Jesus no longer answered at all, so that Pilate was amazed.

Now at the feast he released one prisoner to them whom they pardoned. And there was one called Barabbas who was imprisoned with the insurrectionists who had committed murder in the insurrection. And a crowd arose and began to ask that he do what he had done before for them. And Pilate responded to

3. Paul describes one such experience in 2 Cor. 11:23–24.
4. Acts describes at some length these situations of persecution by secular authorities: Acts 18:12–17; 19:35–41; 21:37–22:29; 23:23–26:32. See also Pliny, *Ep.* 10.96–97. For discussion, see Marcus, *Mark 9–16*, 882–84.
5. Mark 13:26–27.

them, saying, "Do you wish me to release for you the king of the Jews?" For he knew that it was from envy that the chief priests had betrayed him. But the chief priests stirred up the crowd to get him to release Barabbas to them. But Pilate again responded and said to them, "Then what do I do with the king of the Jews?" And they called out again, "Crucify him." But Pilate said to them, "What evil has he done?" But they cried out all the more, "Crucify him." (15:1–14)

The night trial of Jesus before the Jewish council in the residence of the high priest now gives way to the trial before the Roman governor Pilate, apparently on the outside of the Roman palace (*praetorium*; 15:16). As with the betrayal and arrest at Gethsemane, signaling to the readers the imminent return of Christ in Jesus's command to his *sleeping* disciples to *rise* (*egeirō*), so here too Jesus is betrayed by the entire Jewish Sanhedrin to Pilate "*in the early morning [prōi]."* In Mark this is the time of the resurrection (*prōi*; 16:2). The ancient readers of Mark, in the midst of being betrayed by Jewish councils (*synedria*; 13:9), now see Jesus as coming ever closer (13:29).

Pilate now makes an entirely new accusation against Jesus: "Are you the king of the Jews?" Whereas the night trial in the residence of the high priest focused on the intra-Jewish religious charge of blasphemy, the political charge of a claim for sovereignty (kingship), challenging Roman imperial rule, comes to the fore here. In the night trial Jesus identified himself as the "I am [*egō eimi*]" and as the one whose return at the right hand of power with the clouds was imminent (14:62). Here before Pilate, Jesus does not identify himself at all but, ironically, allows Pilate to do so: "You say so" (15:2). The many things which the chief priests accuse Jesus of here before Pilate are, given the context, most likely the attempt to substantiate the charge that Jesus declared himself king when he entered Jerusalem (11:7–10). The readers of course understand the irony here: the crowd declared the coming kingdom of their father David just as Jesus entered the city with complete humility in order to suffer betrayal and death. Pilate, however, misses the irony and emphasizes the seriousness of the political accusation (15:4). For the ancient readers in Mark's churches, how Jesus responds to betrayal and interrogation is how they are to respond. They are not to be anxious about what to say when they are brought up on charges, but to rely in that moment upon the Holy Spirit (13:11).

For the readers of Mark, what happens next in the narrative depends on understanding the choice created by Pilate's practice of releasing one prisoner to the crowd at the feast of Passover.[6] Again the narrative irony is heightened:

6. An otherwise unknown practice, most likely a narrative invention here to create the choice of which prisoner to release and which prisoner to crucify. For discussion, see Marcus, *Mark 9–16*, 1028; A. Y. Collins, *Mark*, 714.

"Barabbas" in Aramaic means "son of the father," and Jesus has entered Jerusalem to shouts of "Blessed is the coming kingdom of our *father* David!" (11:10). Barabbas, however, is already a prisoner with those who rebelled against Rome and committed murder (15:7). Jesus entered Jerusalem in humility and peace.[7]

On the basis of previous practice, the crowd now asks Pilate to release a prisoner to them. And at this point in the narrative the readers know that the crowd previously was supportive of Jesus. Indeed it was fear of the crowd's favor toward Jesus that led to his being arrested in stealth and darkness (12:12, 37; 14:2). So when Pilate asks, "Do you wish me to release for you the king of the Jews?" the narrative signals that both the crowd and Pilate are on the side of Jesus. Pilate, indeed, is willing to release "the king of the Jews," even though the presumptive title suggests political rebellion against Rome. Pilate apparently does not believe the charge or any corroborating testimony brought forth by the chief priests, because he knows it was brought forth from envy (15:3, 10).

At this point the chief priests are able to "stir up [*anaseiō*]" the crowd so that they will turn and prefer the release of Barabbas rather than Jesus. Within the narrative this sudden turn of the crowd is not explained. How or with what arguments are they influenced? The readers do not know. All the readers know is that former allies have now become accusers, perhaps in ways analogous to the ancient readers' own experience of persecution. These ancient readers are starkly aware of situations, for example, in which family members are suddenly willing to betray fellow family members unto death (13:12).

The call for the punishment of crucifixion comes out of nowhere. Pilate's response to the crowd's request to release Barabbas—"Then what do I do with the king of the Jews?"[8]—does not require crucifixion as the alternative. If anything, Jesus might have been put into the same cell from which Barabbas was taken. Yet the crowd now cries out here for crucifixion, and so the cross is introduced into the passion narrative for the first time (15:13).

Pilate's response to the crowd indicates once again that he does not agree with the charge that Jesus claimed to be king of the Jews: "What evil has he done?" signals complete exoneration from Pilate. The reaction of the stirred-up crowd, however, is to cry out for crucifixion more intensely. The narrative clearly indicates a sort of mob mentality at this point. And while a Roman

7. What rebellion the narrative refers to here is unknown. Again, this is possibly a narrative invention to create the contrast between the violent Barabbas and the peaceful Jesus. See A. Y. Collins, *Mark*, 714–19.

8. The strong variant reading here, "What do you wish I do with the man whom you call king of the Jews?" is probably not the text. Up to this point the crowd has never called Jesus king of the Jews. See *Novum Testamentum Graece*, 28th ed., and the comments on this passage.

governor wishing to satisfy an unruly mob by releasing Barabbas, in prison with known insurrectionists against Rome, is an unlikely historical scenario, the readers of the narrative are left with the inescapable conclusion that this mob is indeed responsible for the crucifixion of Jesus. And here again the ancient readers would closely identify their own experience of betrayal by fellow citizens and subsequent martyrdom within the Christian community with what is happening to Jesus in the narrative.

Torture

And Pilate, wishing to make the crowd happy, released to them Barabbas. And having flogged Jesus, he betrayed [*paradidōmi*] him to be crucified.
　　And the soldiers led him inside the courtyard, which was the Praetorium. And they called together the entire cohort. They dressed him in purple, and, weaving a crown of thorns, they put it on him. And they began to salute him: "Hail, king of the Jews!" They struck his head with a reed and spit upon him and bent their knees to him. And when they had mocked him, they stripped him of the purple cloak and put his own cloak back upon him. And they led him out to crucify him. (15:15–20)

The man already in prison is released, and the innocent man, apparently to assuage the stirred-up crowd, is scourged and then *betrayed* (*paradidōmi*) to them by Pilate for crucifixion (15:15). Here the second passion prediction is brought to the attention of the readers, "The Son of Man will be *betrayed* [*paradidōmi*] into the hands of human beings" (9:31). Again in an unlikely historical scenario, the Roman governor Pilate appears to grant the power of capital punishment to the crowd.[9] And although Pilate maintained the innocence of Jesus throughout the encounter with the chief priests and mob, the charge of claiming to be king of the Jews is at the heart of the punishment Jesus receives, both in terms of torture (purple cloak, crown of thorns, bending the knee, 15:17–19) and execution (crucifixion for an act of rebellion against Roman rule). For the liturgical reader of Mark, there are ritual baptismal connotations here: the Roman soldiers strip Jesus of his clothes and place the purple cloak and crown of thorns upon him, and then strip him of these clothes and put his own clothes back upon him (15:17–20). Jesus empties himself into the chaos of torture and again, after this experience, will empty himself into the chaos of his death on a cross. The resurrection and imminent return in glory await on the other side (16:7).

---

9. For discussion, see A. Y. Collins, *Mark*, 721.

10

The Passion of Jesus

The Cross and Tomb

15:21–16:8

Mark 15

Simon the Cyrene

And they pressed into service a certain Simon of Cyrene who was passing by [*paragō*], coming in from the country, the father of Alexander and Rufus, to take up [*airō*] the cross [*stauros*]. (15:21)

In the centuries since Mark was written, there has been speculation as to the identity of Simon of Cyrene. He was a man passing by (15:21), the father of Alexander and Rufus, who was compelled (apparently by the soldiers) to take up (*airō*) the cross (*stauros*). The readers of Mark, both ancient and modern, would note that Simon's action is exactly the fulfillment of 8:34: "He called *the crowd* [*ochlos*] with his disciples and said to them, 'If anyone wishes to follow behind me, let that person deny himself, *take up* [*airō*] *his cross* [*stauros*], and follow me.'" Jesus makes this statement following the second ritual meal in the wilderness (Gentiles eating with Jews in a Gentile place) and on the way to the villages of Caesarea Philippi, clearly a Gentile location. The teaching about taking up the cross, therefore, is directed to the Jewish disciples along with the Gentile crowd (*ochlos*). There is therefore little reason to doubt that the narrative fulfillment of Mark 8:34, Simon of Cyrene taking up the cross at 15:21, is with a *Gentile* taking up (*airō*) the cross (*stauros*). Such a Gentile would here stand in stark contrast with the Jewish Twelve, Judas who betrays and Peter who denies. There is little reason for the Jewish Christians of Mark's churches to withdraw from table fellowship with Gentiles who take up the cross with Jesus.

Cross

The brought him to Golgatha place, which, translated, means "place of the skull." And they gave to him wine mixed with myrrh [*smyrnizō*], which he did not take. And they crucified him and divided his garments, casting lots for who would take what. It was the third hour, and they crucified him. And the inscription of the charge was written down: "The king of the Jews." And they crucified with him two thieves, one on his right and one on his left.

And those passing by blasphemed him, shaking their heads and saying, "So, you who would destroy the temple and rebuild it in three days, save yourself and descend [*katabainō*] from the cross." (15:22–30)

At Golgatha, the place of execution, the soldiers give to Jesus wine mixed with myrrh (*smyrnizō*), but he does not take it. The liturgical reader recalls the faithful woman who *poured out* (*katacheō*) myrrh (*myron*) upon the head of Jesus—as he has now been poured out—and thereby prepared his body for burial (14:3–9). The myrrh (*smyrnizō*) is here mixed with wine, the blood (*haima*) of the covenant (*diathēkē*), which Jesus here pours out (*ekcheō*) for the many (14:24). Yet Jesus does not drink, and the liturgical reader recalls his earlier pronouncement that he will not drink the fruit (*genēma*) of the vine (*ampelos*) until he drinks it new in the kingdom of God (14:25). Jesus here on the cross has not yet been completely poured out (*ekcheō*), and so the final unification of Jesus with the elect is imminent but not yet here (13:27).[1]

Those who passed by the cross blasphemed Jesus by saying, "So, you who would destroy the temple and rebuild it in three days, save yourself and descend

---

1. This scene at the cross brings the reader again to both the night trial at the residence of the high priest and the audience with Pilate in front of the Roman Praetorium. The inscription of the charge against Jesus was simply "The king of the Jews," that is, the answer to the question Pilate initially asked of Jesus: "Are you the king of the Jews?" (15:2). And though the narrative tells us that Pilate thought Jesus innocent of such political insurrection (15:14), both the reported torture given by the Roman soldiers and the inscription here suggest that Jesus was in fact killed by the Romans on a charge of political insurrection. For discussion, see A. Y. Collins, *Mark*, 747.

[*katabainō*] from the cross" (15:29–31). At the night trial before the Sanhedrin, the initial accusation against Jesus was that he had said he would destroy the temple made with hands and in the course of three days build another not made with hands (14:58). The liturgical reader therefore knows the hidden truth within both that accusation and the taunting of Jesus here. Earlier in the narrative Peter recognized the destruction of the temple on the third day, the day of resurrection: "The fig tree which you cursed is withered" (11:21). The readers of Mark also know the new temple will be a "house of prayer for all the Gentiles" (11:17) located in the ritual meal gathering of Jews and Gentiles, men and women, sharing the one loaf (8:14–21), the resurrected body (*sōma*) of Christ (14:22).

Even more, at the opening of the Gospel Jesus went into the waters of the Jordan and then *ascended* (*anabainō*) from those baptismal waters (chaos) to receive the Spirit and to be declared the beloved Son (1:10–11). So the liturgical reader knows that here Jesus now enacts the baptism with which the narrative of Mark began: Jesus here must *descend* (*katabainō*) into chaos and death in order to rise after the third day and become the house of prayer for all the Gentiles (11:17). The irony of this narrative scene at the cross is therefore complete: if Jesus does *descend* (*katabainō*) from the cross, then he cannot *ascend* (*anabainō*) from the waters of death (chaos) at his baptism to receive the Spirit (*pneuma*; 1:10) which he will now give out to the churches at the moment of his death (*ekpneō*; 15:37, 39). This is the Spirit (*pneuma*) being poured out (*ekcheō*) from the liturgical act of Christ on the cross (baptism) that establishes the church, the body of Christ, Jews and Gentiles, men and women, to eat the meal of the one loaf.[2] Unlike the characters taunting Jesus in the narrative, the liturgical reader knows that *it is necessary* (*dei*) for Jesus to suffer greatly and be killed (8:31). Just like those being persecuted and martyred in the inclusive house churches of Mark's time, if Jesus does *descend* (*katabainō*) to save himself, he will lose his life, but if he loses his life he will save it (8:35).

> At the same time the chief priests and the scribes mocked him among themselves and said, "He saved [*sōzō*] others, yet he is unable to save [*sōzō*] himself." (15:31)

Ironically, the only way that Jesus can save others is to not save himself. Now the chief priests, the Jewish leadership responsible for stirring up the

---

2. This, of course, is the very heart of the narrative plot of Mark. Jesus rises from (baptismal) death to receive the Spirit of new creation and thereby to establish the house churches of Jews and Gentiles, men and women. And so he then must die in order to be the very death which, ritually enacted in baptism, establishes participation in the ritual meal, the new creation of the church itself.

crowd against Jesus outside of the Praetorium, are suddenly joined there by the scribes so that together they may now taunt Jesus on the cross.[3] These two groups begin their taunt with a surprising admission: "He saved [*sōzō*] others." The liturgical readers of Mark here recognize the irony: Jesus *saved* (*sōzō*) the Jewish man with the withered hand in the synagogue (3:4) and with that restoration brought out the hatred that would eventually bring him here to the cross (3:6). Later the Gentile blind man Bartimaeus (son of Timaeus) was *saved* (*sōzō*) and chose to follow Jesus on the way (*hodos*) that has also ended here at the cross (10:52). Most important, these ancient readers of Mark know, in the midst of horrendous persecution by both the Jewish councils and Roman authorities (13:9), and in light of the imminence of God's wrath upon all flesh (13:20), that only those who endure to the end will be *saved* (*sōzō*; 13:13). The implication for the original readers of Mark is clear. Jesus could choose to come down (*katabainō*) from the cross. Like these readers now suffering persecution, Jesus would save his life but then lose his life: "Whoever wishes to *save* [*sōzō*] his life will destroy it; and but whoever would destroy his life on account of me and the gospel will save [*sōzō*] it" (Mark 8:35). Those caught up in the persecution at the time of Mark's writing can choose not to die. They can deny Christ.[4] But as with the flask of myrrh, destroyed by the anonymous woman (14:4) and poured out (14:3) for the many (14:3, 24), Jesus and the martyrs of Mark's churches will save themselves and others only by not saving themselves.

> "Let the Christ [*christos*], the King of Israel, descend [*katabainō*] now from the cross so that we might see [*horaō*] and have faith [*pisteuō*]." (15:32)

For the ancient readers of Mark, the taunt here reflects both the night trial in the residence of the high priest ("Are you the Christ?" in 14:61) and Pilate's investigation of Jesus in front of the Praetorium, asking Jesus if he was the "king of the Jews" (15:2, 9, 12). They are also brought again to recall Peter's confession of Jesus as the Christ (*christos*) at Mark 8:29, followed immediately by Jesus's prediction of both the night trial, suffering, and rejection by the elders, chief priests, and scribes and Pilate's handing over of

---

3. The scribes previously had been part of the night trial but appear to have been absent from the scene before Pilate at the Praetorium (15:3–11).

4. Perhaps the most interesting historical example of this opportunity to deny Christ and so be freed comes from the famous response of the emperor Trajan to Pliny, the governor of Bithynia, in the early second century: "They are not to be sought out. Yet if they are referred to you and convicted, they must be punished. Even so, whosoever denies himself to be a Christian and makes this plain, that is, by worshiping our gods, shall have pardon from punishment, whatever the previous suspicion was" (Pliny, *Ep.* 10.97, my translation).

Jesus to be killed (8:31). These readers see again that the necessity of Jesus's death, resisted mightily by Peter (8:32), has now come to pass in the trial and crucifixion of Jesus.

The use of the title "King of Israel" is a subtle change from Pilate's question to Jesus in front of the Praetorium: "Are you the king of the Jews?" (15:2). Pilate's question drove to the heart of Rome's concern over a rival political claim. The taunt here concerns what the chief priests and scribes consider to be a false claim of Jewish messianic authority. The liturgical readers of Mark are again reminded of the episode in which Jesus defended his disciples' clearing the way (hodos) on the Sabbath with a similar claim of royal authority:

> "Have you not read what David did when he was in need and was hungry, and those with him, how he entered the house of God when Abiathar was high priest and ate the loaves of offering, which are not permitted to be eaten by any but the priests, and gave them to those who were with him?" (2:25–26)

For these readers, the irony of the present taunt is now inescapable. If Jesus descends (katabainō) from the cross now, there will be no basis for Jesus's authority as David, or as Lord of the Sabbath, to give the loaves to Jews and Gentiles, men and women, that is, "to those who [are] with him" (2:26). It is the death of Jesus here on the cross which is the ransom for the many (10:45), the cup which is *poured out* for the many (14:23). It is the death of Christ which brings about this royal authority even surpassing the royal authority of David (12:35–37). It is this death on the cross which brings the imminent resurrection to gather the elect, Jews and Gentiles, men and women, from the four winds (13:27).

The chief priests and scribes do not in fact see (horaō). The ancient readers of Mark, on the other hand, know that when they see (horaō) the outbreak of persecution and martyrdom, the resurrection of Christ draws near (engys), indeed is at the very gates (13:29).[5] The chief priests and scribes do not *have faith* (pisteuō). They are unlike the blind man Bartimaeus, who recognized Jesus as Son of David, threw off his cloak in a gesture of baptismal disrobing, and asked to be able to see (10:47–52). Bartimaeus's *faith* (pistis) saved (sōzō) him (10:52). He was able to see and follow Jesus on the way (hodos) of his crucifixion and death (10:52), the way (hodos) which was enacted by Jesus in his ritual baptism by John (1:2–3) and which now ends here on the cross and the imminent resurrection.

---

5. These readers would see (horaō) as well that the moment of the betrayal and arrest of Jesus, as with their own arrests and betrayals, marks the imminence of the resurrection of the martyrs at the return of Jesus: "Rise, let us go. See [horaō], my betrayer draws near [engizō]" (14:42).

And those crucified with him also reproached him. And at the sixth hour darkness came upon the entire earth until the ninth hour. (15:32–33)

At the scene of crucifixion, darkness descends for three hours from noon until three. Creation is reversed. Whereas God in Genesis separated the darkness from the darkness to create light as the absence of darkness,[6] now the darkness comes back together to cover the whole earth. In the narrative, the liturgical readers are reminded of the descending darkness of the first sea voyage to the Gentile mission (4:35), the lateness of the hour of the first ritual meal in the wilderness (6:35), and the descending darkness within which Jesus walks upon the water (6:47). Jesus rises from his baptismal death in the sea, his immersion into chaos, to begin the Gentile mission on Gentile soil (4:39–5:1). The meal in the Jewish wilderness is held, and Gentiles become part of the Jewish story of the exodus and wilderness (6:43). The disciples, and so the readers of Mark, should understand that in the inclusive meal, the loaves which have become one loaf (8:14–21), the resurrection is manifest, and the waters of chaos are calmed (6:51). So here at the cross darkness descends, but the resurrection, the domination of chaos in the resurrected body of Christ (14:22), the final gathering of the church (the elect), is imminent (13:27).

And in the ninth hour Jesus called out in a loud voice, "Eloi, Eloi, lema sabachthani," which, translated, means, "My God, my God, why have you abandoned me?" (15:34)

The desperate cry of Jesus at the ninth hour (three in the afternoon) in the Aramaic of Psalm 22:2, "My God, my God, why have you abandoned me?" (15:34), captures in the narrative the desperation of the Christian martyrs of Mark's churches, betrayed by countrymen and strangers as well as family (13:9, 12), hated by everyone on account of the name of Christ (13:13). It is just at this moment, the darkest hour, in which the resurrected Christ is set to appear at the very gates (13:29).

And some who were standing by, when they heard this, said, "See [horaō], he calls to Elijah." And someone ran and soaked a sponge with sour wine and, having placed it upon a reed, gave it to him to drink, saying, "Wait, let us see if Elijah comes [erchomai] to pull him down." (15:35–36)

In the narrative some bystanders, apparently not able to understand Aramaic, determine that Jesus in this moment of anguish is calling upon Elijah

6. Gen. 1:4 LXX.

to take him down from the cross. They prepare a drink of sour wine on a sponge, that is, the fruit of the vine (14:25), in order to see whether Elijah will come to pull Jesus down from the cross, that is, to save him. But Jesus does not actually drink this sour wine. Just before this the chief priests and scribes have taunted Jesus to come down from the cross under his own power to save himself; now these bystanders suggest that the prophet Elijah might pull Jesus down from the cross. In both cases, however, to come down or to be pulled down, the ancient readers of Mark are again challenged to acknowledge the necessity of the death of Christ: he must die in order to be raised. He must die in order to drink the fruit of the vine new in the kingdom of God (14:25). And because Jesus stays on the cross to die these readers should expect the imminent return of the resurrected Christ to gather the elect, the inclusive house churches of Mark's time, in the midst of their own suffering and martyrdom.

These readers also know that Elijah has already appeared, not to save Jesus from this death, but to baptize Jesus *into* this death (1:9–10). Thus Elijah marks the beginning of the messianic age not merely by arriving (*erchomai*) but by ritually baptizing Jesus to receive the Spirit and begin his mission to gather Jews and Gentiles, men and women, into the churches. In Mark, John the Baptist is Elijah (1:6; 2 Kings 1:8), who died a martyr's death (6:14–29; 9:12); Elijah will return to be with Jesus and Moses in the imminent resurrection (9:4). The readers of Mark know that if Elijah were to come (*erchomai*) and pull Jesus down from the cross, there would be no death and thus no resurrection, no ritual drink to mark the in-breaking of the kingdom of God (14:25).

And with a loud voice Jesus released the spirit [*ekpneō*]. (15:37)

At the moment of death, Jesus, in a loud voice, *released the spirit* (*ekpneō*; 15:37). Immediately the readers of Mark are brought back to the very beginning of the narrative. They recall the promise made by the Baptist at the outset of Jesus's ministry: "He will baptize you with the Holy Spirit [*pneuma*]" (1:8). These readers also know that up to this point in the narrative Jesus has not baptized anyone at any time in the Holy Spirit. Here at his death the Spirit is now released, and the reader is brought again to the beginning of the narrative. This is the Spirit of creation, the dove that after the chaos of the flood returned to the heavens and so now returns in the narrative of Mark to enact the new creation (Gen. 8:12). When Jesus rises (*anabainō*) from the waters of chaos in his baptism (1:10), it is this Spirit that will defeat the unclean spirits inhabiting both Jews (1:26–27) and Gentiles (5:8–13), and Gentile women (7:29). It is this Spirit that gives the martyrs their voice to witness during persecution (13:11). This is the Spirit, released now by Jesus's death, that inhabits the inclusive and persecuted house churches of Mark's time, churches that now anxiously await the return of Jesus in the resurrection, coming on the clouds with power and glory (13:26).

> And the veil of the temple was split into two [*schizō*] from top to bottom. (15:38)

At the death of Jesus, the veil of the temple was split in two (*schizō*) from top to bottom. The ancient readers know that this is the veil that separated the holy of holies, the inner sanctum of the temple, from the rest of the temple; it was the space within which the high priest, and only the high priest, would sprinkle the blood of the great sacrifice of atonement (forgiveness) one time per year (Lev. 16:6) and with that ritual bring creation from chaos.[7] At the beginning of the narrative, Jesus, baptized into his own death as the sacrificed Son of Man, receives the Spirit from the sky split into two (*schizō*; 1:10), and so receives the power to forgive the sins of the Gentile paralytic and restore the order of creation (2:1–12). His death establishes the community which can, in the act of forgiveness of one another in the conduct of the sacred meal, become the house of prayer for all the Gentiles (11:17–25) and replace the now-withered sacrificial ritual of the temple (11:23). It is Jesus who, anointed by a woman, is poured out as sacrifice (*katacheō*; 14:3), a ransom for the many (10:45). It is Jesus whose sacrificial death creates the ritual meal of the one loaf, the resurrected *body of Christ*, Jews and Gentiles, men and women (14:22). It is the blood of Jesus which is poured out in sacrifice to establish the new covenant in his blood for the many (14:12, 24).

> And a centurion standing opposite to him saw that he let forth the spirit [*ekpneō*] and said, "Truly this man was the Son of God." (15:39)

It is a Gentile at the foot of the cross, a Roman centurion, who, within the narrative, specifically notices that Jesus "released the spirit" (15:37). On that basis the Gentile declares, "Truly this man was the Son of God" (15:39). The original liturgical readers of Mark would now be brought back to the very first verse of the Gospel, "The beginning of the gospel of Jesus Christ, *the Son of God*."[8] For these readers, the declaration, coming from a Gentile and noting the release of the Spirit, perfectly illustrates the narrative purpose of

---

7. For detailed commentary on the veil, see Marcus, *Mark 9–16*, 1056–57.

8. The manuscripts are divided on whether "Son of God" is part of the original text of Mark. The strongest argument for including "Son of God" is precisely the inclusio it provides with the ending of the Gospel, a literary technique popular in antiquity. For discussion of the evidence and a contrary conclusion, see A. Y. Collins, *Mark*, 130–32.

the Gospel. The death of Jesus, through ritual baptism and the in-breaking of the Spirit into the world, brings Gentiles and Jews into the meal of the one loaf, the ritual space of the new creation. This is the church which is now undergoing persecution and now expects the imminent return of Christ to save and gather it from the four winds (13:27).

> And there were women there watching from a distance. Among them were Mary Magdalene and Mary the mother of James the younger and Joses, and Salome. These women, when he was in Galilee, followed him and served him. And there were many other women who ascended [*synanabainō*] with him to Jerusalem. (15:40–41)

It is not just the Gentile centurion who acts with faith at the final moment of Jesus's life. The narrative notes here that there were also three women who were watching from a distance (15:40): Mary Magdalene, Mary the mother of James the younger and Joses, and Salome. The narrative also mentions that there were many other women who served Jesus and followed him and came up with him to Jerusalem (15:41). The readers recall here the faith of the woman with a hemorrhage who knew that if she only touched the garment of Jesus she would be saved (5:28, 34); the resurrection of a twelve-year-old girl from the dead (5:41); the insistence of the Syrophoenician woman to be included at the one table (7:25–30); and the anonymous woman who anointed Jesus for his burial (14:3–9).

The narrative cycle of the two ritual meals in the wilderness is also carefully structured to show the faith and place of women at the table. The first ritual meal description notes that five thousand *males* were fed (6:44), while the second ritual meal description, following the story of the Syrophoenician woman's insistence on being fed and Jesus's exorcism of her daughter, carefully omits the exclusive reference to males and then notes that four thousand—symbolic of Gentiles and women—were in attendance. Finally, the readers of Mark would note that the widow at the temple gave everything she possessed (*echō*) for others, "her whole life [*holos bios*]" (12:44), on the model of Christ on the cross and the witness of Christian martyrs in the persecution of Mark's community. She is matched by the anonymous woman who, in an extraordinary act of imitating Jesus's action on the cross, poured out (*katacheō*) everything she had (*echō*) to anoint Jesus for both his royal Davidic claim (pouring oil on his head) and his death (pouring oil on his body, 14:3–9).

In this way the narrative of Mark makes an extraordinarily strong claim that the community rituals of baptism and meal established by the death of Christ include not just Jewish men and women but Gentile men and women as well. Many women went up (*synanabainō*) with Jesus to Jerusalem, joining him on the way (*hodos*) to his passion, death, and resurrection. Three of those women specifically will minister to his burial needs and, ostensibly, be the first to witness to others concerning the resurrection of Christ. Here at the cross no male disciples are to be found, not even watching from a distance.

Everything about the characters and events surrounding the death of Jesus on the cross points to what the narrative seeks to accomplish to convince the ancient readers, especially the Jewish ancient readers, of the necessary suffering, rejection, and death of Jesus as the basis upon which the Gentiles, men and women, have now been joined with Jews in the one loaf of the Lord's Supper. The opportunities Jesus had to save himself, or to have Elijah come and save him, are, in the world of the narrative, real opportunities. And in the very real world of the persecution of early Christian churches there also would have been the opportunity to recant, to deny Christ and go free.[9] Mark's insistence that Jesus must suffer and die, and that any person who would follow Jesus must "take up his cross" and "destroy his life on account of [Jesus] and the gospel" (8:34–35), is set within the real possibility of apostasy in Mark's churches. Only endurance to the end will result in being swept up in the *imminent* return of Christ to gather the elect from the four winds (13:13, 27).

Yet the narrative purpose of Mark is not merely to create martyrs, but to tie the act of martyrdom to the church of Jews and Gentiles, men and women, that is, to the inclusive church Jesus himself created and implored his Jewish disciples to serve (6:37; 8:7; 10:42–45). For Mark, to be faithful, and even to be a martyr for Christ, is to be a member of this particular embodiment of the church (13:27), one who is gathered at the ritual table of the one loaf (8:14–21) and so a member of the inclusive body of Christ (14:22).

> And when it was already evening on the day of preparation before the Sabbath, Joseph of Arimathea came. He was a prominent member of the council and was himself waiting for the kingdom of God. He dared to go to Pilate and ask for the body of Jesus. Pilate was amazed that he was already dead and summoned the centurion and asked him if he had died. And learning this from the centurion, he gave the body to Joseph. And Joseph bought a fine linen and took him down. He wrapped him in the linen and placed him in a tomb hewn from a

---

9. Precisely as this is described in Gal. 5:11, it is eating at one table (Gal. 2:12–13) with Jews and Gentiles that apparently triggers persecution (whether by Jewish or Roman authorities is not clear). Pliny's letters to Trajan make clear that the Roman authorities were interested in making apostasy quite easy for Christians: "From this, in my opinion, it is quite easy to suggest that a large number would recant if given the opportunity for penance [*Ex quo facile est opinari, quae turba hominem emendari possit, si fiat paenitentiae locus*]" (Pliny, *Ep.* 10.96, my translation).

rock, and he rolled a stone across the door of the tomb. And Mary Magdalene and Mary mother of Joses observed where he was laid. (15:42–47)

Joseph of Arimathea asks for the body of Jesus. And it is the Gentile centurion, the Roman soldier who testified at the release of the Spirit that Jesus was "the Son of God," who here testifies that Jesus is in fact dead. As the first of the martyrs, Jesus has in fact endured to the end. And even his persecutor, the Roman soldier, recognized his claim to be Son of God in that very endurance. Here the Gospel of Mark speaks directly to its ancient readers, in the midst of persecution, expectantly waiting for the resurrected Jesus to appear and save (*sōzō*) them: they too must endure to the end.

Mark 16

The First Day of the Week

When the Sabbath was over, Mary Magdalene, Mary the mother of James, and Salome bought spices so that they might come [to the tomb] and anoint him. And very early [*prōi*] on the first day of the week, they came to the tomb at the rising [*anatellō*] of the sun. And they said amongst themselves, "Who will roll away the stone from the entrance to the tomb?" And when they looked up, they saw that the stone was rolled back. It was very large. (16:1–4)

These disciples of Jesus abide by Jewish law. The women wait until after the Sabbath (sundown Saturday) to purchase spices. Mary Magdalene, Mary the mother of James, and Salome are to use the spices to anoint the body of Jesus in the tomb. The readers of Mark, however, know that the anonymous woman in the house of Simon the leper, during the course of the ritual meal, had already anointed Jesus's body for burial (14:8).

Of the women here, only Mary Magdalene knows the location of the tomb (15:47). She and the other Mary and Salome come to the tomb very early (*prōi*), at the time the sun is rising (*anatellō*). The stone on the tomb is very large. And yet they discover that that large stone has already been rolled back. The liturgical reader of Mark now realizes that the resurrection, Christ leaving the tomb, must have taken place sometime between sundown on the Sabbath and the rising of the sun; the darkness of chaos has been defeated. This reader is again drawn to see the resurrected Christ within the narrative, when he rises (*anistēmi*) very early (*prōi*) and prays in the wilderness before going out on his mission to gather the church of Jews and Gentiles (1:35); to see the resurrected Christ early in the morning (*prōi*) declare the temple withered, the sacrificial system no longer useful for the forgiveness of sins (11:20), and the rise of a new house of prayer for the Gentiles, a new place of atonement, the ritual meal of the house church (11:17–25); to see the resurrected Christ walking upon the sea in the fourth watch of the night, in the darkness before dawn (6:48–50); and now, having followed the narrative through the suffering and death of Christ, to understand the loaves, that gathering of the Gentiles with the Jews, the defeat of chaos (water and wind), and the presence in the meal and on the boat of the one loaf, the resurrected body of Christ (6:52; 14:22).

> When they entered the tomb, they saw a young man [*neaniskos*] sitting on the right [*dexios*] side wrapped in a white robe [*stolē*], and they were amazed. And he said to them, "Do not be amazed. You seek Jesus of Nazareth, the one who was crucified. He is risen [*egeirō*]. He is not here. See the place where they placed him. But go, tell the disciples and Peter, he goes before you to Galilee. There you will see [*horaō*] him as he told you." And they left and fled from the tomb. They were shaking and ecstatic. And they said nothing to anyone, for they were afraid. (16:5–8)

Who is the *young man* (*neaniskos*), wrapped in a white robe (*stolē*), sitting on the right side of the tomb, whom these women encounter when they enter the tomb? Liturgical readers can imagine that this is the young man (*neaniskos*) who at the arrest of Jesus in Gethsemane disrobed (*kataleipō*) from his linen cloth (*sindōn*) and ran away naked (14:52). Now rehabilitated, he has been baptized into the death of Christ and sits here at the right (*dexios*) side of the tomb reclothed in a white robe (*stolē*). Perhaps this is a Gentile martyr for whom this place on the right (*dexios*) of the resurrected Christ has been prepared (10:40).[10]

It would serve the purpose of the narrative well if the young man who first proclaims the resurrection ("he is risen") and the fact of the empty tomb ("he is not here") were such a narrative figure. The one who has himself been baptized can now forgive the other disciples who fled, and Peter, who denied Jesus. And so the *Gentile* would tell the *women* to tell the Jewish Peter and the other Jewish disciples that Jesus is going before them to Galilee. And once again the resurrected Christ will be leading the disciples toward their mission (6:48), this time to Galilee, the probable location of the house churches for whom Mark writes this Gospel (14:28). There they will *see* (*horaō*) him. There in the midst of their trials before the synagogues and Roman authorities

10. It is probably not worth probing the narrative further for exactly what these women were amazed by as they entered the tomb and encountered the young man on the right side in a white robe: The fact that the large stone has been rolled back by someone or something? The apparent features of the young man dressed in white? The fact that Jesus's body was apparently not in the tomb, but the burial cloths were (16:6)?

(13:9), they will *see* (*horaō*) what Jesus described in his own trial before the Jewish authorities: the Son of Man, the "I am" of Exodus 3:14, sitting at the right hand of power and coming with the clouds of heaven (14:62). They have only to endure as the young man here dressed in white has endured. They will see (*horaō*) the resurrected Christ on the clouds with great power and glory coming to gather them, the elect, from the four winds and ends of heaven (13:26–27).

The Gospel of Mark ends with the report that the women fled from the tomb, shaking and ecstatic. They said nothing to anyone, "for they were afraid" (16:8). Yet something was said. The narrative of Mark was in fact written. The women did in fact overcome their fear and repeat the proclamation of the resurrection and their witness of the empty tomb. The narrative of Mark tells us that the Jewish house churches of Mark's time and place, despite some hesitation, began to include Gentiles and women at the Lord's Supper on the basis of their understanding of the necessary death and resurrection of Christ (14:3–9). This was the death and resurrection of Christ ritually enacted in baptismal death and sacred meal. In the Lord's Supper this inclusive community would eat of the one loaf, the body of Christ, and drink the blood poured out by Christ for the inclusion of the many (14:22–24).

Opposition among some Jews, who ironically end up in the narrative being responsible for the death of Jesus, and hesitation among some Jewish Christians concerning the connection of the necessity of Jesus's death and the consequent ritual practices of baptism and inclusive meal, were also part of the experience of these churches. At the time of the Jewish revolt against Rome (AD 66–73), probably in Galilee, this question of identity must have come to a sharp climax. The need to draw sharper distinctions between the synagogue and Christian house churches, the need for clearer lines of communal identity, would have intensified persecution from both Jewish synagogues and Roman authorities. Such a moment would have created a crisis in some house churches in the area of Galilee and southern Syria.

The Gospel of Mark provided, in creating this particular story of Jesus and his mission from baptism to death, a narrative explanation of the true identity of these house churches: Jews and Gentiles, women and men, baptized into the death of Christ and gathered as the meal of the resurrected body of Christ (8:1–9; 14:22–25), the original order of creation itself (10:5–9). In the narrative story of his mission to gather the elect, Jews and Gentiles, men and women, Jesus encounters hostility from fellow Jews and resistance from his Jewish disciples, family, and kin. He is finally executed by the Romans at the behest of some strong Jewish opposition. It is in his suffering and death on account of that mission that the beleaguered Christians of Mark's time would have found their own story and subsequently the identity of their churches as inclusive and rooted in the death and imminent return of the resurrected Christ. These inclusive churches, Jew and Greek, male and female, were now caught up in the suffering of Christ himself and so also, as the narrative of Mark teaches them, the sure expectation of his imminent return from the empty tomb to gather them from the four winds into a new creation (13:26–27).

Epilogue

An interpretation of Mark's narrative purpose such as the one proposed here cannot be understood apart from an attempt to re-create imaginatively at least a semblance of the reality of the ritual setting—baptism and meal—experienced in the earliest Christian house churches. It would have been within that ritual setting, especially in the breaking and giving of the one loaf at the Lord's Supper, that the experience of the mission, death, and resurrection of Jesus would become a reality in present circumstance and not just past event. And only within the performance of such a ritual could a narrative be generated that would retell the story of Jesus as a story to teach the present community about its own identity. These were the gatherings within the house churches, probably in Galilee and areas close by, of Jews with Gentiles, men and women on their way (*hodos*) to follow Jesus to persecution and martyrdom. Within the tension created by the threat of persecution, these particular Christians practiced rituals that performed unity, martyrdom, and the expectation of resurrection and final judgment.

The dynamic ritual setting of the earliest house churches makes the most sense as the place from which a narrative such as the Gospel of Mark would be generated and in which it would be experienced as reality. Only within such a ritual setting would this narrative about Jesus be understood as presenting at once the real experience of the resurrected Christ within the situation of the churches of Mark's day as well as the past story of Jesus and his disciples, while all the while anticipating Jesus's imminent return to end time. This book, therefore, ends with the argument that the narrative purpose of the Gospel of Mark was generated from within the ritual setting of baptismal death and gathered meal of Jews with Gentiles, men with women, time outside of time and place outside of place, the very qualities of ritual performance.[1]

Far from modern interpretations of Mark's Gospel, most often based in an attempt to understand the narrative character of Jesus as an individual and the disciples and opponents in relationship to that individual, I have tried to present the Gospel as a creative, even brilliant, adaptation of the story of Jesus to a particular ritual and communal situation in a historical context largely lost to us. But it cannot remain there. I have argued throughout this book that the creativity displayed in Mark's narrative was directly tied to the experience of liturgy, baptismal death, and resurrection gathering. And it goes without saying that this experience is still at the heart of the Christian church today. As in Mark's time, our preaching and teaching of the living Christ must be the creative, even brilliant, adaptation of the story of Jesus to our own time and place.

1. For discussion, see Doty, *Mythography*; J. Z. Smith, "Influence of Symbols"; J. Z. Smith, *To Take Place*.

General Bibliography

Achtemeier, Paul J. "And He Followed Him: Miracles and Discipleship in Mark 10:46–52." *Semeia* 11 (1978): 115–45.

———. "He Taught Them Many Things: Reflections on Markan Christology." *CBQ* 42 (1980): 465–81.

———. *Invitation to Mark.* Garden City, NY: Doubleday, 1978.

———. *Mark.* 2nd ed. Philadelphia: Fortress, 1986.

———. "Mark as Interpreter of the Jesus Traditions." *Int* 32 (1978): 339–52.

———. "The Origin and Function of Pre-Marcan Miracle Catenae." *JBL* 91 (1972): 198–221.

———. "Toward the Isolation of Pre-Markan Miracle Catenae." *JBL* 89 (1970): 265–91.

Adams, Daniel J. "Towards a Theological Understanding of Postmodernism." *CC* 47 (1998): 518–30.

Ahearne-Kroll, Stephen P. *The Psalms of Lament in Mark's Passion: Jesus' Davidic Suffering.* Cambridge: Cambridge University Press, 2007.

———. "Who Are My Mother and My Brothers? Family Relationships and Family Language in the Gospel of Mark." *JR* 81 (2001): 1–25.

Aichele, George. *Jesus Framed.* London: Routledge, 1996.

———. *The Phantom Messiah: Postmodern Fantasy and the Gospel of Mark.* New York: T&T Clark, 2006.

Allison, Dale. "Elijah Must Come First." *JBL* 103 (1984): 256–58.

Alter, Robert. *The Art of Biblical Narrative.* London: G. Allen & Unwin, 1981.

Ambrozic, Aloysius M. *The Hidden Kingdom: A Redaction-Critical Study of the References to the Kingdom of God in Mark's Gospel.* Washington, DC: Catholic Biblical Association of America, 1972.

———. "New Teaching with Power (Mark 1:27)." In *Word and Spirit: Essays in Honor of David Michael Stanley, S.J., on His 60th Birthday,* edited by J. Plevnik, 113–49. Willowdale, ON: Regis College, 1975.

Anderson, Bernhard W. "Exodus Typology in Second Isaiah." In *Israel's Prophetic Heritage: Essays in Honor of James Muilenburg,* edited by Bernhard W. Anderson and Walter Harrelson, 177–95. New York: Harper, 1962.

Anderson, Hugh. *The Gospel of Mark.* Grand Rapids: Eerdmans, 1981.

Anderson, Janice Capel. "Feminist Criticism: The Dancing Daughter." In *Mark and Method,* 2nd ed., edited by Janice Capel Anderson and Stephen D. Moore, 111–143. Minneapolis: Fortress, 2008.

Anderson, Janice Capel, and Stephen D. Moore, eds. *Mark and Method,* 2nd ed. Minneapolis: Fortress, 2008.

Auerbach, Erich. *Memesis: The Representation of Reality in Western Literature.* Princeton: Princeton University Press, 1953.

Aune, David E. "The Problem of the Messianic Secret." *NovT* 11 (1969): 1–31.

———. *"Septem Sapientium Convivium (Moralia* 146B–164D)." In *Plutarch's Ethical Writings and Early Christian Literature,* edited by Hans Dieter Betz, 51–105. Leiden: Brill, 1978.

Baarlink, Heinrich. *Anfängliches Evangelium: Ein Beitrag zur näheren Bestimmung der theologischen Motive im Markusevangelium.* Kok: Kampen, 1977.

Bacon, B. W. *The Gospel of Mark: Its Composition and Date.* London: Oxford University Press, 1925.

Baird, J. A. "A Pragmatic Approach to Parable Exegesis: Some New Evidence on Mark 4:11, 33–34." *JBL* 76 (1957): 201–7.

Balabanski, Vicky. *Eschatology in the Making: Mark, Matthew, and the Didache.* Cambridge: Cambridge University Press, 1997.

Balslev, Anindita N., ed. *Religion and Time.* Leiden: Brill, 1993.

Balthasar, Hans Urs von. *Explorations in Theology.* San Francisco: Ignatius Press, 1989.

———. *Mysterium Paschale: The Mystery of Easter.* Edinburgh: T&T Clark, 1990.

Barth, Karl. *Christ and Adam.* Translated by T. M. Smail. New York: Macmillan, 1956.

Barton, Stephen C. "Can We Identify the Gospel Audiences?" In *The Gospels for All Christians: Rethinking the Gospel Audiences,* edited by Richard Bauckham, 173–94. Grand Rapids: Eerdmans, 1998.

———. *Discipleship and Family Ties in Mark and Matthew.* Cambridge: Cambridge University Press, 1994.

———. "Mark as Narrative: The Story of the Anointing Woman (Mark 14:3–9)." *ExpTim* 102 (1991): 230–34.

Batto, Bernard. "Creation Theology in Genesis." In *Creation in the Biblical Traditions,* edited by John Collins and Richard J. Clifford, 16–38. Washington, DC: Catholic Biblical Association of America, 1992.

Bauckham, Richard. *Jesus and the Eyewitnesses: The Gospels as Eyewitness Testimony.* Grand Rapids: Eerdmans, 2006.

Baudoz, Jean François. "Mc 7,31–37 Et Mc 8:22–26: Géographie et théologie." *RB* 102 (1995): 560–69.

———. *Les miettes de la table.* Paris: Gabalda, 1995.

Bauernfeind, O. *Die Worte der Dämonen im Markusevangelium.* Stuttgart: Kohlhammer, 1927.

Beasley-Murray, G. R. *Jesus and the Last Days: The Interpretation of the Olivet Discourse.* 2nd ed. London: Macmillan, 1954. Reprint, Peabody, MA: Hendrickson, 1993.

Beavis, M. A. *Mark's Audience: The Literary and Social Setting of Mark 4:11–12.* Sheffield: Sheffield Academic, 1989.

———. "The Trial before the Sanhedrin (Mark 14:53–65): Reader Response and the Greco-Roman Readers." *CBQ* 49 (1987): 581–96.

Beck, N. A. "Reclaiming a Biblical Text: The Mark 8:14–21 Discussion about Bread in the Boat." *CBQ* 43 (1981): 49–56.

Best, Ernest. *Disciples and Discipleship: Studies in the Gospel of Mark.* Edinburgh: T&T Clark, 1986.

———. "Discipleship in Mark: Mark 8:22–10:52." *SJT* 23 (1970): 323–37.

———. *Following Jesus: Discipleship in Mark's Gospel.* Sheffield: JSOT Press, 1981.

———. "Mark's Narrative Technique." *JSNT* 37 (1989): 43–58.

———. "Mark's Preservation of the Tradition." In *The Interpretation of Mark,* edited by William R. Telford, 153–68. Edinburgh: T&T Clark, 1995.

———. "Mark's Readers: A Profile." In *The Four Gospels 1992: Festschrift Frans Neirynck,* edited by F. Van Segbroeck, 839–58. Leuven: Leuven University Press, 1992.

———. "Mark's Use of the Twelve." *ZNW* 69 (1977): 11–35.

———. *Mark: The Gospel as Story.* Edinburgh: T&T Clark, 1983.

———. "Peter in the Gospel according to Mark." *CBQ* 40 (1978): 547–58.

———. "The Role of the Disciples in Mark." *NTS* 23 (1977): 377–401.

———. *The Temptation and the Passion: The Markan Soteriology.* 2nd ed. Cambridge: Cambridge University Press, 1990.

Betsworth, Sharon. *The Reign of God Is Such as These: A Socio-Literary Analysis of Daughters in the Gospel of Mark.* London: T&T Clark, 2010.

Betz, Hans Dieter. "Jesus as Divine Man." In *Jesus and the Historians,* edited by F. T. Trotter, 114–33. Philadelphia: Westminster, 1968.

Bilezikian, Gilbert G. *The Liberated Gospel: A Comparison of the Gospel of Mark and Greek Tragedy.* Grand Rapids: Baker, 1977.

Black, C. Clifton. "Christ Crucified in Paul and Mark: Reflections on an Intercanonical Convention." In *Theology and Ethics in Paul and His Interpreters: Essays in Honor of Victor Paul Furnish,* edited by E. H. Lovering and J. L. Sumney, 80–104. Nashville: Abingdon, 1996.

———. *The Disciples according to Mark: Markan Redaction in Current Debate.* Sheffield: Sheffield Academic, 1989.

———. *Mark.* Nashville: Abingdon, 2011.

———. "Mark as Historian of God's Kingdom." *CBQ* 71 (2009): 64–83.

———. "The Quest of Mark the Redactor: Why It Has Been Pursued and What It Has Taught Us." *JSNT* 33 (1988): 19–39.

———. "Was Mark a Roman Gospel?" *Exp Tim* 105 (1993): 36–40.

Black, David Alan. *Perspectives on the Ending of Mark.* London: Broadman & Holman, 2008.

Black, Matthew. *The Scrolls and Christian Origin: Studies in the Jewish Background of the New Testament.* New York: Scribner, 1961.

Blackburn, B. *Theios Aner and the Markan Miracle Traditions.* Tübingen: Mohr Siebeck, 1991.

Blank, G. K. "Deconstruction: Entering the Bible through Babel." *Neot* 20 (1986): 61–67.

Blatherwicke, David. "The Markan Silhouette." *NTS* 17 (1971): 184–92.

Blevins, J. L. "The Christology of Mark." *RevExp* 75 (1978): 505–17.

———. *The Messianic Secret in Markan Research.* Washington, DC: University Press of America, 1981.

Blount, Brian K. *Cultural Interpretation: Reorienting New Testament Criticism.* Minneapolis: Fortress, 1995.

———. "Preaching the Kingdom: Mark's Apocalyptic Call for Prophetic Engagement." *PSB* 3 (1994): 33–56.

Bobertz, Charles A. "Our Opinion Is in Accordance with the Eucharist and the Eucharist Confirms Our Opinion: Irenaeus and the *Sitz im Leben* of Mark's Gospel." *StPatr* 65 (2013): 79–90.

———. "That by His Passion He Might Purify the Water: Ignatius of Antioch and the Beginning of Mark's Gospel." *FF* 3 (2014): 91–98.

Boer, Martinus C. de. "Paul and Jewish Apocalyptic Eschatology." In *Apocalyptic and the New Testament: Essays in Honor of J. Louis Martyn,* edited by Joel Marcus and Marion L. Soards, 169–90. Sheffield: Sheffield Academic, 1989.

Boismard, M. É. *L'Évangile de Marc: Sa préhistoire.* EBib, n.s., 26. Paris: Gabalda, 1994.

Boobyer, G. H. "Mark II,10a and the Interpretation of the Healing of the Paralytic." *HTR* 48 (1954): 115–20.

Boomershine, Thomas Eugene. "Mark 16:8 and the Apostolic Commission." *JBL* 100 (1981): 225–39.

Boring, M. Eugene. "The Christology of Mark: Hermeneutical Issues for Systematic Theology." *Semeia* 30 (1985): 125–53.

———. "Mark 1:1–15 and the Beginning of the Gospel." *Semeia* 52 (1990): 43–81.

———. *Mark: A Commentary.* NTL. Louisville: Westminster John Knox, 2006.

Borrell, Agustí. *The Good News of Peter's Denial: A Narrative and Rhetorical Reading of Mark 14:54.66–72.* University of South Florida International Studies in Formative Christianity and Judaism. Atlanta: Scholars Press, 1998.

Botha, P. J. J. "The Historical Setting of Mark's Gospel: Problems and Possibilities." *JSNT* 51 (1993): 27–55.

Böttger, J. L. *Der König der Juden: Das Heil für die Völker.* Neukirchen: Neukirchener, 1981.

Boucher, M. *The Mysterious Parable: A Literary Study.* CBQMS 6. Washington, DC: Catholic Biblical Association of America, 1977.

Bourquin, Yvan. *Marc, Une théologie de la fragilité: Obscure clarté d'une narration.* Geneva: Labor et Fides, 2005.

Braaten, Carl. "The Resurrection Debate Revisited." *ProEccl* 8 (1999): 147–58.

Breytenbach, Cilliers. *Nachfolge und Zukunftserwartung nach Markus: Eine methodenkritische Studie.* Zurich: Theologischer Verlag, 1984.

Broadhead, Edwin Keith. *Naming Jesus: Titular Christology in the Gospel of Mark.* Sheffield: Sheffield Academic, 1999.

———. *Prophet, Son, Messiah: Narrative Form and Function in Mark 14–16.* Sheffield: JSOT Press, 1994.

———. *Teaching with Authority: Miracles and Christology in the Gospel of Mark.* Sheffield: JSOT Press, 1992.

Brooks, James A. "An Annotated Bibliography on Mark." *SwJT* 21 (1978): 75–82.

———. *Mark.* Nashville: Broadman, 1991.

Brower, Kent. "Mark 9:1: Seeing the Kingdom in Power." In *The Synoptic Gospels,* edited by Craig A. Evans and Stanley E. Porter, 121–42. Sheffield: Sheffield Academic, 1995.

Brown, Raymond E. *An Introduction to the New Testament.* Garden City, NY: Doubleday, 1997.

———. "Jesus and Elisha." *Per* 12 (1971): 85–104.

Brueggemann, Walter. "The Loss and Recovery of Creation in Old Testament Theology." *ThTo* 53 (1996): 177–90.

Bruns, Gerald L. *Hermeneutics, Ancient and Modern.* New Haven: Yale University Press, 1992.

Bryan, Christopher. *A Preface to Mark: Notes on the Gospel in Its Literary and Cultural Setting.* Oxford: Oxford University Press, 1993.

Büchler, A. "The Law of Purification in Mark VII.1–23." *ExpTim* 21 (1909–10): 34–40.

Budesheim, T. L. "Jesus and the Disciples in Conflict with Jerusalem." *ZNW* 62 (1971): 190–209.

Bultmann, Rudolf. *History and Eschatology: The Presence of Eternity.* New York: Harper, 1955.

———. *The History of the Synoptic Tradition.* Translated by John Marsh. New York: Harper, 1963.

———. *Theologie des Neuen Testaments.* Durchgesehene und ergänzte ed. Neue Theologische Grundisse 3. Berlin: Evangelische Verlagsanstalt, 1959.

Burkett, Delbert Royce. *Rethinking the Gospel Sources from Proto-Mark to Mark.* New York: T&T Clark, 2004.

Burkill, T. A. "The Historical Development of the Story of the Syrophoenician Woman (Mark VII.24–31)." *NovT* 9 (1967): 161–78.

———. "Mark 3:7–12 and the Alleged Dualism of the Evangelist's Miracle Material." *JBL* 87 (1968): 409–17.

———. "The Syrophoenician Woman: The Congruence of Mark 7,24–31." *ZNW* 57 (1966): 23–37.

Burridge, Richard A. *What Are the Gospels? A Comparison with Graeco-Roman Biography.* 2nd ed. Biblical Resource Series. Grand Rapids: Eerdmans, 2004.

Burtchaell, James T. *From Synagogue to Church: Public Services and Offices in the Earliest Christian Communities.* Cambridge: Cambridge University Press, 1992.

Buse, I. "The Markan Account of the Baptism of Jesus and Isaiah LXIII." *JTS* 7 (1956): 74–75.

Busemann, R. *Die Jüngergemeinde nach Markus 10.* Bonn: Hanstein, 1983.

Bynum, Caroline Walker. *Fragmentation and Redemption: Essays on Gender and the Human Body in Medieval Religion.* Cambridge, MA: Zone Books, 1991.

Byrne, Brendan. *A Costly Freedom: A Theological Reading of Mark's Gospel.* Collegeville, MN: Liturgical Press, 2008.

Cadoux, Arthur Temple. *The Sources of the Second Gospel.* New York: Macmillan, 1935.

Cahill, Michael. *The First Commentary on Mark: An Annotated Translation.* Translated by Michael Cahill. Oxford: Oxford University Press, 1998.

Camery-Hoggat, Jerry. *Irony in Mark's Gospel.* Cambridge: Cambridge University Press, 1992.

Cangh, J. M. van. "La Multiplication des pains dans l'Évangile de Marc." In *L'Évangile selon Marc: Tradition et rédaction,* edited by M. Sabbe, 309–46. Leuven: Duculot / Leuven University Press, 1974.

Carey, Holly J. *Jesus' Cry from the Cross: Towards a First-Century Understanding of the Intertextual Relationship between Psalm 22 and the Narrative of Mark's Gospel.* London: T&T Clark, 2009.

Carrington, P. *The Primitive Christian Calendar: A Study in the Making of the Markan Gospel.* Cambridge: Cambridge University Press, 1952.

Carter, Warren. *Households and Discipleship: A Study of Matthew 19–20.* JSNTSup 103. Sheffield: JSOT Press, 1994.

———. "Recalling the Lord's Prayer: The Authorial Audience and Matthew's Prayer as Familiar Liturgical Experience." *CBQ* 57 (1995): 514–30.

Casey, M. "Culture and Historicity: The Plucking of the Grain (Mark 2.23–28)." *NTS* 34 (1988): 1–23.

Castelli, E., Stephen D. Moore, and E. Schwartz, eds. *The Postmodern Bible.* New Haven: Yale University Press, 1995.

Catchpole, David R. "The Fearful Silence of the Women at the Tomb: A Study in Markan Theology." *JTSA* 18 (1977): 3–10.

Chapman, Dean W. "Locating the Gospel of Mark: A Model of Agrarian Biography." *BTB* 25 (1995): 25–36.

———. *The Orphan Gospel.* Sheffield: Sheffield Academic, 1993.

Charlesworth, James H. *Jesus within Judaism: New Light from Exciting Archaeological Discoveries.* New York: Doubleday, 1988.

Charlesworth, James H., Hermann Lichtenberger, and Gerbern S. Oegema, eds. *Qumran-Messianism: Studies on the Messianic Expectations in the Dead Sea Scrolls.* Tübingen: Mohr Siebeck, 1998.

Chilton, Bruce. "The So-Called Trial before the Sanhedrin: Mark 14:53–72." *Forum* 1 (1998): 163–80.

Chilton, Bruce, Darrell L. Bock, and Daniel M. Gurtner. *A Comparative Handbook to the Gospel of Mark: Comparisons with Pseudepigrapha, the Qumran Scrolls, and Rabbinic Literature.* Leiden: Brill, 2010.

Clark, Elizabeth, and Herbert Richardson, eds. *Women and Religion: A Feminist Sourcebook of Christian Thought.* San Francisco: Harper, 1977.

Clerici, Luigi. *Einsammlung der zerstreuten Liturgiegeschichtliche Untersuchung zur Vor- und Nachgeschichte der Fürbitte Für die Kirche in Didache 9,4 und 10,5.* Liturgiewissenschaftliche Quellen und Forschungen. Münster: Aschendorff Verlagsbuchhandlung, 1966.

Clifford, Richard J. "Creation in the Psalms." In *Creation in the Biblical Traditions,* edited by John Collins and Richard J. Clifford, 57–69. Washington, DC: Catholic Biblical Association of America, 1992.

Cole, R. A. *The Gospel according to Mark: An Introduction and Commentary.* 2nd ed. Grand Rapids: Eerdmans, 1989.

Collins, Adela Yarbro. *The Beginning of the Gospel: Probings of Mark in Context.* Minneapolis: Fortress, 1992.

———. *The Combat Myth in the Book of Revelation.* Chico, CA: Scholars Press, 1976.

———. *Cosmology and Eschatology in Jewish and Christian Apocalypticism.* Leiden: Brill, 1996.

———. "From Noble Death to Crucified Messiah." *NTS* 40 (1994): 481–503.

———. "The Genre of the Passion Narrative." *ST* 47 (1993): 3–28.

———. *Mark: A Commentary.* Minneapolis: Fortress, 2007.

———. "Narrative, History, and Gospel: A General Response." *Semeia* 43 (1988): 145–53.

Collins, John, ed. *Apocalypse: Morphology of a Genre.* Atlanta: Society of Biblical Literature, 1979.

———. *The Apocalyptic Imagination: An Introduction to the Jewish Matrix of Christianity*. New York: Crossroad, 1987.

———. "From Prophecy to Apocalypticism: The Expectation of the End." In *The Origins of Apocalypticism in Judaism and Christianity*, vol. 1 of *The Encyclopedia of Apocalypticism*, edited by John Collins, 129–61. New York: Continuum, 1999.

———. *The Scepter and the Star: The Messiahs of the Dead Sea Scrolls and Other Ancient Literature*. New York: Doubleday, 1995.

Collins, John, and Craig A. Evans. *Christian Beginnings and the Dead Sea Scrolls*. ASBT. Grand Rapids: Baker Academic, 2006.

Conzelmann, H., and A. Lindemann. *Interpreting the New Testament*. Translated by Siegfried Schatzmann. Peabody, MA: Hendrickson, 1988.

Cook, John G. *The Structure and Persuasive Power of Mark: A Linguistic Approach*. Atlanta: Scholars Press, 1995.

Cook, Michael J. *Mark's Treatment of the Jewish Leaders*. Leiden: Brill, 1978.

Cook, Stephen L. *Prophecy and Apocalypticism: The Postexilic Social Setting*. Minneapolis: Fortress, 1995.

Countryman, L. William. "How Many Baskets Full? Mark 8:14–21 and the Value of Miracles in Mark." *CBQ* 47 (1985): 643–55.

Couts, John. "The Authority of Jesus and the Twelve in St. Mark's Gospel." *JTS* 8 (1957): 111–18.

Coutsoumpos, Panayotis. *Paul and the Lord's Supper: A Socio-Historical Investigation*. Studies in Biblical Literature. New York: Peter Lang, 2005.

Cranfield, C. E. B. *The Gospel according to Saint Mark: An Introduction and Commentary*. Cambridge: Cambridge University Press, 1959.

Crossan, John Dominic. *The Birth of Christianity: Discovering What Happened in the Years Immediately after the Execution of Jesus*. San Francisco: Harper, 1998.

———. "Empty Tomb and Absent Lord." In *The Passion in Mark: Studies on Mark 14–16*, edited by Werner Kelber, 135–52. Philadelphia: Fortress, 1976.

———. "A Form for Absence: The Markan Creation of Gospel." *Semeia* 12 (1978): 41–55.

———. *The Historical Jesus: The Life of a Mediterranean Jewish Peasant*. San Francisco: Harper, 1991.

———. "Mark and the Relatives of Jesus." *NovT* 15 (1973): 81–113.

Crossan, John Dominic, Werner H. Kelber, and Luke Timothy Johnson. *The Jesus Controversy: Perspectives in Conflict*. Harrisburg, PA: Trinity Press International, 1999.

Crossley, James G. *The Date of Mark's Gospel: Insight from the Law in Earliest Christianity*. JSNTSup 266. London: T&T Clark, 2004.

Culpepper, R. Alan. *Mark*. Smyth & Helwys Bible Commentary. Macon, GA: Smyth & Helwys, 2007.

Cunningham, Phillip J. *Mark: The Good News Preached to the Romans*. New York: Paulist Press, 1995.

Dahl, Nils. *The Crucified Messiah*. Minneapolis: Augsburg, 1974.

Daley, Brian. *The Hope of the Early Church*. Cambridge: Cambridge University Press, 1991.

Daly, Robert J. "The Eucharist and Redemption: The Last Supper and Jesus' Understanding of His Death." *BTB* 11 (1981): 21–27.

Danker, F. W. "Mark 8:3." *JBL* 82 (1963): 215–16.

Danove, Paul L. *The End of Mark's Story: A Methodological Story*. Leiden: Brill, 1993.

———. *Linguistics and Exegesis in the Gospel of Mark: Applications of a Case Frame Analysis*. Sheffield: Sheffield Academic, 2001.

———. *The Rhetoric of the Characterization of God, Jesus, and Jesus' Disciples in the Gospel of Mark*. JSNTSup 290. London: T&T Clark, 2005.

Daube, David. *The Exodus Pattern in the Bible*. London: Faber and Faber, 1963.

. *The New Testament and Rabbinic Judaism*. London: University of London, Athlone Press, 1956.

Dautzenberg, Gerhard. "Die Zeit des Evangeliums: Mark 1,15 und die Konzeption des Markusevangeliums." *BZ* 22 (1978): 76–91.

Davidsen, Ole. *The Narrative Jesus: A Semiotic Reading of Mark's Gospel*. Aarhus: Aarhus University Press, 1993.

Davies, Philip R. *Behind the Essenes: History and Ideology in the Dead Sea Scrolls*. Atlanta: Scholars Press, 1987.

Davies, W. D. *Paul and Rabbinic Judaism*. London: SPCK, 1962.

. "Reflections on Archbishop Carrington's *The Primitive Christian Calendar*." In *The Background of the New Testament and Its Eschatology*, edited by W. D. Davies and David Daube, 124–52. Cambridge: Cambridge University Press, 1956.

. *Torah in the Messianic Age and/or the Age to Come*. Philadelphia: Society of Biblical Literature, 1952.

Davis, Philip G. "Mark's Christological Paradox." In *The Synoptic Gospels*, edited by Craig A. Evans and Stanley E. Porter, 163–77. Sheffield: Sheffield Academic, 1995.

Davis, Stephen, Daniel Kendall, and Gerald O'Collins, eds. *The Resurrection: An Interdisciplinary Symposium on the Resurrection of Jesus*. Oxford: Oxford University Press, 1997.

Delorme, Jean. "Aspects doctrineaux du second Évangile." *AsSeign* 46 (1974): 43–50.

De Mingo Kaminouchi, Alberto. *"But It Is Not So among You": Echoes of Power in Mark 10.32–45*. JSNTSup 249. New York: T&T Clark, 2003.

Derrett, J. D. M. "Contributions to the Study of the Gerasene Demoniac." *JSNT* 3 (1979): 2–17.

. *The Making of Mark: The Scriptural Bases of the Earliest Gospel*. Shipston-on-Stour, UK: Drinkwater, 1985.

Dewey, Joanna. "The Gospel of Mark as an Oral-Aural Event: Implications for Interpretation." In *The New Literary Criticism and the New Testament*, edited by Elizabeth Struthers Malbon and Edgar V. McKnight, 145–63. Sheffield: Sheffield Academic, 1994.

. "The Literary Structure and the Controversy Stories in Mark 2:1–3:6." *JBL* 92 (1973): 394–401.

. "The Literary Structure of the Controversy Stories in Mark 2:1–3:6." In *The Interpretation of Mark*, edited by William R. Telford, 141–51. Edinburgh: T&T Clark, 1995.

. *Markan Public Debate: Literary Technique, Concentric Structure, and Theology in Mark 2:1–3:6*. Chico, CA: Scholars Press, 1980.

. "Mark as Interwoven Tapestry: Forecasts and Echoes for a Listening Audience." *CBQ* 53 (1991): 221–36.

. "Point of View and the Disciples in Mark." *SBLSP* 21 (1982): 97–106.

. "Recent Studies on Mark." *RelSRev* 17 (1991): 12–23.

Dewey, Kim E. "Peter's Curse and the Cursed Peter (Mark 14:53–54, 66–72)." In *The Passion in Mark: Studies on Mark 14–16*, edited by Werner Kelber, 96–114. Philadelphia: Fortress, 1976.

Dibelius, Martin. *Die Formgeschichte des Evangeliums*. 3rd ed. Göttingen: Mohr Siebeck, 1959.

Dihle, A. "The Gospels and Greek Biography." In *The Gospel and the Gospels*, edited by Peter Stuhlmacher, 361–86. Grand Rapids: Eerdmans, 1992.

Dillon, Richard. "As One Having Authority (Mark 1:22): The Controversial Distinction of Jesus' Teaching." *CBQ* 57 (1995): 92–113.

Dippenaar, Michaelis Christoffel. "The Disciples in Mark: Narrative and Theology." *TJT* 17 (1995): 139–209.

DiTomasso, Lorenzo. "Apocalypses and Apocalypticism in Antiquity (Part 1)." *CurBR* 5 (2007): 235–86.

Dodd, C. H. "The Framework of the Gospel Narrative." *ExpTim* 43 (1932): 398–400.

. *New Testament Studies*. Manchester: Manchester University Press, 1954.

Donahue, John R. *Are You the Christ? The Trial Narrative in the Gospel of Mark*. Missoula, MT: Society of Biblical Literature, 1973.

. "Introduction: From Passion Traditions to Passion Narrative." In *The Passion in Mark: Studies on Mark 14–16*, edited by Werner Kelber, 1–20. Philadelphia: Fortress, 1976.

———. "Jesus as the Parable of God in the Gospel of Mark." *Int* 32 (1978): 369–86.

———. "A Neglected Factor in the Theology of Mark." *JBL* 101 (1982): 563–94.

———. "The Quest for the Community of Mark's Gospel." In *The Four Gospels, 1992: Festschrift Frans Neirynck*, edited by F. Van Segbroeck, 819–34. Leuven: Leuven University Press, 1992.

———. "Redaction Criticism: Has the *Hauptstrasse* Become a *Sackgasse*?" In *The New Literary Criticism and the New Testament*, edited by Elizabeth Struthers Malbon and Edgar V. McKnight, 27–57. Sheffield: Sheffield Academic, 1994.

———. "Seeking Ariadne's Thread: Some Unfinished Reflections on Method and the Study of Mark." Catholic Biblical Association Paper, 1997.

———. "Temple, Trial, and Royal Christology." In *The Passion in Mark: Studies on Mark 14–16*, edited by Werner Kelber, 61–79. Philadelphia: Fortress Press, 1976.

———. *The Theology and Setting of Discipleship in the Gospel of Mark*. Milwaukee: Marquette University Press, 1983.

———. "Windows and Mirrors: The Setting of Mark's Gospel." *CBQ* 57 (1995): 1–26.

Donahue, John R., and Daniel J. Harrington. *The Gospel of Mark*. Collegeville, MN: Liturgical Press, 2002.

Donfried, K. "The Feeding Narratives and the Markan Community: Mark 6,30–45 and Mark 8,1–10." In *Kirche: Festschrift für Günther Bornkamm zum 75. Geburtstag*, edited by D. Lührmann and G. Strecker, 95–103. Tübingen: Mohr Siebeck, 1980.

Dormeyer, Detlev. "Die Kompositionsmetapher 'Evangelium Jesu Christi, des Sohnes Gottes' Mk 1:1: Ihre theologische und literarische Aufgabe in der Jesus-Biographie des Markus." *NTS* 33 (1987): 452–68.

———. *Die Passion Jesu als Verhaltensmodell*. Münster: Aschendorff, 1974.

———. *Der Sinn des Leidens Jesu*. Stuttgart: Katholisches Bibelwerk, 1979.

Dormeyer, Detlev, and Hubert Frankemölle. "Evangelium als literarische Gattung und als theologischer Begriff: Tendenzen und Aufgaben der Evangeliumforschung im 20. Jahrhundert mit einer Untersuchung des Markusevangeliums in seinem Verhältnis zur antiken Biographie." *ANRW* 2, no. 25.2 (1984): 1543–704.

Dowd, Sharyn. "The Gospel of Mark as Ancient Novel." *LTQ* 26 (1991): 53–59.

———. "Mark and Isaiah." *LTQ* 30 (1995): 133–43.

———. *Reading Mark: A Literary and Theological Commentary on the Second Gospel*. Reading the New Testament Series. Macon, GA: Smyth & Helwys, 2000.

Driggers, Ira Brent. *Following God through Mark: Theological Tension in the Second Gospel*. Louisville: Westminster John Knox, 2007.

Drury, J. "Mark 1:1–15: An Interpretation." In *Alternative Approaches to New Testament Study*, edited by A. E. Harvey, 25–36. London: SPCK, 1985.

Dschulnigg, Peter. *Sprache, Redaktion, und Intention des Markus-Evangeliums: Eigentumlichkeiten der Sprache des Markus-Evangeliums und ihre Bedeutung für die Redaktionskritik*. Stuttgart: Katholisches Bibelwerk, 1984.

Duling, Dennis C., Norman Perrin, and Robert L. Ferm. *The New Testament: Proclamation and Parenesis, Myth and History*. 3rd ed. under the general editorship of Robert Ferm. Fort Worth: Harcourt Brace, 1994.

Dungan, David Laird. *A History of the Synoptic Problem*. New York: Doubleday, 1999.

Dunn, James D. G. *Christology in the Making: A New Testament Inquiry in the Origins of Doctrine*. Philadelphia: Westminster, 1980.

———. *Jesus, Paul, and the Law: Studies in Mark and Galatians*. Louisville: Westminster John Knox, 1990.

———. "Mark 2:1–3:6: A Bridge between Jesus and Paul on the Question of the Law." *NTS* 30 (1984): 395–415.

———. "The Messianic Secret in Mark." *Tyn Bul* 21 (1970): 92–117.

Dunn, James D. G., and James Mackey. *New Testament Theology in Dialogue: Christology and Ministry*. Philadelphia: Westminster, 1987.

Dupont, J. "Encore la parabole de la semence, qui pousse toute seule (Mk 4,26–29)." In *Jesus und Paulus: Festschrift für Werner Georg Kümmel zum 70. Geburtstag*, edited by E. E. Ellis and E. Grässer, 96–101. Göttingen: Vandenhoeck & Ruprecht, 1975.

Duran, Nicole Wilkinson, Teresa Okure, and Daniel Patte. *Mark*. Minneapolis: Fortress, 2010.

Dwyer, Timothy. *The Motif of Wonder in the Gospel of Mark*. Sheffield: Sheffield Academic, 1996.

Dyer, Keith D. *The Prophecy on the Mount: Mark 13 and the Gathering of the New Community*. New York: Peter Lang, 1998.

Ebeling, Hans Jürgen. *Das Messiasgeheimnis und die Botschaft des Marcus-Evangelisten*. Berlin: Töpelmann, 1939.

Edwards, James R. *The Gospel according to Mark*. Grand Rapids: Eerdmans, 2002.

———. "Markan Sandwiches: The Significance of Interpolations in Markan Narratives." *NovT* 31 (1989): 193–216.

Egger, W. *Frohbotschaft und Lehre: Die Sammelberichte des Wirkens Jesu im Markusevangelium*. Frankfurt: Joseph Knecht, 1976.

———. *Nachfolge als Weg zum Leben*. Klosterneuburg: Österreichisches Katholisches Bibelwerk, 1979.

Ehrman, Bart D. "The Text of Mark in the Hands of the Orthodox." *LQ* 5 (1991): 143–56.

Eilberg-Schwartz, Howard. *The Savage in Judaism: An Anthropology of Israelite Religion in Ancient Judaism*. Bloomington: Indiana University Press, 1990.

Elliott, J. K. "The Conclusion of the Pericope of the Healing of the Leper and Mark 1.45." *JTS* 22 (1971): 153–57.

———, ed. *The Language and Style of Mark*. Leiden: Brill, 1993.

———. "Mark 1:1–3: A Later Addition to the Gospel?" *NTS* 46 (2000): 584–88.

Ellis, E. Earle. "Biblical Interpretation in the New Testament Church." In *Mikra: Text, Translation, Reading, and Interpretation of the Hebrew Bible in Ancient Judaism and Early Christianity*, edited by Martin Mulder, 691–725. Philadelphia: Fortress, 1988.

———. "The Date and Provenance of Mark's Gospel." In *The Four Gospels, 1992: Festschrift Frans Neirynck*, edited by F. Van Segbroeck et al., 801–16. Leuven: Leuven University Press, 1992.

———. "Patterns and Structures in Mark's Gospel." In *Biblical Studies in Contemporary Thought*, edited by M. Ward, 88–103. Somerville, MA: Greeno, Hadden, 1975.

Enslin, Morten Scott. "The Artistry of Mark." *JBL* 66 (1947): 385–99.

Ernst, Josef. *Das Evangelium nach Markus*. Regensburg: Pustet, 1981.

Escaffre, Bernadette. "La mort de Jésus et la venue du royaume dans l'Évangile de Marc." *EstBib* 52 (1994): 329–39.

Evans, Craig A. "Isaiah 6:9–10 in Rabbinic and Patristic Writings." *VC* 36 (1982): 275–81.

———. "Jesus and the Cave of Robbers: Toward a Jewish Context for the Temple Action." *BBR* 3 (1993): 93–100.

———. *Mark 8:27–16:20*. Word Biblical Commentary 34B. Nashville: Thomas Nelson, 2001.

———. *Noncanonical Writings and New Testament Interpretation*. Peabody, MA: Hendrickson, 1992.

———. *To See and Not Perceive: Isaiah 6.9–10 in Early Jewish and Christian Interpretation*. Sheffield: Sheffield Academic, 1989.

Evans, Craig A., and Stanley E. Porter, eds. *The Synoptic Gospels*. Sheffield: Sheffield Academic, 1995.

Farmer, William Reuben. *The Last Twelve Verses of Mark*. Cambridge: Cambridge University Press, 2005.

Farrell, Thomas J. "Kelber's Breakthrough." *Semeia* 39 (1987): 27–45.

Farrer, Austin. *A Study of St. Mark*. London: Dacre Press, 1951.

Fay, G. "Introduction to Incomprehension: The Literary Structure of Mark 4:1–34." *CBQ* 51 (1989): 65–81.

Feldman, Louis H. *Jew and Gentile in the Ancient World.* Princeton: Princeton University Press, 1993.

Feldmeier, R. "Die Syrophönizierin (Mk 7,24–30)—Jesu 'verlorenes' Streitgespräch?" In *Die Heiden: Juden, Christen und das Problem des Fremden,* edited by R. Feldmeier and U. Heckel, 211–27. Tübingen: Mohr Siebeck, 1994.

Fendler, Folkert. *Studien zum Markusevangelium: Zur Gattung, Chronologie, Messiasgeheimnistheorie und Berlieferung des zweiten Evangeliums.* Göttingen: Vandenhoeck & Ruprecht, 1991.

Feneberg, Rupert. *Der Jude Jesus und die Heiden: Biographie und Theologie Jesu im Markusevangelium.* Freiburg: Herder, 2000.

Fenton, J. C. "Paul and Mark." In *Studies in the Gospels: Essays in Memory of R. H. Lightfoot,* edited by D. E. Nineham, 89–112. Oxford: Basil Blackwell, 1957.

Fischer, Cédric. *Les disciples dans l'Évangile de Marc: Une grammaire théologique.* Études Bibliques, n.s., 57. Paris: Gabalda, 2007.

Fledderman, Harry T. "The Discipleship Discourse (Mark 9:33–50)." *CBQ* 43 (1981): 57–75.

———. "The Flight of the Naked Young Man (Mark 14:51–52)." *CBQ* 41 (1979): 412–18.

Fleddermann, Harry T., and F. Neirynck. *Mark and Q: A Study of the Overlap Texts.* BETL. Leuven: Leuven University Press, 1995.

Floyd, Michael H. "Zechariah and Changing Views of Second Temple Judaism in Recent Commentaries." *RelSRev* 25 (1999): 257–63.

Flusser, David. "Healing through the Laying On of Hands in a Dead Sea Scroll." *IEJ* 7 (1957): 107–8.

———. "Psalms, Hymns, and Prayers." In *Jewish Writings of the Second Temple Period,* edited by Michael E. Stone, 551–77. Philadelphia: Fortress, 1984.

Focant, Camille. *L'Évangile selon Marc.* Paris: Cerf, 2004.

———. "La fonction narrative des doublets dans la section des pains: Mc 6.6b–8.26." In *The Four Gospels, 1992: Festschrift Frans Neirynck,* edited by F. Van Segbroeck. 1039–63. Leuven: Leuven University Press, 1992.

———. *The Gospel according to Mark.* Translated by Leslie Robert Keylock. Eugene, OR: Pickwick, 2012.

———. "L'incompréhension des disciples dans le deuxième Évangile: Tradition et rédaction." *RB* 82 (1975): 161–85.

———. "Mc 7,24–31 par Mt 15,21–29: Critique des sources et/ou étude narrative." In *The Synoptic Gospels: Source Criticism and the New Literary Criticism,* edited by C. Focant, 39–75. Leuven: Leuven University Press, 1993.

Fowler, Robert M. *Let the Reader Understand: Reader Response Criticism and the Gospel of Mark.* Minneapolis: Fortress, 1991.

———. *Loaves and Fishes: The Function of the Feeding Stories in the Gospel of Mark.* Chico, CA: Scholars Press, 1981.

———. "The Rhetoric of Direction and Indirection in the Gospel of Mark." In *The Interpretation of Mark,* edited by William R. Telford, 207–27. Edinburgh: T&T Clark, 1995.

———. "Who Is 'the Reader' of Mark's Gospel?" *SBLSP* 22 (1983): 31–53.

France, R. T. *Divine Government: God's Kingship in the Gospel of Mark.* London: SPCK, 1990.

———. *The Gospel of Mark.* New York: Doubleday, 1998.

———. *The Gospel of Mark: A Commentary on the Greek Text.* Grand Rapids: Eerdmans, 2002.

———. "Mark and the Teaching of Jesus." In *Gospel Perspectives,* edited by R. T. France and D. Wenham, 101–36. Sheffield: JSOT Press, 1980.

Fredriksen, Paula. "Did Jesus Oppose Purity Laws?" *BRev* 11 (1995): 18–25, 42–47.

———. "Jesus and the Temple, Mark and the War." *SBLSP* 29 (1990): 293–310.

———. "What You See Is What You Get: Context and Content in Current Research on the Historical Jesus." *ThTo* 52 (1995): 75–97.

Frei, Hans W. *The Eclipse of Biblical Narrative.* New Haven: Yale University Press, 1974.

———. "Epilogue: George Lindbeck and the Nature of Doctrine." In *Theology in*

Dialogue, edited by Bruce Marshall, 275–82. Notre Dame, IN: University of Notre Dame Press, 1990.

———. "Narrative in Christian and Modern Reading." In *Theology in Dialogue*, edited by Bruce Marshall, 149–63. Notre Dame, IN: University of Notre Dame Press, 1990.

Fretheim, Terrence E. "The Plagues as Ecological Signs of Historical Disaster." *JBL* 110 (1991): 385–96.

Freyne, Sean. "At Cross Purposes: Jesus and the Disciples in Mark." *Furrow* 33 (1982): 331–39.

Frickenschmidt, D. *Evangelium als Biographie: Die vier Evangelien in Rahmen antiker Erzählkunst*. Tübingen: Francke, 1997.

Fuller, R. *The Foundations of New Testament Christology*. New York: Scribner, 1965.

Fullmer, Paul M. *Resurrection in Mark's Literary-Historical Perspective*. LNTS. London: T&T Clark, 2007.

Garrett, Susan R. Review of *Christian Origins and Cultural Anthropology: Practical Models for Biblical Interpretation*, by Bruce Malina. *JBL* 107 (1988): 532–34.

———. *The Temptations of Jesus in Mark's Gospel*. Grand Rapids: Eerdmans, 1998.

Gaventa, Beverly Roberts, and Patrick D. Miller, eds. *The Ending of Mark and the Ends of God: Essays in Memory of Donald Harrisville Juel*. Louisville: Westminster John Knox, 2005.

Geddert, Timothy. *Watchwords: Mark 13 in Markan Eschatology*. Sheffield: Sheffield Academic, 1989.

Geertz, Clifford. *The Interpretation of Cultures*. New York: Basic Books, 1973.

Gibson, Jeffrey B. "Jesus' Refusal to Produce a Sign (Mk 8.11–13)." *JSNT* 38 (1990): 37–66.

———. "Jesus' Wilderness Temptation according to Mark." *JSNT* 53 (1994): 3–34.

———. "The Rebuke of the Disciples in Mark 8:14–21." *JSNT* 31 (1986): 31–47.

Gilfillan Upton, Bridget. *Hearing Mark's Endings: Listening to Ancient Popular Texts through Speech Act Theory*. Leiden: Brill, 2006.

Gloer, Hulitt, ed. *Eschatology and the New Testament*. Peabody, MA: Hendrickson, 1988.

Gnilka, Joachim. *Das Evangelium nach Markus*. 3rd ed. Neukirchen: Neukirchener Verlag, 1989.

Gould, Ezra Palmer. *A Critical and Exegetical Commentary on the Gospel according to St. Mark*. ICC. New York: Scribner, 1896.

Goulder, Michael D. *The Evangelist's Calendar: A Lectionary Explanation for the Development of Scripture*. London: SPCK, 1978.

———. "The Pre-Markan Gospel." *SJT* 47 (1994): 453–71.

Graham, Susan. "Silent Voices: Women in the Gospel of Mark." *Semeia* 54 (1991): 145–58.

Grässer, E. "Jesus in Nazareth (Mk VI.1–6a): Notes on the Theology and Redaction of Mark." *NTS* 16 (1969): 1–23.

Grassi, Joseph A. "The Eucharist in the Gospel of Mark." *AER* 168 (1974): 595–608.

Gray, Timothy C. *The Luminous Mysteries: Biblical Reflections on the Life of Christ*. Steubenville, OH: Emmaus Road, 2004.

———. *The Temple in the Gospel of Mark: A Study in Its Narrative Role*. Tübingen: Mohr Siebeck, 2008.

Green, Garrett. *Scriptural Authority and Narrative Interpretation*. Philadelphia: Fortress, 1987.

Green, Joel B. *The Death of Jesus*. Tübingen: Mohr Siebeck, 1988.

Green, William Scott, ed. *Approaches to Ancient Judaism*. Missoula, MT: Scholars Press, 1978.

Greenberg, Irving. *The Jewish Way: Living the Holidays*. New York: Touchstone, 1988.

Greer, Rowan A. *Broken Lights and Mended Lives: Theology and Common Life in the Early Church*. University Park: Pennsylvania State University Press, 1986.

Greer, Rowan A., and James L. Kugel. *Early Biblical Interpretation*. Louisville: Westminster, 1986.

Gregg, David. "A Semantic Voyage." In *Essays on Eucharistic Sacrifice in the Early Church*, edited by Colin Buchanan, 10–14. Bramcote, UK: Grove Books, 1984.

Grundmann, Walter. *Das Evangelium nach Markus*. Berlin: Evangelische Verlagsanstalt, 1989.

Gryson, Roger. *The Ministry of Women in the Early Church.* Collegeville, MN: Liturgical Press, 1976.

Guelich, Robert. "The Beginning of the Gospel: Mark 1:1–15." *BR* 27 (1982): 5–15.

———. "The Gospel Genre." In *Das Evangelium und die Evangelien,* edited by P. Stuhlmacher, 183–219. Tübingen: Mohr Siebeck, 1983.

———. *Mark 1–8:26.* Word Biblical Commentary 34A. Dallas: Word, 1989.

———. "Mark, Gospel of." In *Dictionary of Jesus and the Gospels,* edited by J. B. Green, S. McKnight, and I. H. Marshall, 512–25. Downers Grove, IL: InterVarsity, 1992.

Gundry, Robert H. *Mark: A Commentary on His Apology for the Cross.* Grand Rapids: Eerdmans, 1993.

———. "Recent Investigations into the Literary Genre Gospel." In *New Dimensions in New Testament Study,* edited by R. Longenecker and M. C. Tenney, 97–114. Grand Rapids: Zondervan, 1974.

Gunther, John J. *St. Paul's Opponents and Their Background: A Study of Jewish and Apocalyptic Sectarian Writings.* Leiden: Brill, 1973.

Haenchen, Ernst. "Die Komposition von Mark Viii 27–Ix 1 und par." *NovT* 6 (1963): 81–109.

———. *Der Weg Jesu: Eine Erklärung des Markus-Evangeliums und der kanonischen Parallelen.* 2nd ed. Berlin: Töpelmann, 1960.

Hahn, F. *Frühjüdische und urchristliche Apokalyptik: Eine Einführung.* Neukirchen-Vluyn: Neukirchener, 1998.

———. *The Titles of Jesus in Christology.* Translated by H. Knight and G. Ogg. London: Lutterworth, 1969.

Hahn, Scott, and Curtis Mitch. *The Gospel of Mark.* San Francisco: Ignatius, 2001.

Hall, D. *The Gospel Framework: Fiction or Fact? A Critical Evaluation of "Der Rahmen der Geschichte Jesu" by Karl Ludwig Schmidt.* Carlisle: Paternoster, 1998.

Halverson, J. "Greco-Roman Textuality and the Gospel of Mark: A Critical Assessment of Werner Kelber's *The Oral and Written Gospel.*" *BBR* 7 (1997): 91–106.

Hamerton-Kelly, Robert. *The Gospel and the Sacred Poetics of Violence in Mark.* Minneapolis: Fortress, 1994.

Hamilton, Edith, and Huntingen Cairns, eds. *The Collected Dialogues of Plato.* New York: Pantheon, 1961.

Hamilton, N. O. "Resurrection Tradition and the Composition of Mark." *JBL* 84 (1965): 415–21.

Hanhart, Karel. *The Open Tomb: A New Approach to Mark's Passover Haggada.* Collegeville, MN: Liturgical Press, 1995.

Hanson, James S. *The Endangered Promises: Conflict in Mark.* Atlanta: Society of Biblical Literature, 2000.

Harder, Lydia Marlene. *Obedience, Suspicion, and the Gospel of Mark: A Mennonite-Feminist Exploration of Biblical Authority.* Waterloo, ON: Wilfrid Laurier University Press, 1998.

Hare, Douglas R. A. *Mark.* Louisville: Westminster John Knox, 1996.

Harnack, Adolf von. *Bible Reading in the Early Church.* New York: Putnam, 1912.

———. *Die Lehre der zwölf Apostel.* Leipzig: Hinrichs, 1884.

Harrelson, Walter. *From Fertility Cult to Worship.* Garden City, NY: Doubleday, 1969.

Harrington, Daniel J. "A Map of Books on Mark." *BTB* 15 (1985): 12–16.

———. *Mark.* Collegeville, MN: Michael Glazier / Liturgical Press, 1979.

———. "Sabbath Tensions: Matthew 12:1–14 and Other New Testament Texts." In *The Sabbath in Jewish and Christian Traditions,* edited by T. Eskanazi, D. J. Harrington, and W. H. Shea, 45–56. New York: Crossroad, 1991.

———. "What and Why Did Jesus Suffer according to Mark?" *CS* 34 (1995): 32–41.

Harrington, Hannah K. *The Impurity of Systems of Qumran and the Rabbis.* Atlanta: Scholars Press, 1993.

Harrington, Wilfrid. *Mark.* Wilmington, DE: Michael Glazier, 1979.

Harris, J. Rendel. *The Teaching of the Apostles: Newly Edited with Facsimile Text and Commentary.* Baltimore: Johns Hopkins University Press, 1887.

Hartman, Lars. *Mark for the Nations: A Text- and Reader-Oriented Commentary.* Eugene, OR: Pickwick, 2010.

———. *Prophecy Interpreted: The Formation of Some Jewish Apocalyptic Texts and the Eschatological Discourse in Mark 13 Par.* ConBNT 1. Lund, Sweden: Gleerup, 1966.

Hassler, I. "The Incident of the Syrophoenician Woman (Matt XV,21–28; Mark VII,24–30)." *ExpTim* 45 (1934): 459–61.

Hatina, Thomas R. *In Search of a Context: The Function of Scripture in Mark's Narrative.* London: Sheffield Academic, 2002.

Hawkin, D. J. "The Incomprehension of the Disciples in the Markan Redaction." *JBL* 91 (1972): 491–500.

Hay, Lewis S. "The Son-of-God Christology in Mark." *JBR* 32 (1964): 106–14.

———. "The Son of Man in Mark 2.10 and 2.28." *JBL* 89 (1970): 69–75.

Hayes, John H. "Atonement in the Book of Leviticus." *Int* 52 (1998): 5–15.

Hayward, C. T. R. *The Jewish Temple: A Non-Biblical Sourcebook.* London: Routledge, 1996.

Healy, Mary. *The Gospel of Mark.* Grand Rapids: Baker Academic, 2008.

Hebert, A. J. "History in the Feeding of the Five Thousand." *SE* 2 (1964): 65–72.

Hedrick, C. W. "The Role of 'Summary Statements' in the Composition of the Gospel of Mark: A Dialogue with Karl Schmidt and Norman Perrin." *NovT* 26 (1984): 289–311.

———. "What Is a Gospel? Geography Time and Narrative Structure." *PRSt* 10 (1983): 255–68.

Heid, Stefan. *Chiliasmus und Antichrist-Mythos: Eine frühchristliche Kontroverse um das heilige Land.* Bonn: Borengässer, 1993.

Heil, John Paul. *The Gospel of Mark as Model for Action: A Reader-Response Commentary.* New York: Paulist Press, 1992.

———. *Jesus Walking on the Sea: Meaning and Gospel Functions of Matt. 14:22–32; Mark 6:45–52; John 6:15b–21.* Rome: Biblical Institute Press, 1981.

———. "Mark 14:1–52: Narrative Structure and Reader-Response." *Bib* 71 (1990): 305–32.

———. "The Narrative Strategy and Pragmatics of the Temple Theme in Mark." *CBQ* 59 (1997): 76–100.

Henaut, Barry. *Oral Tradition and the Gospels: The Problem of Mark 4.* Sheffield: Sheffield Academic, 1993.

Henderson, Suzanne Watts. *Christology and Discipleship in the Gospel of Mark.* Cambridge: Cambridge University Press, 2006.

———. "Concerning the Loaves: Comprehending Incomprehension in Mark 6:45–52." *JSNT* 83 (2001): 3–26.

Hengel, Martin. "Entstehungszeit und Situation des Markusevangeliums." In *Markus Philologie*, edited by H. Cancik, 1–45. Tübingen: Mohr Siebeck, 1984.

———. *Studies in the Gospel of Mark.* Philadelphia: Fortress, 1985.

Hofius, O. "Jesu Zuspruch der Sündenvergebung: Exegetische Erwägungen zu Mk 2,5b." *JBT* 9 (1994): 125–45.

Holladay, C. H. *Theios Aner in Hellenistic Judaism: A Critique of the Use of This Category in New Testament Christology.* Missoula, MT: Scholars Press, 1972.

Hooker, Morna D. *The Gospel according to Saint Mark.* Peabody, MA: Hendrickson, 1991.

———. *The Message of Mark.* London: Epworth, 1983.

———. *The Signs of a Prophet: The Prophetic Actions of Jesus.* Harrisburg, PA: Trinity Press International, 1997.

———. *The Son of Man in Mark: A Study of the Background of the Term "Son of Man" and Its Use in St. Mark's Gospel.* London: SPCK, 1967.

———. "Trial and Tribulation in Mark XIII." *BJRL* 65 (1982): 78–99.

Horsley, Richard A. *Hearing the Whole Story.* Louisville: Westminster John Knox, 2001.

Huber, Konrad. *Jesus in Auseinandersetzung: Exegetische Untersuchungen zu den sogenannten jerusalemer Streitgesprächen des Markusevangeliums im Blick auf ihre christologischen Implikationen.* Würzburg: Echter, 1995.

213

Humphrey, Hugh. *A Bibliography for the Gospel of Mark: 1954–1980*. Toronto: Edwin Mellen, 1981.

———. *From Q to "Secret" Mark: A Composition History of the Earliest Narrative Theology*. New York: T&T Clark, 2006.

———. *He Is Risen: A New Reading of Mark's Gospel*. Mahwah, NJ: Paulist Press, 1992.

Humphrey, Robert L. *Narrative Structure and Message in Mark: A Rhetorical Analysis*. Studies in the Bible and Early Christianity. Lewiston, NY: Edwin Mellen, 2003.

Hunter, Archibald Macbride. *The Gospel according to Saint Mark: Introduction and Commentary*. London: SCM, 1951.

Hurtado, Larry W. "Following Jesus in the Gospel of Mark—and Beyond." In *Patterns of Discipleship in the New Testament*, edited by Richard N. Longenecker, 9–29. Grand Rapids: Eerdmans, 1996.

———. "The Gospel of Mark: Evolutionary or Revolutionary Document?" *JSNT* 40 (1990): 15–32.

———. "The Gospel of Mark in Recent Study." *Them* 14 (1989): 47–52.

———. *Mark*. San Francisco: Harper, 1983.

Iverson, Kelly R. *Gentiles in the Gospel of Mark: Even the Dogs under the Table Eat the Children's Crumbs*. LNTS. London: T&T Clark, 2007.

Iverson, Kelly R., and Christopher W. Skinner, eds. *Mark as Story: Retrospect and Prospect*. Atlanta: Society of Biblical Literature, 2011.

Iwe, John Chijioke. *Jesus in the Synagogue of Capernaum: The Pericope and Its Programmatic Character for the Gospel of Mark*. Rome: Editrice Pontificia Universita Gregoriana, 1999.

Jacobs, M. M. "Mark's Jesus through the Eyes of Twentieth Century New Testament Scholars." *Neot* 28 (1994): 53–85.

Jay, Nancy. *Throughout Your Generations Forever: Sacrifice, Religion, and Paternity*. Chicago: University of Chicago Press, 1992.

Johnson, E. S. "Is Mark 15:39 the Key to Mark's Christology?" In *The Synoptic Gospels*, edited by Craig A. Evans and Stanley E. Porter, 143–62. Sheffield: Sheffield Academic, 1995.

———. "Mark 10:46–52: Blind Bartimaeus." *CBQ* 40 (1978): 191–204.

———. "Mark Viii.22–26: The Blind Man from Bethsaida." *NTS* 25 (1979): 370–83.

Johnson, Luke Timothy. *The Writings of the New Testament*. Minneapolis: Fortress, 1999.

Johnson, Sherman E. *A Commentary on the Gospel according to St. Mark*. London: A.&C. Black, 1960.

Johnson, Steven R. "The Identity and Significance of the *Neaniskos* in Mark." *FF* 8 (1992): 123–39.

Jones, C. P. "Joint Sacrifice at Iasus and Side." *JHS* 118 (1998): 183–86.

Joy, David. *Mark and Its Subalterns: A Hermeneutical Paradigm for a Postcolonial Context*. London: Equinox, 2008.

Juel, Donald. *The Gospel of Mark*. Nashville: Abingdon, 1999.

———. *Mark*. Minneapolis: Augsburg, 1990.

———. *A Master of Surprise: Mark Interpreted*. Minneapolis: Fortress, 1994.

———. *Messiah and Temple: The Trial of Jesus in the Gospel of Mark*. Missoula, MT: Scholars Press, 1977.

———. "The Origin of Mark's Christology." In *The Messiah*, edited by James Charlesworth, 449–60. Minneapolis: Fortress, 1992.

Kahl, Werner. *New Testament Miracle Stories in Their Religious-Historical Setting: A Religionsgeschichtliche Comparison from a Structural Perspective*. Göttingen: Vandenhoeck & Ruprecht, 1994.

Kähler, Martin. *The So-Called Historical Jesus and the Historic Biblical Christ*. Translated by Karl Braaten. Philadelphia: Fortress, 1964. Originally published as *Der sogenannte historische Jesus und der geschichtliche, biblische Christus* (Munich: C. Kaiser, 1956).

Käsemann, Ernst. *Perspectives on Paul*. Philadelphia: Fortress, 1971.

Kazmierski, Carl R. *Jesus the Son of God*. Würzburg: Echter, 1979.

———. *Jesus the Son of God: A Study of the Markan Tradition and Its Redaction by the Evangelist*. FB. Wurzburg: Echter Verlag, 1982.

Kealy, Sean P. *A History of the Interpretation of the Gospel of Mark.* Lewiston, NY: Edwin Mellen, 2007.

———. *Mark's Gospel: A History of Its Interpretation from the Beginning until 1979.* New York: Paulist Press, 1982.

Keck, Leander. "The Introduction to Mark's Gospel." *NTS* 12 (1965): 352–70.

———. "Mark 3:7–12 and Mark's Christology." *JBL* 84 (1965): 341–58.

———. "The Spirit and the Dove." *NTS* 17 (1970): 41–67.

Kee, Howard Clark. "Aretalogy and Gospel." *JBL* 92 (1973): 402–22.

———. *Community of the New Age: Studies in Mark's Gospel.* Philadelphia: Westminster, 1977.

———. "The Divine Man as the Key to Mark's Christology: The End of an Era?" *Int* 35 (1981): 243–57.

———. "The Function of Scriptural Quotation and Allusions in Mark 11–16." In *Jesus und Paulus: Festschrift für Werner Georg Kümmel zum 70. Geburtstag,* edited by E. E. Ellis and E. Grässer, 165–88. Göttingen: Vandenhoeck & Ruprecht, 1975.

———. "Mark as Redactor and Theologian: A Survey of Some Recent Markan Studies." *JBL* 90 (1971): 333–36.

———. "Mark's Gospel in Recent Research." In *Interpreting the Gospels,* edited by James Luther Mays, 130–47. Philadelphia: Fortress, 1981.

———. *Miracle in the Early Christian World.* New Haven: Yale University Press, 1983.

———. "The Terminology of Mark's Exorcism Stories." *NTS* 14 (1967): 232–46.

———. *Who Are the People of God? Models of Community in Judaism and the New Testament.* New Haven: Yale University Press, 1995.

Keegan, Terence. *A Commentary on the Gospel of Mark.* Mahwah, NJ: Paulist Press, 1981.

———. "The Parable of the Sower and Mark's Jewish Leaders." *CBQ* 56 (1994): 501–18.

Kelber, Werner H. "Conclusion: From Passion Narrative to Gospel." In *The Passion in Mark: Studies on Mark 14–16,* edited by Werner Kelber, 153–80. Philadelphia: Fortress, 1976.

———. "The Hour of the Son of Man and the Temptation of the Disciples (Mark 14:32–42)." In *The Passion of Mark: Studies in Mark 14–16,* edited by Werner Kelber, 41–60. Philadelphia: Fortress, 1976.

———. *The Kingdom in Mark: A New Place and a New Time.* Philadelphia: Fortress, 1974.

———. "Mark 14:32–34: Gethsemane; Passion Christology and Discipleship Failure." *ZNW* 63 (1972): 166–87.

———. *Mark's Story of Jesus.* Philadelphia: Fortress, 1979.

———. *The Oral and Written Gospel: The Hermeneutics of Speaking and Writing in the Synoptic Tradition, Mark, Paul and Q.* Philadelphia: Fortress, 1983.

———, ed. *The Passion in Mark: Studies on Mark 14–16.* Philadelphia: Fortress, 1976.

Kelber, Werner H., Anitra Kolenkow, and Robin Scroggs. "Reflections on the Question: Was There a Pre-Markan Passion Narrative?" *SBLSP* 22 (1971): 503–85.

Kennedy, George A. *Classical Rhetoric and Its Christian and Secular Tradition from Ancient to Modern Times.* Chapel Hill: University of North Carolina Press, 1999.

Kenney, Garrett C. *Mark's Gospel.* Lanham, MD: University Press of America, 2007.

Kermode, Frank. *The Genesis of Secrecy: On the Interpretation of Narrative.* Cambridge, MA: Harvard University Press, 1979.

Kertelge, Karl. "The Epiphany of Jesus in the Gospel." In *The Interpretation of Mark,* edited by William R. Telford, 105–23. Edinburgh: T&T Clark, 1995.

———. "Die Funktion der 'Zwölf' in Markusevangelium: Eine redaktionsgeschichtliche Auslegung zugleich ein Beitrag zur Frage nach dem neutestamentlichen Amtsverständnis." *TTZ* 78 (1969): 193–206.

———. *Die Wunder Jesu im Markusevangelium: Eine redaktions-geschichtliche Untersuchung.* Munich: Kösel Verlag, 1970.

Kiilunen, Jarmo. *Die Vollmacht im Widerstreit: Untersuchungen zum Werdegang von Mk*

2,1–3,6. AASF. Helsinki: Suomalainen Tiedeakatemia, 1985.

Kilpatrick, George Dunbar. *The Origins of the Gospel according to Saint Matthew*. Oxford: Clarendon, 1946.

Kim, Seong Hee. *Mark, Women, and Empire: A Korean Postcolonial Perspective*. Sheffield: Sheffield Phoenix, 2010.

Kingsbury, Jack Dean. *The Christology of Mark's Gospel*. Philadelphia: Fortress, 1983.

———. *Conflict in Mark: Jesus, Authorities, Disciples*. Minneapolis: Fortress, 1989.

———. "The 'Divine Man' as the Key to Mark's Christology—the End of an Era?" *Int* 35 (1981): 243–57.

———. "The Gospel of Mark in Current Research." *RelSRev* 5 (1979): 101–7.

———. *Matthew as Story*. Philadelphia: Fortress, 1986.

Kinukawa, Hisako. *Women and Jesus in Mark: A Japanese Feminist Perspective*. Maryknoll, NY: Orbis, 1994.

Kirk, Daniel J., and Stephen L. Young. "I Will Set His Hand to the Sea: Psalm 88:26 LXX and Christology in Mark." *JBL* 133 (2014): 333–40.

Klauck, Hans-Josef. "Die erzählerische Rolle der Jünger in Markusevangelium: Eine narrative Analyse." *NovT* 24 (1982): 1–26.

———. "Die Frage der Sündenvergebung in der Perikope von der Heilung des Gelähmten (Mk 2:1–12 Parr.)." *BZ* 25 (1981): 223–48.

Klein, Günther. "Die Berufung des Petrus." *ZNW* 58 (1967): 1–44.

———. "Die Verleugnung des Petrus: Eine traditionsgeschichtliche Untersuchung." *ZTK* 58 (1961): 285–328.

———. *Die zwölf Apostel: Ursprung und Gehalt einer Idee*. FRLANT 59. Göttingen: Vandenhoeck & Ruprecht, 1961.

Klosinski, Lee Edward. "The Meals in Mark." PhD diss., Claremont Graduate School, 1988.

Klostermann, Erich. *Das Markusevangelium*. Tübingen: Mohr Siebeck, 1971.

Knigge, Heinz-Dieter. "The Meaning of Mark: The Exegesis of the Second Gospel." *Int* 22 (1968): 53–70.

Knoch, Otto. "'Do This in Memory of Me' (Luke 22:20; 1 Corinthians 11:24ff.): The Celebration of the Eucharist in the Primitive Christian Communities." In *One Loaf, One Cup: Ecumenical Studies of 1 Corinthians 11 and Other Eucharistic Texts*, edited by Ben F. Meyer, 1–10. Macon, GA: Mercer University Press, 1993.

Koch, Dietrich-Alex. *Die Bedeutung der Wundererzählungen für die Christologie des Markusevangeliums*. Berlin: de Gruyter, 1975.

———. "Inhaltliche Gliederung und geographischer Aufriss im Markusevangelium." *NTS* 29 (1983): 145–66.

Koester, Helmut. "History and Development of Mark's Gospel." In *Colloquy on New Testament Studies*, edited by B. Corley, 35–57. Macon, GA: Mercer University Press, 1983.

Kolarcik, Michael. "Creation and Salvation in the Book of Wisdom." In *Creation in the Biblical Traditions*, edited by John Collins and Richard J. Clifford, 97–107. Washington, DC: Catholic Biblical Association of America, 1992.

Kollmann, Bernd. *Ursprung und Gestalten der frühchristlichen Mahlfeier*. Göttingen: Vandenhoeck & Ruprecht, 1990.

Kort, Wesley A. *Take, Read: Scripture, Textuality, and Cultural Practice*. University Park: Pennsylvania State University Press, 1996.

Kuby, Alfred. "Zur Konzeption des Markus-Evangeliums." *ZNW* 49 (1958): 52–64.

Kuhn, Heinz-Wolfgang. *Ältere Sammlungen im Markusevangelium*. Göttingen: Vandenhoeck & Ruprecht, 1971.

Kuhn, Karl George. "Jesus in Gethsemane." *EvT* 12 (1952): 260–85.

Kühschelm, R. *Jüngerverfolgung und Geschick Jesu*. Klosterneuburg: Österreichisches Katholisches Bibelwerk, 1983.

Kürzinger, Josef. *Papias von Hierapolis und die Evangelien des Neuen Testaments*. Regensburg: Eichstätter Materialien, 1983.

Kuthirakkattel, Scaria. *The Beginning of Jesus' Ministry according to Mark's Gospel (1,14–3,6): A Redaction Critical Study*. Rome: Editrice Pontificio Istituto Biblico, 1990.

Lagrange, Marie-Joseph. *Évangile selon saint Marc*. Paris: Librairie Lecoffre, 1929.

Lamarche, Paul. *Évangile de Marc commentaire*. Paris: Gabalda, 1996.

Lambrecht, Jan. "Redaction and Theology in Mark IV." In *L'Évangile selon Marc: Tradition et rédaction*, edited by M. Sabbe, 269–307. Leuven: Duculot / Leuven University Press, 1974.

———. *Die Redaktion der Markus-Apokalypse: Literarische Analyse und Strukturuntersuchung*. Rome: Pontifical Biblical Institute, 1967.

———. "The Relatives of Jesus in Mark." *NovT* 16 (1974): 241–58.

Lane, William Lister. "From Historian to Theologian: Milestones in Markan Scholarship." *RevExp* 75 (1978): 601–17.

———. *The Gospel according to Mark: The English Text with Introduction, Exposition, and Notes*. Grand Rapids: Eerdmans, 1974.

Lang, F. G. "Kompositionsanalyse des Markusevangeliums." *ZTK* 74 (1977): 1–24.

———. "Über Sidon mitten ins Gebiet der Dekapolis: Geographie und Theologie in Markus 7,31." *ZDPV* 94 (1978): 145–60.

Larsen, Kevin W. "'Do You See Anything?' (Mark 8:23): Seeing and Understanding Jesus; A Literary and Theological Study of Mark 8:22–9:13." PhD diss., Catholic University of America, 2002.

———. "The Structure of Mark's Gospel: Current Proposals." *CurBR* 3 (2004): 140–60.

Lash, Nicholas. *Theology on the Way to Emmaus*. London: SCM, 1986.

Laufen, Rudolf. *Die Doppelüberlieferungen: Der Logienquelle und des Markusevangeliums*. BBB. Bonn: Peter Hanstein, 1980.

LaVerdière, Eugene. *The Beginning of the Gospel: Introducing the Gospel of Mark*. Collegeville, MN: Liturgical Press, 1999.

Lee, David. *Luke's Stories of Jesus: Theological Reading of Narratives and the Legacy of Hans Frei*. Sheffield: Sheffield Academic, 1999.

Lee, Dorothy A. *The Symbolic Narratives of the Fourth Gospel: The Interplay of Form and Meaning*. Sheffield: JSOT Press, 1994.

Légasse, Simon. "Approche de l'épisode pré-évangelique des fils de Zébédée (Marc X.35–40 par.)." *NTS* 20 (1974): 161–77.

———. "Tout quitter pour suivre le Christ: Mc 10, 17–30." *AsSeign* 59 (1974): 43–54.

Lemcio, E. E. "The Intention of the Evangelist Mark." *NTS* 32 (1986): 187–206.

Lentzen-Deis, F. *Die Taufe Jesu nach den Synoptikern*. Frankfurt: Knecht, 1970.

Levenson, Jon D. *Creation and the Persistence of Evil: The Jewish Drama of Divine Omnipotence*. San Francisco: Harper, 1987. Reprint, Princeton: Princeton University Press, 1994.

———. *The Death and Resurrection of the Beloved Son: The Transformation of Child Sacrifice in Judaism and Christianity*. New Haven: Yale University Press, 1993.

———. *Sinai and Zion*. San Francisco: Harper, 1987.

———. "Theological Consensus or Historicist Evasion: Jews and Christians in Biblical Studies." In *Hebrew Bible or Old Testament? Studying the Bible in Judaism and Christianity*, edited by John J. Collins and Roger Brooks, 109–45. Notre Dame, IN: University of Notre Dame Press, 1990.

———. "The Unexamined Commitments of Criticism." *FT* 30 (1993): 24–33.

Levine, Amy-Jill, and Marianne Blickenstaff. *A Feminist Companion to Mark*. FCNTECW. Sheffield: Sheffield Academic, 2001.

Lewis, P. B. "Indications of a Liturgical Source in the Gospel of Mark." *Enc* 39 (1978): 385–94.

Liew, Tat-Siong Benny. *Politics of Parousia: Reading Mark Inter(con)textually*. BibInt. Leiden: Brill, 1999.

Lightfoot, R. H. *The Gospel Message of St. Mark*. Oxford: Clarendon, 1950, 1962.

———. *Locality and Doctrine in the Gospels*. New York: Harper, 1937.

Lincoln, Andrew T. "The Promise and the Failure: Mark 16:7,8." In *The Interpretation of Mark*, edited by William R. Telford, 229–51. Edinburgh: T&T Clark, 1995.

Lincoln, Bruce. *Discourse and the Construction of Society: Comparative Studies of Myth, Ritual, and Classification*. New York: Oxford University Press, 1989.

Lindbeck, George. "The Gospel's Uniqueness: Election and Untranslatability." *MT* 13 (1997): 423–50.

———. "Scripture Consensus and Community." *TW* 23 (1988): 5–24.

———. "The Story-Shaped Church: Critical Exegesis and Theological Interpretation." In *The Theological Interpretation of Scripture: Classic and Contemporary Readings*, edited by Stephen E. Fowl, 39–52. Cambridge: Blackwell, 1997.

Linnemann, Eta. *Studien zur Passionsgeschichte*. Göttingen: Vandenhoeck & Ruprecht, 1970.

Linton, O. "The Demand for a Sign from Heaven: Mark 8,11–12 and Parallels." *ST* 19 (1965): 112–29.

Lohmeyer, Ernst. *Das Evangelium nach Markus*. Göttingen: Vandenhoeck & Ruprecht, 1967.

———. *Galiläa und Jerusalem*. Göttingen: Vandenhoeck & Ruprecht, 1936.

Loisy, Alfred Firmin. *L'Évangile selon Marc*. Paris: E. Nourry, 1912.

Lührmann, Dieter. "Markus 14:55–65: Christologie und Zerstörung des Temples in Markusevangelium." *NTS* 27 (1981): 457–74.

———. *Das Markusevangelium*. Tübingen: Mohr Siebeck, 1987.

———. "Die Pharisäer und die Schriftgelehrten im Markusevangelium." *ZNW* 78 (1987): 169–85.

Luz, Ulrich. "Das Geheimnismotiv und die markinische Christologie." *ZNW* 56 (1965): 9–30.

———. "Markusforschung in der Sackgasse?" *TLZ* 105 (1980): 641–55.

MacDonald, Dennis Ronald. *The Homeric Epics and the Gospel of Mark*. New Haven: Yale University Press, 2000.

Mack, Burton L. *A Myth of Innocence: Mark and Christian Origins*. Philadelphia: Fortress, 1988.

Mackay, Ian D. *John's Relationship with Mark: An Analysis of John 6 in the Light of Mark 6–8*. WUNT. Tübingen: Mohr Siebeck, 2004.

Madigan, Kevin J., and Jon D. Levenson. *Resurrection: The Power of God for Christians and Jews*. New Haven: Yale University Press, 2008.

Magness, J. Lee. *Sense and Absence: Structure and Suspension in the Ending of Mark's Gospel*. SemeiaSt. Atlanta: Scholars Press, 1986.

Maier, Gerhard. *Markus-Evangelium*. Neuhausen-Stuttgart: Hänssler Verlag, 1995.

Maier, Johann, ed. and trans. *The Temple Scroll*. Sheffield: Sheffield Academic, 1985.

Malbon, Elizabeth Struthers. *Between Author and Audience in Mark: Narration, Characterization, Interpretation*. Sheffield: Sheffield Phoenix, 2009.

———. "Characters in Mark's Story: Changing Perspectives in the Narrative Process." In *Mark as Story: Retrospect and Prospect*, edited by Kelly R. Iverson and Christopher W. Skinner, 45–69. Atlanta: Society of Biblical Literature, 2011.

———. "Disciples/Crowds/Whoever: Markan Characters and Readers." *NovT* 28 (1986): 104–30.

———. "Echoes and Foreshadowing in Mark 4–8." *JBL* 112 (1993): 211–30.

———. "Fallible Followers: Women and Men in the Gospel of Mark." *Semeia* 28 (1983): 29–48.

———. "Galilee and Jerusalem: History and Literature in Markan Interpretation." In *The Interpretation of Mark*, edited by William R. Telford, 253–68. Edinburgh: T&T Clark, 1995.

———. *In the Company of Jesus: Characters in Mark's Gospel*. Louisville: Westminster John Knox, 2000.

———. "The Jesus of Mark and the Sea of Galilee." *JBL* 103 (1984): 363–77.

———. "The Major Importance of the Minor Characters in Mark." In *The New Literary Criticism and the New Testament*, edited by Elizabeth Struthers Malbon and Edgar V. McKnight, 58–86. Sheffield: Sheffield Academic, 1994.

———. "Mark: Myth and Parable." *BTB* 16 (1986): 8–17.

———. *Narrative Space and Mythic Meaning in Mark*. Sheffield: Sheffield Academic, 1991.

————. "TE OIKIA AUTOU: Mark 2.15 in Context." *NTS* 31 (1985): 282–92.

————. "Texts and Contexts: Interpreting the Disciples in Mark." *Semeia* 62 (1992): 81–102.

Malina, Bruce. "Christ and Time: Swiss or Mediterranean?" *CBQ* 51 (1989): 1–31.

Maloney, Elliott C. *Semitic Interference in Marcan Syntax*. Chico, CA: Scholars Press, 1981.

Mann, Christopher Stephen. *Mark: A New Translation with Introduction and Commentary*. Garden City, NY: Doubleday, 1986.

Mansfield, M. R. *Spirit and Gospel in Mark*. Peabody, MA: Hendrickson, 1987.

Marcus, George E., and Michael M. J. Fischer. *Anthropology as Cultural Critique: An Experimental Moment in the Human Sciences*. Chicago: University of Chicago Press, 1986.

Marcus, Joel. "Jesus's Baptismal Vision." *NTS* 41 (1995): 512–21.

————. "Jesus Walking on the Water: Mark 6:45–52." In *The Gospels and the Scriptures of Israel*, edited by C. Evans and W. Stegner, 196–211. Sheffield: Sheffield Academic, 1994.

————. "The Jewish War and the *Sitz Im Leben* of Mark." *JBL* 111 (1992): 441–62.

————. *Mark 1–8*. New York: Doubleday, 2000.

————. "Mark 4:10–12 and Marcan Epistemology." *JBL* 103 (1984): 557–74.

————. *Mark 9–16*. New York: Doubleday, 2008.

————. "Mark 9, 11–13: As It Has Been Written." *ZNW* 80 (1989): 42–63.

————. "Mark 14:61: Are You the Messiah-Son-of-God?" *NovT* 31 (1988): 125–41.

————. "Mark and Isaiah." In *Fortunate the Eyes That See: Essays in Honor of David Noel Freedman on His Seventieth Birthday*, edited by Astrid Beck et al., 449–66. Grand Rapids: Eerdmans, 1995.

————. *The Mystery of the Kingdom of God*. Atlanta: Scholars Press, 1986.

————. "Scripture and Tradition in Mark 7." In *The Scriptures in the Gospels*, edited by C. Tuckett, 145–63. Leuven: Leuven University Press, 1997.

————. "'The Time Has Been Fulfilled' (Mark 1:15)." In *Apocalyptic in the New Testament: Essays in Honor of J. Louis Martyn*, edited by J. Marcus and M. Soards, 49–68. Sheffield: Sheffield Academic, 1989.

————. *The Way of the Lord: Christological Exegesis of the Old Testament in the Gospel of Mark*. Louisville: Westminster John Knox, 1992.

Marshall, Christopher D. *Faith as a Theme in Mark's Narrative*. Cambridge: Cambridge University Press, 1989.

Martin, Ralph P. *Mark*. Atlanta: John Knox, 1981.

————. *Mark: Evangelist and Theologian*. Grand Rapids: Zondervan, 1973.

Marxsen, Willi. *Mark the Evangelist: Studies on the Redaction History of the Gospel*. Nashville: Abingdon, 1969.

————. "Redaktionsgeschichtliche Erklärung der sogenannten Parabeltheorie des Markus." *ZTK* 52 (1955): 255–71.

Matera, Frank J. "The Crucified Son of God: Introducing the Gospel according to Mark." *CS* 34 (1995): 6–16.

————. *The Kingship of Jesus: Composition and Theology of Mark 15*. Chico, CA: Scholars Press, 1982.

————. "The Prologue as the Interpretive Key to Mark's Gospel." *JSNT* 34 (1988): 3–20.

————. *What Are They Saying about Mark?* New York: Paulist Press, 1987.

Mathews, Victor H., and Donald C. Benjamin. *The Social World of Ancient Israel*. Peabody, MA: Hendrickson, 1993.

Maurer, C. "Knecht Gottes und Sohn Gottes im Passionsbericht des Markusevangeliums." *ZTK* 50 (1953): 1–39.

Mauser, Ulrich. *Christ in the Wilderness: The Wilderness Theme in the Second Gospel and Its Basis in the Biblical Tradition*. SBT. London: SCM, 1963.

Mays, James Luther, ed. *Interpreting the Gospel*. Philadelphia: Fortress, 1981.

Mazza, Enrico. *The Origins of the Eucharistic Prayer*. Collegeville, MN: Liturgical Press, 1995.

McKenna, Megan. *On Your Mark: Reading Mark in the Shadow of the Cross*. Maryknoll, NY: Orbis, 2006.

McKnight, Scot, and Matthew C. Williams. *The Synoptic Gospels: An Annotated Bibliography*. Grand Rapids: Baker Books, 2000.

Meagher, John C. *Clumsy Construction in Mark's Gospel: A Critique of Form- and Redaktionsgeschichte*. TST. New York: Edwin Mellen, 1979.

Meeks, Wayne. "The Image of the Androgyne: Some Uses of a Symbol in Earliest Christianity." *JHR* 13 (1973): 165–208.

Mell, Ulrich. *Die anderen Winzer: Eine exegetische Studie zur Vollmacht Jesu Christi nach Markus 11.27–12.34*. Tübingen: Mohr Siebeck, 1994.

———. "Jesu Taufe durch Johannes (Markus 1:9–15)—zur narrativen Christologie von neuen Adam." *BZ* 40 (1996): 161–78.

———. *Die Zeit der Gottesherrschaft zur Allegorie und zum Gleichnis von Markus 4, 1–9*. Stuttgart: Kohlhammer, 1998.

Meye, Robert. *Jesus and the Twelve: Discipleship and Revelation in Mark's Gospel*. Grand Rapids: Eerdmans, 1968.

———. "Mark 16:8: The Ending of Mark's Gospel." *BR* 14 (1969): 33–43.

Meyer, Ben F. *Critical Realism and the New Testament*. Allison Park, PA: Pickwick, 1989.

Miller, Dale, and Patricia Miller. *The Gospel of Mark as Midrash on Earlier Jewish and New Testament Literature*. Lewiston, NY: Edwin Mellen, 1990.

Miller, James. "The Literary Structure of Mark: An Interpretation Based on 1 Corinthians 2:1–8." *ExpTim* 106 (1995): 296–99.

Mills, Watson E. *The Gospel of Mark*. BiBR 2. Lewiston, NY: Mellen Biblical Press, 1994.

———. *St. Mark*. London: SCM, 1963.

Minor, Mark. *Literary Critical Approaches to the Bible: An Annotated Bibliography*. West Cornwall, CT: Locust, 1992.

Mitchell, Joan L. *Beyond Fear and Silence: A Feminist-Literary Approach to the Gospel of Mark*. New York: Continuum, 2001.

Moeser, Marion C. *The Anecdote in Mark, the Classical World, and the Rabbis*. Sheffield: Sheffield Academic, 2002.

Moloney, Francis J. *A Body Broken for a Broken People: Eucharist in the New Testament*. Peabody, MA: Hendrickson, 1997.

———. *The Gospel of Mark*. Grand Rapids: Baker Academic, 2003.

———. *Mark: Storyteller, Interpreter, Evangelist*. Peabody, MA: Hendrickson, 2004.

———. "The Vocation of the Disciples in the Gospel of Mark." *Salesianum* 43 (1981): 487–516.

Montague, George. "Hermeneutics and the Teaching of Scripture." *CBQ* 41 (1979): 1–17.

Moore, C. A. "Mk 4,12: More Like the Irony of Michaiah Than Isaiah." In *Light unto My Paths: Old Testament Studies in Honor of Jacob M. Meyers*, edited by Howard N. Bream, Ralph D. Heim, and Carey A. Moore, 335–44. Philadelphia: Temple University Press, 1971.

Moore, Stephen D. *Mark and Luke in Post-structuralist Perspectives: Jesus Begins to Write*. New Haven: Yale University Press, 1992.

Morton, A. Q. *The Making of Mark*. Lewiston, NY: Mellen Biblical Press, 1996.

Moule, Charles Francis Digby. *The Gospel according to Mark*. Cambridge: Cambridge University Press, 1965.

———. *The Phenomenon of the New Testament*. London: SCM, 1967.

Mudiso Mbâ Mundla, Jean-Gaspard. *Jesus und die Führer Israels: Studien zu den sogenannten Jerusalemer Streitgesprächen*. Münster: Aschendorf, 1984.

Müller, U. B. "Die christologische Absicht des Markusevangeliums und die Verklärungsgeschichte." *ZNW* 64 (1973): 159–93.

Munro, Winsome. "Women Disciples in Mark." *CBQ* 44 (1982): 225–41.

Murphy, Nancey. *Anglo-American Postmodernity: Philosophical Perspectives on Science, Religion, and Ethics*. Boulder, CO: Westview Press, 1997.

Mussner, F. "Ein Wortspiel in Mk 1,24?" *BZ* 4 (1960): 285–86.

Myers, Ched. *Binding the Strong Man: A Political Reading of Mark's Story of Jesus*. Maryknoll, NY: Orbis, 1988.

Neirynck, Frans. *Duality in Mark: Contributions to the Study of the Markan Redaction*. Leuven: Leuven University Press, 1972.

———. *L'Évangile de Marc: À propos du commentaire de R. Pesch*. ALBO. Leuven: Peeters, 1979.

———. "L'Évangile de Marc: À propos d'un nouveau commentaire." *ETL* 53 (1977): 153–81.

———. "La fuite du jeune homme en Mc 14,51–52." *ETL* 55 (1979): 43–66.

———. *The Gospel of Mark: A Cumulative Bibliography, 1950–1990*. BETL. Leuven: Leuven University Press, 1992.

———. "Jesus and the Sabbath: Some Observations on Mark II,27." In *Jésus aux origines de la christologie*, edited by J. Dupont, 227–70. Leuven: Leuven University Press, 1975.

———. "The Redactional Text of Mark." *ETL* 57 (1981): 144–62.

Neirynck, Frans, Theo Hansen, and Frans van Segbroeck. *The Minor Agreements of Matthew and Luke against Mark with a Cumulative List*. BETL. Leuven: Leuven University Press, 1974.

Neville, David J. *Mark's Gospel: Prior or Posterior? A Reappraisal of the Phenomenon of Order*. London: Sheffield Academic, 2002.

Newheart, Michael Willett. *My Name Is Legion: The Story and Soul of the Gerasene Demoniac*. Collegeville, MN: Liturgical Press, 2004.

Neyrey, Jerome. *Christ Is Community: The Christologies of the New Testament*. Collegeville, MN: Michael Glazier / Liturgical Press, 1985.

———. "Questions, Chreiai, and Challenges to Honor: The Interface of Rhetoric and Culture in Mark's Gospel." *CBQ* 60 (1998): 657–81.

Nickelsburg, George W. "The Genre and Function of the Markan Passion Narrative." *HTR* 73 (1980): 153–84.

Nineham, Dennis E. "The Order of Events in St. Mark's Gospel: An Examination of Dr. Dodd's Hypothesis." In *Studies in the Gospels: Essays in Honor of R. H. Lightfoot*, edited by D. E. Nineham, 223–39. Oxford: Blackwell, 1957.

———. *Saint Mark*. Philadelphia: Westminster, 1963.

Novum Testamentum Graece. Edited by Kurt Aland and Eberhard Nestle et al. 28th ed. Stuttgart: German Bible Society, 2013. http://www.nestle-aland.com/en/read-na28-online/.

O'Brien, Kelli. *The Use of Scripture in the Markan Passion Narrative*. London: T&T Clark, 2010.

O'Connor, Jerome Murphy. "The Essenes and Their History." *RB* 81 (1974): 215–44.

Oden, Thomas C., and Christopher A. Hall, eds. *Mark*. Downers Grove, IL: InterVarsity, 1998.

Øland, Jorunn. *Women in Their Place: Paul and the Corinthian Discourse of Gender and Sanctuary Space*. London: T&T Clark, 2004.

Olekamma, Innocent Uhuegbu. *The Healing of Blind Bartimaeus (Mk 10,46–52) in the Markan Context: Two Ways of Asking*. Frankfurt am Main: Peter Lang, 1999.

Olyan, Saul. "'Anyone Blind or Lame Shall Not Enter the House': On the Interpretation of Second Samuel 5:8b." *CBQ* 60 (1998): 218–27.

Ong, Walter. "Text as Interpretation: Mark and After." *Semeia* 39 (1987): 7–25.

———. "The Writer's Audience Is Always a Fiction." In *Interfaced of the Word: Studies in the Evolution of Consciousness and Culture*, 53–81. Ithaca, NY: Cornell University Press, 1977.

O'Rourke, J. J. "A Note concerning the Use of EIS and EN in Mark." *JBL* 85 (1966): 348–51.

Orton, David E. *The Composition of Mark's Gospel: Selected Studies from Novum Testamentum*. BRBS. Leiden: Brill, 1999.

Ossom-Batsa, George. *The Institution of the Eucharist in the Gospel of Mark: A Study of* the Function of Mark 14, 22–25 within the Gospel Narrative. Bern: Peter Lang, 2001.

Osterley, W. O. E. *The Jewish Background of the Christian Liturgy*. Gloucester, MA: Peter Smith, 1965.

Painter, John. *Mark's Gospel: Worlds in Conflict*. London: Routledge, 1997.

———. "When Is a House Not a Home? Disciples and Family in Mark 3:13–35." *NTS* 45 (1999): 498–513.

Park, Yoon-Man. *Mark's Memory Resources and the Controversy Stories (Mark 2:1–3:6): An Application of the Frame Theory of Cognitive Science to the Markan Oral-Aural Narrative*. Leiden: Brill, 2010.

Parrott, Rod. "Conflict and Rhetoric in Mark 2:23–28." *Semeia* 64 (1993): 117–37.

Patella, Michael. *Lord of the Cosmos: Mithras, Paul, and the Gospel of Mark*. New York: T&T Clark, 2006.

Patterson, Stephen J. *The God of Jesus: The Historical Jesus and the Search for Meaning*. Harrisburg, PA: Trinity Press International, 1998.

Peabody, David Barrett. *Mark as Composer*. NGS 1. Macon, GA: Mercer University Press, 1987.

Peristiany, J. G., ed. *Honour and Shame: The Values of Mediterreanean Society*. Chicago: University of Chicago Press, 1966.

Perrin, Norman. "The Christology of Mark." In *L'Évangile selon Marc: Tradition et rédaction*, edited by M. Sabbe, 471–85. Leuven: Duculot / Leuven University Press, 1974.

———. "The Christology of Mark: A Study in Methodology." In *The Interpretation of Mark*, edited by William R. Telford, 125–40. Edinburgh: T&T Clark, 1995.

———. "The Creative Use of the Son of Man Traditions in Mark." *USQR* 23 (1968): 357–65.

———. "The Interpretation of the Gospel of Mark." *Int* 30 (1976): 115–24.

———. "Towards an Interpretation of the Gospel of Mark." In *Christology and a Modern Pilgrimage*, edited by Hans Dieter Betz, 1–78. Claremont, CA: New Testament Colloquium, 1971.

———. "The Wredestrasse Becomes the Hauptstrasse: Reflections on the Reprinting of the Dodd Festschrift." *JR* 46 (1966): 299.

Pesch, Rudolf. "Berufung und Sendung, Nachfolge und Mission: Eine Studie zu Mk 1, 16–20." *ZKT* 91 (1969): 1–31.

———. "The Markan Version of the Healing of the Gerasene Demoniac." *ER* 21 (1971): 349–76.

———. *Das Markusevangelium*. HTKNT. Freiburg: Herder, 1976.

———. *Das Markusevangelium: Einleitung und Kommentar zu Kap. 1:1–8:26*. 6th ed. Freiburg: Herder, 1977.

———. *Das Markusevangelium: Kommentar zu Kap. 8:27–16:20*. 6th ed. Freiburg: Herder, 1977.

———. "Das Messiasbekentniss des Petrus (MK 8, 27–30): Neuverhandlung einer alten Frage." *BZ* 18 (1974): 20–31.

———. *Naherwartungen: Tradition und Redaktion in Mk 13*. KBANT. Düsseldorf: Patmos, 1968.

———. "Ein Tag vollmächtige Wirkens Jesu in Kapharnaum (Mk 1,21–34.35–39)." *BibLeb* 9 (1968): 114–95.

Petersen, N. R. "The Composition of Mark 4:1–8:26." *HTR* 93 (1980): 185–217.

———, ed. *Perspectives on Mark's Gospel*. Atlanta: Society of Biblical Literature, 1980.

———. "Point of View in Mark's Narrative." *Semeia* 12 (1978): 97–121.

———. "When Is the End Not the End? Literary Reflections on the Ending of Mark's Gospel." *Int* 34 (1980): 151–66.

Peterson, Dwight N. *The Origins of Mark: The Markan Community in Current Debate*. BibInt. Leiden: Brill, 2000.

Peterson, Karl. "Zu den Speisungs- und Abendmahlsberichten." *ZNW* 32 (1933): 217–18.

Phillips, John. *Contested Knowledge: A Guide to Critical Theory*. London: Zed Books, 2000.

Pilch, John J. "Healing in Mark: A Social Science Analysis." *BTB* 15 (1985): 142–50.

Placher, William C. *Mark*. Louisville: Westminster John Knox, 2010.

Poetker, Katrina. "Domestic Domains in the Gospel of Mark." *Direction* 24 (1995): 14–27.

Pokorny, P. "From a Puppy to a Child: Some Problems of Contemporary Biblical Exegesis." *NTS* 41 (1995): 321–37.

———. "Das Markusevangelium: Literarische und theologische Einleitung mit Forschungsbericht." *ANRW* 2, no. 25.3 (1983): 1970–2035.

Powell, J. Enoch. *The Evolution of the Gospel: A New Translation of the First Gospel with Commentary and Introductory Essay.* New Haven: Yale University Press, 1994.

Powell, Mark Allan. "Narrative Criticism." In *Hearing the New Testament*, edited by Joel B. Green, 239–55. Grand Rapids: Eerdmans, 1995.

———. "Toward a Narrative-Critical Understanding of Mark." *Int* 47 (1993): 341–46.

Pryke, E. J. *Redactional Style in the Markan Gospel: A Study of Syntax and Vocabulary as Guides to Redaction in Mark.* Cambridge: Cambridge University Press, 1978.

Quesnell, Quentin. *The Mind of Mark: Interpretation and Method through the Exegesis of Mark 6,52.* Rome: Pontifical Biblical Institute Press, 1969.

Radcliffe, T. "The Coming of the Son of Man: Mark's Gospel and the Subversion of the Apocalyptic Imagination." In *Language, Meaning, and God: Essays in Honor of Herbert McCabe O.P.*, edited by B. Davies, 167–89. London: Chapman, 1987.

Radermakers, J. "L'Évangile de Marc: Structure et théologie." In *L'Évangile selon Marc: Tradition et rédaction*, edited by M. Sabbe, 221–39. Leuven: Duculot / Leuven University Press, 1974.

Räisänen, Heikki. "Jesus and the Food Laws: Reflections on Mark 7:15." In *Jesus, Paul, and Torah: Collected Essays*, edited by H. Räisänen, 127–48. Sheffield: Sheffield Academic, 1992.

———. The *"Messianic Secret" in Mark.* Edinburgh: T&T Clark, 1990.

———. *Das 'Messiasgeheimnis' im Markusevangelium.* Helsinki: LänsiSuomi, 1976.

Rau, G. "Das Markusevangelium: Komposition und Intention der ersten Darstellung der christlicher Mission." *ANRW* 2, no. 3.15 (1985): 2036–257.

Rawlinson, A. E. *St. Mark: With Introduction, Commentary and Additional Notes.* London: Methuen, 1925.

Récanati, François. *Meaning and Force: The Pragmatics of Performative Utterances.* CSP. Cambridge: Cambridge University Press, 1987.

Reiser, M. *Syntax und Stil des Markusevangeliums im Licht der hellenistischen Volksliteratur.* Tübingen: Mohr, 1984.

Reploh, Karl-Georg. *Markus, Lehrer der Gemeinde.* Stuttgart: Katholisches Bibelwerk, 1969.

Rhoads, David. "Jesus and the Syrophoenician Woman in Mark." *JAAR* 62 (1994): 343–75.

———. "Narrative Criticism and the Gospel of Mark." *JAAR* 50 (1982): 411–34.

———. *Reading Mark, Engaging the Gospel.* Minneapolis: Fortress, 2004.

———. "Social Criticism: Crossing Boundaries." In *Mark and Method*, 2nd ed., edited by Janice Capel Anderson and Stephen D. Moore, 145–79. Minneapolis: Fortress, 2008.

Rhoads, David, Joanna Dewey, and Donald Michie. *Mark as Story: An Introduction to the Narrative of a Gospel.* 2nd ed. Minneapolis: Fortress, 1999.

Richardson, Alan. "The Feeding of the Five Thousand." *Int* 9 (1955): 144–49.

———. *An Introduction to the Theology of the New Testament.* New York: Harper & Row, 1958.

Riches, John K. *A Century of New Testament Study.* Valley Forge, PA: Trinity Press International, 1993.

———. *Conflicting Mythologies: Identity Formation in the Gospels of Mark and Matthew.* Edinburgh: T&T Clark, 2000.

Robbins, Vernon K. *Exploring the Texture of Texts: A Guide to Socio-Rhetorical Interpretation.* Valley Forge, PA: Trinity Press International, 1996.

———. *Jesus the Teacher: A Socio-Rhetorical Interpretation of Mark.* Minneapolis: Augsburg, 1992.

————. *New Boundaries in Old Territory: Form and Social Rhetoric in Mark.* New York: Peter Lang, 1994.

————. "Text and Context in Recent Studies of the Gospel of Mark." *RelSRev* 17 (1991): 16–23.

————. "The Woman Who Touched Jesus' Garment: Social Rhetorical Analysis of the Synoptic Accounts." In *New Boundaries in Old Territory: Form and Social Rhetoric in Mark*, edited by D. B. Gowler, 155–84. New York: Peter Lang, 1994.

Robinson, James M. "The Literary Composition of Mark." In *L'Évangile selon Marc: Tradition et rédaction*, edited by M. Sabbe, 11–19. Leuven: Duculot / Leuven University Press, 1974.

————. *A New Quest of the Historical Jesus.* London: SCM, 1959.

————. *The Problem of History in Mark and Other Marcan Studies.* Philadelphia: Fortress, 1982.

————. "The Problem of History in Mark Reconsidered." *USQR* 20 (1965): 131–47.

Robinson, William C. "The Quest for Wrede's Secret Messiah." *Int* 27 (1973): 10–30.

Rodd, Cyril S. *The Gospel of Mark.* Epworth Commentaries. London: Epworth, 2005.

Rohrbaugh, R. I. "The Social Location of the Markan Audience." *BTB* 23 (1993): 114–27.

Roloff, Jürgen. "Das Markusevangelium als Geschichtsdarstellung." *EvT* 29 (1969): 73–93.

Romaniuk, K. "Le problème des paulinismes dans l'Évangile de Marc." *NTS* 23 (1976): 266–74.

Rordorf, Willy. *Sunday: The History of the Day of Rest and Worship in the Earliest Centuries of the Christian Church.* London: SCM, 1968.

Roskam, Hendrika N. *The Purpose of the Gospel of Mark in Its Social and Historical Context.* Leiden: Brill, 2004.

Roth, Wolfgang. *Hebrew Gospel: Cracking the Code of Mark.* Oak Park, IL: Meyer Stone Books, 1988.

Rowe, Robert D. *God's Kingdom and God's Son: The Background in Mark's Christology from Concepts of Kingship in the Psalms.* Leiden: Brill, 2002.

Rowland, C. *The Open Heaven: A Study of Apocalyptic in Judaism and Early Christianity.* New York: Crossroad, 1982.

Rubenstein, Jeffrey L. *The History of Sukkot in the Second Temple and Rabbinic Periods.* BJS. Atlanta: Scholars Press, 1995.

Russell, D. S. *The Method and Message of Jewish Apocalyptic.* Philadelphia: Westminster, 1964.

Sabin, Marie Noonan. *The Gospel according to Mark.* Collegeville, MN: Liturgical Press, 2006.

————. *Reopening the Word: Reading Mark as Theology in the Context of Early Judaism.* Oxford: Oxford University Press, 2002.

Samuel, Simon. *A Postcolonial Reading of Mark's Story of Jesus.* LNTS. London: T&T Clark, 2007.

Sanders, E. P. *The Historical Figure of Jesus.* London: Penguin Books, 1993.

————. *Judaism: Practice and Belief, 63 BCE–63 CE.* Philadelphia: Trinity Press International, 1992.

Sandmel, Samuel. "Prologomena to a Commentary on Mark." In *New Testament Issues*, edited by Richard A. Batey, 45–56. New York: Harper & Row, 1970.

Santos, Narry F. *Slave of All: The Paradox of Authority and Servanthood in the Gospel of Mark.* JSNTSup 237. London: Sheffield Academic, 2003.

Sariola, Heikki. *Markus und das Gesetz: Eine redaktionskritische Untersuchung.* AASF. Helsinki: Suomalainen Tiedeakatemia, 1990.

Sawyer, Harry. "The Marcan Framework." *SJT* 14 (1961): 279–94.

Schenk, Wolfgang. *Der Passionsbericht nach Markus.* Gütersloh: Mohn, 1974.

Schenke, Ludger. *Das Markusevangelium.* Stuttgart: Kohlhammer, 1988.

————. *Studien zur Passionsgeschichte des Markus: Tradition und Redaktion in Markus 14, 1–42.* Würzburg: Echter, 1971.

————. *Die Wundererzählungen des Markusevangeliums.* Stuttgart: Katholisches Bibelwerk, 1975.

Schierling, Marla Jean. "Women as Leaders in the Marcan Communities." *List* 15 (1980): 250–56.

Schiffman, Lawrence. *The Eschatological Community of the Dead Sea Scrolls*. Atlanta: Scholars Press, 1989.

———, ed. *Texts and Traditions: A Source Reader for the Study of Second Temple and Rabbinic Judaism*. Hoboken, NJ: Ktav, 1998.

Schildgen, Brenda Dean. *Crisis and Continuity: Time in the Gospel of Mark*. Sheffield: Sheffield Academic, 1998.

———. *Power and Prejudice: The Reception of the Gospel of Mark*. Detroit: Wayne State University Press, 1999.

Schmahl, Günther. *Die Zwölf im Markusevangelium*. Trier: Paulinus Verlag, 1974.

Schmid, Hans Heinrich. "Creation, Righteousness, and Salvation: 'Creation Theology' as the Broad Horizon of Biblical Theology." In *Creation in the Old Testament*, edited by Bernard W. Anderson, 102–17. Philadelphia: Fortress, 1984.

Schmid, J. *The Gospel according to Mark*. Staten Island, NY: Alba, 1968.

Schmidt, Daryl D. *The Gospel of Mark*. Sonoma, CA: Polebridge Press, 1990.

Schmidt, Hans. *Eucharisterion: Studien zur Religion und Literatur des alten und neuen Testaments. 2. Teil: Zur Religion und Literatur des Neuen Testaments*. Göttingen: Vandenhoeck & Ruprecht, 1923.

Schmithals, Walter. *Das Evangelium nach Markus*. 2nd ed. Gütersloh: Mohn, 1986.

Schnackenburg, Rudoph. *Jesus in the Gospels: A Biblical Christology*. Louisville: Westminster John Knox, 1995.

Schneck, Richard. *Isaiah in the Gospel of Mark I–VIII*. Vallejo, CA: Bibal Press, 1994.

Schnelle, Udo. *The History and Theology of the New Testament Writings*. Translated by M. Eugene Boring. Minneapolis: Fortress, 1998.

Scholtissek, Klaus. *Die Vollmacht Jesu: Traditions- und redaktionsgeschichtliche Analysen zu einem Leitmotiv markinischer Christologie*. Münster: Aschendorff, 1992.

Scholtissek, Klaus, and Thomas Söding. *Der Evangelist als Theologe: Studien zum Markusevangelium*. Stuttgart: Katholisches Bibelwerk, 1995.

Schreiber, Johannes. "Die Christologie des Markusevangeliums." *ZTK* 58 (1961).

Schulz, Siegfried. "Mark's Significance for the Theology of Early Christianity." In *The Interpretation of Mark*, edited by William R. Telford, 197–206. Edinburgh: T&T Clark, 1995.

Schweizer, Eduard. "Anmerkungen zur Theologie des Markus." In *Neotestimentica: Deutsche und Englische Aufsätze (1951–1963)*, edited by Eduard Schweizer, 93–104. Zürich: Zwingli, 1963.

———. *Erniedrigung und Erhöhung bei Jesus und seinen Nachfolgern*. 2nd ed. Zürich: Zwingli, 1962.

———. *Das Evangelium nach Markus*. Göttingen: Vandenhoeck & Ruprecht, 1978.

———. *The Good News according to Mark*. Richmond: John Knox, 1970.

———. "Mark's Theological Achievement." In *The Interpretation of Mark*, edited by William R. Telford, 63–87. Edinburgh: T&T Clark, 1995.

———. "The Portrayal of the Life of Faith in the Gospel of Mark." *Int* 32 (1978): 387–99.

———. "The Question of the Messianic Secret in Mark." In *The Messianic Secret in Mark*, edited by C. Tuckett, 65–74. Philadelphia: Fortress, 1983.

———. "The Son of Man." *JBL* 79 (1960): 119–29.

———. "Die theologische Leistung des Markus." In *Beiträge zur Theologie des Neuen Testaments: Neutestamentliche Aufsätze (1955–1970)*, edited by Eduard Schweizer, 21–42. Zürich: Zwingli, 1970.

———. "Towards a Christology of Mark." In *God's Christ and His People: Studies in Honor of Nils Alstrup Dahl*, edited by Jacob Jervell and Wayne Meeks, 29–42. Oslo: Universitetsforlaget, 1977.

———. "Zur Frage des Messiasgeheimnisses." *ZNW* 56 (1965): 1–8.

Scott, Alan. *Origen and the History of the Stars*. Oxford: Oxford University Press, 1991.

Scott, M. Phillip. "Chiastic Structure: A Key to the Interpretation of Mark's Gospel." *BTB* 15 (1985): 17–26.

Scroggs, Paul. "Paul and the Eschatological Woman." *JAAR* 40 (1972): 283–303.

———. "Paul and the Eschatological Woman Revisited." *JAAR* 42 (1974): 532–37.

Scroggs, Robin, and K. I. Groff. "Baptism in Mark: Dying and Rising with Christ." *JBL* 92 (1973): 513–48.

Seal, Welton O. "Norman Perrin and His School: Retracing a Pilgrimage." *JSNT* 20 (1984): 87–107.

Sellew, Philip. "Aphorisms of Jesus in Mark: A Stratigraphic Analysis." FF 8 (1992): 141–60.

———. "Composition of Didactic Scenes in Mark's Gospel." *JBL* 108 (1989): 613–34.

———. "Secret Mark and the History of Canonical Mark." In *The Future of Early Christianity: Essays in Honor of Helmut Koester*, edited by B. A. Pearson, 242–57. Minneapolis: Fortress, 1991.

Selvidge, Marla Jean. "And Those Who Followed Feared (Mark 10.32)." *CBQ* 45 (1983): 385–400.

———. "Mark 5:25–34 and Leviticus 15: A Reaction to Restrictive Purity Regulations." *JBL* 103 (1984): 619–23.

Senior, Donald. "The Eucharist in Mark: Mission, Reconciliation, Hope." *BTB* 12 (1982): 67–72.

———. *The Passion of Jesus in the Gospel of Mark*. Wilmington, DE: Michael Glazier, 1984.

———. "The Struggle to Be Universal: Mission as Vantage Point for New Testament Investigation." *CBQ* 46 (1984): 63–81.

———. "With Swords and Clubs: The Setting of Mark's Community and His Critique of Abusive Power." *BTB* 17 (1987): 10–20.

Shepherd, Tom. *Markan Sandwich Stories: Narration, Definition, and Function*. Berrian Springs, MI: Andrews University Press, 1993.

———. "The Narrative Function of Markan Intercalation." *NTS* 41 (1995): 522–40.

Shim, Ezra. "A Suggestion about the Genre or Text-Type of Mark." *Scriptura* 50 (1994): 69–89.

Shiner, Whitney. *Follow Me: Disciples in Markan Rhetoric*. Atlanta: Scholars Press, 1995.

———. *Proclaiming the Gospel: First Century Performance of Mark*. Philadelphia: Trinity Press International, 2003.

Sloyan, Gerard. *The Gospel of Saint Mark*. Collegeville, MN: Liturgical Press, 1952.

Smit, Johannes. "A Semiological Reading of Mark as Mythology." *Scriptura* 50 (1994): 55–67.

———. "Theoretical Considerations: Reading Mark as Mythology." *Scriptura* 50 (1994): 41–54.

Smith, D. Moody. "The Use of the Old Testament in the New." In *The Use of the Old Testament in the New, and Other Essays: Studies in Honor of William Franklin Stinespring*, edited by James Efird, 3–65. Durham, NC: Duke University Press, 1972.

Smith, Jonathan Z. *To Take Place: Toward Theory in Ritual*. Chicago: University of Chicago Press, 1987.

Smith, Mark. *The Pilgrimage Pattern in Exodus*. Sheffield: Sheffield Academic, 1997.

Smith, Morton. *The Aretalogy Used by Mark*. Berkeley: Center for Hermeneutical Studies, 1975.

———. "Prolegomena to a Discussion of Aretalogies, Divine Men, the Gospels, and Jesus." *JBL* 90 (1971): 174–99.

———. *The Secret Gospel: The Discovery and Interpretation of the Secret Gospel according to Mark*. New York: Harper & Row, 1973.

Smith, Stephen H. "Bethsaida via Gennesaret: The Enigma of the Sea Crossing in Mark 6:45–53." *Bib* 77 (1996): 349–74.

———. *A Lion with Wings: A Narrative Critical Approach to Mark's Gospel*. Sheffield: Sheffield Academic, 1996.

———. "Mark 3,1–6: Form, Redaction and Community Function." *Bib* 74 (1994): 153–74.

Smith, W. Robertson. *Lectures on the Religion of the Semites*. New ed. rev. throughout by the author. London: Adam and Charles Black, 1894.

Snoy, T. "Mark 6,48: '. . . et il voulait les dépasser.'" In *L'Évangile selon Marc: Tradition et rédaction*, edited by M. Sabbe, 347–63. Leuven: Duculot / Leuven University Press, 1974.

Söding, Thomas. *Glaube bei Markus: Glaube an das Evangelium, Gebetsglaube und Wunderglaube im Kontext der markinischen Basileiatheologie und Christologie*. Stuttgart: Katholisches Bibelwerk, 1985.

Spatafora, Andrea. *From the Temple of God to God as the Temple: A Biblical Theological Study of the Temple in the Book of Revelation*. Rome: Editrice Pontificia Universita Gregoriana, 1997.

Spell, David. *Miracles in Mark*. Boston: Wipf and Stock, 2009.

Standaert, Benoît. *L'Évangile selon Marc: Commentaire*. 3rd ed. Paris: Cerf, 1997.

———. *L'Évangile selon Marc: Composition et genre littéraire*. Nijmegen: Stichting Studentenpers, 1978.

Starobinski, Jean. "An Essay in Literary Analysis: Mark 5:1–20." *ER* 23 (1971): 377–97.

St. Clair, Raquel Annette. *Call and Consequences: A Womanist Reading of Mark*. Minneapolis: Fortress, 2008.

Steichele, Hans. *Der leidende Sohn Gottes: Eine Untersuchung einiger alttestamentlicher Motive in der Christologie des Markusevangeliums; Zugleich ein Beitrag zur Erhellung des überlieferungsgeschichtlichen Zusammenhangs zwischen Altem und Neuem Testament*. Regensburg: F. Pustet, 1980.

Stein, Robert Henry. *Mark*. Grand Rapids: Baker Academic, 2008.

———. "The Proper Methodology for Ascertaining a Markan Redaction History." *NovT* 13 (1971): 181–98.

Steinmetz, David C. "The Superiority of Pre-Critical Exegesis." In *The Theological Interpretation of Scripture: Classic and Contemporary Readings*, edited by Stephen E. Fowl, 26–38. Cambridge: Blackwell, 1997.

Stendahl, Krister. *Paul among Jews and Gentiles, and Other Essays*. Philadelphia: Fortress, 1976.

Stèokl Ben Ezra, Daniel. *The Impact of Yom Kippur on Early Christianity: The Day of Atonement from Second Temple Judaism to the Fifth Century*. WUNT. Tübingen: Mohr Siebeck, 2003.

Stevens, Bruce A. "Why Must the Son of Man Suffer? The Divine Warrior in the Gospel of Mark." *BZ* 31 (1987): 101–10.

Stevenson, Gregory. *Power and Place: Temple and Identity in the Book of Revelation*. BZNW. Berlin: de Gruyter, 2001.

Stewart-Sykes, Alistair. "TAXEI in Papias: Again." *JECS* 3 (1995): 487–92.

Stock, Augustine. *Call to Discipleship: A Literary Study of Mark's Gospel*. Wilmington, DE: Michael Glazier, 1982.

———. "Hinge Transitions in Mark's Gospel." *BTB* 15 (1985): 27–31.

———. *The Method and Message of Mark*. Wilmington: Michael Glazier, 1989.

Stock, K. *Boten aus dem Mit-Ihm Sein: Das Verhältnis zwischen Jesus und den Zwölf nach Markus*. Rome: Pontifical Biblical Institute Press, 1975.

Stoldt, Hans-Herbert. *History and Criticism of the Marcan Hypothesis*. Edited and translated by Donald L. Niewyk. Macon, GA: Mercer University Press, 1980. Originally published as *Geschichte und Kritik der Markus-Hypothese* (Göttingen: Vandenhoeck & Ruprecht, 1977).

Stone, Michael, ed. *Jewish Writings of the Second Temple Period*. Philadelphia: Fortress, 1984.

Strecker, George. "The Passion and Resurrection Predictions in Mark's Gospel." *Int* 22 (1968): 421–42.

Streeter, B. H. *The Four Gospels: A Study of Origins*. New York: Macmillan, 1925.

Strelan, Richard E. "The Fallen Watchers and the Disciples in Mark." *JSP* 20 (1999): 73–92.

Stuhlmacher, Peter. *Historical Criticism and the Theological Interpretation of Scripture*. Translated by Roy A. Harrisville. Philadelphia: Fortress, 1977.

Stuhlmann, R. "Beobachtungen und Überlegungen zu Markus 4.26–29." *NTS* 19 (1973): 153–62.

Styler, G. M. "The Priority of Mark." In *The Birth of the New Testament*, 3rd ed., edited by C. F. D. Moule, 285–316. San Francisco: Harper & Row, 1982.

Such, W. A. *The Abomination of Desolation in the Gospel of Mark: Its Historical Reference in Mark 13:14 and Its Impact in the Gospel*. Lanham, MD: University Press of America, 1999.

Suhl, Alfred. *Die Funktion der alttestamentlichen Zitate und Anspielungen in Markusevangelium*. Gütersloh: Mohn, 1965.

Svartvik, Jesper. *Mark and Mission: Mk 7:1–23 in Its Narrative and Historical Contexts*. ConBNT 32. Stockholm: Almqvist & Wiksell International, 2000.

Swanson, D. *The Temple Scroll and the Bible*. Leiden: Brill, 1995.

Swanson, Reuben J. *Mark*. Vol. 2 of *New Testament Greek Manuscripts: Variant Readings Arranged in Horizontal Lines against Codex Vaticanus*. Sheffield: Sheffield Academic, 1995.

Swartley, Willard. *Israel's Scripture Traditions and the Synoptic Gospels: Story Shaping Story*. Peabody, MA: Hendrickson, 1994.

———. "The Role of Women in Mark's Gospel: A Narrative Analysis." *BTB* 27 (1997): 16–22.

Swetnam, J. "Some Remarks on the Meaning of HO DE EXELTHON in Mark 1.45." *Bib* 68 (1987): 245–49.

Tagawa, Kenzo. *Miracles et Évangile: La pensée personnelle de l'Évangéliste Marc*. EPR. Paris: Presses Universitaires de France, 1966.

Talbert, Charles. *What Is a Gospel? The Genre of the Canonical Gospels*. Philadelphia: Fortress, 1977.

Tannehill, Robert C. "The Disciples in Mark: The Function of a Narrative Role." In *The Interpretation of Mark*, edited by William R. Telford, 169–95. Edinburgh: T&T Clark, 1995.

———. "The Gospel of Mark as Narrative Christology." *Semeia* 16 (1979): 57–92.

Tate, Randolph. *Reading Mark from the Outside: Eco and Iser Leave Their Marks*. Bethesda, MD: Christian Universities Press, 1995.

Taylor, Vincent. *The Gospel according to St. Mark*. 2nd ed. New York: Macmillan, 1952. Reprint, Grand Rapids: Baker, 1981.

Telford, William R. *The Barren Temple and the Withered Tree: A Redaction-Critical Analysis of the Cursing of the Fig-Tree Pericope in Mark's Gospel and Its Relation to the Cleansing of the Temple Tradition*. Sheffield: JSOT Press, 1980.

———, ed. *The Interpretation of Mark*. 2nd ed. Edinburgh: T&T Clark, 1995.

———. *Mark*. Sheffield: Sheffield Academic, 1995.

———. *Mark*. TTCSG. London: T&T Clark, 2003.

———. *The Theology of the Gospel of Mark*. Cambridge: Cambridge University Press, 1998.

———. *Writing on Mark*. Boston: Deo, 2009.

Theissen, Gerd. *The Gospels in Context: Social and Political History in the Synoptic Tradition*. Translated by L. Maloney. Minneapolis: Fortress, 1991. Originally published as *Lokalkolorit und Zeitgeschichte in den Evangelien* (Göttingen: Vandenhoeck & Ruprecht, 1989).

———. *The Miracle Stories of the Early Christian Tradition*. Edited by F. McDonagh. Translated by John Riches. Philadelphia: Fortress, 1983.

———. *Urchristliche Wundergeschichten*. Gütersloh: Mohn, 1974.

———. "'Wir haben alles verlassen' (Mc. X.28): Nachfolge und soziale Entwurzelung in der jüdisch-palästinischen Gesellschaft des I, Jahrhunderts N. Ch." *NovT* 14 (1977): 161–96.

Thiselton, Anthony C. *New Horizons in Hermeneutics: The Theory and Practice of Transforming Biblical Reading*. Grand Rapids: Zondervan, 1992.

———. *The Two Horizons*. Grand Rapids: Eerdmans, 1980.

Thissen, W. *Erzählung der Befreiung*. Würzburg: Echter, 1976.

Thurston, Bonnie Bowman. *Preaching Mark*. Fortress Resources for Preaching. Minneapolis: Fortress, 2002.

Thyen, H. "Baptisma Metanoias eis Aphesin Hamartion." In *Zeit und Geschichte: Dankesgabe an Rudolph Bultmann zum 80. Geburtstag*, edited by E. Dinkler, 97–125. Tübingen: Mohr Siebeck, 1964.

Tiede, David L. *The Charismatic Figure as Miracle Worker*. Missoula, MT: Society of Biblical Literature, 1972.

Titley, Robert. *A Poetic Discontent: Austin Farrer and the Gospel of Mark*. London: T&T Clark, 2010.

Tobin, Thomas H. "Interpretations of the Creation of the World in Philo of Alexandria." In *Creation in the Biblical Traditions*, edited by John Collins and Richard J. Clifford, 108–28. Washington, DC: Catholic Biblical Association of America, 1992.

Tolbert, Mary Ann. "The Gospel of Mark." In *The New Testament Today*, edited by Mark Allan Powell, 45–57. Louisville: Westminster John Knox, 1999.

———. "Is It Lawful on the Sabbath to Do Good or to Do Harm? Mark's Ethics of Religious Practice." *PRSt* 23 (1996): 199–214.

———. *Sowing the Gospel: Mark's World in Literary-Historical Perspective*. Minneapolis: Fortress, 1989.

Trainor, Michael F. *The Quest for Home: The Household in Mark's Community*. Collegeville, MN: Liturgical Press, 2001.

Trible, Phyllis. *Rhetorical Criticism: Context, Method, and the Book of Jonah*. Minneapolis: Fortress, 1994.

Trocmé, Etienne. *L'Évangile selon saint Marc*. CNT. Geneva: Labor et Fides, 2000.

———. *The Formation of the Gospel according to Mark*. Philadelphia: Westminster, 1975.

———. "Is There a Markan Christology?" In *Christ and Spirit in the New Testament*, edited by B. Lindars and S. Smalley, 3–13. Cambridge: Cambridge University Press, 1973.

Tuckett, C. M., ed. *The Messianic Secret*. Phildadelphia: Fortress, 1983.

Tyson, Joseph B. "The Blindness of the Disciples in Mark." *JBL* 80 (1961): 261–68.

Ulansey, David. "The Heavenly Veil Torn: Mark's Cosmic *Inclusio*." *JBL* 101 (1991): 123–25.

Van Cangh, Jean-Marie. "La Galilée dans l'Évangile de Marc: Un lieu théologique?" *RB* 79 (1972): 59–75.

VanderKam, James C. *Calendars in the Dead Sea Scrolls: Measuring Time*. London: Routledge, 1998.

VanderKam, James C., and William Adler, eds. *The Jewish Apocalyptic Heritage in Early Christianity*. Minneapolis: Fortress, 1996.

Van Henten, J. W. "The First Testing of Jesus: A Rereading of Mark 1.12–13." *NTS* 45 (1999): 349–66.

Van Iersel, Bastiaan M. F. "Failed Followers in Mark: Mark 13:12 as a Key for the Identification of the Intended Readers." *CBQ* 58 (1996): 244–63.

———. "The Gospel according to St. Mark—Written for a Persecuted Community?" *NedTT* 34 (1980): 15–36.

———. "Locality, Structure, and Meaning in Mark." *LB* 53 (1983): 45–54.

———. *Mark: A Reader-Response Commentary*. Sheffield: Sheffield Academic, 1998.

———. *Reading Mark*. Collegeville, MN: Liturgical Press, 1988.

———. "Die wunderbare Speisung und das Abendmahl in der synoptischen Tradition." *NovT* 7 (1965): 167–94.

Van Linden, P. *The Gospel according to Mark*. Collegeville, MN: Liturgical Press, 1983.

Van Oyen, G. *The Interpretation of the Feeding Miracles in the Gospel of Mark*. Turnhout: Brepols, 1999.

Van Segbroeck, F., et al., eds. *The Four Gospels, 1992: Festschrift Frans Neirynck*. Leuven: Leuven University Press, 1992.

Vermes, Géza. *Jesus the Jew: A Historian's Reading of the Gospels*. London: Collins, 1973.

Via, Dan O. *The Ethics of Mark's Gospel: In the Middle of Time*. Philadelphia: Fortress, 1985.

Vines, Michael E. *The Problem of Markan Genre: The Gospel of Mark and the Jewish Novel*. Atlanta: Society of Biblical Literature, 2002.

Vööbus, Arthur. *Liturgical Traditions in the Didache*. Stockholm: ETSE, 1968.

229

Vorster, Dan O. "Literary Reflections on Mark 13:5–37: A Narrated Speech of Jesus." In *The Interpretation of Mark*, edited by William R. Telford, 268–88. Edinburgh: T&T Clark, 1995.

Vorster, W. S. "The Historical Paradigm: Its Possibilities and Limitations." *Neot* 18 (1984): 104–23.

———. "Kerygma, History, and the Gospel Genre." *NTS* (1983): 87–95.

———. "Mark: Collector, Redactor, Author, Narrator?" *JTSA* 31 (1980): 46–61.

———. "The Production of the Gospel of Mark: An Essay on Intertextuality." *HvTSt* 49 (1993): 385–96.

Votaw, C. W. *The Gospels and Contemporary Biographies in the Greco-Roman World.* Philadelphia: Fortress, 1970.

Waetjen, Herman C. *A Reordering of Power: A Sociopolitical Reading of Mark's Gospel.* Minneapolis: Fortress, 1989.

Wallace, Mark I. "Parsimony of Presence in Mark: Narratology, the Reader, and Genre Analysis in Paul Ricoeur." *SR* 18 (1989): 201–12.

Watson, David F. *Honor among Christians: The Cultural Key to the Messianic Secret.* Minneapolis: Fortress, 2010.

Watson, Duane Frederick. *The Intertexture of Apocalyptic Discourse in the New Testament.* Atlanta: Society of Biblical Literature, 2002.

Watson, F. "The Social Function of Mark's Secrecy Theme." *JSNT* 24 (1985): 49–69.

Watts, Rikki E. *Isaiah's New Exodus in Mark.* Tübingen: Mohr Siebeck, 1997.

Webb, Geoff R. *Mark at the Threshold: Applying Bakhtinian Categories to Markan Characterisation.* Leiden: Brill, 2008.

Webb, R. L. *John the Baptizer and Prophet: A Social Historical Study.* Sheffield: JSOT Press, 1991.

Weber, R. "Christologie und 'Messiasgeheimnis': Ihr Zusammenhang und Stellenwert in der Darstellungsintention des Markus." *EvT* 43 (1983): 108–25.

Weeden, Theodore J. "The Heresy That Necessitated Mark's Gospel." In *The Interpretation of Mark*, edited by William R. Telford, 89–104. Edinburgh: T&T Clark, 1995.

———. *Mark: Traditions in Conflict.* Philadelphia: Fortress, 1971.

Wegener, Mark I. *Cruciformed: The Literary Impact of Mark's Story of Jesus and His Disciples.* Lanham, MD: University Press of America, 1995.

———. "Reading Mark's Gospel Today: A Cruciforming Experience." *CurTM* 20 (1993): 462–80.

Weiss, Johannes. *Das älteste Evangelium.* 4th ed. Göttingen: Vandenhoeck & Ruprecht, 1917.

Weiss, Wolfgang. *"Eine neue Lehre in Vollmacht": Die Streit- und Schulgespräche des Markus-Evangeliums.* Berlin: de Gruyter, 1989.

Wendling, E. *Die Entstehung des Marcus-Evangeliums.* Tübingen: Mohr Siebeck, 1908.

Werner, Martin. *Der Einfluss paulinischer Theologie im Markusevangelium: Eine Studie ur neutestamentlichen Theologie.* Giessen: Töpelmann, 1923.

Wilder, Amos. *Early Christian Rhetoric: The Language of the Gospels.* Cambridge, MA: Harvard University Press, 1964.

Williams, James G. *Gospel against Parable: Mark's Language of Mystery.* Sheffield: Almond, 1985.

———. "Sacrifice and the Beginning of Kingship." *Semeia* 67 (1994): 73–92.

Williams, Joel. *Other Followers of Jesus: Minor Figures as Major Characters in Mark's Gospel.* Sheffield: Almond, 1994.

Williamson, Lamar. *Mark.* Atlanta: John Knox, 1983.

Wills, Lawrence M. *The Quest of the Historical Gospel: Mark, John, and the Origins of the Gospel Genre.* London: Routledge, 1997.

Wilson, Andrew P. *Transfigured: A Derridean Rereading of the Markan Transfiguration.* LNTS. New York: T&T Clark, 2007.

Wilson, Barrie A. *About Interpretation: From Plato to Dilthey; A Hermeneutic Anthology.* New York: Peter Lang, 1989.

Winn, Adam. *Mark and the Elijah-Elisha Narrative: Considering the Practice of Greco-Roman Imitation in the Search for Markan Source Material.* Eugene, OR: Pickwick, 2010.

———. *The Purpose of Mark's Gospel: An Early Christian Response to Roman Imperial Propaganda.* WUNT. Tübingen: Mohr Siebeck, 2008.

Witherington, Ben. *The Gospel of Mark: A Socio-Rhetorical Commentary.* Grand Rapids: Eerdmans, 2001.

Wolmarans, J. L. P. "Who Asked Jesus to Leave the Territory of Gerasa (Mark 5:17)?" *Neot* 28 (1994): 87–92.

Wrede, William. *The Messianic Secret.* Translated by J. C. J. Greig. 1905. Reprint, Greenwood, SC: Attic, 1971.

———. *Das Messiasgeheimnis in den Evangelien.* Göttingen: Vandenhoeck & Ruprecht, 1901.

Wright, N. T. *Mark for Everyone.* 2nd ed. London: SPCK / Louisville: Westminster John Knox, 2004.

Wuellner, Wilhelm. *The Meaning of "Fishers of Men."* Philadelphia: Westminster, 1967.

Yadin, Y. "The Temple Scroll." In *New Directions in Biblical Archaeology,* edited by D. N. Freedman and J. C. Greenfield, 156–66. Garden City, NY: Doubleday, 1971.

Yang, Yong-Eui. *Jesus and the Sabbath in Matthew's Gospel.* Sheffield: Sheffield Academic, 1997.

Young, George W. *Subversive Symmetry: Exploring the Fantastic in Mark 6:45–56.* Leiden: Brill, 1999.

Ziesler, J. A. "Which Is the Best Commentary? The Gospel according to Mark." *ExpTim* 98 (1987): 263–67.

Bibliography of Ritual and Liturgical Studies

Ackerman, Robert. "Frazer on Myth and Ritual." *JHI* 36 (1975): 115–34.

Alexander, Bobby C. "An Afterword on Ritual in Biblical Studies." *Semeia* 67 (1994): 209–25.

Aune, David E. *The Cultic Setting of Realized Eschatology in Early Christianity.* Leiden: Brill, 1972.

———. "The Problem of the Genre of the Gospels: A Critique of C. H. Talbert's *What Is a Gospel?*" In *Studies of History and Tradition in the Four Gospels*, vol. 2 of *Gospel Perspectives*, edited by D. Wenham and R. T. France, 9–60. Sheffield: JSOT Press, 1981.

Aus, Roger David. *Water into Wine and the Beheading of John the Baptist.* Atlanta: Scholars Press, 1988.

Austin, J. L. *How to Do Things with Words.* Cambridge, MA: Harvard University Press, 1955.

Barker, Margaret. *On Earth as It Is in Heaven: Temple Symbolism in the New Testament.* Edinburgh: T&T Clark, 1995.

Bassler, J. M. "The Parable of the Loaves." *JR* 66 (1986): 157–72.

Bell, Catherine. *Ritual: Perspectives and Dimensions.* Oxford: Oxford University Press, 1997.

———. *Ritual Theory, Ritual Practice.* Oxford: Oxford University Press, 1992.

Bennett, Clinton. *In Search of the Sacred: Anthropology and the Study of Religions.* New York: Cassell, 1996.

Benoît, André, and Charles Munier. *Die Taufe in der alten Kirche.* Bern: Peter Lang, 1994.

Bobertz, Charles A. "Prolegomena to a Ritual/ Liturgical Reading of the Gospel of Mark." In *Reading in Christian Communities: Essays on Interpretation in the Early Church*, 174–87. Notre Dame, IN: University of Notre Dame Press, 2002.

Boers, Hendrikus. "Reflections on the Gospel of Mark: A Structural Investigation." *SBLSP* 26 (1987): 255–67.

Boobyer, G. H. "The Eucharistic Interpretation of the Miracles of the Loaves in St. Mark's Gospel." *JTS* 3 (1952): 161–71.

Booth, Roger P. *Jesus and the Laws of Purity: Tradition History and Legal History in Mark 7.* Sheffield: JSOT Press, 1986.

Bouyer, Louis. *Liturgy and Architecture.* Notre Dame, IN: University of Notre Dame Press, 1967.

Bowman, J. W. *The Gospel of Mark: The New Jewish Christian Passover Haggadah.* Leiden: Brill, 1965.

233

Bradshaw, Paul F. *Eucharistic Origins*. Oxford: Oxford University Press, 2004.

———. *The Search for the Origins of Christian Worship: Sources and Methods for the Study of the Early Liturgy*. Oxford: Oxford University Press, 1992.

Bradshaw, Paul, and John Melloh. *Foundations in Ritual Studies: A Reader for Students of Christian Worship*. Grand Rapids: Baker Academic, 2007.

Brawley, R. L. "Table Fellowship: Bane and Blessing for the Historical Jesus." *PRSt* 22 (1995): 13–31.

Caldwell, Sarah. "Transcendence and Culture: Anthropologists Theorize Religion." *Rel SRev* 25 (1999): 227–32.

Chauvet, Louis-Marie. *Symbol and Sacrament: A Sacramental Reinterpretation of Christian Existence*. Translated by Patrick Madigan and Madeleine Beaumont. Collegeville, MN: Liturgical Press, 1995.

Chilton, Bruce. *The Temple of Jesus: His Sacrificial Program within a Cultural History of Sacrifice*. University Park: Pennsylvania State University Press, 1992.

Christiansen, Ellen. *The Covenant in Judaism and Paul: A Study of Ritual Boundaries as Identity Markers*. Leiden: Brill, 1995.

Chronis, H. L. "The Torn Veil: Cultus and Christology in Mark 15:37–39." *JBL* (1982): 97–114.

Collins, Adela Yarbro. "The Origin of Christian Baptism." *SL* 19 (1989): 28–46.

Collins, John. "Jerusalem and the Temple in Jewish Apocalyptic Literature of the Second Temple Period." *IRGLS* 1 (1998): 3–31.

Collins, John, and Richard J. Clifford, eds. *Creation in the Biblical Traditions*. Washington, DC: Catholic Biblical Association of America, 1992.

Corley, Kathleen E. *Private Women, Public Meals: Social Conflict in the Synoptic Tradition*. Peabody, MA: Hendrickson, 1993.

Cullmann, Oscar. *Baptism in the New Testament*. London: SCM, 1950.

———. *Early Christian Worship*. London: SCM, 1953.

———. *Salvation in History*. London: SCM, 1965.

Cullmann, Oscar, and F. J. Leenhardt. *Essays on the Lord's Supper*. Translated by J. G. Davies. London: Lutterworth, 1958.

Davies, Philip R. "Leviticus as a Cultic System in the Second Temple Period: Remarks on the Paper by Hannah K. Harrington." In *Reading Leviticus: A Conversation with Mary Douglas*, edited by John Sawyer, 231–37. Sheffield: Sheffield Academic, 1996.

Davila, James R. *Liturgical Works*. Eerdmans Commentaries on the Dead Sea Scrolls. Grand Rapids: Eerdmans, 2000.

DeMaris, Richard E. *The New Testament in Its Ritual World*. London: Routledge, 2008.

Diess, Lucien. *Springtime of the Liturgy: Liturgical Texts of the First Four Centuries*. Translated by Matthew J. O'Connell. Collegeville, MN: Liturgical Press, 1967.

Dix, Dom Gregory. *The Shape of the Liturgy*. New York: Seabury Press, 1982.

Doty, William G. *Mythography: The Study of Myths and Rituals*. 2nd ed. Tuscaloosa: University of Alabama Press, 2000.

Douglas, Mary. "Atonement in Leviticus." *JSQ* 1 (1994): 109–30.

———. *Natural Symbols: Explorations in Cosmology*. New York: Pantheon, 1970.

———. *Risk and Blame: Essays in Cultural Theory*. London: Routledge, 1994.

———. "Sacred Contagion." In *Reading Leviticus: A Conversation with Mary Douglas*, edited by John Sawyer, 86–106. Sheffield: Sheffield Academic, 1996.

Draper, Jonathan. "Ritual Process and Ritual Symbol in Didache 7–10." *VC* 54 (2000): 121–58.

———. "The Role of Ritual in the Alternation of Social Universe: Jewish-Christian Initiation of Gentiles in the Didache." *List* 32 (1997): 48–67.

Driver, T. F. *The Magic of Ritual: Our Need for Liberating Rites That Transform Our Lives and Our Communities*. San Francisco: Harper, 1991.

Duchesne, Louis. *Christian Worship: Its Origin and Evolution.* 5th ed. Translated by M. I. McClure. London: SPCK, 1919.

Duran, Nicole Wilkinson. *The Power of Disorder: Ritual Elements in Mark's Passion Narrative.* London: T&T Clark, 2008.

Durkheim, Émile. *The Elementary Forms of the Religious Life.* New York: Free Press, 1995.

Eichhorn, Albert. *The Lord's Supper in the New Testament.* Translated by Jeffrey F. Cayzer. Atlanta: Society of Biblical Literature, 2007.

Eliade, Mircea. *The Myth of the Eternal Return.* Translated by Willard R. Trask. Princeton: Princeton University Press, 1954.

———. *The Sacred and the Profane.* Translated by William R. Trask. New York: Harcourt Brace Jovanovich, 1959.

Farwell, Lyndon. "Betwixt and Between: The Anthropological Contributions of Mary Douglas and Victor Turner toward a Renewal of Roman Catholic Ritual." PhD diss., Claremont Graduate School, 1976.

Finn, Thomas M. *From Death to Rebirth: Ritual and Conversion in Antiquity.* Mahwah, NJ: Paulist Press, 1997.

Firth, Raymond. *Religion: A Humanist Interpretation.* London: Routledge, 1996.

Fisher, Eugene, ed. *The Jewish Roots of Christian Liturgy.* Mahwah, NJ: Paulist Press, 1990.

Gärtner, Bertil. *The Temple and the Community in Qumran and the New Testament: A Comparative Study in the Temple Symbolism of the Qumran Texts and the New Testament.* Cambridge: Cambridge University Press, 1965.

Giles, Kevin. *Patterns of Ministry among the First Christians.* Blackburn, Australia: Collins Dove / HarperCollins, 1989.

Gorman, Frank H. *Divine Presence and Community: A Commentary on the Book of Leviticus.* Grand Rapids: Eerdmans, 1997.

———. *The Ideology of Ritual.* Sheffield: JSOT Press, 1990.

———. "Priestly Ritual of Founding: Time, Space and Status." In *History and Interpretation: Essays in Honour of John H. Hayes,* edited by M. Patrick Graham, William P. Brown, and Jeffery K. Kuan, 47–64. Sheffield: JSOT Press, 1993.

———. "Ritual Studies and Biblical Studies: Assessment of the Past, Prospects for the Future." *Semeia* 67 (1994): 13–36.

Grassi, Joseph A. *Loaves and Fishes.* Collegeville, MN: Michael Glazier / Liturgical Press, 1991.

Gregg, David. "A Semantic Voyage." In *Essays on Eucharistic Sacrifice in the Early Church,* edited by Colin Buchanan, 10–14. Bramcote: Grove Books, 1984.

Grimes, Ronald L. *Beginnings in Ritual Studies.* Columbia: University of South Carolina Press, 1995.

———. "Infelicitous Performances and Ritual Criticism." *Semeia* 41 (1988): 103–22.

———. *Readings in Ritual Studies.* Upper Saddle River, NJ: Prentice Hall, 1996.

———. "Reinventing Ritual." *Soundings* 75 (1992): 21–41.

———. *Research in Ritual Studies: A Programmatic Essay and Bibliography.* Metuchen, NJ: Scarecrow Press, 1985.

———, ed. *Ritual Criticism: Case Studies in Its Practice, Essays on Its Theory.* Columbia: University of South Carolina Press, 1990.

———. "Ritual Studies." In *The Encyclopedia of Religion,* edited by Mircea Eliade and Charles J. Adams, 422–25. New York: Macmillan, 1987.

Gruenwald, Ithamar. "Paul and Ritual Theory: The Case of the Lord's Supper in 1 Corinthians 10 and 11." In *Antiquity and Humanity: Essays on Ancient Religion and Philosophy,* edited by Adela Yarbro Collins and Margaret Mitchell, 159–87. Tübingen: Mohr Siebeck, 2001.

Hancock, Christopher. "Christ's Priesthood and Eucharistic Sacrifice: An Historical Axe to a Metaphorical Root." In *Essays on Eucharistic Sacrifice in the Early Church,* edited by Colin Buchanan, 15–21. Bramcote: Grove Books, 1984.

Hanson, K. C. "Transformed on the Mountain: Ritual Analysis and the Gospel of Matthew." *Semeia* 67 (1994): 147–70.

Hanson, R. P. C. *Eucharistic Offering in the Early Church*. Bramcote: Grove Books, 1979.

Hardin, Richard F. "'Ritual' in Recent Criticism: The Elusive Sense of Community." *PMLA* 98 (1983): 846–62.

Harrington, Hannah K. "Interpreting Leviticus in the Second Temple System." In *Reading Leviticus: A Conversation with Mary Douglas*, edited by John Sawyer, 214–29. Sheffield: Sheffield Academic, 1996.

Hartman, Lars. "Das Markusevangelium: Für die *Lectio sollemnis* im Gottesdienst abgefasst?" In *Geschichte-Tradition-Reflexion: Festschrift für Martin Hengel zum 70. Geburtstag*, edited by H. Cancik, 3:147–71. Tübingen: Mohr Siebeck, 1996.

Heising, Alkuin. *Die Botschaft der Brotvermehrung*. Stuttgart: Katholisches Bibelwerk, 1966.

Hill, Charles E. *Regnum Caelorum*. 2nd ed. Grand Rapids: Eerdmans, 2001.

Holman, Charles L. *Till Jesus Comes: Origins of Christian Apocalyptic*. Peabody, MA: Hendrickson, 1996.

Hurtado, Larry W. *At the Origins of Christian Worship*. Grand Rapids: Eerdmans, 1999.

———. *Lord Jesus Christ: Devotion to Jesus in Earliest Christianity*. Grand Rapids: Eerdmans, 2003.

Jenson, Philip Peter. *Graded Holiness: A Key to the Priestly Conception of the World*. Sheffield: JSOT Press, 1992.

Jeremias, Joachim. *The Eucharistic Words of Jesus*. Translated by Norman Perrin. London: SCM, 1966.

Joncas, Jan Michael. *Tasting the Reign of God: The Meal Ministry of Jesus and Its Implications for Christian Worship and Life*. Collegeville, MN: St. John's University Press, 2000.

Jones, Cheslyn, et al., eds. *The Study of the Liturgy*. London: SPCK, 1992.

Jungmann, Josef A. *The Early Liturgy: To the Time of Gregory the Great*. Notre Dame, IN: University of Notre Dame Press, 1959.

Kapferer, Bruce. "Performance and the Structuring of Meaning and Experience." In *The Anthropology of Experience*, edited by V. W.

Turner and E. M. Bruner, 188–203. Urbana: University of Illinois Press, 1986.

Kelly, Henry Ansgar. *The Devil at Baptism: Ritual, Theology, and Drama*. Ithaca, NY: Cornell University Press, 1985.

Kirk, Alan. "Crossing the Boundary: Liminality and Transformative Wisdom in Q." *NTS* 45 (1999): 1–18.

Kirk, G. S. *Myth: Its Meaning and Function in Ancient and Other Cultures*. Berkeley: University of California Press, 1970.

Klass, Morton. *Ordered Universe: Approaches to the Anthropology of Religion*. Boulder, CO: Westview, 1995.

Klauser, Theodor. *A Short History of the Western Liturgy*. Translated by John Halliburton. London: Oxford University Press, 1969.

Klawans, J. "Idolatry, Incest, and Impurity: Moral Defilements in Ancient Judaism." *JSJ* 29 (1998): 391–415.

Klingbeil, Gerald A. *Bridging the Gap: Ritual and Ritual Texts in the Bible*. Winona Lake, IN: Eisenbrauns, 2007.

———. *A Comparative Study of the Ritual of Ordination as Found in Leviticus 8 and Emar 369*. Lewiston, NY: Edwin Mellen, 1998.

Kluckhohn, Clyde W. "Myths and Rituals: A General Theory." *HTR* 35 (1942): 45–79.

Kodell, Jerome. *The Eucharist in the New Testament*. Collegeville, MN: Liturgical Press, 1988.

Koenig, John. *The Feast of the World's Redemption: Eucharistic Origins and the Christian Mission*. Harrisburg, PA: Trinity Press International, 2000.

Koester, Craig. *The Dwelling of God: The Tabernacle in the Old Testament, Intertestamental Jewish Literature, and the New Testament*. Washington, DC: Catholic Biblical Association of America, 1989.

Ladrière, Jean. "The Performativity of Liturgical Language." In *Liturgical Experience of Faith*, edited by Herman Schmidt and David Power, 50–62. New York: Herder, 1973.

LaHurd, Carol Schersten. "Exactly What's Ritual about Hearing and/or Reading Mark's Gospel?" *Semeia* 67 (1994): 199–208.

———. "Reader Response to Ritual Elements in Mark 5:1–20." *BTB* 20 (1990): 154–60.

Lang, Bernhard. *Sacred Games: A History of Christian Worship.* New Haven: Yale University Press, 1997.

Lathrop, Gordon. *Holy Ground: A Liturgical Cosmology.* Minneapolis: Fortress, 2003.

LaVerdière, Eugene. *The Eucharist in the New Testament and the Early Church.* Collegeville, MN: Liturgical Press, 1996.

Léon-Dufour, Xavier. *Sharing the Eucharistic Bread: The Witness of the New Testament.* Translated by Matthew J. O'Connell. Mahwah, NJ: Paulist Press, 1987.

Lietzmann, Hans. *Mass and the Lord's Supper.* Translated by H. G. Reeve. Leiden: Brill, 1979.

Malina, Bruce. *The New Testament World: Insights from Cultural Anthropology.* 3rd ed. Louisville: Westminster John Knox, 2001.

Marr, Andrew. "Violence and the Kingdom of God: Introducing the Anthropology of René Girard." *AThR* 80 (1998): 590–603.

Martimort, A. G., I. H. Dalmais, and P. Jounel. *The Liturgy and Time.* Translated by Matthew J. O'Connell. 4 vols. Collegeville, MN: Liturgical Press, 1986.

Martin, Ralph. *Worship in the Early Church.* Grand Rapids: Eerdmans, 1964.

McDonnell, Kilian. *The Baptism of Jesus in the Jordan.* Collegeville, MN: Liturgical Press, 1996.

McDonnell, Kilian, and George Montague. *Christian Initiation and Baptism in the Holy Spirit: Evidence from the First Eight Centuries.* Collegeville, MN: Michael Glazier / Liturgical Press, 1991.

McGowan, Andrew. *Ancient Christian Worship: Early Church Practices in Social, Historical, and Theological Perspective.* Grand Rapids: Baker Academic, 2014.

———. *Ascetic Eucharists: Food and Drink in Early Christian Ritual Meals.* Oxford: Oxford University Press, 1999.

———. "Is There a Liturgical Text in This Gospel? The Institution Narratives and Their Early Interpretive Communities." *JBL* 118 (1999): 73–87.

McLean, Bradley H. *The Cursed Christ: Mediterranean Expulsion Rituals and Pauline Soteriology.* JSNTSup 126. Sheffield: Sheffield Academic, 1996.

McVann, Mark. "Baptism, Miracles, and Boundary Jumping in Mark." *BTB* 21 (1991): 151–57.

———. "Introduction." *Semeia* 67 (1994): 7–12.

———. "The Passion in Mark: Transformation Ritual." *BTB* 18 (1988): 96–101.

———. "Reading Mark Ritually: Honor, Shame, and the Ritual of Baptism." *Semeia* 67 (1994): 179–98.

———, ed. *Transformations, Passages, and Processes: Ritual Approaches to Biblical Texts.* Atlanta: Scholars Press, 1994.

Meeks, Wayne. *The First Urban Christians: The Social World of the Apostle Paul.* New Haven: Yale University Press, 1983.

Meissner, W. W. *The Cultic Origins of Christianity: The Dynamics of Religious Development.* Collegeville, MN: Liturgical Press, 2000.

Milgrom, Jacob. "The Changing Concept of Holiness in the Pentateuchal Codes with Emphasis on Leviticus 19." In *Reading Leviticus: A Conversation with Mary Douglas,* edited by John Sawyer, 65–83. Sheffield: Sheffield Academic, 1996.

Minear, Paul S. *Christians and the New Creation: Genesis Motifs in the New Testament.* Louisville: Westminster John Knox, 1994.

Mitchell, Nathan D. *Liturgy and the Social Sciences.* Collegeville, MN: Liturgical Press, 1999.

———. "Who Is at the Table? Reclaiming Real Presence." *Commonweal* 122 (January 1995): 10–15.

Nelson, Richard D. *Raising Up a Faithful Priest.* Louisville: Westminster John Knox, 1993.

Nicol, Iain G. "Event and Interpretation: Oscar Cullmann's Concept of Salvation History." *Theology* 77 (1974): 14–21.

Niditch, Susan. *From Chaos to Cosmos: Studies in Biblical Patterns of Creation.* Chico, CA: Scholars Press, 1985.

Oesterley, W. O. E. *The Jewish Background of the Christian Liturgy*. Gloucester, MA: Peter Smith, 1965.

Owen, Dennis E. "Ritual Studies as Ritual Practice: Catherine Bell's Challenge to Students of Ritual." *RelSRev* 24 (1998): 23–30.

Parmentier, Richard J. Review of *Ritual Theory, Ritual Practice*, by Catherine Bell. *HR* 33 (1993): 92–94.

Pfatteicher, Philip H. *Liturgical Spirituality*. Valley Forge, PA: Trinity Press International, 1997.

Pickstock, Catherine. *After Writing: On the Liturgical Consummation of Philosophy*. Oxford: Blackwell, 1998.

Price, Simon. *Rituals and Power*. Cambridge: Cambridge University Press, 1984.

Rappaport, Roy A. *Ecology, Meaning, and Religion*. Richmond, CA: North Atlantic Books, 1979.

———. *Ritual and Religion in the Making of Humanity*. Cambridge: Cambridge University Press, 1998.

Richardson, Robert Douglas. Introduction to *Mass and the Lord's Supper*, edited by Hans Lietzmann. Leiden: Brill, 1979.

Rordorf, Willy. *The Eucharist of the Early Christians*. Translated by Matthew J. O'Connell. New York: Pueblo, 1978.

———. *Sabbat und Sonntag in der alten Kirche*. Traditio Christiana. Zurich: Theologischer Verlag, 1972.

Russell, David M. *The "New Heavens and New Earth": Hope for the Creation in Jewish Apocalyptic and the New Testament*. Philadelphia: Visionary Press, 1996.

Sagovsky, Nicholas. "Doing Theology in Heaven." In *Essays on Eucharistic Sacrifice in the Early Church*, edited by Colin Buchanan, 22–25. Bramcote: Grove Books, 1984.

Scott, J. Julius. *Customs and Controversies: Intertestamental Jewish Backgrounds of the New Testament*. Grand Rapids: Baker, 1995.

Segal, Robert A., ed. *Myth and Ritual Theory: An Anthology*. Oxford: Blackwell, 1999.

Sheerin, Daniel J. *The Eucharist*. Wilmington, DE: Michael Glazier, 1986.

Shepherd, M. H. *The Paschal Liturgy and the Apocalypse*. London: Lutterworth, 1960.

Smith, Dennis E. *From Symposium to Eucharist: The Banquet in the Early Christian World*. Minneapolis: Fortress, 2003.

Smith, Dennis E., and Hal Taussig. *Many Tables: The Eucharist in the New Testament and Liturgy Today*. Philadelphia: Trinity Press International, 1990.

Smith, Jonathan Z. *Drudgery Divine: On the Comparison of Early Christianities and the Religions of Late Antiquity*. Jordan Lectures in Comparative Religion. Chicago: University of Chicago Press, 1990.

———. "The Influence of Symbols upon Social Change: A Place on Which to Stand." *Worship* 44 (1970): 457–74.

Srawley, J. H. *The Early History of the Liturgy*. 2nd ed. Cambridge: Cambridge University Press, 1957.

Stacey, David. "The Lord's Supper as Prophetic Drama." In *The Signs of a Prophet: The Prophetic Actions of Jesus*, edited by Morna Hooker, 80–95. Harrisburg, PA: Trinity Press International, 1997.

Stevenson, Kenneth. "Eucharistic Sacrifice: What Can We Learn from Christian Antiquity?" In *Essays on Eucharistic Sacrifice in the Early Church*, edited by Colin Buchanan, 26–33. Bramcote: Grove Books, 1984.

Stewart, Eric Clark. *Gathered around Jesus: Alternative Spiritual Practices in the Gospel of Mark*. Cambridge: James Clarke, 2009.

Strenski, Ivan. "Between Theory and Speciality: Sacrifice in the 90's." *RelSRev* 22 (1996): 10–20.

Talley, Thomas J. *The Origins of the Liturgical Year*. New York: Pueblo, 1986.

Taussig, Hal. *In the Beginning Was the Meal: Social Experimentation and Early Christian Identity*. Minneapolis: Fortress, 2009.

Thiering, Barbara. "Inner and Outer Cleansing at Qumran as a Background to New Testament Baptism." *NTS* 26 (1980): 266–77.

Turner, Victor. *The Drums of Affliction: A Study of Religious Processes among the Ndembu of Zambia*. Oxford: Clarendon, 1968.

———. "Passages, Margins, and Poverty: Religious Symbols of Communitas." *Worship* 46 (1972): 390–412.

———. "Rites of Passage." In *The Encyclopedia of Religion*, edited by Mircea Eliade and Charles J. Adams, 380–87. New York: Macmillan, 1987.

———. *The Ritual Process: Structure and Antistructure*. Lewis Henry Morgan Lectures. Chicago: Aldine, 1969.

Van de Sandt, Huub. "'Do Not Give What Is Holy to Dogs' (Did 9:5D and Matt 7:6A): The Eucharistic Food of the Didache in Its Jewish Purity Setting." *VC* 56 (2002): 223–46.

Vasey, Michael. "Eucharist, Sacrifice, and Scripture." In *Essays on Eucharistic Sacrifice in the Early Church*, edited by Colin Buchanan, 3–10. Bramcote: Grove Books, 1984.

Versnel, H. S., ed. *Transition and Reversal in Myth and Ritual*. Leiden: Brill, 1993.

Watson, Alan. "Leviticus in Mark: Jesus' Attitude toward the Law." In *Reading Leviticus: A Conversation with Mary Douglas*, edited by John Sawyer, 263–74. Sheffield: Sheffield Academic, 1996.

Watts, James W. "Ritual Legitimacy and Scriptural Authority." *JBL* 124 (2005): 401–17.

Whitaker, E. C. *Documents of the Baptismal Liturgy*. London: SPCK, 1970.

White, Hugh. "Introduction: Speech Act Theory and Literary Criticism." *Semeia* 41 (1988): 1–24.

Whitekettle, Richard. "Leviticus 12 and the Israelite Woman: Ritual Process, Liminality, and the Womb." *ZAW* 107 (1995): 393–408.

Winch, Peter. "Understanding a Primitive Society." In *Religion and Understanding*, edited by D. Z. Phillips, 9–42. New York: Macmillan, 1967.

Wright, N. T. *The Resurrection of the Son of God*. Minneapolis: Fortress, 2003.

Young, Francis M. *The Use of Sacrificial Ideas in Greek Christian Writers from the New Testament to John Chrysostom*. Cambridge, MA: Philadelphia Patristic Foundation, 1979.

Zimmerman, Joyce Ann. *Liturgy and Hermeneutics*. Collegeville, MN: Liturgical Press, 1999.

Zizioulos, John D. *Being as Communion: Studies in Personhood and the Church*. Crestwood, NY: St. Vladimir's Seminary Press, 1985.

Author Index

Scripture and Ancient Writings Index

245

Subject Index